F

The Top
100
International
Growth
Stocks

Your Guide to Creating a
Blue-Chip International Portfolio for
Higher Returns and Reduced Risk

Peggy Edersheim Kalb
and Scott E. Kalb

A Fireside Book
Published by Simon & Schuster

FIRESIDE
Rockefeller Center
1230 Avenue of the Americas
New York, NY 10020

Copyright © 1998 by Peggy Edersheim Kalb and Scott E. Kalb
All rights reserved,
including the right of reproduction
in whole or in part in any form.

FIRESIDE and colophon are registered trademarks
of Simon & Schuster Inc.

Designed by Irving Perkins Associates

Manufactured in the United States of America

1   3   5   7   9   10   8   6   4   2

Library of Congress Cataloging-in-Publication Data

Kalb, Peggy Edersheim.
  The top 100 international growth stocks : your guide to creating a
blue-chip international portfolio for higher returns and reduced
risk / Peggy Edersheim Kalb and Scott E. Kalb.
      p.   cm.
  "A Fireside book."
  Includes index.
    1. Corporations—Finance—Directories.   2. Stocks—Prices.
I. Kalb, Scott E.   II. Title.
HG4009.K355   1998
332.63'222—dc21   98-15189
                                                                CIP

ISBN 0-684-84339-0

Acknowledgments

We wish to thank senior management at Salomon Smith Barney for their guidance and support, particularly Tom Jones, Jeff Lane, and George Saks. We would also like to thank Scott's colleagues in the Salomon Smith Barney International Money Management division, including Maurits Edersheim, Jim Conheady, Jeff Russell, Rein Van Der Does, David Ishibashi, Don Elefson, and his associate Nina Gene. The following individuals helped us gather data on various companies and we wish to express our appreciation for their efforts: Francisco Chevez, Lore Serra, Laura Forte, Derek Hughes, Trish McCall, Jeremy Attard Manche, Luanne Zurlo, Justine Roberts, Charlene Wang, Rachel Hamwee, Daniel Carraso, Celeste Tambaro, Daniel Lerner, Julie Allen, Brian Mariscal. Our agent, Laurie Liss, our editor, Becky Cabaza, and reader Peggy O provided valuable insights and advice. Finally, we would like to thank the management and staff of all the companies in the Top 100 whose help made this book possible.

We wish to dedicate this book to our children
Henry Howard and Ariel Jisu,
who own shares in some of these companies
and who we hope will have fun with this book.

Contents

1

Going Global with the Top 100 International Growth Stocks

There are two times in a man's life when he should not speculate: when he can't afford it and when he can.

—MARK TWAIN (1897)

What do most investors want? The best possible returns for the least possible worry. Our advice: Go global. In this book we have carefully chosen 100 top international growth stocks all suitable for a well-diversified portfolio: stocks that complement domestic growth stocks and, when added to a solid U.S. portfolio, should help to increase returns with no added risk.

Why Stocks and Why Go Global?

Stocks Versus Bonds and Cash

Investors often ask why they should put their savings into risky stocks instead of bonds, or instead of into bank instruments. The answer? Over time the return on stocks has been higher than on either of those alternatives. As inflation lowers the value of the dollar, the fixed rates of return offered by bank deposits and bonds actually decrease in value. Stocks, on the other hand, appreciate based on the earnings performance of the company, valuations accorded to those earnings, *and* inflation. Provided management is able to raise prices, maintain margins, and increase earnings successfully over time, a company's share price should—at the very least—provide an attractive real return over the rate of inflation.

The impact of this inflation effect is enormous. As can be seen in Chart 1, $10,000 invested broadly in the U.S. stock market during the five-year period 1991–1995 recorded an average return of 17.3% per annum, including dividends, amounting to $22,207 in all. The average annual return on bonds during this period was high at 14.7%, yielding $19,853 for the same investment but still lower than the return on stocks. The return on money market funds was even lower, at 4.5% per annum, yielding $12,462. And remember that most of the return on bonds and all of the return on money market funds is subject to income tax, while most of the return on stocks is capital gains, free of tax until a sale is made. Cash dividend payments on stock are subject to income tax but make up only a small percentage of total returns for stock holdings. Thus, because of taxes, the *effective* return on bonds and cash, when compared with stocks, is lower than the above figures suggest.

It is worth noting that timing can be a big factor in calculating these returns. For example, look at Chart 2. During the three-year period 1992–1994, the average annual return on stocks (including dividends) was just 6.3%, while for the four-year period 1992–1995, it was as high as 14.1%. An investor who threw in the towel on stock investments at the end of 1994, after having suffered low returns during the previous three years, would have missed out on the boom in 1995 that effectively helped to smooth stock returns back to the long-term average. That is why we say investors should invest for the long term: markets are notoriously difficult to predict. Even professionals have trouble timing short-term investments effectively.

Of course, it is also a good idea for investors to keep some cash around. We would suggest keeping enough to cover three to six months of living expenses, just in case. You never want to have to sell when the market is down and out. We also advise keeping some money in bonds—anywhere from 10% to 40%, de-

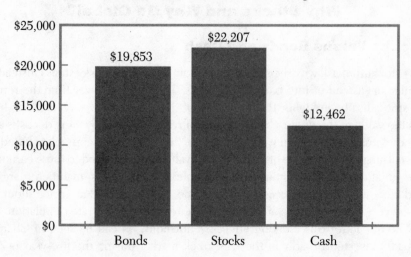

CHART 1   Value of $10,000 Invested in U.S. During 1991–1995

Source: Salomon Smith Barney

CHART 2   Average Annual Return on U.S. Stocks for Two Periods

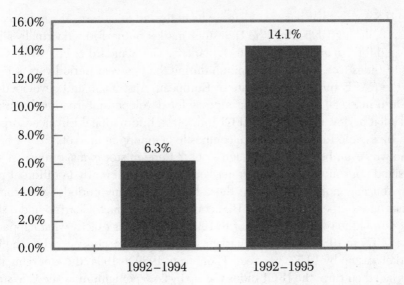

Source: Salomon Smith Barney

pending on your age, your net worth, your income, and your tolerance for risk. The lion's share of your nest egg, however, should be in stocks. Of course, if you are near or past retirement age, you may prefer a higher weighting in bonds.

Stocks Versus Mutual Funds

If stocks are the best alternative, why not invest in them through mutual funds? For some investors, mutual funds are the way to go. For example, if you are investing less than $15,000 in foreign stocks, you would be hard pressed to achieve a well-diversified portfolio (we reached $15,000 by assuming that a diversified portfolio should have at least six different stock holdings, that the average share price is $25, and that normally stocks are purchased in 100-share blocks). You also need to have the time and inclination to research and learn about companies you want to invest in. Finally, you have to be willing to follow your portfolio once you have begun investing (see Chapter 4 for advice on following foreign stocks). All that is much easier when you put money into a mutual fund: a professional will then be choosing and managing a diversified portfolio of stocks for you.

But if you're interested and have the capital to invest, investing directly in stocks allows you to make your own decisions about portfolio weightings, prudent investing, tax planning, and cost control. Besides, investing can be a lot of fun—a challenging, stimulating, and rewarding experience.

Global Versus Domestic Portfolio

The U.S. market has been the place to be in the last few years. As can be seen in Chart 3, during 1995–1996 the U.S. stock market outperformed virtually all developed foreign and emerging stock markets. The Standard & Poor's 500 Composite Index rose by 31% per annum during the two-year period versus 17.6% for the EAFE Index (a composite of European, Australian, and developed Far Eastern markets, usually used as a proxy for developed international markets) and a flat performance for the IFCI Index (the International Finance Corporation Investable Index, based on a composite of emerging markets).

So why even bother with foreign stocks? Foreign stocks make sense in a diversified portfolio because stock markets perform differently in different periods. You may not realize it, but there have been many periods when foreign stocks have outperformed their U.S. counterparts. In fact, Charts 4 and 5 show that during the twenty years prior to 1995–1996, that is exactly what happened. From 1977 to 1988, the EAFE markets were up by 23% per year, while the U.S. market was up by 12.5% per year. Then, from 1989 to 1994, the emerging markets had their turn: the IFCI Index was up by 24% per annum, while U.S. stocks again increased by about 12.5%.

Here's a concrete example: If you had invested $10,000 in a broadly diversified international portfolio during the ten-year period 1985–1994, your investment would have been worth $66,721 at the end of the period, appreciating by

CHART 3   **Annualized Return in U.S. Dollars (%), 1995–1996**

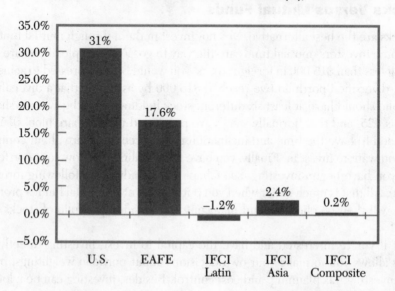

Source: Salomon Smith Barney

21% per annum, versus $40,455, or 15% per annum, for a portfolio based on the S&P Composite. We do not mean to frown on those nice returns generated by U.S. stocks; far from it. It just makes sense to own at least a few foreign stocks in your portfolio, given that stock markets sometimes outperform and sometimes underperform one another.

Another reason to think about foreign stocks: the United States does not have a monopoly on high-growth companies. As you read through our Top 100, you'll see how easy it is to find attractive international companies that are accessible to U.S. investors. After all, the U.S. stock market accounts for only 40% of world stock market capitalization. There is a lot of opportunity in that other 60% of the world.

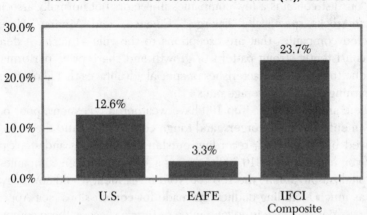

CHART 4   Annualized Return in U.S. Dollars (%), 1977–1988

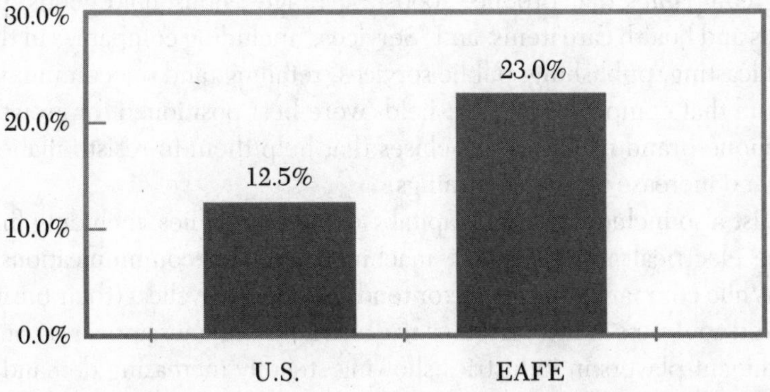

Source: Salomon Smith Barney

CHART 5   Annualized Return in U.S. Dollars (%), 1989–1994

Source: Salomon Smith Barney

Go for Growth

Year in, year out, during booms or busts, in times of political turmoil or relative calm, growth stocks have performed better than any other group. What are growth stocks? They are stocks of companies that have demonstrated over time an ability to record consistent above-average gains in sales and earnings. And in the end, superior sales and earnings growth is rewarded by superior share price performance.

To compile the list of our favorite growth stocks, we looked at a long list of growth-oriented characteristics, including consistent unit volume growth, high operating and net profit margins, an above-average ROE (return on equity), a strong balance sheet, and a commitment to reinvesting in the business. The list is dominated by companies in two noncyclical sectors: "Consumer Goods," including companies that produce foods, beverages, household goods, pharmaceuticals and health care items; and "Services," including companies in the fields of broadcasting, publishing, public services, retailing, and telecommunications. We found that companies in these fields were best positioned for growth. Most have unique brand names or franchises that help them to resist inflation, raise prices, and increase sales and earnings.

Our list also includes select "Capital Goods" companies, including firms that produce electrical and electronic machinery and telecommunications equipment. While companies in this sector tend to be more cyclical (their business expands and contracts as interest rates rise and fall), the ones appearing on our list are dominant players in industries showing steadily increasing demand trends. Take Ericsson (ERICY—NASDAQ), for example. Ericsson is a Swedish company that has a 40% global market share in cellular and wireless infrastructure equipment, an area in which hundreds of billions of dollars are expected to be spent by the end of the century.

Finally, our list contains a few companies in sectors not normally associated with growth stocks, specifically "Energy," "Finance," and "Mining." Here we have selected companies that are exceptions to the rule—that have demonstrated a consistently strong pattern of growth and share price performance, generally due to unique characteristics or special advantages that allow them to increase earnings at above average rates.

All of the companies in the Top 100 have weathered recessions, poor political environments, difficult mergers, and tough competition. And they have not only survived but prospered, recording outstanding earnings and stock price growth. If you had invested $10,000 ten years ago in the top ten companies (by market capitalization) among the Top 100, your investment would now be worth 9.5 times as much including deductions made for commissions (see Appendix B). While past performance is no guarantee of future success, these companies are rock solid and likely, in our view, to thrive for many years to come.

Digging into the Top 100

Here's a simple suggestion for investors: Look for products you like and understand. In searching out investments anywhere in the world, try to find companies that produce or distribute your favorite drinks, your favorite foods, even your favorite medicines.

Missed out on the Wal-Mart boom in the United States? How about France-based Carrefour (CRERF—OTC), a French "hypermarket" that has successfully expanded into ten other countries, including Spain, Argentina, Brazil, China, and South Korea. This strategy of aggressive growth overseas has paid off big for Carrefour, enabling the company to increase its earnings by 20% per annum over the last ten years. Foreign markets, where the penetration of first-rate retailing operations is low, still represent tremendous growth potential for firms such as Carrefour. Retailers comprise an important part of the Top 100 list.

Now take a look at pharmaceutical giant Novartis (NVTSY—OTC). This Swiss company was created in 1996 by two old-time industry rivals, Sandoz and Ciba-Geigy. Novartis has a 4.4% share of the global pharmaceutical market—the second largest in the world. Each of our favorite drug companies has a strong presence in overseas markets where medical practices are less developed than in the United States and where the potential for growth is enormous. Nine of the top pharmaceutical companies in the world, in terms of market share and sales, are among the Top 100.

Near the top of our list: always Coca-Cola. "America's favorite soft drink" does a great business around the world. There are ten "anchor," or primary, bottlers in the Coca-Cola system worldwide, which are charged with expanding the Coca-Cola franchise globally. Nine of them are based overseas, and *seven* are publicly traded. Four of those are on our list: Coca-Cola Amatil (CCLAY—OTC), one of the largest Coca-Cola bottlers outside the United States (in terms of cases sold), with operations in Australia, Indonesia, the Philippines, and South Korea; Panamco (PB-NYSE), the Coca-Cola bottler for Brazil, Colombia, Costa Rica, Mexico, and Venezuela; Fraser & Neave (FRNVF—OTC), the dominant Coca-Cola bottler in Vietnam, Laos, Burma, and Singapore; and Coca-Cola Femsa (KOF—NYSE), one of the top two Coca-Cola bottlers in Mexico and Argentina. These four companies have one thing in common: earnings growth exceeding that of Coca-Cola in the United States.

Here's another suggestion: Look for companies in attractive new industries, particularly in the service sector, that you believe have bright growth prospects. Two new areas we like are outsourcing and information technology. Try to find companies that have established an edge in their respective fields and that are well positioned to grow with rising demand trends.

One example: Germany-based SAP (SAPHY—OTC), a leading supplier of management software worldwide. SAP lists among its clients such blue-chip companies as Coca-Cola Enterprises, Microsoft, and Deutsche Telekom. Just as the information technology sector is becoming a major factor in the U.S. economy, so too is its importance rising overseas. If anything, opportunities for growth internationally are even better than in the United States. Information technology (IT) companies are an important part of the Top 100.

Compass Group (CMSGY—OTC), one of the world's leading contract catering companies, is another example of a business with an edge in a rapidly growing service industry. Compass Group provides food services from the United Kingdom to Malaysia for everything from horse races to school lunches. It is thriving with the corporate shift toward "outsourcing," a theme we think will continue to be important for years to come. Outsourcing firms also account for a big part of the Top 100.

In emerging markets we like infrastructure companies, companies that have been and are likely to continue to be integral to economic growth. On our list are companies such as Enersis (ENI—NYSE), the Chilean energy giant, and Cheung Kong (Holdings) (CHEUY—OTC), a Hong Kong conglomerate with extensive involvement in many of Hong Kong's major businesses, as well as business development in China.

2

Company Selection and Grading

Speculation is the romance of trade, and casts contempt upon all its sober realities. It renders the stock jobber a magician, and the exchange a region of enchantment.

—WASHINGTON IRVING (1855)

Company Selection

We reviewed about 10,000 companies to find the top 100 firms that are presented in this book. First we eliminated companies with short histories (see page 48 for companies we think have bright prospects but that had trading histories that were too short for them to be included in the Top 100), companies that have a market capitalization of less than $500 million, and companies whose shares are difficult to trade. We felt that any companies that did not meet those basic criteria could pose undue settlement and trading risks to individual investors. That knocked about half the companies out of the running. Next we focused on both operating income and net income growth, eliminating companies with less than 12% compound annual growth over ten years in these two areas. We chose operating income, or earnings before interest expenses and taxes (EBIT), because it is a great way to look at the underlying results of a company before they have been "dressed up" through special financing methods or tax breaks. At the same time, it is important to focus on net income because it is the base upon which earnings per share are calculated and tends to be the number focused on by the marketplace. This brought the number of companies on our list down to about 1,000.

The next phase of our selection process was more qualitative: we looked at other financial factors, such as revenue growth, share price performance, operating margins, and balance sheet strength. We also examined franchise strength, market position, and management quality. Finally, we made an effort to include companies from both industrially advanced and emerging markets and to spread our choices to include nations around the world—although to do so we had to make exceptions to some of our rules (see Chapter 5 for more details on exceptions).

The result of these efforts is a geographically diverse list of 100 companies (81 from developed markets and 19 from emerging markets) that have shown an exceptional ability to grow their businesses at superior rates in all kinds of conditions, climates, and political environments. From these you can put together a balanced and attractive group of foreign stocks that complements your domestic portfolio.

Grading

After selecting our companies, we graded them based on their performance over ten years (or as many years as possible) in six categories, with a maximum point score of 100. Four of these categories emphasize growth: revenue growth, operating income growth, EPS growth, and share price growth. The fifth, return on equity (ROE), measures quality of management. The sixth, long-term debt divided by total capital (the sum of long-term liabilities and shareholders' equity), measures balance sheet risk. At the beginning of each company profile, there is a box summarizing the results of this grading process that looks like the following:

SUMMARY GRADING BOX, SAMPLE COMPANY

Growth Categories		Quality of Management	
Revenue Growth	20 pts	Return on Equity	5 pts
Operating Income Growth	20 pts	**Risk**	
Earnings per Share Growth	20 pts	Long-Term Debt/Total Capital	10 pts
Share Price Growth	15 pts	**Total QM&R (maximum 20)**	**15 pts**
Total Growth (maximum 80)	**75 pts**	**FINAL GRADE**	**90 pts**

Growth

Given our emphasis on selecting premium growth companies for the long haul, we decided that our grading system should emphasize growth characteristics. Thus, four of the six categories are devoted to measuring critical components of company growth: revenues, operating income, earnings per share, and share price. Each of these categories carries a maximum grade of 20 points for a total of 80 points out of a possible 100. In each category up to 10 points are awarded for a high average growth rate and 10 points for consistent performance during past years. This methodology prevents companies with wild swings in growth (for example, up 50% one year, down 10% the next) from being rewarded with maximum points, even though their average growth rates may be high. Below we explain why we believe each of these categories is critical for investors and present tables illustrating how points are awarded.

Revenues. No matter how good a company's management is at cutting costs and improving productivity, it is impossible for any company to cut its way to prosperity forever. In other words, a company cannot be successful in the long run without steady top-line growth, achieved through a combination of pricing power and unit volume growth. We awarded 20 points to companies with compound annual revenue growth of 12% or better during their histories, while recording consecutive growth in at least eight out of ten years, or 80% of the time.

REVENUES

Growth		Consistency	
Compound Annual Rate of Growth	**Points Awarded**	Year-over-Year Increases During Period	**Points Awarded**
0%–8%	0	Up to 60% of the time	0
8%–12%	5	60%–80%	5
12% or higher	10	80%–100%	10

Operating Income. Operating income, sometimes referred to as EBIT (earnings before interest payments and taxes), gives an important snapshot of a company's underlying performance. After operating income on a company's income statement are shown nonoperating gains and losses, financing gains and losses, and taxes. The problem with these items is that they may not recur at the same rate on a regular basis and can temporarily inflate or depress earnings. Moreover, different accounting standards in different countries make it difficult to compare these items across borders. Operating income, on the other hand, is a pretty good measure of core business trends, and accounting treatment of it is similar in all countries. Note that, when possible, we add back depreciation and/or amortization to earnings to get EBDIT (earnings before depreciation, interest, and tax) or EBITDA (earnings before interest, tax depreciation, and amortization), other common measures of operating performance that are even more accurate. Companies qualified for the maximum 20 points in this category by recording compound annual operating income growth of 15% or higher during past years and showing consecutive increases at least 80% of the time.

OPERATING INCOME

Growth		Consistency	
Compound Annual Rate of Growth	Points Awarded	Year-over-Year Increases During Period	Points Awarded
0%–12%	0	Up to 60% of the time	0
12%–15%	5	60%–80%	5
15% or higher	10	80%–100%	10

Earnings per Share (or per ADR). Ultimately, both the marketplace and investors focus on earnings per share. EPS reflect distortions that occur from year to year as a result of rights issues or extraordinary items, which may not be reflected in net income. EPS growth remains the litmus test for stock investors and a critical category in our grading system. Companies showing compound annual EPS growth of 15% or higher and at least eight consecutive years of growth during the last ten years (or increases over 80% of historic years) receive the maximum 20-point award. (For an explanation of ADRs see Glossary on page 54, and Chapter 3, Getting Started.)

EARNINGS PER SHARE

Growth		Consistency	
Compound Annual Rate of Growth	Points Awarded	Year-over-Year Increases During Period	Points Awarded
0%–12%	0	Up to 60% of the time	0
12%–15%	5	60%–80%	5
15% or higher	10	80%–100%	10

Share (or ADR) Price Performance. Superior earnings growth should be reflected in superior share price performance over time, and even with market swings, share price trends are important to evaluate. If share price growth does not reflect earnings growth historically, it may be a sign the marketplace has concerns about the company and is pessimistic about its future prospects. Among the growth categories, share price performance has the highest standards for a company to receive the maximum award. It requires at least 20% compound annual growth over ten years and consecutive increases during 80% of the period.

We quote ADR prices for our stocks whenever possible because ADRs are the easiest class of foreign shares for U.S. investors to buy and sell. For example, it may be possible to buy local shares of Astra, but it is much easier to buy the New York Stock Exchange–listed ADR. The ADR prices we show are often translated from the foreign share price using the appropriate dollar exchange rate and ADR ratio. These prices may not correspond exactly to the historical prices of the U.S.-listed ADR, but they should be very close and more than enough to give readers a good assessment of performance. In cases where the company has launched an ADR only recently, we show the theoretical ADR price going back as far as possible, based on the local shares, the ratio of local shares per ADR and the U.S. dollar exchange rate. For example, Danka (DANKY—NASDAQ) has an ADR that started trading in 1992 (one ADR = four foreign shares). On the financial tables we show the ADR price going back to 1988, with prices before 1992 translated from the local shares using the British pound–U.S. dollar year-end exchange rate and multiplying by four to reach the appropriate ratio of local shares to ADRs.

SHARE PRICE PERFORMANCE

Growth		Consistency	
Compound Annual Rate of Growth	Points Awarded	Year-over-Year Increases During Period	Points Awarded
0%–15%	0	Up to 60% of the time	0
15%–20%	5	60%–80%	5
20% or higher	10	80%–100%	10

Quality of Management

Evaluating a company's management is a subjective exercise, and most investors simply look at earnings growth as a guide to how well senior officers are doing their job. However, earnings growth alone may not tell the whole story. Growth factors do not reveal, for instance, whether or not management is doing the best it can to maximize returns for shareholders, for example getting the most out of a great brand name or strong franchise. One of the best ways of evaluating management is by examining the return it is generating on money that is invested in the business. This return should be well above the return investors could make from putting cash into a bank account or into bonds, in order to compensate for stock market and business risk. To measure performance in this area, we have divided net profit by shareholders' equity (otherwise known as return on equity or ROE).

Shareholders' equity represents money that was invested in the company to start the business, money that has been raised from time to time through the sale of new stock, and the portion of earnings (after dividends are paid) that are retained and reinvested. A steady, high-level ROE indicates that management is doing a good job for shareholders in generating consistent returns on capital invested in the company. We award a maximum of 10 points to companies with an ROE averaging 18% or higher over their historical period. We recognize that this is not a perfect measure, since average return on equity can vary substantially from industry to industry. The average ROE of a bank, for example, is very different from the average ROE for a software company. Nevertheless, ROE is still a time-honored way to evaluate management and remains an important valuation tool.

RETURN ON EQUITY (ROE)

Shareholders' Equity Divided by Net Income, Historical Average	Points Awarded
0%–12%	0
12%–18%	5
18% or higher	10

Risk

No company evaluation would be complete without some measure of risk. While there are many ways to look at risk, we feel that financial strength and level of indebtedness are critical factors for any business. For grading purposes, we examined the balance sheet of the companies on our list and gave high marks to those with low levels of debt, using a ratio of long-term debt divided by total capital (total capital is the sum of all long-term liabilities and shareholders' equity).

This measure is also not perfect because some businesses (for example, equipment manufacturing) are capital intensive, requiring large investments and usually higher debt levels in the normal course of operations. In addition, a successful business will sometimes increase its debt temporarily to take advantage of a special opportunity (an acquisition or plant expansion), then pay the debt down over time. Nevertheless, we believe that companies that can keep debt at moderate levels over the long run are less risky because they are less exposed to business downturns, interest rate hikes, and currency fluctuations. Successful growth companies with lower debt levels should be rewarded for their prudent business practices. We awarded companies a maximum of 10 points for low risk, based on a debt-to-capital ratio averaging less than 25% over a ten-year period.

RISK

Long-Term Debt Divided by Total Capital, Historical Average	Points Awarded
35% or higher	0
25%–35%	5
0%–25%	10

One caveat. The grading system is based on past performance and cannot take into account new corporate developments, changes in industry conditions, or macro-economic turmoil. For example, many of the Asian companies in the Top 100 scored highly in our grading system but this did not prevent them from suffering badly during the "Asian contagion" of 1997, a series of currency devaluations and bankruptcies that devastated the region. On the other hand the grading system does give us confidence that the Asian companies in the Top 100 should survive this contagion and go on to prosper in the future. For advice on how to choose an international stock or on when to sell, turn to the next chapter.

3

Getting Started

'Tis sweet to know that stocks will stand / When we with daisies lie, / That commerce will continue, / And trades as briskly fly.
— EMILY DICKINSON

Narrowing the Field

You will not want to buy all of our favorite stocks at the same time. After all, overdiversification can be as much of a problem as underdiversification. How would you keep track of 100 stocks? Besides, overdiversification tends to blunt returns: the low weighting of outperformers prevents them from having much of an impact on the overall portfolio.

You'll want to start by reading through the "Company Descriptions" section at the end of this chapter. This is an alphabetical listing including the country each company is based in and a brief summary of each company's business. This section should give you a quick feel for the companies in the Top 100 and may save you some time in narrowing down your choices.

Next, read through the detailed company write-ups and note the ones that interest you the most. And ask yourself some questions about the companies that catch your eye: Are they in businesses you like? Do they operate in industries that you believe look good for the future? Review the financial tables and the performance section to see how they have done over time. Eventually, you should try to narrow your selections to six to ten companies, making sure they are reasonably well diversified by industry (you don't want to own just cellular phone companies), by geography (you don't want to own all British companies), and by market capitalization (try to include large-, small-, and medium-capitalization companies). You might want to own an emerging market firm or two, but be sure you can tolerate the risk. Before making any final decisions, try to do a little outside research (note the sources shown in the next section).

Other Sources of Information

Some of the best material available to help you make your decision includes annual reports, company press releases, and quarterly or interim result statements. You can usually call or write a company or its U.S. investor relations firm to ask for information the company releases regularly (details are shown at the head of each company section). You also might want to take a look at the company's 10K and 10Q (if the stock is traded on a U.S. exchange, those documents will have been filed with the Securities and Exchange Commission [SEC] and should be available from the stock exchange, as well as over the Internet at http://www.sec.gov). Another source of information is the public library. Search for recent articles on the company in publications such as *Barron's, The Wall Street Journal, Money, SmartMoney, Forbes, Fortune,* and *Business Week.* You might also take a look at some trade publications. *Moody's International Handbook* is your best bet for an international company, but Standard & Poor's, ValueLine, and Morningstar are also likely to have written on the larger foreign names, particularly those with ADRs (American Depository Receipts) trading on a U.S. exchange. Many foreign companies also have begun posting information on the Internet; when available, we have included company Web sites. Of course, there are also more subjective sources of information: brokerage reports, investment advisers, and investment newsletters, each of which can help you narrow the field.

ADRs and Ticker Symbols

Many investors ask what an ADR actually is and what the difference is between an ADR and a share. Then they want to know which one they should buy. An ADR (American Depository Receipt) is a receipt issued by a depository bank, such as Citibank or Bank of New York, that is equivalent to a local foreign share (or a specified number of foreign shares) the bank holds on deposit in the foreign country. ADRs are bought and sold in dollars and are traded through normal channels just as other U.S. securities. In general, it is easier and less costly to purchase ADRs, either those that trade on a U.S. exchange, on NASDAQ, or those that trade over the counter (OTC), than it is to buy local foreign shares, because it eliminates the need to go through a foreign broker and execute foreign currency transactions.

You can identify companies in the Top 100 that have ADRs by the ticker symbol (the code by which a security is referred to) and the exchange abbreviation shown at the head of each company write-up. If the symbol is followed by a U.S. exchange, such as NYSE (New York Stock Exchange) or NASDAQ (National Association of Securities Dealers Automatic Quotation), you are home free. For example, "TEF—NYSE" shows the ticker for Telefónica de España's ADR, which trades on the New York Stock Exchange. "ADECY–NASDAQ" shows the ticker for Adecco's ADR, which trades on NASDAQ. Some companies have ADRs that trade over the counter, and these will show a five-letter ticker ending in the letter Y, followed by "OTC." For example, SBWRY—OTC signifies the ticker symbol for South African Breweries' ADR, which trades over the counter rather than on a listed exchange. All ADRs are assigned a CUSIP Number (see Glossary) for settlement purposes.

Some foreign companies have no ADR, but they trade so frequently in the United States that they have a ticker symbol anyway, usually a five-letter symbol ending in F (for "foreign share"). A good example of this is GRMBF, the ticker for Gruma shares in the United States, which also trade over the counter. Finally, some foreign shares do not trade much in the United States, even though they may be very liquid in their home country, and have no ticker symbol here. For these companies, at the head of the write-up we have substituted the Reuters symbol and show the local exchange where the shares trade. Example: "BARBt.BR–BRUSSELS" is the Reuters symbol for Barco, which trades on the Brussels exchange. Foreign shares are assigned a SEDOL Code (see Glossary), which is used for tracking and settlement purposes.

While you should not let the lack of an ADR dissuade you from buying a foreign stock, you need to be aware of a few things before plunging in. First think about your own tolerance for risk; then check out the market capitalization (in the basic information box at the top of every company write-up). If a company has a large market capitalization and a high trading volume, it is likely to be easier to buy and sell (that actually applies to all stocks, wherever they may trade). You don't want to put together a portfolio of all small foreign stocks, but one or two could give your performance a kick (for good or for bad!).

When *Not* to Buy

Avoid buying a stock when it is at an all-time high or when a company is trading at a price/earnings (P/E) ratio that is significantly higher than its historic average (at least the recent average). It is also a good idea to steer clear of companies based in any country in which there is a great deal of turmoil—everything from political and economic upheaval to natural catastrophes (unless you have a very strong stomach).

Dollar-Cost Averaging

This time-honored investment tool has not lost its luster. If you invest the same amount of money in the shares of a company on a regular basis (using monthly, quarterly or semiannual payments) regardless of market movements, your average cost is likely to be lower than if you invest all at once.

Currency Hedging

In the course of doing your research, you are likely to hear about currency hedging, or buying "contracts" to lock in a given exchange rate to the dollar and protect yourself from the vagaries of foreign exchange. In practice, hedging is difficult and expensive. You will be better off in the long run (and will probably sleep better at night) if you stick with strong growth companies and avoid trying to time the currency markets. Moreover, if you make your investments geographically diverse, you will be building a naturally hedged portfolio without incurring extra expenses.

Purchasing Shares

Once you have decided on which stocks you want to buy, you should be able to call your broker and make a purchase. Be sure to tell your broker the name of the company, the ticker symbol, and the exchange where it is traded, all of which are shown at the top of the company write-up. You may also want to give your broker the CUSIP Number if you are purchasing an ADR that trades over the counter, or the SEDOL Code if it is a local foreign share, to help the broker locate the stock.

A few foreign companies with ADRs have set up direct-purchase stock plans that allow investors to purchase ADRs directly without having to go through a broker. Depository banks that participate in and administer these programs include J. P. Morgan (Shareholders Services Program) and Bank of New York (Global BuyDIRECT). Thirteen companies in the Top 100 participate in one of these programs, among them: Adecco, AEGON, Astra, Fresenius, Luxottica, Novo Nordisk, Reuters, Sony, and Vodafone. We expect that more international companies will offer direct-purchase plans in the future. To find out if an ADR you are interested in has a direct-purchase stock plan, call (800) 749-1687 (for J. P. Morgan ADRs) or (800) 345-1612 (for Bank of New York ADRs); you can also find a current list of participating companies on the Internet at http://www.netstockdirect.com.

Once You Have Invested . . .

Be a Patient Investor

As we have said before, once you're in, be prepared to hold your stocks for a long time. A "buy and hold" strategy gives your solid investments time to grow and spares you from the impossible task of trying to predict short-term market movements. Besides, moving into and out of stocks can cost you a great deal in commission dollars and (if you've been reasonably successful) capital gains taxes; those are dollars you would be better off keeping invested in your solid growth stocks.

When to Throw in the Towel

Of course, there are exceptions. If a stock is not working out, if a company has gone into new businesses it knows nothing about, or if you think management has fundamentally changed for the worse, *sell*. If revenues or earnings growth is slowing, or margins appear to be deteriorating, make sure it is a temporary development. Otherwise, it may be prudent to switch into a stock that is more attractive fundamentally. And be wary of adverse political or economic changes. In general, keep an eye out for stocks that have fallen relative to their local market. Shares often rise and fall for less than valid reasons, but an isolated price decline should be enough to trigger a review of a company if not an outright sale. Many investors use the "20–20 Rule," automatically selling if the shares decline by 20% in value and 20% relative to the local market.

There is one other, happier, reason to sell: your shares surge in price during a short period of time. Then you might consider taking your profits and reinvesting in a more reasonably valued company. But you should sell in this case only if the rapid appreciation and new valuation of your stock clearly exceed the long-term growth potential of the company. Resist the temptation to sell your winners just because they are up.

Brief Descriptions of Our Top 100 Companies

1. **Adecco,** Switzerland:
   One of the world's largest temporary agencies.
2. **AEGON,** Netherlands:
   Eighth largest insurer in the world in terms of assets; operates in the Netherlands, Germany, Belgium, Hungary, Spain, the United States, and the United Kingdom.

3. **Ahold,** Netherlands:
   A giant in the food-retailing business, operating in its home market the Netherlands, Portugal, the Czech Republic, Poland, and the United States. Ahold is the fifth largest food retailer in the United States.

4. **Airtours,** United Kingdom:
   Runs forty-one hotels, three cruise ships, two charter airlines, and tour operations in the United Kingdom, the United States, Canada, and Scandinavia; 30% owned by United States cruise giant Carnival Corporation.

5. **Astra,** Sweden:
   One of the largest drug companies in the world, with top-selling ulcer and asthma medicines worldwide.

6. **Bangkok Bank,** Thailand:
   Largest commercial bank in Thailand, with one of the most extensive branch networks in Southeast Asia.

7. **Bank of Ireland,** Ireland:
   Innovative bank using dominant market position and strong cash flows in Ireland to fund successful expansion in the United Kingdom and the United States.

8. **Bank of the Philippine Islands,** Philippines:
   A leading Philippine retail and corporate bank.

9. **Barco,** Belgium:
   Top manufacturer of specialized components including projectors and display systems and equipment for graphics and automation; 60% of sales in Europe.

10. **Bombardier**, Canada:
    Leading manufacturer worldwide of transportation equipment, including subway cars, high-speed trains, and regional and luxury airplanes.

11. **Canon,** Japan:
    One of the world's largest manufacturers of copying machines and a leader in cameras and printers.

12. **Carrefour,** France:
    France-based hypermarket company that is now global in scope, with 175 stores in Europe, 57 in Latin America, and 13 in Asia.

13. **Castorama,** France:
    The Home Depot of France.

14. **Cheung Kong (Holdings)**, Hong Kong:
    One of the largest Hong Kong property development and infrastructure companies, founded and run by legendary billionaire Li Ka-shing.

15. **Cifra**, Mexico:
    Largest food retailer and hypermarket company in Mexico; joint venture with Wal-Mart.

16. **Citic Pacific,** Hong Kong:
    The investment arm of the People's Republic of China; a holding company with interests in the major infrastructure companies of Hong Kong as well as projects in China.

17. **City Developments**, Singapore:
    Largest property development company in Singapore; recently expanded aggressively into the hotel business under the name Millennium Hotels; bought NYC's Plaza Hotel and twenty hotels in Europe.

18. **Coca-Cola Amatil**, Australia:
    An anchor bottler for Coke and one of the largest bottlers based outside of the United States, operating in Australia, Indonesia, New Zealand, among others. 1997 deal to buy Coke bottler in the Philippines. 1998 deal to buy Korean Coke bottler and spin off European operations.

19. **Coca-Cola Femsa,** Mexico:
    Anchor bottler in the Coke system with $1 billion in sales, operating fifteen beverage plants and fifty distribution centers in Mexico and Argentina.

20. **Colruyt**, Belgium:
    Leading food retailer in Belgium with more than 150 outlets, expanding elsewhere in Europe.

21. **Compañía de Telecomunicaciones de Chile,** Chile:
    Chile's dominant telecommunications company (44% owned by Telefónica de España).

22. **Compass Group,** United Kingdom:
    One of the largest contract catering companies in the world.

23. **CRH**, Ireland:
    One of the world's largest manufacturers and suppliers of building materials; nearly 70% of its revenues derived from mainland Europe, North America, and Argentina.

24. **Cycle & Carriage,** Singapore:
    Holds the Mercedes-Benz, Mitsubishi, and Proton franchises in Singapore; expanding throughout Asia. Also involved in Singapore property development

25. **Danka Business Systems,** United Kingdom:
    The world's largest independent supplier of and service provider for photocopiers, facsimile machines, and other automated office equipment; operates in more than 30 countries around the world.

26. **Dimension Data,** South Africa:
    Leading information technology company in South Africa, operating in communications, software, and services; distributes Cisco products and has a joint venture with U.S.-based EDS.

27. **Edison,** Italy:
Accounts for 5% of Italy's electric power and 5.6% of Italy's natural gas output; joint ventures in Russia, France, Egypt, and Pakistan.

28. **Endesa,** Spain:
Electric utility accounting for more than half of the total energy output of Spain; has expanded into the electricity business in Argentina, Venezuela, and Peru, the cable TV business in Spain and France, and the solid waste business in Spain.

29. **Enersis,** Chile:
The largest publicly held electric power conglomerate in Latin America, with operations in various countries throughout the region.

30. **Ericsson,** Sweden:
One of the world's largest manufacturers of telecommunications equipment for wired and mobile systems.

31. **Eurotherm,** United Kingdom:
One of the world's largest manufacturers of industrial control equipment.

32. **Fairey Group,** United Kingdom:
Manufactures and distributes worldwide specialized components for industrial electronics, electrical power, aerospace, and defense filtration and ceramics.

33. **Fraser & Neave,** Singapore:
Coke anchor bottler with seventeen soft drink plants in eight countries, including Singapore, Malaysia, Brunei, Cambodia, and Vietnam.

34. **Fresenius Medical Care,** Germany:
The largest fully integrated producer of kidney dialysis machines in the world.

35. **Gas Natural,** Spain:
Leading supplier and distributor of natural gas in Spain; has a joint venture to explore opportunities in Mexico, Colombia, Argentina, Uruguay, and Brazil.

36. **GEHE,** Germany:
One of the world's leading wholesalers of pharmaceuticals; 70% of sales are generated outside Germany, mainly in Europe.

37. **Gruma,** Mexico:
Largest producer of corn flour in the Western Hemisphere; 20% owned by Archer Daniels Midland.

38. **Hagemeyer,** Netherlands:
A classic Dutch trading firm with 1996 sales of $4.7 billion in businesses ranging from auto parts to commercial vehicles to gourmet foods.

39. **Heineken,** Netherlands:
A world powerhouse in the brewing industry with brand names such as

Heineken and Amstel Light; operations in 70 countries and sales of $7 billion per annum.

40. **Hellenic Bottling,** Greece:
    Dominant Coke bottler in Greece, Bulgaria, and Armenia; holds stakes in Coke-bottling operations in Ireland, Moldova, Romania, Russia, and Nigeria.

41. **Hennes & Mauritz,** Sweden:
    A leading fashion retailer in Europe with stores in Sweden, Austria, Belgium, the Netherlands, Norway, Denmark, France, Switzerland, and the United Kingdom.

42. **HSBC Holdings,** Hong Kong:
    One of the largest banks in the world, headquartered in the United Kingdom since 1991, still gets more than 30% of revenues from Asia; a global force in the financial industry.

43. **Hutchison Whampoa,** Hong Kong:
    Hong Kong–based conglomerate active in ports, retailing, telecommunications, electricity, hotels, and consumer goods manufacturing.

44. **IHC Caland,** Netherlands:
    Leading oil services company with more than 60% of sales generated outside Europe.

45. **Independent Newspapers,** Ireland:
    A media and communications group with businesses in Ireland, South Africa, Britain, France, Portugal, Australia, New Zealand, and Mexico.

46. **Investec Bank,** South Africa:
    Fifth largest bank in South Africa, specializing in niche services and now expanding overseas; has grown net income at compound rate of 37% per annum over the last ten years.

47. **Leighton Holdings,** Australia:
    A major civil engineering, construction, and contract mining firm in Australia with business in Hong Kong, Thailand, Indonesia, Malaysia, and Vietnam.

48. **L'Oréal,** France:
    World's largest cosmetics company with 1996 sales of $11.8 billion and brand names such as Lancôme, Helena Rubenstein, and L'Oréal.

49. **Lukoil,** Russia:
    Russia's largest vertically integrated oil company; owns vast crude oil reserves.

50. **Luxottica,** Italy:
    World leader in the design and manufacture of mid- to premium-priced eyeglass frames and sunglasses; also owns LensCrafters, the largest optical retailer in the world.

51. **Magna International,** Canada:
    A world leader in automotive parts and an independent supplier to some of the world's largest auto companies.

52. **Magnum,** Malaysia:
    Has 44% share of the gaming market in Malaysia with monopoly on traditional games favored by Chinese ethnic minority; expanding into the Philippines and China.
53. **Mannesmann,** Germany:
    Conglomerate with 43% of revenues in machinery, 22% in automotive engineering, 21% in tubular steel and 8% in telecommunications; telecommunications is this company's high-growth business.
54. **Manutan,** France:
    One of the world's largest mail-order companies specializing in industrial equipment; sixty percent of revenues derived outside France.
55. **Marschollek,** Germany:
    Rapidly growing financial group providing insurance and financial management services to professionals in Germany.
56. **Misys,** United Kingdom:
    Supplies software, management systems, and services to corporate information technology departments.
57. **Natuzzi,** Italy:
    World leader in leather-upholstered furniture; distributes unique designs through 15,000 points of sale in 118 countries.
58. **Nokia,** Finland:
    Second largest manufacturer of mobile phones in the world.
59. **Novartis,** Switzerland:
    One of the world's largest drug companies, formed in 1996 by the merger of Ciba-Geigy and Sandoz.
60. **Novo Nordisk,** Denmark:
    World leader in products used for treatment of diabetics and world's largest producer of industrial enzymes.
61. **Nutricia,** Netherlands:
    Producer of infant formula with dominant market share in Europe; specializes in use of natural materials.
62. **Panamco,** Panama:
    Anchor bottler for Coca-Cola; the largest soft drink bottler in Latin America and one of the largest Coca-Cola bottlers in the world; operates in Mexico, Brazil, Colombia, Costa Rica, and Venezuela.
63. **Perez Companc,** Argentina:
    Dynamic Latin American energy company with core business in oil and gas; expanding into telecommunications and electricity.
64. **Perpetual,** United Kingdom:
    One of the top-performing mutual fund companies in the United Kingdom with nearly £7 billion of assets under management.

65. **Petrobras,** Brazil:
    Monopoly integrated oil company in Brazil; is beginning to exploit vast untapped reserves and benefit from governmental reform.

66. **Phoenix Mecano,** Switzerland:
    One of the world's largest and most cost-efficient suppliers of parts and components to equipment manufacturers.

67. **PolyGram,** Netherlands:
    Entertainment company with recording labels including Mercury, Motown, Island, Verve, and Deutsche Grammophon; recent movies have included *Mr. Holland's Opus* and *Fargo;* 75% owned by Philips.

68. **Potash Corporation of Saskatchewan,** Canada:
    Largest producer of potash in the world, second largest producer of nitrogen, third largest producer of phosphate; all three are key ingredients of fertilizer.

69. **Powerscreen,** Ireland:
    Leading manufacturer of machinery used for screening, crushing, and recycling materials used for the construction and building industries; 50% of revenues come from exports.

70. **Provident Financial,** United Kingdom:
    Financial services company specializing in home credit, provided door to door, and auto insurance.

71. **Psion,** United Kingdom:
    High-tech firm with 33% of the world market for handheld computers.

72. **Randstad,** Netherlands:
    The fourth largest employment agency in the world, with 960 offices in nine countries.

73. **Renaissance,** Canada:
    Oil and gas company centered in the Western Canadian Sedimentary Basin; abundant proven reserves and 10.6 million acres of unexplored land.

74. **Rentokil Initial,** United Kingdom:
    The largest business services group in the world, specializing in pest control, timber treatment, security, cleaning, machine maintenance, tropical plants, contract catering, and personnel.

75. **Reuters,** United Kingdom:
    The world's biggest news and financial information company, reaching 225,000 computer screens daily with live information—well ahead of its nearest competitor.

76. **Rexel,** France:
    One of the world's leading distributors of electrical parts and supplies, such as wires, cables and ducts, particularly to electrical contractors.

77. **Roche,** Switzerland:
100-year-old pharmaceutical company with drugs such as Aleve, Invirase (an AIDS drug), and Accutane.

78. **Rohm,** Japan:
Manufacturer of specialized, custom-designed semiconductors.

79. **SAP,** Germany:
World's fourth largest software company; clients include Coca-Cola, Compaq, Microsoft, IBM, and Deutsche Telekom.

80. **SEB,** France:
World leader in cookware, bakeware, and small household electric appliances; more than two thirds of revenues are generated outside France.

81. **Sema Group,** United Kingdom:
One of Europe's leading information technology companies with businesses in the United Kingdom, France, Scandinavia, and Asia.

82. **Seven-Eleven Japan,** Japan:
The largest chain of convenience stores in Japan with 6,400 outlets; a dominant retailing force in a country where mom-and-pop retailers predominate.

83. **Siebe,** United Kingdom:
The United Kingdom's largest diversified engineering group and the European market leader in temperature controls.

84. **Sodexho Alliance,** France:
The largest contract food services group in the world, handling the food needs of businesses ranging from the Kowloon and Canton Railway Corporation to the Sydney Opera House to Wimbledon.

85. **Sony,** Japan:
The company that brought you the camcorder, the Walkman, and *Jerry Maguire,* now moving headlong into digital technologies.

86. **Sophus Berendsen,** Denmark:
Business service group; owns 36% of Rentokil and has separate businesses in textile services (laundry), power and motion control (hydraulics), and electronics and data (marketing of electronic goods).

87. **Soquimicha,** Chile:
One of the world's largest producers of specialty fertilizers.

88. **South African Breweries,** South Africa:
Fourth largest brewer in the world, with 98.6% share of the South African beer market and 50% share of continental Africa's beer market, as well as brewing plants in Hungary, Romania, Poland, and China.

89. **Sun Hung Kai Properties**, Hong Kong:
Largest and most successful property company in Hong Kong—where property is king.

90. **Synthelabo,** France:
    Third largest drug company in France, 56% owned by L'Oréal; specializes in urology, gastroenterology, and allergy drugs.

91. **Telebras,** Brazil:
    The primary supplier of telecommunications services in Brazil and the largest publicly traded company in Latin America by market capitalization.

92. **Telecom Italia,** Italy:
    The sixth-largest provider of telecommunications services in the world.

93. **Telecom New Zealand,** New Zealand:
    The primary supplier of telecommunications services in New Zealand with a large percentage of revenues in high-margin, value-added services.

94. **Telefónica de España,** Spain:
    Spain's dominant telecommunications company with extensive operations in Latin America and a booming mobile phone business.

95. **Teva,** Israel:
    Manufacturer of Copaxone, used in the treatment of multiple sclerosis; third largest maker of generic drugs in the United States and largest pharmaceutical company in Israel.

96. **Tomra,** Norway:
    Has 80% share of the world market for can- and bottle-recycling machines.

97. **VNU,** Netherlands:
    Publishing and information giant in magazines, newspapers, marketing and trade shows, and business information services; operates in the Netherlands, the United Kingdom, Belgium, the Czech Republic, Hungary, and the United States.

98. **Vodafone,** United Kingdom:
    Largest provider of mobile telecommunications services in the United Kingdom; investments in mobile service businesses in twelve countries.

99. **WM-data,** Sweden:
    Information technology outsourcing firm operating in Sweden, Denmark, Finland, the Netherlands, and Norway.

100. **Zodiac,** France:
    Leading supplier of parts and products to the civil and military aerospace industry worldwide.

4

Following Your
International Companies

There is nothing like the tickertape . . . nothing that promises hour after hour, day after day, such sudden developments; nothing that disappoints so cruelly or occasionally fulfills with such unbelievable, passionate magnificence.

—WALTON KNOWLETON GUTMAN, 1960

Following Your Stocks

As we have said before, it is always good to keep an eye on your investments. Many business journals and newspapers report share price movements and basic data for foreign stocks, particularly those that have ADRs listed on one of the U.S. exchanges. Below we discuss how to follow your stocks in *The Wall Street Journal* ("the *Journal*"), which is widely available and published every business day. Stock tables in many daily publications use the same general format.

For those foreign companies with ADRs listed on a major U.S. stock exchange, investors can find basic share price information in the "C" Section of the *Journal* under the heading of the exchange on which the shares trade (these include the New York Stock Exchange; the American Stock Exchange; and the National Association of Securities Dealers Automated Quotation national market system, or NASDAQ).

The following sample listing, for Dutch supermarket giant Ahold, was selected from the *Journal*, Section C, on June 19, 1996, under the heading "New York Stock Exchange Composite Transactions," where companies are listed alphabetically. Take a look at the *Journal* clip on page 40, focusing on the line for Ahold. The first two columns show the high ($56.25) and the low ($34.63) price at which Ahold's stock traded over the previous fifty-two weeks. The next column gives the name (or an abbreviated version of the name) of the company.

	52 Weeks Hi	Lo	Stock	Sym	Div	Yld %	P.E	Vol 100s	Hi	Lo	Close	Net Chg
	56¼	34⅝	Ahold	AHO	.89e	1.6	...	25	55⅜	54¾	55¼	– ¼
	60⅞	49¾	AirProduct	APD	1 10f	2.0	15	2194	57⅞	56⅜	56⅜	–1¼
	29½	19¼	AirbornFrght	ABF	.30	1.2	24	255	26⅛	25⅜	25⅞	+ ⅜
s	22½	11½	♣ Airgas	ARG		...	34	460	20¼	20	20⅛	...
	18⅞	15	Airlease	FLY	1.80m	10.5	11	72	17⅛	17	17⅛	+ ⅛
	35⅝	25⅝	AirTouch	ATI		...	cc	10032	29¾	29	29⅛	– ¾
	44⅛	26⅛	AK Steel	AKS	.45e	1.0	5	263	43⅛	42⅞	43⅛	+ ⅛
	40⅜	27¾	AK Steel pf		2.15	5.6	...	8	38⅝	38⅝	38⅝	...
n	25½	23¼	AL PwrCap TOPrS		1.84	7.9	...	9	23⅜	23¼	23⅜	...
	26⅛	24⅞	AlaPwr pfA		1.90	7.6	...	36	25¼	25	25	...
	25⅛	21⅝	AlaPwr pfC		1.60	7.2	...	1	22¼	22¼	22¼	– ¼
	25	21½	AlaPwr pfB		1.70	7.4	...	1	23⅛	23⅛	23⅛	...
	26¼	24⅞	AlaPwr pfH		1.90	7.6	...	17	25	25	25	...
	19⅞	15⅞	AlamoGp	ALG	.40	2.3	13	34	17⅝	17⅝	17⅝	– ⅛
	30¾	13⅝	AlaskaAir	ALK		...	14	1022	28⅝	28	28⅛	– ⅜
	26½	17⅛	♣ AlbanyInt	AIN	.40	2.0	14	131	20¼	20	20¼	+ ⅛
	24⅛	15	Albemarle	ALB	.22	1.0	8	699	22½	22⅛	22½	+ ½
n	20⅛	15	AlbEnrg g	AOG	.40	...	...	4	18⅜	18⅜	18⅜	– ⅛
	43¾	27⅞	♣ AlbertoCl	ACV	.36	.9	20	474	41½	40¾	41	+1⅜
	38⅞	24¾	♣ AlbertoCl A	ACVA	.36	1.0	18	750	37	36⅜	36⅜	+1¼
	41½	28⅝	Albertsons	ABS	.60	1.5	21	2193	40¾	39¾	40	– ⅝
	36⅝	28⅜	♣ Alcan	AL	.60	1.9	15	4524	31⅛	30½	31	+ ½
	22⅛	16	AlcatelAsthom	ALA	.92e	5.2	...	375	17¾	17⅝	17¾	...

Next to that you'll see the ticker symbol (AHO), under which the stock trades in the United States on the New York Stock Exchange. Under "Div" is shown the annualized dividend payment ($0.89) based on the last monthly, quarterly, semi-annual, or annual payment. In this case, the lowercase "e" after $0.89 indicates that a dividend was declared in the last twelve months but the *Journal* does not have a record of regular dividend payments. Accordingly, the annualized rate shown may not be the most up-to-date figure available. The letter "e" may also signify that the dividend payment shown was adjusted for a stock split or bonus. "Yld %" shows the dividend yield for the company (1.6%) based on the annualized dividend payment shown in the table. The formula for calculating dividend yield is dividend payment divided by share price.

Under "PE," you will see the current price/earnings (P/E) ratio of the company, calculated by dividing the most recent share price by the total earnings of the last four quarters. This is commonly known as the trailing, or historic, P/E ratio, since it is based on historic data, not projections for future earnings. (In the case of Ahold, the *Journal* did not have enough data to show the P/E ratio.) Moving over to the next column, headed "Vol 100s," you'll see how many shares were traded the previous trading day on that exchange, divided by 100. Accordingly, 2,500 Ahold shares changed hands on the previous day. The next two columns show the high ($55.38) and low ($54.75) prices Ahold's shares traded at during the day. Finally, the last two columns show the price at which Ahold

PARIS
(in French francs)

	Close	Net Chg.
Accor	725.00	− 2.00
Air Liquide	897.00	+ 2.00
Alcatel Alstm	454.20	− 1.50
AXA Group	287.00	− 2.20
Bic	721.00	+ 5.00
BNP	184.00	− 1.00
Carrefour	2854.00	+ 8.00
Club Med	458.20	− 9.70
Danone	769.00	− 4.00
Dassault Avitn	715.00	− 1.00
Elf Aquitaine	x372.60	+ 7.20

shares closed at the end of the day ($55.25) and the change from the previous day (down $0.25).

Note that the table may contain many kinds of notations and footnotes. For example, you can see a small "s" before Airgas, signifying an adjustment to the numbers because of a stock split or stock dividend. These notes are explained in detail in a box called "Explanatory Notes" published in Section C of the *Journal* every day at the beginning of the NYSE listings. Keep an eye out for the three-leaf clover that appears next to the name of select companies (for example, next to Airgas in our sample). That little symbol (explained in "Explanatory Notes") indicates that you can get a free copy of the company's annual report by calling (800) 654-CLUB, or (800) 654-2582. Details of this service also appear in the same section of the *Journal*.

If you want to follow a foreign stock that has no ADR listed and does not trade OTC, look at the "World Markets" page, also in Section C of the *Journal*. You'll see a table called "Foreign Markets" showing the local share price, in foreign currency terms, of more than 500 foreign companies. These companies are listed alphabetically under the name of the foreign city where the stock exchange is located (if the country has more than one stock exchange) or country (if the country only has one stock exchange) where the company's shares are listed and trade.

Above we show a selection of French companies, under the listing "Paris," from the "Foreign Markets" table in the *Journal* on June 19, 1996. Note that only the closing price and change from the previous day are shown. The shares of Carrefour, a French retailer, closed at 2,854 French francs, up 8 francs from the previous day.

In order to calculate the share price in dollars, turn to the "Foreign Exchange" page and find the "Currency Trading" table. A sample from this table, also taken from the June 19, 1996, *Journal*, is shown on page 42. This table lists exchange rates for every major world currency vis-à-vis the U.S. dollar. The last two columns of the table show the amount of foreign currency that would be equivalent to $1.00, over the previous two days. Divide the foreign currency–denominated share price by this figure (use the one from the most recent day available) to get a dollar price for the shares. For example, in the selection from the "Currency Trading" table shown below, we see that $1.00 traded for 5.1353 French francs on Tuesday (note that we use the simple exchange rate for the franc rather than the forward rates). Dividing Carrefour's share price of 2,854 French francs by this rate, we get a U.S. dollar price of $555.76 per share.

The *Journal* also has many other useful tables for investors interested in following foreign stocks, particularly on the "World Markets" page. For example, there is a table called "Stock Market Indices" that gives the daily price change and level of all major world stock markets in local currency terms. The "Dow Jones World Stock Index" gives a daily update of price changes in individual world markets and regional indices in U.S. dollar terms (it also includes percentage change over twelve months and since the beginning of the year, as well as yearly highs and lows). The "Dow Jones World Industry Groups" table shows how various industry groups have performed daily and year to date, on both a global and a regional basis.

Country	U.S. $ equiv.		Currency per U.S. $	
	Tues.	Mon.	Tues.	Mon.
Canada (Dollar)	.7306	.7314	1.3688	1.3672
30-Day Forward	.7309	.7318	1.3681	1.3665
90-Day Forward	.7317	.7327	1.3666	1.3649
180-Day Forward	.7327	.7336	1.3649	1.3631
Chile (Peso)	.002451	.002441	408.05	409.75
China (Renminbi)	.1195	.1199	8.3690	8.3422
Colombia (Peso)	.0009497	.0009510	1053.00	1051.50
Czech. Rep. (Koruna) .	....	....	....	....
Commercial rate	.03610	.03599	27.704	27.784
Denmark (Krone)	.1714	.1710	5.8352	5.8467
Ecuador (Sucre)	....	....	....	....
Floating rate	.0003229	.0003224	3097.00	3102.00
Finland (Markka)	.2161	.2148	4.6283	4.6552
France (Franc)	.1947	.1937	5.1353	5.1625
30-Day Forward	.1951	.1939	5.1264	5.1560
90-Day Forward	.1955	.1945	5.1157	5.1425
180-Day Forward	.1962	.1952	5.0961	5.1228

5

Trends and Observations

If I buy stocks on Smith's tips I must sell those same stocks on Smith's tip. . . . Suppose Smith is away on holiday when the selling time comes around? . . . I know from experience that no-one can give me a tip that will make more money for me than my own judgement.
— REMINISCENCES OF A STOCK OPERATOR, EDWIN LEFEVRE (1923)

Making Exceptions

As we selected companies for the Top 100, we realized we would have to make exceptions in order to wind up with a balanced list. For example, if we had stuck strictly with our criteria across the board, we would not have been able to include any Japanese companies. The Japanese economy and stock market suffered badly from 1989 to 1996, and our screens would have knocked Japan off our lists. But to ignore Japan would be a mistake; after all, Japan's economic woes are not going to last forever.

So we bent the rules a little. In Japan, we looked for companies that have performed well relative to the local economy and to the local stock market, which is still 50% below its peak. The Japanese companies we chose, firms such as Canon (CANNY—NASDAQ) and Seven-Eleven Japan (SVELY—OTC) may not have rewarded investors as well as some of the other companies on our list, but they have prospered during very difficult times, a testament to their resilience. Japan remains one of the most developed economies in the world and its stocks still represent around 30% of world stock market capitalization. Sooner or later, this market will rebound, and when it does, we think the companies in the Top 100 could be winners.

We also made exceptions for the emerging market companies in the Top 100 after finding that very few emerging market companies have long-term track records. Of course, emerging markets are a relatively young asset class. Ten years ago, emerging stock markets represented only 1 to 2% of world stock market capitalization. For equity investors, there just were not a lot of companies to choose from. It's a different story today, however. By the end of 1996 emerging markets accounted for 9% of world stock market capitalization (18% if the United States is not included). Not surprisingly, we were able to find some terrific companies with relatively short histories as publicly traded companies (far more than we could include in this book), and we determined to include a selection of the best in the Top 100.

For example, Mexico-based corn flour producer Gruma (GRMBF—OTC) has been publicly traded for only the last three years, and these have been three difficult years for the Mexican economy and stock market. Had we stuck to our rules, Gruma would have been eliminated. But we did not want to do that. GRUMA is the largest producer of corn flour in the Western Hemisphere, with 50% of its business in the United States, and it has an exceptionally strong market position. Management has done a good job of steering the company through adversity and is preparing to take advantage of better years ahead, particularly as the demand for Mexican food in the United States and prepackaged tortillas in Latin America continues to rise.

That said, emerging market stocks are not right for everyone. They generally offer greater-than-average returns but also greater risk. Only you can determine just how much risk you feel comfortable with.

Grading Financial Companies

Banks and insurance companies operate differently than industrial firms do, and thus they need to be judged by different criteria. We had to adjust our grading formula for those firms that made it into the Top 100. There are only a few—five banks and one insurance company, to be exact—but they are well worth making exceptions for. Take HSBC Holdings (HSBHY—OTC), for example, the largest bank in Hong Kong and now among the top five banks in the world. HSBC makes a great deal of money in Asia, but it is no slouch in the rest of the world either; it also owns banks in the Middle East, Canada, the United States, and Brazil.

You'll notice that on the tables accompanying the bank stocks we substituted net revenues (defined as net interest income plus other revenues such as fees and commissions) for sales. We also substituted gross profit (net revenues minus operating expenses) for EBITDA or operating income, as neither applies to a bank or insurance firm. Finally, we decided to use two measures for quality of management and drop the risk category for lack of data. We stuck with return on equity (ROE) as it is a good measure of efficiency for banks. However, we adjusted the scoring, awarding no points for 0 to 12% ROE, 5 points for 12 to 16% returns, and 10 points for anything over 16%. We also added the category of return on assets (ROA), a standard measure of performance for financial concerns that use loans and investments to generate profits. Here, a return of 1.0 to 1.25% was good enough to merit 5 points, while anything above 1.25% was excellent and garnered ten points.

Note that financial services firms are not the same as banks or insurance firms. Their income statements and balance sheets are similar to other service companies appearing in the Top 100, and they were graded according to our standard formulas.

Trends Among the Top 100

Who would have thought that two of our three companies involved in "printing and publishing" (we used 28 industry categories) would turn out to be in the Netherlands: PolyGram (the entertainment giant) and VNU. The third, Independent Newspapers, is based in Ireland. On the other hand, it came as no surprise that four of the eleven retail stocks on our list are French: Carrefour, Castorama, Manutan, and Rexel—though none of them is involved in high fashion, which would be closer to the general perception of French retailing. Ironically, our one trendy retailer, Hennes & Mauritz, is based in Sweden, a country not particularly well known as a pacesetter in the world of fashion.

Switzerland is home to some of the biggest and most successful pharmaceutical firms in the world. Not surprisingly, two out of the four Swiss firms in the Top 100 are pharmaceutical companies, Roche (ROHHY—OTC) and Novartis (NVTSY—OTC). Interestingly, it might have been three out of five if Sandoz and Ciba-Geigy had not merged and formed Novartis.

In the emerging markets, we mostly came up with companies involved in infrastructure development: electric utilities and oil and gas, telecommunications, construction, and property development companies. These may not be the kinds of industries in which you would expect to find classic growth companies, but it makes sense when you are dealing with rapidly developing economies. Companies with strong brand-name recognition in the food and beverage sector (i.e., the Coca-Cola bottlers) also kept showing up on our lists. Finally, because credit growth is an important component of economic development, we found that companies in the financial sector in many emerging markets showed strong earnings growth relatively consistently.

The Top Sectors in the Top 100

The "Services" sector topped our list, with thirty-five of the Top 100. Within that group, the leading industry group is retailing, with eleven companies that made the cut. This did not surprise us. The retailers on our list are classic growth companies, with the kind of characteristics we are trying to emphasize: steady revenue growth, strong cash flow generation, consistent margins, reasonable debt levels, and limited regulation to impede opportunistic expansion. Besides, the introduction of the hypermarket concept and new technologies in retailing have revolutionized the business and brought big profits to those companies smart enough and entrepreneurial enough to lead the charge.

The "Consumer Goods" sector came in second, with 20 companies in the Top 100. In that group, the health and personal care industry (mostly pharmaceutical companies) led the way, with nine companies on our list. This makes sense to us, too: the global marketplace has a voracious appetite for better drugs, medical treatment, and specialized equipment. And there are a number of global pharmaceutical companies that have consistently invested in research and development and just as consistently produced new "blockbuster" drugs. These companies have outstanding track records and are prized by investors around the world.

"Outsourcing," one of our favorite themes, cuts across sectors. We thought we would find a lot of "outsourcing" companies among our Top 100, but we were surprised at just how many showed up and at the breadth of the trend toward contracting out noncore business functions, particularly in western Europe. It runs the industrial gamut from Rentokil's pest control business to Phoenix Mecano's industrial component business, Compass Group's contract catering business, and Dimension Data's information technology business and is a worldwide phenomenon. Even a company such as Finland's Valmet, which did not make it into the Top 100 because of the cyclical nature of the paper industry, has said it could outsource up to 40% of production.

The country with the most companies in the Top 100 is the United Kingdom, with 15. Given that the United Kingdom is home to the third largest stock market in the world outside of the United States and Japan, that makes sense. The selection of U.K. firms is dominated by service providers rather than manufacturers, reflecting technological and industrial trends in Great Britain. Six of these service providers are "outsourcing firms"—again, an area that has performed well and appears to have strong growth prospects.

France and the Netherlands are tied for second, with nine companies in the Top 100, and Hong Kong and Germany are tied for third. Selections from all four of these countries are noted above. With only five firms in the Top 100, Germany is underrepresented relative to the size of its economy, but we found few companies that met our criteria. The country has only recently begun to establish an equity culture, and stock market investing is relatively undeveloped. Most local investment portfolios have been dominated by bonds. It was not until 1997 that the national telephone company (Deutsche Telekom) was privatized, allowing local investors to own shares in the German equivalent of "Ma Bell." Of course, there are exceptions. One German company that has handsomely rewarded investors, found great success on the world stage, and scored highly in our grading system is enterprise software producer SAP (SAPHY—OTC).

For a detailed breakdown of the Top 100 by country, sector, and industry, see Appendix page 360.

A Few Final Notes

We were happy to discover that as we were writing this book more and more of our companies were developing Web-sites. A number of companies that did not have one when we started this project asked us to include their Web addresses by the time we were done. Others said their Web sites would go up within the next few months. Although it's a trend that's more prevalent among larger-capitalization companies in developed nations (as opposed to small-capitalization companies in emerging markets), it's a heartening sign for investors. Having a company's annual report at your fingertips can make your search for information that much easier. We included all the company Web sites we knew about at the time of publication.

Of course, every company on the Top 100 publishes an annual report or some equivalent and offers information in English as well as the local language.

A few "housekeeping" points for you to keep in mind as you review the Top 100. First, a number of companies objected to their industry classification, which appears at the top of each write-up; however, in an effort to standardize the information, we chose to use the sector descriptions used by Morgan Stanley Capital International (MSCI). While in some cases a little broad and in others a little narrow, these classifications are widely used in the financial industry and they do the job, allowing us to define a company's general business in just a few words and using a defined number of categories.

Second, some of the tables for companies in the Top 100 with the most impressive growth rates may be a little misleading. It is important to keep in mind that if a company was tiny ten years ago, not only would it have been difficult (and riskier) to invest in it then, but in the future it will be that much more difficult to match past performance. That does not mean the company has lost its glow. We are just pointing out that 40% compound annual EPS growth, while amazing, is easier to achieve in the early years of a successful (and sometimes niche) company than later on, when a company is bigger and a bit more mature. You can love a company and not expect it to repeat that kind of performance. Instead, look for signs of strong management, such as consistency, and make sure the company is in an industry you think has potential for the future.

Finally, we would like to give you our "watch list"—companies that did not make the cut because they did not have long enough track records as publicly traded companies (and we did not think they would be appropriate exceptions to our rules). Keep an eye on these companies (see the list that follows) . . . some of them could very well be among tomorrow's Top 100.

Company Name	Country	Business Description
1. Adidas	Germany	Sportswear, sports shoes
2. Assa Abloy	Sweden	World leader in locks
3. Autoliv	Sweden	World leader in air bags, seat belts
4. Baan	Netherlands	Enterprise software, networking
5. Banco Frances	Argentina	Banking and insurance
6. Bulgari	Italy	Jewelry and watches
7. CMG	U.K.	Consulting, computer services
8. Deutsche Telekom	Germany	Telecommunications
9. ENI	Italy	Oil and gas
10. Gedeon Richter	Hungary	Pharmaceuticals
11. Gucci	Italy	Handbags, fine leather goods
12. Hermès	France	Ties, silks, luxury goods
13. ING	Netherlands	Banking and insurance
14. Irish Permanent	Ireland	Banking and insurance
15. Mosenergo	Russia	Oil and gas
16. Petroleum Geo Services	Norway	Oil services
17. Sage	U.K.	Software development
18. SGL Carbon	Germany	Materials used for steel
19. SM Prime	Philippines	Retailing, mall development
20. Sol Melia	Spain	Hotel management; 180 properties worldwide
21. Telecom Italia Mobile	Italy	World's largest cellular company in terms of number of users
22. Vendex	Netherlands	Food retail and business services
23. Wolford	Austria	Hosiery
24. Zeneca	U.K.	Pharmaceuticals

6

Understanding the Financial Tables

"A business without profit is not a business any more than a pickle is a candy."

—CHARLES ABBOTT

The tables included with each of our company write-ups provide historical data and are intended to be used as starting points in your stock research. Some of the information presented in these tables was used in the grading system for the Top 100. Other information is provided solely for your use and interest. As you will hear again and again, past performance is no guarantee of future success, but the historical data in these tables can give you a good idea of the kind of performance you should be expecting from one of our Top 100 companies. Most important, the tables provide a yardstick against which the current prospects and valuations of a company can be measured. Below we explain how the tables are organized and give a few suggestions on how to use them effectively.

Standardized Format and Reference Tools

The financial tables have a standardized format that is easy to follow once you become familiar with it. And we have included two additional reference tools to help readers analyze the numbers: an **Annotated Stock Chart,** on the following pages, which illustrates how the information is organized, and a **Glossary,** which precedes the company list and explains all financial terms.

The financial tables are divided into five sections and contain ten years of data or as many years as we could find. The first section is a **Header**, including company name and ticker symbol, the stock exchange where the stock is traded, and an identification number. Next is **Box I,** containing operating and per share data in each company's local currency. This box contains items such as sales, EBIT (earnings

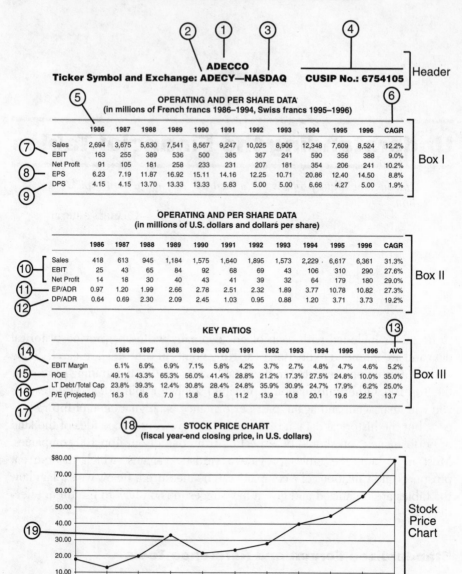

ADECCO
Ticker Symbol and Exchange: ADECY—NASDAQ   CUSIP No.: 6754105   Header

OPERATING AND PER SHARE DATA
(in millions of French francs 1986–1994, Swiss francs 1995–1996)

	1986	1987	1988	1989	1990	1991	1992	1993	1994	1995	1996	CAGR
Sales	2,694	3,675	5,630	7,541	8,567	9,247	10,025	8,906	12,348	7,609	8,524	12.2%
EBIT	163	255	389	536	500	385	367	241	590	356	388	9.0%
Net Profit	91	105	181	258	233	231	207	181	354	206	241	10.2%
EPS	6.23	7.19	11.87	16.92	15.11	14.16	12.25	10.71	20.86	12.40	14.50	8.8%
DPS	4.15	4.15	13.70	13.33	13.33	5.83	5.00	5.00	6.66	4.27	5.00	1.9%

Box I

OPERATING AND PER SHARE DATA
(in millions of U.S. dollars and dollars per share)

	1986	1987	1988	1989	1990	1991	1992	1993	1994	1995	1996	CAGR
Sales	418	613	945	1,184	1,575	1,640	1,895	1,573	2,229	6,617	6,361	31.3%
EBIT	25	43	65	84	92	68	69	43	106	310	290	27.6%
Net Profit	14	18	30	40	43	41	39	32	64	179	180	29.0%
EP/ADR	0.97	1.20	1.99	2.66	2.78	2.51	2.32	1.89	3.77	10.78	10.82	27.3%
DP/ADR	0.64	0.69	2.30	2.09	2.45	1.03	0.95	0.88	1.20	3.71	3.73	19.2%

Box II

KEY RATIOS

	1986	1987	1988	1989	1990	1991	1992	1993	1994	1995	1996	AVG
EBIT Margin	6.1%	6.9%	6.9%	7.1%	5.8%	4.2%	3.7%	2.7%	4.8%	4.7%	4.6%	5.2%
ROE	49.1%	43.3%	65.3%	56.0%	41.4%	28.8%	21.2%	17.3%	27.5%	24.8%	10.0%	35.0%
LT Debt/Total Cap	23.8%	39.3%	12.4%	30.8%	28.4%	24.8%	35.9%	30.9%	24.7%	17.9%	6.2%	25.0%
P/E (Projected)	16.3	6.6	7.0	13.8	8.5	11.2	13.9	10.8	20.1	19.6	22.5	13.7

Box III

STOCK PRICE CHART
(fiscal year-end closing price, in U.S. dollars)

Stock Price Chart

Notes: 1995–96 figures are pro forma before the amortization of goodwill, reflecting the impact of the merger between Adia and Ecco, which occurred in 8/96. Figures for 1986 to 1994 are for Ecco only and are not comparable to the new company's. 1995 dividend and 1996 long-term debt to total capital ratio are estimated. The share prices shown are for Ecco only and are not comparable to the ADR prices.

Key to Reading the Charts

Header

1. Company name.
2. Ticker symbol or code by which the stock is traded. If no ticker is available, Reuters code is shown.
3. Stock exchange on which the shares trade.
4. The CUSIP No. is the code number used to identify all stocks that trade in the United States. If the CUSIP No. is unavailable, the SEDOL Code (international identification number provided by International Stock Exchange in London) is shown.

Box I: Company results in local currency terms (if available)

5. Fiscal year-end. If no month is shown, company fiscal year ends in December.
6. Compound annual growth rate.
7. Earnings before interest and tax, similar to operating income. When possible, EBDIT (EBIT plus depreciation) or EBITDA (EBIT plus depreciation and amortization) is shown.
8. Earnings per share.
9. Dividends per share.

Box II: Company results in U.S. dollar terms

10. Consistency and CAGR of Sales, EBIT, and EPS; these form an important part of the company grade.
11. Earnings per ADR (if company has ADRs).
12. Dividends per ADR (if company has ADRs).

Box III: Ratios

13. Average growth rate.
14. EBIT divided by sales, similar to operating margin; a measure of profitability.
15. Return on equity (net profit divided by shareholders' equity); used to grade quality of management.
16. Long-term debt divided by total capital; used to grade risk.
17. Share price divided by following year's (projected) earnings per share; a measure of stock value.

Stock price chart: Fiscal year-end share price in dollar terms

18. Chart reflects foreign share prices in U.S. dollars or ADR prices, if available.
19. Consistency and CAGR of share price in dollars used in company grade.
20. Notes explain any unusual aspects of the company.

before interest and tax, similar to operating income), net profit, EPS (earnings per share), and DPS (dividends per share) on an annual basis. In the last column, the compound annual growth rate (CAGR) for each of these items is shown.

Third is **Box II,** which shows the same data as in Box I but in U.S. dollar terms. Note that if the company has an ADR, earnings and dividend per ADR are shown. Sometimes no local currency data are available and Box 1 is omitted, but U.S. dollar data are always included in the tables. Generally, we used fiscal year-end exchange rates to translate data into U.S. dollars, but there are exceptions (for example, France, where currency swings have been so dramatic that we decided to use average exchange rates for the French companies). Check the **Notes** at the bottom of the page for exceptions or special information on the company. We used the dollar data in Box II in our grading system, since U.S. investors are more interested in dollar returns. In particular, we looked at sales, EBIT, and EPS (or EP/ADR) growth, giving high marks for both consistent performance and superior absolute growth.

Box III presents four key ratios: EBIT Margin (EBIT divided by sales), ROE (return on equity), LT Debt/Total Capital (long-term debt divided by total capital), and the projected P/E Ratio (share price divided by the following year's earnings). At the end of each line the average for each ratio is shown. Two of these items are used in our grading system: ROE as an indication of management performance and LT Debt/Total Capital as a measure of balance sheet risk. The other ratios, EBIT Margin and P/E, are useful guides to profitability and valuation, respectively.

Note that data for each item are based on the company's fiscal year-end. Many companies have calendar fiscal years (ending in December), but some do not. If a company does not have a calendar fiscal year or if the fiscal year-end changes, a specific month is shown in the date lines in the tables and on the chart (for example, Sony has a fiscal year ending in May). Otherwise, if no month is shown the company has a calendar fiscal year.

The final box contains the **Stock Price Chart,** which shows the stock price (or ADR price) at the end of the fiscal year, in U.S. dollars. Share price performance also formed an important part of our grading system, with each company evaluated for both consistent share price appreciation and compound annual price growth.

Using the Tables to Evaluate Companies

1. The first thing to do is look over the tables and become comfortable with them. Refer to the diagram and Glossary to make sure you understand all the items shown and why they are important.

2. You should then look at the operating items in the first two boxes. As you

go over these boxes, the first thing to look for is consistency. In other words, look for steady increases year over year in the sales line, the EBIT line, the net profit line, and the EPS line. Consistency is the hallmark of a well-managed company. Then examine the compound annual growth figures at the end of each of the rows. Look for above-average growth in each of these categories. If you are not sure what this is, turn to Chapter 2 for details on the grading system regarding what we consider to be high growth numbers. In particular, after you have had a chance to read up on the company and check out current forecasts, see how estimated sales, EBIT, and EPS growth compare with past growth rates. Are they in line or higher than in the past? If lower, what is the reason?

3. Next turn your attention to the ratios, starting with the top row. Ideally, you should see a steady, high EBIT margin or an increasing trend, but keep in mind that margins vary from industry to industry. And low margins do not necessarily mean a company is poorly managed—they might be the result of a temporary situation, such as a merger, or a change in long-term strategy. Compare the average EBIT margin figure, or the margin over the last few years, with current EBIT margin forecasts. It should be similar or better. If the margin looks as if it is declining, watch out: it could be a sign of deterioration in the company's core business.

4. Evaluating ROE is easy: the higher the better. Look for an ROE that is at least as high as the return you could make from putting cash in the bank plus a healthy equity risk premium. And make sure the current ROE of the company is similar to or better than past years.

5. The ratio of long-term debt to total capital, on the other hand, should not be excessively high—and certainly should not be growing consistently. Look for debt to be shrinking rather than growing (one caveat: a high debt level might be related to strategic developments and could be temporary).

6. The P/E ratios shown on a table give you an idea of how the market has valued a company over time. Check the current P/E ratio (the current share price divided by projected earnings per share) and compare it with its historic range. If the current P/E ratio is much higher than the historic average, the shares may be overvalued and you may want to wait before buying.

7. Finally, at the bottom of the page is a stock price chart for each company; this is a clear indication of how the market has responded to the company's performance. In general, try not to buy a company's shares when they are trading at an all-time high. If the earnings outlook for the company looks bright and the valuation is reasonable, this may not be important. But caution is usually warranted when the shares are trading at lofty heights.

7

Glossary

ADR (American Depository Receipt) A receipt issued against a share of a foreign company held in the vault of a U.S. bank that entitles the holder to all dividends and capital gains of the foreign share. U.S. investors can buy the shares of a foreign company in the form of an ADR and save on transaction costs and foreign exchange fees.

AMEX (American Stock Exchange) See Exchange.

Amortization The write-down in value in set amounts over a period of years of intangible assets that have a limited life, including goodwill (see Goodwill). Goodwill usually exists when one company buys another; it represents the intangible parts of the company acquired that have value besides the tangible assets—for example a company's strong name in the marketplace. The concept of amortization is similar to that of depreciation (see Depreciation), which is the gradual write-down in value of tangible assets, such as plant or equipment, over a period of years. The purpose of both amortization and depreciation is to reflect accurately the resale value of the asset. Both are tax-deductible.

Assets Anything a company owns that has commercial or exchangeable value is an asset. Assets are usually divided into two parts: fixed assets (sometimes referred to as noncurrent assets), including property, plant and equipment (PP&E), construction in progress, and leasehold improvements; and current assets, including cash, marketable securities, inventories, receivables (money owed to the company for products or services sold), and deferred charges. Intangible assets, such as trademarks, patents, copyrights, and goodwill, are usually shown under fixed assets.

Balance sheet A statement that shows the financial position of a company at a given point in time. The balance sheet is divided into two parts that are equal or "balanced": total assets (both fixed and current) must be equal to total liabilities (both long- and short-term) plus shareholders' equity. The balance sheet is a detailed listing of the items that make up the two sides of this equation.

Book value The value of a company's assets after depreciation.

Book value per share The book value of a company divided by the total number of shares outstanding.

CAGR Compound annual growth rate.

CUSIP Number Stands for Committee on Uniform Securities Identification Procedures Number. All stocks and registered bonds that trade in the United States are identified by a CUSIP Number.

Depreciation Refers to the charges a company makes for the loss of value on property, plant, and equipment (PP&E, collectively known as the company's fixed assets) each year due to wear and tear or obsolescence. Equipment is deemed to have a useful life (of, say, ten to twenty years), after which it will have to be replaced. Rather than take a big charge all at once when the equipment needs to be replaced, a company divides the charge into equal installments and deducts a set amount each year. In this way, depreciation more accurately reflects the impact on a company's operations of the gradual loss of value on equipment. Depreciation is considered a noncash charge, since the amount being deducted has not been spent yet on the new equipment while the company retains the cash. The good news for companies is that depreciation is tax-deductible; the bad news is that it reduces reported earnings.

If you are having difficulty grasping the concept of depreciation, think of the annual decline in value of your car or personal computer, based on what you could sell them for in any given year. As time passes, you would have to value them at lower levels in your personal statement of net worth. That's depreciation in a nutshell.

DP/ADR (dividends per ADR) Dividends paid by the company divided by total ADRs outstanding.

DPS (dividends per share) Dividends paid by the company divided by the total shares outstanding.

EBDIT or EBITD Earnings before depreciation, interest, and tax. This is the same as EBIT (operating income), except that it includes depreciation. Not all companies publish their depreciation figures, but when they are available, analyzing EBDIT can be even more useful than analyzing EBIT because it helps to smooth yet another potential difference in cross-border accounting. Depreciation schedules may vary from country to country, and this sometimes distorts income comparisons of international firms. By adding back depreciation to EBIT, we remove this potential distortion and can make more accurate cross-border comparisons. In addition, since depreciation is a noncash charge, EBDIT gives us a better picture of the cash being generated by a company's core businesses than does EBIT.

EBIT (earnings before interest and tax) Another way of expressing operating income. Shows the income generated by the company after costs of production (costs of goods sold) and overhead (sales, general, and administrative costs, or SG&A) are deducted, but before financing charges or nonoperating gains. EBIT is important to look at because it shows the profit of the company from its underlying businesses without contributions (or deductions) from noncore operations (for example, disposal of land or shares) that may not recur, or from financial items (such as taxes), which can be variable. It is worth noting that accounting standards differ from country to country, as does the treatment of nonoperating and financial items on income statements. However, treatment of EBIT or operating income is almost universally the same. Thus, analyzing EBIT accomplishes two goals: it helps to evaluate the strength of a company's core business franchise, and it eliminates distortions that may occur from comparing income statements prepared under different accounting regimes.

EBIT/interest expense (also EBDIT/interest expense and EBITDA/interest expense) EBIT (or EBDIT, EBITDA) divided by interest expenses. Used instead of long-term debt to total capital ratio to measure risk for some British companies whose shareholders' equity has been distorted by acquisitions. This ratio measures the ability of a company to cover interest payments on its debts with internally generated cash flow. The higher the coverage ratio, the easier it is for a company to support its debt and the less likely it is to default.

EBITDA (earnings before interest, tax, depreciation, and amortization) This is the same as EBDIT or EBITD, except that it also includes amortization. International companies do not always publish amortization figures, but when they do, this is the best measure to use for evaluating a company's core business rather than EBDIT. Amortization is also one of those items that differs from country to country in how it is treated; by adding it back to EBDIT, it removes all potential distortions from this measure of operating income. EBITDA is often used by analysts to measure the cash flow or underlying cash-generating capability of a company.

EBIT margin (also EBDIT and EBITDA margin) EBIT (or EBDIT, EBITDA) divided by revenues. This ratio measures the profitability of a company's core business before nonoperating and financial items. The net margin (net income divided by revenues) is also a critical measure of profitability, but it can be misleading when comparing international companies because net income is impacted by things such as tax rates and financial income, which are treated differently from country to country.

EP/ADR (earnings per ADR) Net income divided by total ADRs outstanding.

EPS (earnings per share) Net income divided by total shares outstanding.

Exchange Short form for "stock exchange." A stock exchange is an organized marketplace in which stocks, bonds, and their equivalents are bought and sold by members of the exchange, who act as agents (brokers) or principals (dealers or traders). Each exchange sets its own requirements for membership as well as for listing of securities.

Expenses to assets ratio Used for insurance companies in this book, it is expenses divided by total assets. This ratio is used to analyze how well an insurance company is managing its costs.

FY (fiscal year) The twelve-month reporting period for a company. Not all companies have a fiscal year that coincides with the calendar year ending in December. For example, Danka's fiscal year ends on July 31.

Goodwill What is the value attached to a business besides its physical properties, such as buildings, equipment, and cash? What about the intangible properties, such as a brand name, nationwide distribution capability, or especially talented management? When a company acquires another company and pays more than the value of the physical assets, the premium paid for such intangibles is referred to as goodwill.

Gross Profit Used for banks in this book; it stands for gross operating profit and is net revenues minus operating expenses. This is similar to operating income for an industrial company.

Investment Income Used for insurance companies in this book; it is the money an insurance company generates from its investment portfolio.

Liabilities The debt or loans of a company. On the balance sheet, liabilities are usually divided into two categories: long-term liabilities (defined as debt that is payable after more than one year), including long-term credits, loans, notes, and bonds; and short-term liabilities, including short-term loans, credits, the current portion of long-term debt, payables (money owed to suppliers or others in the course of business), and deferred income.

Long-term debt to total capital ratio Long-term debt (defined as debt payable after a year) divided by shareholders' equity plus long-term debt. This ratio, used as a measure of risk in this book, tells shareholders how much of the total capital invested in the business is debt. If the ratio is too high, it may indicate that more equity is needed in the business, which could lead to dilution for existing shareholders. In addition, a long-term debt to total capital ratio that is too high may mean the company could face trouble in the event business slows.

Market capitalization, or market cap The total number of shares outstanding multiplied by the share price.

N/A (not applicable or not available) Used on financial tables when figures are not applicable for a certain category or are not available.

NASDAQ (National Association of Securities Dealers Automated Quotation system) A computerized system that provides brokers and dealers with price quotations for securities that are traded "over the counter" (OTC). OTC stocks traded on the NASDAQ National Market System have "live" price quotations that are updated throughout the trading day on computer screens. Other OTC stocks may have prices that are printed only once a day and that need to be checked directly by telephone.

Net income Synonymous with net earnings and net profit; sometimes called the "bottom line." Net income is the sum remaining after all costs and expenses have been deducted from revenues.

Net revenues Used for banks in this book; it is interest income plus other income (fees, commissions, etc.) minus interest expenses. This is similar to revenues for an industrial company.

N/M (not meaningful) Used on financial tables when the figure available is irrelevant; for example, a negative P/E ratio.

NYSE (New York Stock Exchange) See Exchange.

Operating income See EBIT.

OTC (Over the Counter) A security that is not listed on a U.S. stock exchange but that trades on NASDAQ. In the United States this usually applies to smaller or newer companies that do not meet the stringent listing requirements of one of the major stock exchanges such as the AMEX or NYSE. As for foreign companies, many have not listed their shares on a U.S. exchange, even though they may be able to meet the requirements. Interested U.S. investors must purchase the shares of these foreign companies either directly or OTC.

P/E ratio Price per share divided by earnings per share. A common ratio used to value an investment. Tells the investor how many years of earnings are represented in the share price or how many years of earnings the market is willing to pay for a share of the company. A trailing P/E ratio is the latest fiscal year's earnings divided by the current share price. A projected or estimated P/E ratio uses estimated earnings for the coming fiscal year (provided by analysts) divided into the current share price. Investors favor using a projected P/E because they are more interested in how a share is trading relative to expected earnings than in what it has earned in the past.

Premiums Used for insurance companies in this book; these are similar to revenues for an industrial company. Insurance companies record the money they take in from selling insurance products as premiums.

Pretax profit The profits of a company after all expenses are deducted except taxes and extraordinary items. Comparing pretax profit growth or margins of international companies may be less problematic than comparing net profit growth or margins because of the difference in tax rates around the world, but it is not as accurate as comparing EBITDA or EBIT figures.

Price to book (P/B) ratio The share price divided by the book value per share of a company. This ratio tells an investor how many times book value the shares are trading at and gives an indication of what the shares might be worth if the company were to be broken up and sold off.

ROA (return on assets) Net income divided by total assets. This measure is useful for analyzing banks or insurance companies. A large part of their income comes from loans and investments, which are recorded as assets on a financial company's balance sheet. This ratio tells investors how well the bank or insurance company is using its loan book or investment portfolio to generate income.

ROE (return on equity) Net income divided by shareholders' equity. ROE tells investors what kind of return a company is making on money that has been invested in the business by shareholders. Strong net income growth is important, but if a company is recording a low ROE, it shows that management may not be doing as good a job as it could with the money invested in the business. ROE should be at least as high as the return generated by cash in the bank plus a healthy equity risk premium.

SEDOL Code Stock Exchange Daily Official List Code. The SEDOL Code is the identification number assigned to all foreign stocks by the International Stock Exchange of London. A foreign stock that does not have a CUSIP Number and does not trade actively in the United States can be identified by its SEDOL Code.

Shareholders' equity Also known as stockholders' equity, equity, or net worth. It is the ownership interest of shareholders in a corporation. Besides any debt, shareholders' equity shows how much money has been invested in the company. Rather than pay out all of net income in the form of dividends, a company usually holds back some to reinvest in the business. These "retained earnings" are added to shareholders' equity.

Total capital Shareholders' equity plus long-term debt (liabilities). Tells shareholders the total amount of money, both cash and debt, that has been invested in a company.

8

The Top 100

ADECCO (ADECY—NASDAQ)

Address: Grand-Pont 12/Ch-1002 Lausanne, Switzerland
Tel.: (011) 41 21 321 66 66   **Fax:** (011) 41 21 321 66 28   **Web site:** http://www.adecco.com

BASIC INFORMATION

Country: Switzerland
Industry: Temporary employment
Investment thesis: One of the world's largest temporary agencies

Market capitalization: $5.3 billion
Share status: ADRs trade on NASDAQ

COMPANY GRADING BOX

Growth Categories		Quality of Management	
Revenue Growth	20	Return on Equity	10
Operating Income Growth	15	**Risk**	
Earnings per Share Growth	15	Long-Term Debt/Total Capital	10
Share Price Growth	15	**Total QM&R (maximum 20)**	20
Total Growth (maximum 80)	65	**FINAL GRADE**	85

BACKGROUND

If you had invested in the giant of U.S. temporary agencies, Manpower, five years ago, you would know how business is booming. Here is an opportunity to participate in Manpower's European counterpart, as European regulatory reform is now making possible the kind of industry growth we have already seen in the United States. The Adecco Group came into being in 1996, the result of a merger between France-based Ecco and Switzerland-based Adia. Together the two companies form one of the largest temporary employment companies in the world, about even with Manpower in terms of market share and second to Manpower in terms of revenues. The combined company reported annual sales of $6.4 billion for 1996.

Ecco's real revenue center has been France, where it dominates the market (only the United States has a larger market for temporary workers). Adia, on the other hand, is number four in the United States and the market leader in Australia, Germany, and Switzerland. Adecco staffs about 250,000 jobs a day through 2,500 offices for 200,000 clients, and management is optimistic about future growth prospects. Trends in the world economy, particularly in Europe, look very favorable for Adecco.

Regulatory reform in Europe, allowing for more flexible work practices, has already led to explosive growth for firms such as Adecco and is just gathering steam. A temporary workforce is something we know and accept in the United States, but it is relatively new in the rest of the world. As corporations try to make their workforces more flexible, they are turning to temporary agencies—and a dominant company such as Adecco is well positioned to benefit. Although this is a business affected by the ups and downs of the economic cycle, Adecco is positioning itself for the future. Wall Street analysts expect to hear about acquisitions going forward.

COMPANY STATEMENT (from the 1996 annual report)

"In personnel services, one of the fastest growing industries in the world, Adecco leads the field. As never before, customers require a precise match between the temporary associate and required skills. The greater need for speed, flexibility and response time in supplying associates is putting new, more stringent demands on our people and systems.

In addition, clients are demanding increasingly skilled workers—experienced and ready to adapt to their own ever-changing organizations. Against these enhanced requirements we balance the desires of our temporary associates—we are committed to delivering the right job, when and where they want, with all the right rewards. On both fronts, Adecco's programs for clients and associates define the industry standards.

"Adecco offers a range of human resource services and staffing solutions in mainstream clerical and industrial areas, as well as specialty skills such as accounting, information technology and engineering. We also operate highly regarded brands offering out-placement and career management services. Increasingly, big customers are demanding these services be delivered as a single coherent offering. We are uniquely positioned to satisfy this need."

PERFORMANCE

Adecco came into being in 1996, the product of the merger between Adia and Ecco. The problem for us? Neither company's historic numbers tell the whole picture. Even so, we wanted to give you an understanding of at least part of management's track record. Hence our tables: We used company-provided pro forma numbers, in Swiss francs, for 1995 and 1996; these show results as if the companies had been merged from the beginning of 1994. We used Ecco's numbers, in the original French francs, for the previous eight years and Ecco's share price over the last decade.

That said, Adecco received a total score of 85 points in our grading system—with high marks for growth and ROE. In the years before the merger, Ecco's EPS and EBDIT in dollars increased from 1986 to 1990, then trended downward until 1994 (of course, with the restated numbers, it looks as if both jumped in 1995—but the numbers are for the two companies combined). Revenue in dollars increased in each of the seven years before the restated numbers, with recorded compound annual growth of 31% through 1996. ROE declined when the companies were combined, from Ecco's 17% in 1993 to Adecco's 10% in 1996. However, that could be as a result of the merger itself and is likely to improve as the companies are integrated. The ratio of long-term debt to total capital was just 6% in 1996.

If you had invested $10,000 in Ecco at the end of 1986, you would have purchased around 40 shares at about $250 each (excluding commissions). Over the next ten years, there were a number of small capital changes, a ten-for-one stock split in October 1989, and a one-for-five bonus issue in June 1995. By the end of 1996, you would have had 556 shares worth about $44,000. You would also have received dividend payments of around $11,000. Note that the share price for Ecco is useful only for getting an idea of how you would have fared from investing in the company over time. The Ecco share price is not directly comparable with the Adecco ADR price.

ADECCO

Ticker Symbol and Exchange: ADECY—NASDAQ   **CUSIP No.: 6754105**

OPERATING AND PER SHARE DATA
(in millions of French francs 1986–1994, Swiss francs 1995–1996)

	1986	1987	1988	1989	1990	1991	1992	1993	1994	1995	1996	CAGR
Sales	2,694	3,675	5,630	7,541	8,567	9,247	10,025	8,906	12,348	7,609	8,524	12.2%
EBIT	163	255	389	536	500	385	367	241	590	356	388	9.0%
Net Profit	91	105	181	258	233	231	207	181	354	206	241	10.2%
EPS	6.23	7.19	11.87	16.92	15.11	14.16	12.25	10.71	20.86	12.40	14.50	8.8%
DPS	4.15	4.15	13.70	13.33	13.33	5.83	5.00	5.00	6.66	4.27	5.00	1.9%

OPERATING AND PER SHARE DATA
(in millions of U.S. dollars and dollars per share)

	1986	1987	1988	1989	1990	1991	1992	1993	1994	1995	1996	CAGR
Sales	418	613	945	1,184	1,575	1,640	1,895	1,573	2,229	6,617	6,361	31.3%
EBIT	25	43	65	84	92	68	69	43	106	310	290	27.6%
Net Profit	14	18	30	40	43	41	39	32	64	179	180	29.0%
EP/ADR	0.97	1.20	1.99	2.66	2.78	2.51	2.32	1.89	3.77	10.78	10.82	27.3%
DP/ADR	0.64	0.69	2.30	2.09	2.45	1.03	0.95	0.88	1.20	3.71	3.73	19.2%

KEY RATIOS

	1986	1987	1988	1989	1990	1991	1992	1993	1994	1995	1996	AVG
EBIT Margin	6.1%	6.9%	6.9%	7.1%	5.8%	4.2%	3.7%	2.7%	4.8%	4.7%	4.6%	5.2%
ROE	49.1%	43.3%	65.3%	56.0%	41.4%	28.8%	21.2%	17.3%	27.5%	24.8%	10.0%	35.0%
LT Debt/Total Cap	23.8%	39.3%	12.4%	30.8%	28.4%	24.8%	35.9%	30.9%	24.7%	17.9%	6.2%	25.0%
P/E (Projected)	16.3	6.6	7.0	13.8	8.5	11.2	13.9	10.8	20.1	19.6	22.5	13.7

STOCK PRICE CHART
(fiscal year-end closing price, in U.S. dollars, adjusted for capital changes)

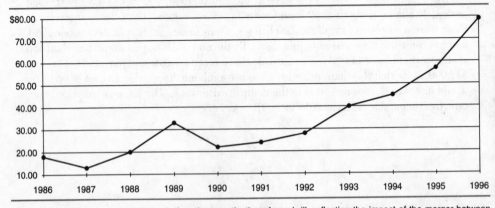

Notes: 1995–96 figures are pro forma before the amortization of goodwill, reflecting the impact of the merger between Adia and Ecco, which occurred in 8/96. Figures for 1986 to 1994 are for Ecco only and are not comparable to the new company's. 1995 dividend and 1996 long-term debt to total capital ratio are estimated. The share prices shown are for Ecco only and are not comparable to the ADR prices.

AEGON (AEG—NYSE)

Address: Mariahoeveplein 50 / P.O. Box 202 / 2501 CE The Hague / Netherlands
Tel.: (011) 31 70 344 3210   **Fax:** (011) 31 70 347 5238

BASIC INFORMATION

Country: Netherlands
Industry: Insurance
Investment thesis: Eighth largest insurer in the world in terms of assets

Market capitalization: $17.04 billion
Share status: ADRs trade on NYSE

COMPANY GRADING BOX

Growth Categories		Quality of Management	
Revenue Growth	20	Return on Equity	10
Operating Income Growth	20	Investment Income/Total Investments	10
Earnings per Share Growth	10	**Total QM (maximum 20)**	**20**
Share Price Growth	20		
Total Growth (maximum 80)	**70**	**FINAL GRADE**	**90**

BACKGROUND

American investors buy a lot of insurance stocks, but many do not even know AEGON exists—that despite the company's $3.5 billion purchase of the insurance operations of U.S.-based Providian in 1996. With the Providian acquisition, AEGON became a major player in the U.S. life insurance market. This Netherlands-based company is the eighth largest listed insurer in the world in terms of assets (excluding mutual insurers), the eleventh largest insurer in the United States in terms of assets, and the ninth largest in the world in terms of market capitalization. Annual revenues are more than $14.5 billion; premiums are about $10 billion.

The European insurance and pension markets are undergoing radical changes, and AEGON is well positioned to jump in when opportunities present themselves. As state welfare programs are scaled back, deregulation takes hold, and consumers become better educated, AEGON's efficiencies of scale and ability to tailor products to both corporate and individual customers should give it ample ammunition to compete—both with less flexible older competitors and with nimble new entrees. Of AEGON's revenues, 77% come from life insurance, including its pension, investment, and savings plans (from asset management to plan management). In addition, with the ongoing unification of the European marketplace AEGON sees tremendous potential for cross-border business in markets that are less competitive than the Netherlands.

Markets in which AEGON has a presence: the Netherlands, Germany, Belgium, Hungary, Spain, the United States, and the United Kingdom—where AEGON's 80% holding in Scottish Equitable, a provider of pension and personal investment products, has been particularly profitable. In addition, AEGON has a joint venture in Mexico, where the pension industry is in its infancy. And in 1996 AEGON management said it is looking to expand in Asia, where it has had operations since 1992 and markets are rife with opportunity for both the insurance and the pension plan business. Toward that end, in 1996 AEGON received a license for insurance activities in the Philippines.

COMPANY STATEMENT (from the 1996 annual report)

"Our expertise lies in insurance, particularly life insurance and the related areas of pensions and investment products. Last year, these activities accounted for 77% of revenues and an even higher proportion of income. These core competencies put us in markets that are large, fast-growing and international: we do not lack for growth opportunities, as our record attests. Therefore, facing increasing competition from banks and other financial service providers in deregulating markets, we have decided to build on our core expertise rather than dilute it.

"In 1996, we participated in the benefits of 'bancassurance' distribution through joint ventures with banks, such as Seguros Banamex AEGON, and through specialized subsidiaries, such as Spaarbeleg. However, we also kept our identity as an insurer. In fact, inspired by the competitive challenges, our operating units are developing a range of relevant new skills in such areas as asset management and financial data-base management to complement their traditional insurance skills. This is why general insurance and accident and health insurance are also playing an important role in markets where we expect long-term profitability from these product lines. The distribution channels, the databases, the coverage of overhead expenses; it all combines to improve our market position and profitability."

PERFORMANCE

AEGON recorded an overall score of 90 points on our grading system, making it a top performer. Note that as an insurance company, its grading categories and performance benchmarks are different from other firms'. For example, instead of revenues we look at premium growth, and here the company got a perfect score. AEGON's premiums increased every year over the last ten and showed compound growth of 16%. Another category unique to insurance companies is investment income, and here AEGON also gets high marks. Investment income in dollars increased in nine of ten years, with compound annual growth of 12%. EP/ADR were equally consistent, rising in nine of ten years, and grew by 11.4% per annum, just one tenth of a point short of scoring full marks. Dividends per ADR have been very strong, rising from $0.29 to $1.60 over the decade and growing by 19% per annum. The average payout ratio during the period was 38% of earnings.

Return on equity averaged 16%, high for an insurance company. And return on assets averaged 1.1% in an industry where anything over 1% is considered excellent. AEGON's shares have also performed well for investors, rising at a compound rate of 24% per annum and closing at new highs in nine out of ten years.

If you had invested $10,000 in AEGON at the end of 1986, you would have purchased around 260 ADRs (or ADR equivalents) at about $38 each (excluding commissions). Over the next ten years, there were a one-for-eleven rights issue in 1989, a two-for-one stock split in 1992, and a two-and-a-half-for-one stock split in 1995. By the end of 1996, you would have owned around 1,300 ADRs worth an estimated $83,000. You would also have received around $11,000 in dividends.

AEGON

Ticker Symbol and Exchange: AEG—NYSE   **CUSIP No.: 007924103**

OPERATING AND PER SHARE DATA
(in millions of Dutch guilders and guilders per share)

	1986	1987	1988	1989	1990	1991	1992	1993	1994	1995	1996	CAGR
Premiums	4,817	5,201	6,018	6,947	7,192	7,942	8,789	12,351	13,998	13,768	16,703	13.2%
Invest. Income	2,589	2,850	3,283	3,855	4,182	5,026	5,823	5,591	5,684	5,833	6,429	9.5%
Net Profit	450	466	573	662	726	815	913	1,009	1,151	1,323	1,568	13.3%
EPS	2.53	2.61	3.15	3.36	3.46	3.60	3.73	4.00	4.50	5.05	5.93	8.9%
DPS	0.63	0.74	0.92	1.14	1.40	1.46	1.50	1.60	1.94	2.37	2.79	16.0%

OPERATING AND PER SHARE DATA
(in millions of U.S. dollars and dollars per ADR)

	1986	1987	1988	1989	1990	1991	1992	1993	1994	1995	1996	CAGR
Premiums	2,210	2,938	3,014	3,637	4,281	4,644	4,829	6,334	8,091	8,552	9,599	15.8%
Investment Income	1,188	1,610	1,644	2,018	2,489	2,939	3,199	2,867	3,286	3,623	3,695	12.0%
Net Profit	206	263	287	347	432	477	502	517	665	822	901	15.9%
EP/ADR	1.16	1.47	1.58	1.76	2.06	2.11	2.05	2.05	2.60	3.14	3.41	11.4%
DP/ADR	0.29	0.42	0.46	0.60	0.83	0.85	0.82	0.82	1.12	1.47	1.60	18.7%

KEY RATIOS

	1986	1987	1988	1989	1990	1991	1992	1993	1994	1995	1996	AVG
Expenses/Assets	4.3%	4.3%	3.9%	3.8%	3.6%	3.6%	3.4%	2.9%	2.3%	2.0%	2.0%	3.3%
ROE	15.3%	12.0%	18.5%	16.3%	14.8%	17.9%	16.1%	16.4%	13.5%	17.3%	20.5%	16.2%
ROA	1.15%	1.15%	1.22%	1.24%	1.24%	1.24%	1.18%	0.95%	0.87%	0.92%	0.94%	1.10%
P/E (Projected)	6.5	3.5	5.4	6.4	5.9	6.4	7.5	9.4	8.8	12.0	17.2	8.1

STOCK PRICE CHART
(fiscal year-end closing price, in U.S. dollars, adjusted for capital changes)

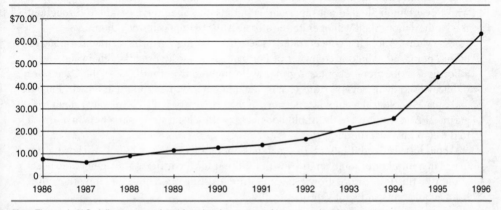

Note: Figures in U.S. dollars are translated from local currency using year-end exchange rates.

AHOLD (AHO—NYSE)

Address: Albert Heijnweg 1 / P.O. Box 3050 / 1500 HB Zaandam / Netherlands
Tel.: (011) 31 75 659 56 48   **Fax:** (011) 31 75 659 83 55

BASIC INFORMATION

Country: Netherlands
Industry: Retailing, food
Market capitalization: $11.49 billion
Share status: ADRs trade on NYSE
Investment thesis: Dutch food retailing giant expanding overseas; fifth largest in the United States

COMPANY GRADING BOX

Growth Categories		Quality of Management	
Revenue Growth	20	Return on Equity	10
Operating Income Growth	20	**Risk**	
Earnings per Share Growth	10	Long-Term Debt/Total Capital	0
Share Price Growth	15	**Total QM&R (maximum 20)**	10
Total Growth (maximum 80)	65	**FINAL GRADE**	75

BACKGROUND

You probably didn't know that when you shop in a U.S. supermarket, you have a one-in-five chance of visiting a Dutch owned chain. And on the East Coast, the odds are better than fifty-fifty. Netherlands-based Ahold is a giant of the food-retailing industry. Its operations include fifteen retail chains in the United States, the Netherlands, Portugal, the Czech Republic, and Poland—with more than 2,800 supermarkets, specialty stores, hypermarkets, discount stores, and cash-and-carry outlets; it employs 200,000 people and has annual revenues of more than $21 billion. With its 1996 acquisition of New England's Stop & Shop chain (1995 revenues: $4.1 billion), Ahold became the largest supermarket retailer on the East Coast of the United States—and the fifth largest in the country. Its other U.S. holdings include BI-LO, Giant Food Stores, Finast, Edwards Super Food Stores, and Tops Markets.

In its home market, the Netherlands, Ahold dominates the market with six retail companies operating more than 1,600 stores. The largest of the six, Albert Heijn, is the country's leading supermarket chain. The other five are specialty retailers, liquor stores, confectioners, and health and beauty stores. In early 1997 Ahold signed an agreement with Royal Dutch Shell to put supermarket outlets into Shell service stations throughout the Netherlands. Shell will operate the stores; Albert Heijn will stock them.

Elsewhere, Ahold has concentrated its activities on "high-growth" markets. Among its other operations, Ahold is co-owner of Portugal's leading supermarket chain and—with a Portuguese partner—operates a group of Portuguese hypermarkets. In the Czech Republic, Ahold owns several store chains, including a group of supermarkets. In Poland and Spain, Ahold is developing a network of hypermarkets and supermarkets along with partners. And, most recently, Ahold hooked up with a local supermarket chain in Brazil to develop business there.

Ahold has also said it intends to expand its operations in Asia, where it already participates in a number of joint ventures with different local partners. Management expects about two thirds of future growth to come from existing operations and the other third from acquisitions and joint ventures.

COMPANY STATEMENT (from the 1995 annual report)

"As a retail organization specialized in producing and distributing fresh foods, groceries and other consumer goods, Royal Ahold serves large numbers of customers directly through its stores in the Netherlands, other European countries and the United States. The company's objective is to continue to perform this role in society in both current and new market areas, and in so doing, achieve a reasonable return on its investment, while at the same time providing substantial employment. To achieve its objective and meet its related responsibilities, the company needs to ensure its continuity. Ahold wants to determine its own future, and therefore strives to maintain its independence and unique identity.

"We are taking an innovative approach to our international development, particularly in areas such as Asia where we are not yet established, but which offer major opportunities for a group with our strengths and skills. We are strongly focused on growth, and ambitious in our goals. Furthermore, we are highly skilled and experienced in all aspects of food retailing, production and distribution, and have demonstrated our ability to adapt ourselves successfully, and sensitively, to different cultures and operating environments."

PERFORMANCE

Over the last ten years, Ahold gets top marks for revenues, operating income, and ROE, but its overall grade of 75 points was pulled down by low scores on EP/ADR performance and risk. Ahold's revenues and EBDIT had compound annual growth of 16% and 21%, respectively, in dollars, and both set new highs every year over the last decade. EP/ADR, however, did not grow as fast or consistently as these top-line numbers, because rights offerings to raise cash for acquisitions diluted profits somewhat. On the other hand, management demonstrated that it can make a good return on money invested in its businesses, as ROE averaged 18% over the decade and rose to a high of 26% in 1996 from 14% in 1986. The company has had to increase debt to fund acquisitions too, and while cash flows and interest coverage are very strong, the average long-term debt to total capital ratio of 38% means that Ahold has a slightly higher risk level than other companies on our list.

Investors have appreciated management's strong efforts, driving the ADR price to close at higher levels in nine out of ten years and to grow at a compound rate of 18% per annum. Dividends per ADR increased from $0.20 in 1986 to $0.93 in 1996, increasing by 17% per annum, and achieved a dividend payout ratio averaging 30% over the decade.

If you had invested $10,000 in Ahold at the end of 1986, you would have purchased 210 ADRs (or ADR equivalents) at around $47.50 each (excluding commissions). During the following ten-years, there were a two-for-one-hundred bonus issue in 1987, a two-for-one bonus issue in 1990, a one-for-ten rights issue in 1993, and a two-for-one stock split in 1993. By the end of 1996, you would have had 865 ADRs worth about $54,700. You would also have received around $4,600 in dividend payments.

AHOLD

Ticker Symbol and Exchange: AHO—NYSE   **CUSIP No.: 500467303**

OPERATING AND PER SHARE DATA
(in millions of Dutch guilders and guilders per share)

	1986	1987	1988	1989	1990	1991	1992	1993	1994	1995	1996	CAGR
Sales	10,864	11,067	14,638	17,075	16,920	20,122	21,594	27,093	28,978	29,617	36,600	12.9%
EBDIT	390	407	547	606	706	879	992	1,232	1,381	1,556	2,076	18.2%
Net Profit	130	131	145	195	244	276	305	343	410	457	632	17.1%
EPS	1.74	1.58	1.74	2.06	2.51	2.75	2.94	2.95	3.41	3.74	4.30	9.5%
DPS	0.44	0.42	0.45	0.56	0.79	0.89	0.98	1.10	0.77	0.89	1.62	13.9%

OPERATING AND PER SHARE DATA
(in millions of U.S. dollars and dollars per ADR)

	1986	1987	1988	1989	1990	1991	1992	1993	1994	1995	1996	CAGR
Sales	4,983	6,253	7,330	8,940	10,071	11,767	11,865	13,894	16,750	18,396	21,034	15.5%
EBDIT	179	230	274	317	420	514	545	632	798	966	1,193	20.9%
Net Profit	60	74	73	102	145	161	167	176	237	284	363	19.8%
EP/ADR	0.80	0.89	0.87	1.08	1.49	1.61	1.62	1.51	1.97	2.32	2.47	12.0%
DP/ADR	0.20	0.24	0.23	0.29	0.47	0.52	0.54	0.56	0.45	0.55	0.93	16.5%

KEY RATIOS

	1986	1987	1988	1989	1990	1991	1992	1993	1994	1995	1996	AVG
EBDIT Margin	3.6%	3.7%	3.7%	3.6%	4.2%	4.4%	4.6%	4.5%	4.8%	5.3%	5.7%	4.4%
ROE	14.4%	15.0%	14.1%	13.5%	16.6%	21.4%	20.5%	16.1%	18.4%	20.4%	26.2%	17.9%
LT Debt/Total Cap	28.6%	34.1%	35.0%	27.3%	24.1%	42.5%	42.9%	40.9%	40.1%	56.4%	49.5%	38.3%
P/E (Projected)	15.9	8.4	10.8	13.4	12.0	13.1	14.7	13.8	14.4	15.2	21.1	13.9

STOCK PRICE CHART
(fiscal year-end closing price, in U.S. dollars, adjusted for capital changes)

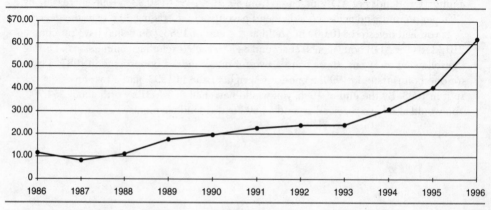

Note: Figures in U.S. dollars are translated from local currency using year-end exchange rates.

AIRTOURS (ATORF—OTC)

Address: Parkway 3 / Parkway Business Center / 300 Princess Road / Manchester M14 7QU / England

Tel.: (011) 44 161 232 6519   **Fax:** (011) 44 161 232 6575

BASIC INFORMATION

Country: United Kingdom

Industry: Leisure and tourism

Investment thesis: Runs 34 hotels, three cruise ships, two charter airlines, and tour operations

Market capitalization: $2.1 billion

Share status: Foreign shares trade OTC

COMPANY GRADING BOX

Growth Categories		Quality of Management	
Revenue Growth	20	Return on Equity	10
Operating Income Growth	20	**Risk**	
Earnings per Share Growth	15	Long-Term Debt/Total Capital	10
Share Price Growth	20	**Total QM&R (maximum 20)**	**20**
Total Growth (maximum 80)	**75**	**FINAL GRADE**	**95**

BACKGROUND

As its name implies, U.K.-based Airtours is a tour operator—for Caribbean, European, and U.S. destinations. More than half of its more than $2 billion in annual revenues is generated in the United Kingdom, and most of the rest in Scandinavia, where it has been expanding aggressively. Airtours recently launched businesses in North America as well (three subsidiaries in Canada, one in the United States), but they are not yet significant in terms of overall performance. However, Airtours made headlines in the United States in 1996, when Carnival Corporation, owner of the largest U.S. cruise line, bought a 29.6% stake, then teamed up with the U.K. company to buy Italian cruise operator Costa Crociere for $300 million (Airtours' stock price has doubled since the Carnival investment). Costa has about 30% of the Italian cruise market.

Altogether, Airtours runs 34 hotels, three cruise ships (in addition to the eight Italian ships owned by the Costa Crociere joint venture), and two charter airlines, as well as tour operations in the United Kingdom (with the United Kingdom's largest network of foreign exchange bureaus), Canada, and Scandinavia. It recently moved into the United States through a California-based subsidiary called Sunquest Holdings and has begun selling package holidays from southern California to the Caribbean, Mexico, and Hawaii. Airtours added the Sunquest name in the mid-1990s, when it bought a Canadian tour operator called Sunquest Vacations. Airtours is also exploring opportunities for expansion in the time-share market, with its first project, a joint venture, now under construction in Orlando, Florida; and, in 1998, launched tour operations in Poland, under the brand name Ving.

COMPANY STATEMENT (from the 1996 annual report)

"Three years ago we concluded that in order to maintain our rate of growth we would need to develop our business overseas. At that time we stated our objectives of achieving, in the medium term, an even split of profits between UK and overseas businesses.

"Our move into overseas markets began with the acquisition of the Scandinavian Leisure Group (SLG) in 1994 followed a year later by the acquisition of Sunquest Vacations (Sunquest) in Canada. In 1996 we strengthened our positions in Scandinavia and North America by the acquisition of Simon Spies Holding A/S (Spies) and Alba Tours International Inc (Alba) respectively.

"In a short period of time, Airtours has transformed itself from a purely UK based company into an internationally diversified leisure group which is now the largest air inclusive tour operator in the world. The growth of the Group continues to produce economies of scale and by managing capacity across our different markets we obtain the maximum utilization of our aircraft, cruise ships and hotels.

"Our strategy for future growth is relatively straightforward. We shall seek to develop or acquire businesses operating in markets which we understand, where we can add value and where the acquired business has high quality management or alternatively can be readily integrated into our existing management infrastructures. We believe there will be significant opportunities for further expansion which we shall exploit as they arise."

PERFORMANCE

Airtours is one of our top-scoring companies, with 95 points in our grading system. Its growth has been phenomenal, ROE excellent, and debt level reasonable. Revenues in dollars increased in each of the last ten years, with an extraordinary compound annual growth rate of around 40%. EBDIT in dollars increased in nine of the last ten years, with compound annual growth of 51%. EPS growth was less consistent but still increased at a compound annual rate of 38%. Dividends kept pace, recording compound annual growth of 37% over the eight years since the company went public—with an average payout of 31%. Over ten years, ROE averaged an impressive 37%. As for risk, the long-term debt to total capital ratio averaged 11% (it spiked up in 1995 but started coming down again in 1996).

If you had invested $10,000 in Airtours in September 1988, you would have bought around 4,150 shares at about $2.40 each (excluding commissions). During the following ten years, there were a three-for-ten rights issue in April 1991, a three-for-one bonus issue in January 1992, and a one-for-five bonus issue in April 1994. By September 1996, you would have had about 18,900 shares worth an estimated $178,000. You would also have received dividend payments of around $16,400.

AIRTOURS

Ticker Symbol and Exchange: ATORF—OTC   **SEDOL Code: 10979**

OPERATING AND PER SHARE DATA
(in millions of British pounds and pounds per share)

	Sep 86	Sep 87	Sep 88	Sep 89	Sep 90	Sep 91	Sep 92	Sep 93	Sep 94	Sep 95	Sep 96	CAGR
Sales	66	68	103	156	183	290	406	616	972	1,318	1,718	38.5%
EBDIT	1.8	1.9	4.0	4.2	7.2	25.8	28.9	41.5	77.4	70.2	105.7	50.3%
Net Profit	1.3	1.3	2.8	3.3	4.4	18.2	22.3	27.9	49.4	43.0	64.9	47.9%
EPS	0.02	0.02	0.04	0.05	0.07	0.24	0.24	0.26	0.42	0.33	0.46	37.3%
DPS	0.00	0.01	0.01	0.02	0.02	0.06	0.07	0.09	0.12	0.14	0.16	42.6%

OPERATING AND PER SHARE DATA
(in millions of U.S. dollars and dollars per share)

	Sep 86	Sep 87	Sep 88	Sep 89	Sep 90	Sep 91	Sep 92	Sep 93	Sep 94	Sep 95	Sep 96	CAGR
Sales	96	110	174	253	343	507	724	921	1,533	2,086	2,689	39.6%
EBDIT	2.6	3.1	6.8	6.8	13.5	45.1	51.6	62.0	122.1	111.1	165.4	51.4%
Net Profit	1.9	2.1	4.7	5.3	8.3	31.8	39.8	41.7	77.9	68.1	101.6	49.0%
EPS	0.03	0.03	0.07	0.08	0.12	0.42	0.43	0.39	0.66	0.52	0.71	38.4%
DPS	0.01	0.01	0.02	0.03	0.04	0.10	0.13	0.13	0.19	0.22	0.25	37.0%

KEY RATIOS

	Sep 86	Sep 87	Sep 88	Sep 89	Sep 90	Sep 91	Sep 92	Sep 93	Sep 94	Sep 95	Sep 96	AVG
EBDIT Margin	2.7%	2.8%	3.9%	2.7%	3.9%	8.9%	7.1%	6.7%	8.0%	5.3%	6.2%	5.3%
ROE	54.2%	22.4%	35.0%	32.4%	33.8%	43.5%	43.3%	41.5%	36.1%	36.2%	31.3%	37.2%
LT Debt/Total Cap	22.6%	6.5%	1.2%	9.7%	7.1%	1.2%	2.3%	2.9%	6.4%	36.7%	28.4%	11.4%
P/E (Projected)	N/A	N/A	6.2	5.7	1.2	7.8	9.2	9.6	13.7	8.4	11.4	8.1

STOCK PRICE CHART
(fiscal year-end closing price, in U.S. dollars, adjusted for capital changes)

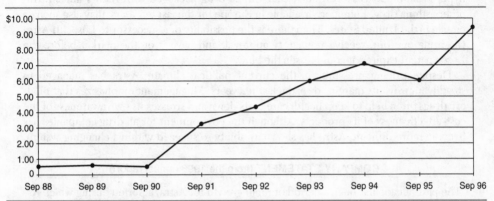

Notes: 1992–95 data restated for change in accounting policy. Figures prior to 1992 remain unadjusted. Figures in U.S. dollars are translated from local currency using year-end exchange rates.

ASTRA (A—NYSE)

Address: 151 85 Sodertalje / Sweden
Tel.: (011) 46 8 553 260 00   **Fax:** (011) 46 8 553 290 00   **Web site:** http://www.astra.com

BASIC INFORMATION

Country: Sweden
Industry: Health and personal care
Investment thesis: A leading global pharmaceutical company

Market capitalization: $26.5 billion
Share status: ADRs trade on NYSE

COMPANY GRADING BOX

Growth Categories		Quality of Management	
Revenue Growth	20	Return on Equity	10
Operating Income Growth	20	**Risk**	
Earnings per Share Growth	20	Long-Term Debt/Total Capital	10
Share Price Growth	20	**Total QM&R (maximum 20)**	20
Total Growth (maximum 80)	**80**	**FINAL GRADE**	**100**

BACKGROUND

You've loved Merck, Pfizer, and Abbott Laboratories. Astra is their Swedish counterpart, a giant among equals—with a market capitalization of $26.5 billion and $5.6 billion in revenues. It is a global competitor in the pharmaceutical business with blockbuster drugs, tremendous distribution, and 20% of resources (financial and human) devoted to research and development. It is even tied to Wall Street's darling Merck through a fifty-fifty joint venture set up to distribute Astra products in the United States.

Astra's best-selling product is the ulcer drug Losec, marketed in the United States under the name Prilosec and one of the top-selling prescription medicines in the world in 1996. Although analysts worry that Astra will become too dependent on revenues from Losec (now accounting for about 45% of Astra's total sales), management has said it is preparing itself for the inevitable. Astra's U.S. patent on Losec expires in 2001, opening the door to competition. In anticipation, this cash-rich company is pouring money into research, and Astra management has said to expect three new product launches a year. Among the drugs now in Astra's arsenal: Naropin, a new anesthetic; Atacand, a drug for hypertension; and Oxis Turbuhaler, an asthma drug packaged with Astra's inhaler. Another asthma drug, Pulmicort, available in Europe for the last ten years, may also soon go on sale in the United States. Then there is the possibility of a successor to Losec. If Astra can bring one out, receive regulatory approval, and have it on the market before the Losec patent expires, it could lessen the blow.

Despite pricing pressures in the current political climate, Astra has managed to steadily improve its margins over the last ten years. Management emphasizes that modern drugs often help to keep health care costs down and stresses its own awareness of the cost-effectiveness of its products. Although the environment for all drug companies has become more difficult, Astra has shown its ability to succeed within a changing system.

COMPANY STATEMENT (from the 1996 annual report)

"The past decade has been a period of rapid growth for Astra, a period during which Astra's board approved investments of 30 billion kroner to make this growth possible. During this time we have created approximately 13,000 new jobs in the Astra Group, as well as a large number of new jobs with subcontractors. Astra's exports from Sweden have grown from roughly 2 billion kroner a year to approximately 15 billion kroner in 1996. The company's market capitalization has risen from 14 billion kroner to more than 200 billion kroner. The number of stockholders during the period has increased by 90,000 to about 115,000. Astra has a strong financial position with liquid assets of 18 billion kroner and an equity ratio of 73 percent.

"This rapid development makes Astra one of the most successful companies in international business. We compete with the global elite in our industry. Our pharmaceuticals are examined and compared on a regular basis with the very best in different countries and cultures. Coming second or third behind the competition is not enough. Astra's products must be the number one alternative. . . .

"In its small home market in Sweden, Astra has become one of the most international companies, with operations in some 50 countries and more than 90 percent of sales in foreign markets. Two-thirds of the work force are employed by Astra's foreign operations."

PERFORMANCE

Astra gets high marks in every category and a total score of 100—making it one of our star companies. Over the last ten years, revenues and EBDIT in dollars have grown every year, with compound annual growth of 23% and 28% respectively. EP/ADR increased from $0.18 in 1986 to $2.23 in 1996, with compound annual growth of 29%. Despite some difficult years for health care stocks overall, Astra's ADR price performance also has been excellent, with the shares rising at a compound annual rate of 29%. Regarding management, the record is strong: the operating margin averaged 31% and increased in eight of the last ten years. ROE averaged 27% during the period, a very strong return. As for risk, the long-term debt to total capital ratio declined from a high of 27% in 1987 to 11% in 1996.

If you had invested $10,000 in Astra at the end of 1986, you would have purchased around 135 ADRs (or ADR equivalents) at about $73.25 each (excluding commissions). During the following ten years, there were a one-for-five bonus issue in June 1987, a two-for-one stock split in June 1987, a one-for-four bonus issue in October 1989, a one-for-three bonus issue in August 1991, and a five-for-one stock split in June 1993. By the end of 1996, you would have had around 2,700 ADRs worth an estimated $130,700. You would also have received around $5,900 in dividend payments.

ASTRA

Ticker Symbol and Exchange: A—NYSE   **CUSIP No.: 46298105**

OPERATING AND PER SHARE DATA
(in millions of Swedish kronor and kronor per share)

	1986	1987	1988	1989	1990	1991	1992	1993	1994	1995	1996	CAGR
Sales	4,960	5,406	6,278	7,457	9,420	12,501	15,568	22,600	28,030	35,800	38,988	22.9%
EBDIT	1,262	1,482	1,700	2,078	2,728	3,642	4,924	7,689	10,444	13,133	14,598	27.7%
Net Profit	752	635	747	991	1,432	2,182	3,527	6,092	6,795	8,764	9,449	28.8%
EPS	1.20	1.03	1.21	1.62	2.38	3.60	5.76	9.92	11.05	14.22	15.33	29.0%
DPS	0.19	0.24	0.30	0.37	0.48	0.65	1.00	1.60	2.25	3.00	4.00	35.6%

OPERATING AND PER SHARE DATA
(in millions of U.S. dollars and dollars per ADR)

	1986	1987	1988	1989	1990	1991	1992	1993	1994	1995	1996	CAGR
Sales	727	935	1,027	1,203	1,673	2,252	2,199	2,710	3,773	5,392	5,683	22.8%
EBDIT	185	256	278	335	485	656	695	922	1,406	1,978	2,128	27.7%
Net Profit	110	110	122	160	254	393	498	730	915	1,320	1,377	28.7%
EP/ADR	0.18	0.18	0.20	0.26	0.42	0.65	0.81	1.19	1.49	2.14	2.23	28.9%
DP/ADR	0.03	0.04	0.05	0.06	0.09	0.12	0.14	0.19	0.30	0.45	0.58	35.5%

KEY RATIOS

	1986	1987	1988	1989	1990	1991	1992	1993	1994	1995	1996	AVG
EBDIT Margin	25.5%	27.4%	27.1%	27.9%	29.0%	29.1%	31.6%	34.0%	37.3%	36.7%	37.4%	31.2%
ROE	23.9%	18.9%	19.3%	20.2%	23.9%	27.3%	31.9%	37.7%	31.0%	30.4%	31.0%	26.9%
LT Debt/Total Cap	17.4%	26.7%	26.0%	25.6%	21.1%	19.6%	16.2%	11.4%	10.1%	10.4%	10.5%	17.7%
P/E (Projected)	24.3	18.8	17.0	26.5	19.4	20.5	14.6	16.8	13.3	17.2	18.3	18.8

STOCK PRICE CHART
(fiscal year-end closing price, in U.S. dollars, adjusted for capital changes)

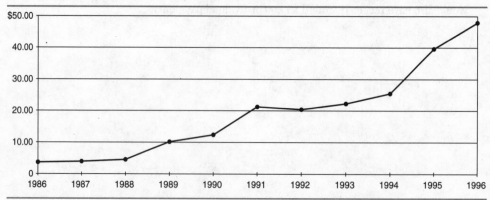

Note: Figures in U.S. dollars are translated from local currency using year-end exchange rates.

BANGKOK BANK (BKKPF—OTC)

Address: 333 Silom Road / P.O. Box 95 BMC / Bangkok 10000 / Thailand
Tel.: (011) 66 2 231 4333   **Fax:** (011) 66 2 231 4692

BASIC INFORMATION

Country: Thailand
Industry: Banking
Investment thesis: Largest commercial bank in Thailand; extensive branch network

Market capitalization: $9.9 billion
Share status: Foreign shares trade OTC

COMPANY GRADING BOX

Growth Categories		Quality of Management	
Revenue Growth	20	Return on Equity	10
Operating Income Growth	20	Return on Assets	5
Earnings per Share Growth	20	**Total QM (maximum 20)**	**15**
Share Price Growth	15		
Total Growth (maximum 80)	**75**	**FINAL GRADE**	**90**

BACKGROUND

In the second half of 1996, as foreign investors fled the tumbling Thai market, Bangkok Bank managed to retain its status as a core Thai holding (likely to be a long-term investment proposition). It was one bank that investors did not expect would need a government bailout, even though a property crash threatened to bring down some of its peers. Over the last five decades it has grown from a small commercial bank into Thailand's largest, with one of the most extensive branch networks in Southeast Asia.

The bank was started in 1944 to give Thailand a financial institution that could compete with the foreign banks that were doing the nation's banking—on the initiative of members of the royal family, businessmen, and landowners (a number of the founders were former government officials). Thai and Chinese bank customers, who were not as well served by foreign banks, helped Bangkok Bank survive the foreign competition. After disastrous land investments almost brought down the bank in the early 1950s, a new management team was installed, and it was determined that this bank would stay out of land speculation. Since then, Bangkok Bank has focused on the commercial banking activities that have helped fuel Thailand's growth and its own success. Despite Thailand's recent problems, from 1989 to 1995 it was one of the most dynamic economies in the world, with GDP growth in the high single digits. The expected further deregulation of the Thai economy, while likely to create a more competitive environment, should also open new opportunities for the bank (e.g., underwriting and more fee-based products).

Recent turmoil in the region has clearly been devastating to the Thai economy; however, as with our other Asian picks, Bangkok Bank is a company we believe will survive and offer an interesting investment opportunity when the Thai economy turns around.

COMPANY STATEMENT (from the 1996 annual report)

"Thai financial institutions have had to quickly adjust in order to keep pace and conduct their business efficiently. Bangkok Bank, for its part, has made preparations and has adapted its organization and operations in order to increase its efficiency in the rapidly changing marketplace: these are as follows.

1. To urgently develop and expand its branch network into all parts of the region, because the financial system reform and liberalization will affect the Thai financial market so that it will become a regional market with international implications, and thus become more integrated with the global financial market. . . .
2. To urgently develop the system and improve the efficiency of operations so as to be able to fully meet the many needs of all our customers. The Bank will especially develop new financial services and provide fully integrated services. The Bank will also make greater effort to take advantage of communication and information technology in its services and management.
3. Be fully prepared for the changes taking place in the banking business by sharpening our ability to handle new financial businesses. In the future, the traditional service of accepting deposits and extending credits will become less important, whereas fee-based income will increase. . . .
4. Urgently develop and prepare our personnel for the future environment. Financial liberalization will greatly enhance the need for well-qualified and capable staff members."

PERFORMANCE

Bangkok Bank's score of 90 points in our grading system reflects strong consistent growth. In dollars, revenues and gross profit increased in each of the last ten years, with compound annual growth of 22% and 24%, respectively. EPS in dollars increased in nine of the last ten years, recording compound annual growth of 25%. Share price performance was a little less consistent but still impressive, rising at a compound annual rate of 23%. The ratio of profits to revenues averaged 58%. ROE averaged 17%, a very high rate of return for a bank. Similarly, ROA averaged 1.2%, also very impressive. Although dividends increased at a slower rate than EPS, the dividend payout still averaged an impressive 45%.

If you had invested $10,000 in Bangkok Bank at the end of 1986, you would have purchased around 940 shares at about $10.50 each (excluding commissions). During the following ten years, there were a one-for-ten rights issue in May 1990, a one-for-ten rights issue in March 1991, a one-for-twenty rights issue in July 1991, and a ten-for-one stock split in May 1992. By the end of 1996, you would have had around 10,200 shares worth an estimated $76,100. You would also have received dividend payments of around $14,400.

BANGKOK BANK

Ticker Symbol and Exchange: BKKPF—OTC　　　　　　**SEDOL Code: 6077019**

OPERATING AND PER SHARE DATA
(in millions of Thai baht and baht per share)

	1986	1987	1988	1989	1990	1991	1992	1993	1994	1995	1996	CAGR
Net Revenues	7,807	9,833	13,264	15,411	22,786	25,712	33,651	40,403	47,845	51,805	57,505	22.1%
Gross Profit	4,432	5,636	6,321	7,648	11,163	15,747	21,013	25,323	31,250	33,179	37,267	23.7%
Net Income	932	1,525	1,843	2,475	4,689	7,255	10,540	13,904	17,360	19,702	20,747	36.4%
EPS	2.14	2.81	2.83	3.80	6.60	9.52	10.54	13.90	17.36	19.68	20.72	25.5%
DPS	1.61	2.02	2.12	2.21	2.42	2.80	3.10	3.70	6.50	5.50	6.00	14.1%

OPERATING AND PER SHARE DATA
(in millions of U.S. dollars and dollars per share)

	1986	1987	1988	1989	1990	1991	1992	1993	1994	1995	1996	CAGR
Net Revenues	306	392	524	603	906	1,018	1,319	1,584	1,906	2,056	2,246	22.1%
Gross Profit	174	225	250	299	444	623	824	993	1,245	1,317	1,456	23.7%
Net Income	37	61	73	97	186	287	413	545	692	782	810	36.3%
EPS	0.08	0.11	0.11	0.15	0.26	0.38	0.41	0.55	0.69	0.78	0.81	25.4%
DPS	0.06	0.08	0.08	0.09	0.10	0.11	0.12	0.15	0.26	0.22	0.23	14.0%

KEY RATIOS

	1986	1987	1988	1989	1990	1991	1992	1993	1994	1995	1996	AVG
Profit/Revenues	56.8%	57.3%	47.7%	49.6%	49.0%	61.2%	62.4%	62.7%	65.3%	64.0%	64.8%	58.3%
ROE	7.6%	10.2%	10.2%	13.0%	17.5%	19.2%	23.2%	20.8%	22.2%	21.2%	19.3%	16.8%
ROA	0.34%	0.51%	0.53%	0.60%	0.90%	1.22%	1.58%	1.78%	1.93%	1.90%	1.80%	1.2%
P/E (Projected)	8.9	10.4	7.2	4.4	3.3	4.2	6.7	12.6	10.5	10.4	8.8	7.9

STOCK PRICE CHART
(fiscal year-end closing price, in U.S. dollars, adjusted for capital changes)

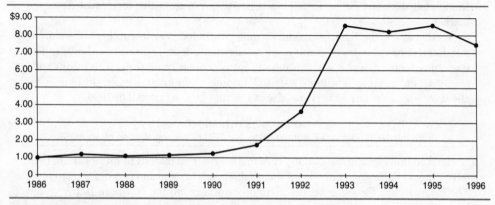

Notes: Foreigners can buy only a certain class of shares in Thailand; these are limited in number and trade at a premium to regular shares. Figures in U.S. dollars are translated from local currency using year-end exchange rates.

BANK OF IRELAND (IRE—NYSE)

Address: Lower Baggot Street / Dublin 2 / Ireland
Tel.: (011) 353 1 661 5933   **Fax:** (011) 353 1 661 5105

BASIC INFORMATION

Country: Ireland
Industry: Banking

Market capitalization: $4.77 billion
Share status: ADRs trade on NYSE

Investment thesis: Innovative bank with dominant market position; expanding in United Kingdom and United States

COMPANY GRADING BOX

Growth Categories		Quality of Management	
Revenue Growth	15	Return on Equity	5
Gross Profits	15	Return on Assets	0
Earnings per Share Growth	10	**Total QM (maximum 20)**	**5**
Share Price Growth	15		
Total Growth (maximum 80)	**55**	**FINAL GRADE**	**60**

BACKGROUND

This is no fly-by-night company. The Bank of Ireland was established by royal charter of King George III in 1783 and has been quoted on the Dublin Stock Exchange since it was formed in 1793 (it was incorporated in 1799). Today the Bank of Ireland is one of the largest commercial banks in the country and offers 1990s-style one-stop shopping. The bank services the personal and commercial sectors with everything from checking and deposit services to loans, mortgages, fund management, international asset financing, stockbroking, and advice on mergers and acquisitions. It's your local bank, your money center bank, and your Wall Street firm all rolled into one Irish company.

In Ireland, the Bank of Ireland has 20% of the market for financial services. And its retail business extends throughout Ireland, Northern Ireland, and Britain (although it also owns a minority stake in Citizens Financial Group in New Hampshire). The bank has used its strong cash flows in Ireland to fund growth internationally, particularly in the United States and the United Kingdom. Most recently the bank bought Bristol & West Building Society, the ninth largest building society in the United Kingdom, with a significant retail deposit base and a strong regional presence in the residential mortgage market.

Another key to the Bank of Ireland's strong growth has been its success in developing non-interest-based income—from asset management, fees, and services. Looking forward, management says it will continue to focus on its core markets, with a continued emphasis on growing non-interest-based income. Non-interest-based income grew about 50% over the last six years to 32% of revenue for the first half of 1996.

COMPANY STATEMENT
(from the 1996 Form 20-F submitted to the SEC re the registration of an ADS)

"Ireland continues to be the Group's core market where it intends to further strengthen its position as the leading provider of financial services to retail and corporate customers. The International Financial Services based businesses and the Northern Ireland retail businesses will also continue to be developed. The Group will also engage in selected financial services activities outside Ireland. The Group's main objective is to be a secure, growth oriented investment in diversified financial services. The Group will seek to achieve this through:

- Continued expansion of the core business, and growth outside Ireland

  The Group intends to expand further its core lending, deposit and money transmission businesses in its domestic market. . . . Outside Ireland, the Group's principal target markets will be Britain and the U.S. . . . The Group aims to grow selectively where it can add value and can achieve competitive advantage. . . .
- Growth in non-interest income

  The Group aims to continue to grow its non-interest income in absolute terms and as a percentage of total income through growth in fee-based activities such as asset management and life insurance. . . .
- Effective cost management

  In the near-term, the Group aims to achieve a cost/income ratio of 60% through a combination of cost reduction programs and restructuring of the Group's business processes. . . .
- Prudent risk management

  The Group aims to maintain the quality of its loan book through the consistent application of credit policies and procedures which emphasize the core objective of balance between long-term performance and portfolio quality and growth."

PERFORMANCE

Consistent, healthy revenue growth has been a hallmark of the Bank of Ireland, which received a total of 60 points in our grading system. Net revenue in dollars increased in each of the last ten years, with compound annual growth of 10%. Less consistent, but stronger, gross profits and EP/ADR in dollars increased in seven of the last ten years, with compound annual growth of around 13%, respectively. Dividends per share increased at a compound annual rate of 12%, with a payout ratio of 56%. ADR price performance surpassed EP/ADR and dividends, increasing at a compound annual rate of 17%. Although ROE averaged a not particularly impressive 13%, it has been improving, increasing to 18% in 1997. ROA averaged a reasonable 0.7% for the decade, but it has been 1% or higher during the last three years.

If you had invested $10,000 in Bank of Ireland in March 1987, you would have purchased around 640 ADRs (or ADR equivalents) at about $15.50 each (excluding commissions). During the next ten years, there were a two-for-nine rights issue in June 1987, a one-for-four rights issue in June 1988, a one-for-three bonus issue in July 1989, a one-for-five bonus issue in July 1991, and a one-for-six rights issue in July 1993. By March 1997, you would have had about 1,200 ADRs worth an estimated $48,000. You would also have received dividend payments of around $8,500.

BANK OF IRELAND

Ticker Symbol and Exchange: IRE—NYSE   **CUSIP No.: 46267Q103**

OPERATING AND PER SHARE DATA
(in millions of Irish punts and punts per share)

	Mar 87	Mar 88	Mar 89	Mar 90	Mar 91	Mar 92	Mar 93	Mar 94	Mar 95	Mar 96	Mar 97	CAGR
Net Revenues	418.0	495.0	564.0	642.0	680.0	714.0	834.0	984.0	931.0	998.0	985.0	8.9%
Gross Profit	127.0	159.5	179.8	180.4	214.1	206.1	276.4	402.5	396.6	430.0	416.2	12.6%
Net Profit	50.9	62.7	82.0	98.8	27.4	29.1	59.8	187.4	224.2	213.6	252.4	17.4%
EPS	0.17	0.18	0.20	0.23	0.06	0.07	0.14	0.41	0.47	0.45	0.52	12.0%
DPS	0.06	0.07	0.07	0.09	0.09	0.09	0.09	0.11	0.13	0.15	0.17	11.1%

OPERATING AND PER SHARE DATA
(in millions of U.S. dollars and dollars per ADR)

	Mar 87	Mar 88	Mar 89	Mar 90	Mar 91	Mar 92	Mar 93	Mar 94	Mar 95	Mar 96	Mar 97	CAGR
Net Revenues	619	798	806	1,019	1,079	1,170	1,283	1,426	1,526	1,647	1,563	9.7%
Gross Profit	188	257	257	286	340	338	425	583	650	710	661	13.4%
Net Profit	75	101	117	157	43	48	92	272	368	352	401	18.2%
EP/ADR	0.99	1.18	1.13	1.48	0.41	0.45	0.86	2.38	3.09	2.94	3.30	12.8%
DP/ADR	0.34	0.42	0.42	0.55	0.55	0.57	0.57	0.61	0.82	1.01	1.06	11.9%

KEY RATIOS

	Mar 87	Mar 88	Mar 89	Mar 90	Mar 91	Mar 92	Mar 93	Mar 94	Mar 95	Mar 96	Mar 97	AVG
Profit/Revenues	12.2%	12.7%	14.5%	15.4%	4.0%	4.1%	7.2%	19.0%	24.1%	21.4%	25.6%	14.6%
ROE	10.8%	11.2%	14.3%	16.5%	4.4%	4.1%	8.0%	20.8%	21.7%	17.4%	17.8%	13.4%
ROA	0.6%	0.7%	0.7%	0.7%	0.2%	0.2%	0.4%	1.1%	1.2%	1.0%	1.3%	0.7%
P/E (Projected)	7.7	8.6	7.4	32.1	24.3	11.0	5.7	5.5	7.0	7.2	10.1	11.5

STOCK PRICE CHART
(fiscal year-end closing price, in U.S. dollars, adjusted for capital changes)

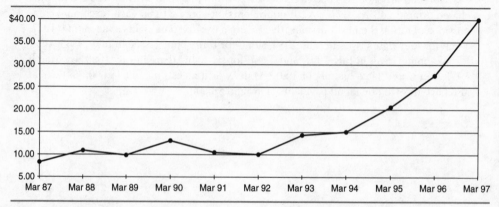

Note: Figures in U.S. dollars are translated from local currency using year-end exchange rates.

BANK OF THE PHILIPPINE ISLANDS
(BPI.PS—PHILIPPINES)

Address: Paseo de Roxas / Corner Ayala Avenue / Makati City / Philippines
Tel.: (011) 63 2 891 6728   **Fax:** (011) 63 2 891 0419
or
Address: 7 East 53rd Street / New York, NY 10022
Tel.: (212) 644-6700   **Fax:** (212) 752-5969

BASIC INFORMATION

Country: The Philippines   **Market capitalization:** $2.8 billion
Industry: Banking   **Share status:** Foreign shares trade on Philippines Exchange
Investment thesis: A leading Philippines financial services firm with a 145-year history

COMPANY GRADING BOX

Growth Categories		Quality of Management	
Revenue Growth	20	Return on Equity	10
Operating Income Growth	20	Return on Assets	10
Earnings per Share Growth	15	**Total QM (maximum 20)**	**20**
Share Price Growth	15		
Total Growth (maximum 80)	**70**	**FINAL GRADE**	**90**

BACKGROUND

Bank of the Philippine Islands (BPI) has been around for a long time. It was founded by decree of the governor general of the Philippines in 1851 as Banco Español de Isabel II, when the Philippines was a colony of Spain—and for years BPI was the Philippines' only domestic commercial bank. Initially, the bank focused on trade financing and extending credit for infrastructure and charitable projects (most of its early shareholders were related to the Catholic Church). In 1908 the bank took on its current name—and kept growing. For a number of years it functioned as the Philippines' central bank, then through the early 1980s it was primarily a corporate bank. Today BPI provides a range of services (having bought the market leader in consumer banking in 1983) through three primary divisions: institutional banking, consumer banking, and investment banking.

In late 1996, BPI merged with a smaller Philippines bank, CityTrust Banking Corporation, consolidating its preeminent position in consumer banking in the Philippines. BPI is now first in consumer lending, number of branches, and assets under management. It also has 50% of the market in auto loans and mortgages. In addition, BPI still is considered one of the Philippines' top corporate banks, and it has recently made inroads into the middle market (with growth rates of over 30% in some parts of the country). Then there is the agribusiness lending, leasing, securities sales and trading, and asset management—including 14 investment funds with money invested for nearly 1,300 institutional clients and more than 15,000 retail investors. During years of turmoil in the Philippines, BPI has helped the country move forward, providing a measure of fiscal stability, while also making a lot of money for shareholders. Although the collapse of Asian markets clearly took its toll on BPI, this is another company which has weathered crises in the past and looks like a good turnaround play.

COMPANY STATEMENT (from the 1996 annual report)

"Looking back, we believe our recent moves to raise new capital and to merge with CityTrust were both based on our underlying faith in the future of the economy and our own readiness to seize the many opportunities in such an expanding environment. The economy is now in an irreversible growth track and this increasingly is reflected in the macroeconomic fundamentals. . . .

"It is in this positive context that we have continued to prime ourselves for the more exciting competitive world ahead. We have grown bigger and stronger than ever before. . . .

"We have managed to grow our balance sheet without eroding the quality of our assets. Our non performing loan level was at a mere 1.3% at year end and well below industry standards, earning for us the continued respect and recognition of international credit rating agencies. . . .

"We have also further tightened our grip on the consumer market. . . . Our corporate banking team further reinforced our position as the top lender and lead banker to the top names in the industry. . . . Our investment banking arm, BPI Capital, also thrived in an environment of stability and growth. . . . Our asset management team preserved its leadership position in the industry. . . . Finally, our growth was also nurtured by the continuing efforts to enhance our delivery systems. Our focus remained on automation and investment banking technology as we pushed our frontiers specifically in phone banking, in our electronic payments system, and in customer call centers."

PERFORMANCE

Bank of the Philippine Islands (BPI) may not be the kind of emerging market company that investors are commonly aware of, but given its track record, perhaps it should be. Despite operating in a very volatile economy and political environment, BPI received 90 points in our grading system and got top marks for revenue and gross profit growth as well as for ROE and ROA. Net revenue and gross profit in dollars increased in eight out of the last ten years, rising at compound annual rates of 18% and 28%, respectively. EPS increased in seven of the last ten years, with compound growth of 16% in dollars. Return on equity averaged a staggering 22%, very high for a bank, and never fell below 18% during the decade. Similarly, ROA averaged 1.6% during the last ten years, also a very high figure, and never came in at less than 1%.

BPI's share price in dollars closed at new highs in seven out of ten years, with compound annual growth of 24%. The dividend payout ratio averaged about 20% for the decade, reaching $0.09 per share in 1996.

If you had invested $10,000 in BPI at the end of 1986, you would have purchased around 500 shares at about $20 each (excluding commissions). In 1994 there was a one-for-five bonus issue, and in October 1995 there were three more corporate actions: a one-for-one bonus issue, a ten-for-one stock split and a one-and-a-half-for-twenty-five rights issue. By the end of 1996, you would have had around 13,700 shares worth an estimated $82,900. You would also have received around $5,700 in dividend payments.

BANK OF THE PHILIPPINE ISLANDS

Ticker Symbol and Exchange: BPI.PS—PHILIPPINES   **SEDOL Code: 6074968**

OPERATING AND PER SHARE DATA
(in millions of Philippine pesos and pesos per share)

	1986	1987	1988	1989	1990	1991	1992	1993	1994	1995	1996	CAGR
Net Revenues	1,669	2,650	2,138	2,974	3,848	4,125	5,031	5,256	6,596	8,823	11,238	21.0%
Gross Profit	355	1,277	499	1,079	1,405	1,378	1,958	2,133	2,983	3,594	5,129	30.6%
Net Income	247	303	393	633	832	952	1,325	1,413	1,754	2,946	4,013	32.2%
EPS	1.14	1.40	1.46	2.34	2.46	2.82	3.14	3.35	4.20	5.43	6.52	19.1%
DPS	0.30	0.36	0.37	0.37	0.37	0.42	0.43	0.59	0.72	1.27	2.40	23.1%

OPERATING AND PER SHARE DATA
(in millions of U.S. dollars and dollars per share)

	1986	1987	1988	1989	1990	1991	1992	1993	1994	1995	1996	CAGR
Net Revenues	81	128	103	137	141	158	205	192	273	337	428	18.1%
Gross Profit	17	62	24	50	52	53	80	78	123	137	195	27.5%
Net Income	12	15	19	29	31	37	54	52	72	112	153	29.0%
EPS	0.06	0.07	0.07	0.11	0.09	0.11	0.13	0.12	0.17	0.21	0.25	16.2%
DPS	0.01	0.02	0.02	0.02	0.01	0.02	0.02	0.02	0.03	0.05	0.09	20.1%

KEY RATIOS

	1986	1987	1988	1989	1990	1991	1992	1993	1994	1995	1996	AVG
Profit/Revenues	21.3%	48.2%	23.3%	36.3%	36.5%	33.4%	38.9%	40.6%	45.2%	40.7%	45.6%	37.3%
ROE	17.8%	18.9%	20.7%	26.0%	26.4%	24.4%	26.4%	22.9%	23.2%	18.8%	19.2%	22.2%
ROA	1.0%	1.1%	1.2%	1.3%	1.5%	1.5%	1.8%	1.7%	1.8%	2.4%	2.3%	1.6%
P/E (Projected)	10.7	11.0	7.7	7.3	7.1	4.7	5.3	7.1	11.7	15.8	19.9	9.8

STOCK PRICE CHART
(fiscal year-end closing price, in U.S. dollars, adjusted for capital changes)

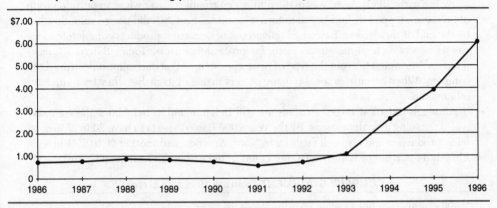

Notes: 1986–88 year-end share prices are estimated from high and low. Figures in U.S. dollars are translated using year-end exchange rates.

BARCO (BARBT.BR—BRUSSELS)

Address: President Kennedypark 35 / 8500 Kortrijk / Belgium
Tel.: (011) 32 56 262 611   **Fax:** (011) 32 56 262 262

BASIC INFORMATION

Country: Belgium   **Market capitalization:** $1.72 billion
Industry: Electrical and electronic   **Share status:** Foreign shares trade on Brussels Exchange
Investment thesis: Top manufacturer of specialized components for high-tech systems

COMPANY GRADING BOX

Growth Categories		Quality of Management	
Revenue Growth	20	Return on Equity	10
Operating Income Growth	15	**Risk**	
Earnings per Share Growth	20	Long-Term Debt/Total Capital	0
Share Price Growth	15	**Total QM&R (maximum 20)**	**10**
Total Growth (maximum 80)	**70**	**FINAL GRADE**	**80**

BACKGROUND

Belgium is hardly synonymous with high tech, but Silicon Valley's brightest growth stocks have nothing over Belgium-based Barco, with a market capitalization of $1.7 billion and 1996 revenues of almost $600 million. After five years of double-digit growth, with sales up 50% since 1992, this once stodgy old Belgian company has proven Belgium skeptics wrong. Barco's specialty? Being a niche player in a range of high-value-added niches: a maker of specialized components developed through its extensive research and development program. Among its products: projectors and display systems used by air traffic controllers, doctors, and shipping companies for training and tracking; management systems for telecommunications and cable television companies; and specialty equipment for graphics and automation, used in everything from publishing to textiles.

Founded as a radio manufacturer back in 1934, the Belgian American Radio Corporation quickly added televisions to its product line. By the 1940s it was one of the largest television manufacturers in Europe, making the only product compatible with all the European systems. But the advent of cable—which made Barco's technology unnecessary—along with the arrival of cheaper Japanese televisions in the 1970s sent Barco into a tailspin.

By the early 1980s Barco was in deep financial trouble. That's when an outside group of investors stepped in, and began to turn it around. The 1980s did not go smoothly, but by the end of the decade, Barco had moved out of consumer products completely to focus its efforts on high-margin products for professional users. Today, Barco's management is determined to avoid the type of price competition that once almost destroyed the company. When executives see too many players in one of its niches, they try to find another niche.

Although Barco's strongest markets are still Belgium and its neighbors, the company is also pursuing growth overseas. By the year 2000 Barco expects to have 20 to 25% of its sales, production and research facilities in North America, and another 20 to 25% in Asia. Already 44 percent of Barco's revenues come from outside the European Union.

COMPANY STATEMENT (from the 1996 annual report)

"1996 was another outstanding year for Barco. . . .

"Barco Projection Systems, strengthened by its new three-pillar structure and the systems skills of its new acquisitions, concentrated on developing comprehensive control room systems, and on further gearing up its visualization expertise towards high technology, high added value markets.

"Barco Display Systems increased the synergy between its hardware and software to offer even more flexible solutions in crucial areas of human progress, reinforcing its market position in integrated air traffic control display systems and extending its product range in the high-end medical technology.

"Barco Communication Systems moved further to a systems approach, expanding cable TV management systems in the direction of network monitoring. Particular emphasis was placed on developing original digital compression and transmission technology to prepare the company for the new digital area.

"Barco Graphics is seeking to stand out from the competition through an optimal combination of its linear plotter technology and its software lines. A perfect example is its new FASTLANE concept for high print throughput.

"For Barco Automation, new reference accounts in Korea, China and Mexico, testified to the real potential for its CIM and optical inspection systems in new growth areas.

"Every year Specialized Subcontracting invests in the latest equipment to enable it to offer optimal quality and flexibility to customers both inside and outside the group. Having these facilities in-house also allows each Barco product group to react quickly in rapidly changing electronics markets and to minimize the time to market of innovative products."

PERFORMANCE

Barco received 80 points in our grading system—with its highest marks for revenue and EPS growth and ROE. In dollars, revenues and EPS increased in eight of the last nine years, with compound annual growth of 19% and 22%, respectively. EBDIT in dollars increased in just six of the last ten years but increased at a compound annual rate of 24%. Share price performance was also inconsistent, but over the ten-year period, the share price in dollars increased at a compound annual rate of 20%. ROE averaged 18%, a mark in Barco's favor. As for risk, the ratio of long-term debt to total capital averaged 38%, rather high, but it had fallen to 12% in 1996.

If you had invested $10,000 in Barco at the end of 1986, you would have purchased around 120 shares at $84.00 each (excluding commissions). There was a change in the capital structure in January 1989. By the end of 1996, you would have had about 360 shares worth an estimated $61,100. You would also have received dividend payments of around $2,000.

BARCO

Ticker Symbol and Exchange: BARBt.BR—Brussels   SEDOL Code: 4089049

OPERATING AND PER SHARE DATA
(in millions of Belgian francs and francs per share)

	1986	1987	1988	1989	1990	1991	1992	1993	1994	1995	1996	CAGR
Sales	4,335	4,667	5,837	9,136	10,515	9,720	10,071	10,482	11,624	15,076	18,920	15.9%
EBIT	432	576	805	1,422	928	747	1,286	1,316	1,814	2,636	3,401	22.9%
Net Profit	347	440	603	1,027	513	258	601	805	1,315	1,803	2,358	21.1%
EPS	37.0	46.9	64.3	104.8	51.9	26.0	60.0	78.0	125.0	170.0	193.00	18.0%
DPS	2.8	3.3	4.6	19.5	19.5	19.5	21.0	23.8	29.7	37.5	46.50	32.7%

OPERATING AND PER SHARE DATA
(in millions of U.S. dollars and dollars per share)

	1986	1987	1988	1989	1990	1991	1992	1993	1994	1995	1996	CAGR
Sales	108.2	141.9	156.9	256.6	340.1	310.5	303.0	289.4	365.6	510.9	590.1	18.5%
EBIT	10.8	17.5	21.6	40.0	30.0	23.9	38.7	36.3	57.1	89.3	106.1	25.7%
Net Profit	8.7	13.4	16.2	28.8	16.6	8.2	18.1	22.2	41.4	61.1	73.5	23.8%
EPS	0.92	1.43	1.73	2.94	1.68	0.83	1.81	2.15	3.93	5.76	6.02	20.6%
DPS	0.07	0.10	0.12	0.55	0.63	0.62	0.63	0.66	0.93	1.27	1.45	35.7%

KEY RATIOS

	1986	1987	1988	1989	1990	1991	1992	1993	1994	1995	1996	AVG
EBIT Margin	10.0%	12.3%	13.8%	15.6%	8.8%	7.7%	12.8%	12.6%	15.6%	17.5%	18.0%	13.1%
ROE	19.9%	21.5%	24.2%	26.9%	12.3%	6.2%	12.9%	14.6%	19.0%	22.3%	16.5%	17.8%
LT Debt/Total Cap	30.0%	29.4%	28.4%	33.4%	57.1%	61.3%	53.4%	49.1%	41.6%	18.4%	12.0%	37.7%
P/E (Projected)	23.8	13.0	11.6	41.3	41.2	15.9	16.5	17.6	14.8	18.1	21.4	21.4

STOCK PRICE CHART
(fiscal year-end closing price, in U.S. dollars, adjusted for capital changes)

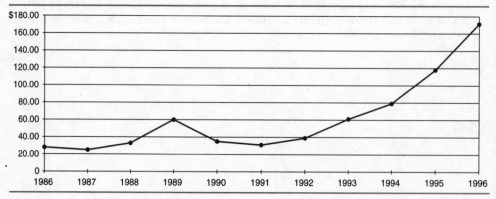

Note: Figures in U.S. dollars are translated from local currency using year-end exchange rates.

BOMBARDIER (BBDA.TO—TORONTO)

Address: 800, Boulevard René-Lévesque West / Montreal, Quebec H3B 1Y8 / Canada
Tel.: (514) 861-9418   **Fax:** (514) 861-7053   **Web site:** http://www.bombardier.com

BASIC INFORMATION

Country: Canada   **Market capitalization:** $6.4 billion
Industry: Industrial equipment   **Share status:** Shares trade on Toronto Exchange
Investment thesis: Leading manufacturer worldwide of transportation equipment

COMPANY GRADING BOX

Growth Categories		Quality of Management	
Revenue Growth	20	Return on Equity	5
Operating Income Growth	20	**Risk**	
Earnings per Share Growth	15	Long-Term Debt/Total Capital	5
Share Price Growth	20	**Total QM&R (maximum 20)**	10
Total Growth (maximum 80)	75	**FINAL GRADE**	85

BACKGROUND

Owning a $9.4 million LearJet (or a brand-new $35 million Global Express) might not be for everybody, but you might be interested in buying a piece of the company that builds them. Founded in 1942 as a snowmobile manufacturer, Montreal-based Bombardier now designs and builds regional airplanes, high-speed trains and business jets—the LearJet among them. Throughout the 1990s, this company has been—to indulge in a cliché—flying high. Today, Bombardier is actually the fourth largest civil aircraft manufacturer with annual revenues of close to $6 billion, 40,000 employees, and a market capitalization of $6.4 billion. Its fifty-seat regional jets are helping to transform the airline industry. This is a company that has successfully diversified—without straying from its expertise as a manufacturer of transportation equipment.

Among the deals inked by Bombardier in 1997: a $921 million contract for 680 rapid transit cars with New York's Metropolitan Transit Authority, replacing part of the city's aging subway fleet, and a $600 million contract with Atlantic Southeast Airlines for thirty regional jets. Other current projects—alone or with partners—include a new tram in a London suburb; regional jets for Lufthansa CityLine, a unit of Germany's largest airline, Lufthansa; a subway system in Ankara, Turkey; and two high-speed train projects in North America.

Moving to grow its markets, Bombardier has also joined up with Lufthansa to provide an executive corporate charter service geared toward European and North American corporate executives who want more flexibility than they can get with a regular airline; it has also partnered with American Airlines to allow customers to purchase a fraction of a business jet with a yearly flight time entitlement. There's more: in another logical extension of its businesses, Bombardier is moving more aggressively into the market for aerospace support services—maintenance, training, and operations management.

There is another twist to the Bombardier story: Bombardier highlights its extensive charitable contributions near the front of its Annual Report. In fact, the company's foundation receives 3% of Bombardier's income before income taxes. For investors looking for socially responsible companies, Bombardier stands out. Last year, the J. Armand Bombardier Foundation, named for the company's founder, donated $2 million to Canadian regional and national organizations active in social services, education, the arts, and health care.

COMPANY STATEMENT (from the 1997 annual report)

"During the past five years, the Corporation's operating income has more than doubled and we have maintained a healthy financial position while making considerable investments. . . .

"Activity in the aerospace segment was intense during the year, marked by a record number of aircraft deliveries and new orders, as well as by the progress achieved in our new aircraft development programs. We delivered 90 regional aircraft during the fiscal year, 70 business aircraft and 8 amphibious aircraft for a total of 168, or 22 more than in the previous year.

"The motorized consumer products segment also posted excellent results due mainly to major increases in market-share. . . . Buoyed by the success of our watercraft, jet boats and snowmobiles, we will continue to rely on innovation and the extension of our product lines to reinforce client loyalty and attract new consumers.

"The transportation group maintained a similar level of activity in 1996–97 as in the previous fiscal year. Its performance suffered, however, from unprofitable orders for tramways, manufactured in our plants in Belgium and Austria. The Group's efforts were nevertheless crowned with success as it obtained major orders. The largest was from Amtrak for the high-speed train linking Washington, New York and Boston."

PERFORMANCE

Through consistency and strong revenue growth, Bombardier garnered 85 points in our grading system. Revenues in dollars increased in every one of the last ten years, with compound annual growth of 23%. Pretax profit in dollars increased in nine of the last ten years, with compound annual growth of 27%. And EPS in dollars increased in eight of the last ten years, with compound annual growth of around 20%. Shareholders did well; the share price in dollars increased at a compound annual rate of 27%, and the dividend payout ratio averaged 25%. Bombardier did not get top marks for ROE, which averaged 16%, or for the ratio of its long-term debt to total capital, which averaged 29%. Although both were acceptable, neither was outstanding compared with some of the other companies in this book.

If you had invested $10,000 in Bombardier in January 1987, you would have purchased around 1,400 shares at about $7.00 (excluding commissions). During the next ten years, there were a one-for-one bonus issue in January 1992 and a two-for-one stock split in July 1995. By January 1997, you would have had around 5,600 shares worth an estimated $105,000. You would also have received dividend payments of around $6,000.

BOMBARDIER

Ticker Symbol and Exchange: BBDA.TO—Toronto

SEDOL Code: 2109723

OPERATING AND PER SHARE DATA
(in millions of Canadian dollars and dollars per share)

	Jan 87	Jan 88	Jan 89	Jan 90	Jan 91	Jan 92	Jan 93	Jan 94	Jan 95	Jan 96	Jan 97	CAGR
Sales	999	1,406	1,426	2,143	2,892	3,059	4,448	4,769	5,943	7,123	7,958	23.1%
Pretax Profit	54	103	109	117	121	121	151	207	346	236	606	27.3%
Net Profit	46	67	68	92	100	108	133	176	242	158	406	24.3%
EPS	0.19	0.30	0.34	0.34	0.35	0.36	0.43	0.56	0.73	0.45	1.16	19.8%
DPS	0.05	0.05	0.06	0.07	0.09	0.09	0.10	0.10	0.15	0.22	0.20	14.9%

OPERATING AND PER SHARE DATA
(in millions of U.S. dollars and dollars per share)

	Jan 87	Jan 88	Jan 89	Jan 90	Jan 91	Jan 92	Jan 93	Jan 94	Jan 95	Jan 96	Jan 97	CAGR
Sales	746	1,107	1,208	1,816	2,495	2,615	3,530	3,785	4,502	5,088	5,809	22.8%
Pretax Profit	40.5	80.9	92.2	99.3	104.0	103.8	119.8	164.4	261.8	168.4	442.6	27.0%
Net Profit	34.4	52.6	57.9	77.5	86.4	92.1	105.4	139.4	183.3	112.9	296.5	24.0%
EPS	0.14	0.24	0.29	0.29	0.30	0.31	0.34	0.44	0.55	0.32	0.85	19.6%
DPS	0.04	0.04	0.05	0.06	0.08	0.08	0.08	0.08	0.11	0.16	0.18	16.9%

KEY RATIOS

	Jan 87	Jan 88	Jan 89	Jan 90	Jan 91	Jan 92	Jan 93	Jan 94	Jan 95	Jan 96	Jan 97	AVG
Operating Margin	5.4%	7.3%	7.6%	5.5%	4.2%	4.0%	3.4%	4.3%	5.8%	3.3%	7.6%	5.3%
ROE	16.2%	19.9%	18.6%	19.7%	15.2%	12.5%	14.0%	13.0%	15.0%	8.7%	18.4%	15.6%
LT Debt/Total Cap	20.2%	15.9%	14.4%	22.0%	26.8%	29.3%	39.7%	41.5%	35.1%	39.4%	36.7%	29.2%
P/E (Projected)	7.9	6.4	9.9	10.9	10.9	19.9	10.4	14.5	25.3	17.1	18.7	13.8

STOCK PRICE CHART
(fiscal year-end closing price, in U.S. dollars, adjusted for capital changes)

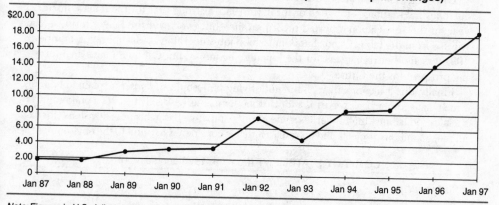

Note: Figures in U.S. dollars are translated from local currency using year-end exchange rates.

CANON (CANNY—NASDAQ)

Address: 30-2 Shimomaruko 3-chome / Ohta-ku / Tokyo 146 / Japan
Tel.: (011) 81 3 3758 2111   **Fax:** (011) 81 3 5482 5134   **Web site:** http://www.canon.com

BASIC INFORMATION

Country: Japan
Industry: Electrical and electronic
Investment thesis: A leading manufacturer of copiers, cameras, and printers

Market capitalization: $18.91 billion
Share status: ADRs trade on NASDAQ

COMPANY GRADING BOX

Growth Categories		Quality of Management	
Revenue Growth	20	Return on Equity	0
Operating Income Growth	20	**Risk**	
Earnings per Share Growth	15	Long-Term Debt/Total Capital	10
Share Price Growth	15	**Total QM&R (maximum 20)**	**10**
Total Growth (maximum 80)	**70**	**FINAL GRADE**	**80**

BACKGROUND

Canon is one of the world's largest manufacturers of copying machines and a leader in cameras and printers. And it has a brand name known around the world, a name first registered in 1935. Canon was incorporated in 1937, its shares have been listed on the Tokyo Stock Exchange since 1949, and the company has had a branch office in New York since 1955. Today Canon seems to be everywhere. Over the last fifty years this company has established a reputation for quality and innovative product design. And Canon has been there every step of the way as the concept of the home office has taken hold (in the interest of full disclosure, we should say that the first draft of this book was printed on our Canon BJC-4200 printer).

Today Canon's product line includes full-color and high-speed digital copying machines, facsimile machines, digital cameras, ink-jet printers, chemicals used in Canon products, a constantly updated line of cameras, semiconductor manufacturing equipment such as steppers, lenses used in television camera equipment . . . the list goes on. In the first half of this decade, Canon was among the top five recipients of U.S. patents every year.

Of course, like any major exporter's, Canon's short-term performance is affected by currency fluctuations—for good or for ill (in 1996, a strong year for the dollar and a bad year for the yen, Canon reported record profits); however, over the longer term, as you will see from the table, Canon has done a good job smoothing out its operating numbers. 1997 was another trying year for the Japanese economy, but Canon remains an interesting prospect for the future.

Finally, this is a company with the underlying philosophy of *kyosei* (explained below), which management says serves as a touchstone for its business activities. It's a philosophy of social responsibility that underlies some of the company's basic business decisions (for example, no military projects and no research that is considered harmful to the environment).

COMPANY STATEMENT (from the 1996 annual report)

"Philosophy:

"Canon's kyosei philosophy—living and working together for the common good—guides its global operations. The 75,000 employees of Canon in many countries around the world respect this ideal as we create innovations in cameras, business machines, and optical products. Through our dedication to customer satisfaction, we aim to make offices more pleasant places to work in, offer individuals a better quality of life, and provide industry with improved productivity.

"Approach:

"As multimedia continues to play an increasingly important role across a wide socioeconomic spectrum in our contemporary lives, a pervasive need has arisen for merging, modifying and exchanging still photographs, moving images and text in ways that allow their dissemination by new means that are both rapid and attractive. We continue to develop technology in diverse areas in order to contribute to improving the quality of life by offering new multimedia environments allowing our customers to communicate as naturally and conveniently as possible.

"Responsibility:

"As a truly global corporation, Canon feels a strong corporate responsibility toward the local communities where we conduct our business operations and toward protecting the natural environment. That we take this responsibility seriously is recognized in our corporate behavior. We place ecology and the environment above the business basics of quality, cost, and delivery, and we make special efforts to contribute to local communities around the world."

PERFORMANCE

Considering the performance of the Japanese equity market over the past ten years, Canon's overall score of 80 in our grading system is remarkable. In particular, Canon got high marks for consistency and revenue growth, despite a difficult domestic economy. Revenues in dollar terms rose every year for the last ten years, with compound annual growth of 15%. EBDIT increased nine out of the last ten years, with compound annual growth of 19%. EP/ADR were inconsistent but increased at a compound annual rate of 24%. ROE, which averaged 6.2%, rose to 9.6% in 1996 (close to its high for the period). As for risk, the long-term debt to total capital ratio declined from a high of 20.0% in 1986 to a low of 7.5% in 1996, averaging 15.3% for the period.

If you had invested $10,000 in Canon at the end of 1986, you would have purchased around 310 ADRs (or ADR equivalents) at about $32 each (excluding commissions). In August 1989, there was a one-for-ten bonus issue. By the end of the ten-year period, you would have had 345 shares worth an estimated $38,600. You would also have received dividend payments of around $1,900.

CANON

Ticker Symbol and Exchange: CANNY—NASDAQ   **CUSIP No.: 138006309**

OPERATING AND PER SHARE DATA
(in billions of Japanese yen and yen per share)

	1986	1987	1988	1989	1990	1991	1992	1993	1994	1995	1996	CAGR
Sales	889	977	1,106	1,351	1,728	1,869	1,914	1,836	1,933	2,166	2,558	11.1%
EBDIT	85.5	103.5	145.5	180.8	237.2	226.4	242.4	199.1	214.0	258.3	338.3	14.7%
Net Profit	10.7	13.2	37.1	38.3	61.4	51.4	35.6	21.1	31.0	55.0	94.2	24.3%
EPS	16.67	19.64	51.30	49.31	78.12	64.30	46.50	26.80	35.80	62.70	106.90	20.4%
DPS	11.36	9.09	11.36	11.93	12.50	12.50	12.50	12.50	12.50	13.00	15.00	2.8%

OPERATING AND PER SHARE DATA
(in millions of U.S. dollars and dollars per ADR)

	1986	1987	1988	1989	1990	1991	1992	1993	1994	1995	1996	CAGR
Sales	5,646	8,074	8,855	9,392	12,762	14,976	15,337	16,422	19,388	20,958	22,432	14.8%
EBDIT	543	855	1,165	1,257	1,751	1,814	1,942	1,781	2,147	2,499	2,966	18.5%
Net Profit	68	109	297	266	453	412	285	189	311	532	826	28.4%
EP/ADR	0.53	0.81	2.05	1.71	2.88	2.58	1.86	1.20	1.80	3.03	4.69	24.4%
DP/ADR	0.36	0.38	0.45	0.41	0.46	0.50	0.50	0.56	0.63	0.63	0.66	6.2%

KEY RATIOS

	1986	1987	1988	1989	1990	1991	1992	1993	1994	1995	1996	AVG
EBDIT Margin	9.6%	10.6%	13.2%	13.4%	13.7%	12.1%	12.7%	10.8%	11.1%	11.9%	13.2%	12.0%
ROE	3.2%	3.6%	8.9%	7.0%	9.9%	7.8%	5.1%	2.9%	4.0%	6.5%	9.6%	6.2%
LT Debt/Total Cap	20.0%	19.6%	15.9%	16.9%	14.4%	15.0%	13.2%	19.9%	13.9%	12.0%	7.5%	15.3%
P/E (Projected)	45.8	16.4	27.5	23.4	19.9	30.3	51.1	43.0	27.0	17.5	25.1	29.7

STOCK PRICE CHART
(fiscal year-end closing price, in U.S. dollars, adjusted for capital changes)

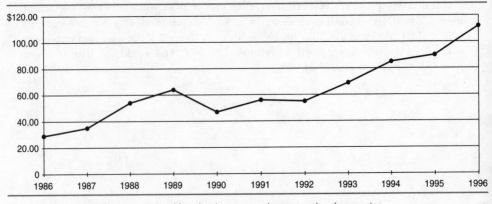

Note: Figures in U.S. dollars are translated from local currency using year-end exchange rates.

CARREFOUR (CRERF—OTC)

Address: B.P. 419-16 / 75769 Paris Cedex 16 / France
Tel.: (011) 33 1 5370 1900   **Fax:** (011) 33 1 5370 8616

BASIC INFORMATION

Country: France
Industry: Retailing, food
Investment thesis: Expansion of hypermarkets in rapidly growing developing nations

Market capitalization: $23.69 billion
Share status: Foreign shares trade OTC

COMPANY GRADING BOX

Growth Categories		Quality of Management	
Revenue Growth	20	Return on Equity	10
Operating Income Growth	20	**Risk**	
Earnings per Share Growth	20	Long-Term Debt/Total Capital	10
Share Price Growth	20	**Total QM&R (maximum 20)**	**20**
Total Growth (maximum 80)	**80**	**FINAL GRADE**	**100**

BACKGROUND

Carrefour is doing around the world what Wal-Mart did in the United States—except that American investors largely have missed out on the Carrefour story. The latest chapter? Carrefour is building its hypermarkets, giant retail outlets (typically 100,000 square feet plus) that sell large volumes of everything from fresh foods to clothing to pharmaceuticals, in rapidly growing developing countries. Already, Carrefour is one of the largest and most successful international hypermarket companies, with sales topping $20 billion, more than 100,000 employees, and a 22% historic annual growth rate. In the thirty years since Carrefour opened its first French hypermarket, the company's management has proven its ability to deliver consistent, profitable, growth.

Today, the company comprises 275 hypermarkets in 14 countries around the globe. In 1995, for the first time, more than half of the hypermarkets owned and operated by the company were located outside France. And management expects that trend to continue. In the years ahead, 75 to 80% of operations will be located outside France. As of the end of 1996, Carrefour had 178 stores in Europe (117 in France, 53 in Spain, 6 in Italy, 2 in Portugal), 72 in Latin America (44 in Brazil, 15 in Argentina, and 13 in Mexico), and 25 in Asia (13 in Taiwan, 3 in China, 3 in South Korea, 2 in Malaysia, 2 in Thailand, and 1 in Hong Kong, and 1 in Turkey). In 1997 and 1998, the company plans to open stores in Poland, Singapore, and Colombia.

In addition, among its other investments Carrefour owns 23% of another top-performing French retail chain, Comptoirs Modernes, 50% of Office Depot France (as well as 6% of Office Depot in the United States), a chain of discount stores, and a line of frozen foods. International expansion is clearly at the top of this company's agenda.

COMPANY STATEMENT (from the 1996 annual report)

"Hypermarkets today are part of consumer habits in developed countries, where choice, optimum price and product quality remain our priority concerns. To meet those requirements our aims are innovation, professionalism, and the on-going enhancement of our sales and management methods.

"Our approach also meets consumer expectations in the new countries where we are present. Based on a few essential hypermarket principles—everything under the same roof, purchasing comfort, and services—our constant concern is to adapt to the marketplace and the specific habits of consumers in every country, assisted by our partnerships with the major players in the local economy.

"Development of this kind would not meet with its current success without the corporate culture inherent to the world of Carrefour: a combination of trade experience, pioneer spirit and management skill. Based on the expertise and know-how of a core group, our teams are rapidly set up on-site. Their own development enables a high-speed opening rate using local managerial staff, thereby furthering the assimilation of our Group in-country. . . .

"The investments we are making mean we can forecast continuing growth in our results, based on both the enhancement of our business activities and the development of new countries."

PERFORMANCE

Carrefour is one of our star companies, with a perfect score of 100 in our grading system. It gets high marks in every category. Over the last ten years, revenues in dollars increased every year, with compound annual growth of 14.3%. EBDIT also increased every year during the period, showing compound annual growth of 26%. EPS in dollars increased from $2.83 in 1986 to $15.89 in 1996, with compound annual growth of 19%. The share price, adjusted for bonus issues, has set a new high every year since 1988 and increased from a low of $42 in 1988 to a high of $665 in 1996. ROE averaged 18% during the period. As for risk, the long-term debt to total capital ratio declined from a high of 28% in 1992 to 12% in 1995. Finally, dividends per share have grown every year, reaching more than $5 in 1996, with an average payout ratio of 31% of earnings during the decade.

If you had invested $10,000 in Carrefour at the end of 1986, you would have purchased 18 shares at $560 each (excluding commissions). During the following ten years, there were a one-for-three bonus issue in April 1989, a one-for-one bonus issue in May 1991, a one-for-one bonus issue in May 1994, and a one-for-two bonus issue in May 1996. By the end of 1996, you would have had around 140 shares worth an estimated $94,000. You would also have received around $4,200 in dividend payments.

CARREFOUR

Ticker Symbol and Exchange: CRERF—OTC   **SEDOL Code: 4177546**

OPERATING AND PER SHARE DATA
(in millions of French francs and francs per share)

	1986	1987	1988	1989	1990	1991	1992	1993	1994	1995	1996	CAGR
Sales (bn)	51.5	56.5	64.8	73.9	75.8	100.4	117.1	123.2	136.3	144.6	154.9	11.6%
EBDIT	1,058	1,263	1,588	2,092	2,374	2,544	3,899	5,123	5,883	6,742	8,106	22.6%
Net Profit	693	761	911	1,214	1,382	1,358	1,638	1,979	2,516	3,038	3,123	16.2%
EPS	18.21	19.98	23.85	31.74	36.10	35.33	42.57	51.43	65.45	79.03	81.19	16.1%
DPS	7.13	7.50	8.75	10.02	10.86	10.82	11.66	13.99	17.34	21.34	26.00	13.8%

OPERATING AND PER SHARE DATA
(in millions of U.S. dollars and dollars per share)

	1986	1987	1988	1989	1990	1991	1992	1993	1994	1995	1996	CAGR
Sales (bn)	8.0	9.4	10.9	11.6	13.9	17.8	22.1	21.8	24.6	29.0	30.3	14.3%
EBDIT	164	211	267	328	436	451	737	905	1,062	1,352	1,586	25.5%
Net Profit	108	127	153	191	254	241	310	350	454	609	611	19.0%
EPS	2.83	3.33	4.00	4.98	6.64	6.26	8.05	9.09	11.81	15.85	15.89	18.8%
DPS	1.11	1.25	1.47	1.57	2.00	1.92	2.20	2.47	3.13	4.28	5.09	16.5%

KEY RATIOS

	1986	1987	1988	1989	1990	1991	1992	1993	1994	1995	1996	AVG
EBDIT Margin	2.1%	2.2%	2.4%	2.8%	3.1%	2.5%	3.3%	4.2%	4.3%	4.7%	5.2%	3.4%
ROE	16.3%	17.6%	16.6%	19.6%	20.2%	16.6%	17.4%	16.6%	19.5%	19.7%	18.0%	18.0%
LT Debt/Total Cap	13.6%	23.6%	19.1%	18.1%	12.8%	26.7%	27.9%	20.8%	18.0%	16.5%	11.9%	19.0%
P/E (Projected)	22.5	12.8	12.8	16.8	15.5	18.1	15.3	21.9	18.6	24.4	31.8	19.1

STOCK PRICE CHART
(fiscal year-end closing price, in U.S. dollars, adjusted for capital changes)

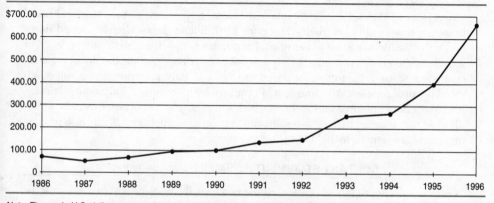

Note: Figures in U.S. dollars are translated from local currency using average exchange rates.

CASTORAMA (CDBFF—OTC)

Address: Z.I. / 59175 Templemars / France
Tel.: (011) 33 2 20 16 75 75   **Fax:** (011) 33 3 20 95 19 17   **Web site:** http://www.castorama.fr.

BASIC INFORMATION

Country: France
Industry: Retailing, specialty
Investment thesis: The Home Depot of France

Market capitalization: $2.47 billion
Share status: Foreign shares trade OTC

COMPANY GRADING BOX

Growth Categories		Quality of Management	
Revenue Growth	20	Return on Equity	10
Operating Income Growth	20	**Risk**	
Earnings per Share Growth	20	Long-Term Debt/Total Capital	5
Share Price Growth	20	**Total QM&R (maximum 20)**	15
Total Growth (maximum 80)	80	**FINAL GRADE**	95

BACKGROUND

Castorama is the Home Depot of France—and it is expanding throughout Europe. It has the largest share of the do-it-yourself market in France (about 17%), has developed new store formats, and consistently has been successful in increasing sales per square meter. Although limited by regulations governing new superstore openings, Castorama has found other venues for growth, including redesigns of old stores (some are being reformatted; others are being expanded), a new chain of smaller stores geared more toward professional customers (an estimated 25% of the market), a building materials warehouse chain, and overseas expansion.

The company's growth over the last ten years has been impressive, from 444,000 square meters of sales space in 1985 to 1,127,000 square meters in 1995. Most of the growth has been within the company, although the company has made a few acquisitions along the way. In 1996 Castorama had 14,300 employees, revenues of $2.9 billion, and a market capitalization of $2.47 billion. Analysts see potential for margin expansion if Castorama reduces its relatively high staff costs (which are not expected to increase as the company expands) and increases its sales of own-label products, which currently account for only about 5% of revenues.

Overseas, in March 1997 Castorama said it would buy an eleven-store Montreal-based home improvement chain, Reno-Depot, for $107 million. It has already opened stores under the Castorama name in Germany, Italy, Poland, and Brazil, with varying levels of success. Although so far results in Germany have been disappointing, the division was recently reorganized. Castorama has been successful in Italy, a market that is still dominated by small retailers. And Brazil and Poland are both promising. Poland, in particular, has tremendous potential for Castorama, with a high percentage of home owners, a middle class that is doing better financially, and very little competition. Brazil, also promising, gives Castorama a toehold in Latin America.

COMPANY STATEMENT (from the 1996 annual report)

"*A paradise for do-it-yourselfers.* At Castorama, a friendly welcome has always been at the heart of our business philosophy. DIY is growing as a recreational activity, but whether they come for business or pleasure, our customers are increasingly demanding. That is why Castorama stores are becoming more information intensive, with more accessible product displays, more readily available sales teams, and more integrated services.

"Everything under one roof. The new superstore concept makes it easier to find everything the customer needs. Product lines have been re-organized into six universes, all located in the same building. Store layout has been changed, but not size; we still need about 12,500 square meters to present the full range of our expertise.

"Fitting seamlessly into the environment. The typical Castorama store is on the outskirts of a metropolitan area with a population of around 200,000. Its architecture and location are very carefully designed to harmonize with the local community, which it also serves by creating jobs.

"Upgrading existing stores. If appropriate, current outlets are being upgraded to the new concept to drive further expansion in their catchment areas. An advantage of the new concept is that it builds upon existing layout to create an enhanced design."

PERFORMANCE

Castorama received a total score of 95, making it one of our top performers. Sales in dollars increased in each of the last ten years, with compound annual growth of almost 17%. EPS in dollars increased in nine of the last ten years, with compound annual growth of 23%. And the share price in dollars has set a new high in each of the last ten years, increasing from a low of $15 in 1986 to a high of $204 in 1996. Dividends per share in dollars rose in nine of the last ten years, from $0.31 in 1986 to $2.15 in 1996. EBDIT growth was also impressive, increasing in nine of the last ten years and showing compound annual growth of 17%. ROE was 15% in 1996 and averaged just under 18% during the decade. The only category in which Castorama lost a few points was "risk"—for a higher-than-ideal average long-term debt to total capital ratio; however, by 1996, that ratio was down to 10%.

If you had invested $10,000 in Castorama at the end of 1986, you would have bought around 95 shares at about $106 each (excluding commissions). During the following ten years, there was a one-for-ten bonus issue in June 1990, a one-for-four stock split in May 1992, and another one-for-ten bonus issue in July 1995. By the end of 1996, you would have had around 450 shares worth an estimated $80,000. You would also have received around $5,500 in dividend payments.

CASTORAMA

Ticker Symbol and Exchange: CDBFF—OTC   **SEDOL Code: 4179144**

OPERATING AND PER SHARE DATA
(in millions of French francs and francs per share)

	1986	1987	1988	1989	1990	1991	1992	1993	1994	1995	1996	CAGR
Sales	4,019	4,661	5,569	6,298	7,486	8,751	10,401	11,616	12,614	13,788	14,922	14.0%
EBDIT	346	358	425	519	618	791	904	1,030	1,140	1,316	1,348	14.6%
Net Profit	50	86	109	152	182	255	307	393	474	546	554	27.2%
EPS	5.60	8.70	11.00	12.80	15.00	18.60	22.10	25.80	31.00	34.80	34.90	20.1%
DPS	1.97	3.38	4.50	5.40	5.75	6.80	8.10	9.40	10.60	11.00	11.00	18.8%

OPERATING AND PER SHARE DATA
(in millions of U.S. dollars and dollars per share)

	1986	1987	1988	1989	1990	1991	1992	1993	1994	1995	1996	CAGR
Sales	624	777	935	989	1,376	1,552	1,966	2,052	2,277	2,765	2,920	16.7%
EBDIT	54	60	71	81	114	140	171	182	206	264	264	17.3%
Net Profit	7.8	14.3	18.2	23.9	33.4	45.3	58.1	69.4	85.5	109.5	108.5	30.2%
EPS	0.87	1.45	1.85	2.01	2.76	3.30	4.18	4.56	5.60	6.98	6.83	22.9%
DPS	0.31	0.56	0.76	0.85	1.06	1.21	1.53	1.66	1.91	2.21	2.15	21.5%

KEY RATIOS

	1986	1987	1988	1989	1990	1991	1992	1993	1994	1995	1996	AVG
EBDIT Margin	8.6%	7.7%	7.6%	8.2%	8.3%	9.0%	8.7%	8.9%	9.0%	9.5%	9.0%	8.6%
ROE	12.9%	19.5%	20.6%	19.2%	16.8%	18.6%	17.9%	18.2%	17.5%	17.0%	14.9%	17.6%
LT Debt/Total Cap	55.6%	52.5%	52.7%	40.2%	43.5%	34.6%	31.1%	13.4%	11.1%	10.8%	10.0%	32.3%
P/E (Projected)	16.1	16.4	15.6	16.0	11.5	17.7	17.3	25.9	17.4	23.0	21.3	18.0

STOCK PRICE CHART
(fiscal year-end closing price, in U.S. dollars, adjusted for capital changes)

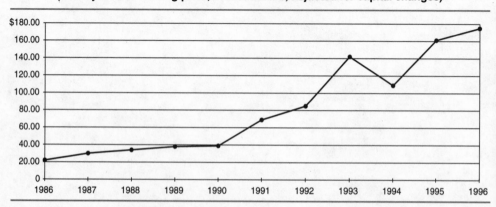

Note: Figures in U.S. dollars are translated from local currency using average exchange rates.

CHEUNG KONG (HOLDINGS) (CHEUY—OTC)

Address: China Building, 18–22 Floors / 29 Queens Road Central / Hong Kong
Tel.: (011) 852 2526 6911   **Fax:** (011) 852 2845 2057

BASIC INFORMATION

Country: Hong Kong
Industry: Multi-industry
Investment thesis: A leading Hong Kong property developer and infrastructure company

Market capitalization: $19.99 billion
Share status: ADRs trade OTC

COMPANY GRADING BOX

Growth Categories		Quality of Management	
Revenue Growth	15	Return on Equity	10
Operating Income Growth	20	**Risk**	
Earnings per Share Growth	20	Long-Term Debt/Total Capital	10
Share Price Growth	15	**Total QM&R (maximum 20)**	**20**
Total Growth (maximum 80)	**70**	**FINAL GRADE**	**90**

BACKGROUND

Cheung Kong (Holdings), a Hong Kong–based holding company, is the creation of Li Ka-shing, who is chairman, the single largest shareholder, and one of the richest men in the world. Over the years, Mr. Li has made a fortune through Cheung Kong, and it seems pretty likely that, through the company, he is going to keep on making money. Cheung Kong has several lines of business. First and foremost, it is a major Hong Kong property developer with an impressive track record in developing and selling property and a rich land-bank for future development. Management has focused on large-scale developments of small- to medium-sized apartments, as well as on commercial and industrial properties. Recently, Cheung Kong has begun growing its investment property business to ensure a steady stream of rental income.

Second, Cheung Kong owns a 44.2% stake in Hong Kong conglomerate Hutchison Whampoa (see page 186), also a Li Ka-shing company. Hutchison Whampoa's operations include ports, property investment, retailing, telecommunications, and oil.

Third, Cheung Kong has been developing commercial and residential properties in China since the early 1990s. In 1996 Cheung Kong bundled together its twenty China infrastructure projects, including the Shenzhen-Shantou Highway, the Shantou Bay Bridge, and three Shantou power plants, into a company called CKI (Cheung Kong Infrastructure) and floated it on the Hong Kong Stock Exchange. Of course, Cheung Kong still has its hand in CKI through Hutchison Whampoa. Shortly after taking it public, Cheung Kong sold Hutchison Whampoa its 75% CKI stake. Separately, Cheung Kong is still developing residential property in China.

Although hard hit by the "Asian contagion" in 1997, Cheung Kong should be well positioned for any turnaround.

COMPANY STATEMENT (from the 1995 annual report—statement by Li Ka-Shing)

"As the economies of China and Hong Kong continue to improve, the property market is expected to follow suit. Further, given Hong Kong's continuous prosperity over the past years, the average citizen should have amassed savings to improve his living environment, resulting in a strong underlying demand for residential properties. As confidence in the economy revives, the local property market will become active again. I am particularly optimistic in this respect.

"During the period of consolidation over the past year or so, the Company has acquired several sites at reasonable costs through different channels, namely, government auctions, government tenders, joint ventures with statutory corporations and acquisitions from private parties. These acquisitions have greatly boosted our land bank and will provide a solid base for the Company's development for several years beyond 1998. . . .

"The Group's various projects on the mainland are making good progress. Among them, the hotels and certain rental properties have been in operation for years, while several completed power plant and highway-bridge projects will begin to make a profit contribution in 1996."

PERFORMANCE

Cheung Kong received a score of 90 in our grading system—with impressive growth in EP/ADR and EBDIT in dollars; both of these increased in every one of the last ten years. While revenue had a moderately impressive compound annual growth of 14%, EBDIT showed compound annual growth of 24% and EP/ADR showed compound growth of 28%. Dividends per ADR also increased in every one of the last ten years, with compound annual growth of 28%. ROE averaged 20% and was 24% in 1996. And the long-term debt to total capital ratio averaged a moderate 14%. Reflecting the ups and downs of property in general and the Hong Kong equity market in specific, ADR price performance has been somewhat inconsistent; however, growth has been excellent, with the ADR price rising at a compound annual rate of 24%.

If you had invested $10,000 in Cheung Kong at the end of 1986, you would have purchased around 1,500 ADRs (or ADR equivalents) at about $6.50 each (excluding commissions). In 1987, there were a four-for-one stock split, a one-for-four bonus issue, and a one-for-ten rights issue. By 1996, you would have had about 9,700 ADRs worth an estimated $86,300. You would also have received dividend payments of around $8,100.

CHEUNG KONG (HOLDINGS)

Ticker Symbol and Exchange: CHEUY—OTC   **CUSIP No.: 166744201**

OPERATING AND PER SHARE DATA
(in millions of Hong Kong dollars and dollars per share)

	1986	1987	1988	1989	1990	1991	1992	1993	1994	1995	1996	CAGR
Sales	3,648	2,323	2,258	5,044	4,413	9,990	10,278	10,693	14,841	12,122	13,202	13.7%
PBT	1,615	1,793	2,281	3,143	3,602	5,738	7,563	11,932	13,150	12,573	14,220	24.3%
Net Profit	1,283	1,581	2,090	2,775	3,251	4,886	6,266	9,781	10,113	11,125	12,251	25.3%
EPS	0.51	0.77	0.95	1.26	1.48	2.22	2.85	4.45	4.60	5.06	6.02	28.0%
DPS	0.12	0.22	0.29	0.38	0.48	0.68	0.80	1.00	1.10	1.20	1.38	27.7%

OPERATING AND PER SHARE DATA
(in millions of U.S. dollars and dollars per ADR)

	1986	1987	1988	1989	1990	1991	1992	1993	1994	1995	1996	CAGR
Sales	468	299	289	647	566	1,284	1,328	1,383	1,917	1,568	1,708	13.8%
EBDIT	207	231	292	403	462	738	977	1,544	1,699	1,627	1,840	24.4%
Net Profit	165	204	268	356	417	628	810	1,265	1,307	1,439	1,585	25.4%
EP/ADR	0.07	0.10	0.12	0.16	0.19	0.29	0.37	0.58	0.59	0.65	0.78	28.1%
DP/ADR	0.02	0.03	0.04	0.05	0.06	0.09	0.10	0.13	0.14	0.16	0.18	27.8%

KEY RATIOS

	1986	1987	1988	1989	1990	1991	1992	1993	1994	1995	1996	AVG
EBDIT Margin	44.3%	77.2%	101.0%	62.3%	81.6%	57.4%	73.6%	111.6%	88.6%	103.7%	107.7%	82.6%
ROE	17.5%	14.3%	16.2%	17.0%	17.2%	21.5%	22.9%	27.6%	23.4%	21.4%	24.0%	20.3%
LT Debt/Total Cap	18.3%	14.1%	9.4%	11.5%	14.1%	10.0%	7.1%	16.6%	26.8%	13.6%	15.0%	14.2%
P/E (Projected)	10.4	7.1	6.4	6.5	5.7	6.9	4.2	10.3	6.2	7.8	8.9	7.3

STOCK PRICE CHART
(fiscal year-end closing price, in U.S. dollars, adjusted for capital changes)

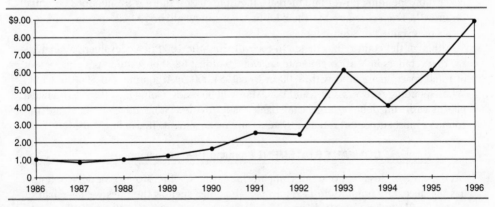

Note: Figures in U.S. dollars are translated from local currency using year-end exchange rates.

CIFRA (CFRAY—OTC)

Address: José María Castorena 470 / Delegación Cuajimalp / 05200 Mexico D.F.
Tel.: (011) 52 5 327 9211   **Fax:** (011) 52 5 327 9259

BASIC INFORMATION

Country: Mexico
Industry: Retailing, food
Investment thesis: Giant food retailer and hypermarket company; majority owned by Wal-Mart

Market capitalization: $5.51 billion
Share status: ADRs trade OTC

COMPANY GRADING BOX

Growth Categories		Quality of Management	
Revenue Growth	20	Return on Equity	10
Operating Income Growth	20	**Risk**	
Earnings per Share Growth	20	Long-Term Debt/Total Capital	10
Share Price Growth	15	**Total QM&R (maximum 20)**	**20**
Total Growth (maximum 80)	**75**	**FINAL GRADE**	**95**

BACKGROUND

Cifra is Mexico's largest and most successful retailer. Now it is also controlled by U.S. discount retailing giant Wal-Mart. In June 1997, Wal-Mart announced plans to buy a majority of Cifra's voting stock as its first direct investment in a foreign partner. Prior to the deal, a six-year-old joint venture between the two companies operated 145 of Cifra's more than 370 units, including 18 Wal-Mart Supercenters and 28 Sam's Clubs. Other holdings (belonging to Cifra alone and the joint venture) include 35 Aurrera hypermarkets, 60 Aurrera Bodega discount stores, 36 Superama supermarkets, 156 Vips restaurants, and 36 Suburbia clothing department stores.

Like all Mexican retailers, Cifra was hard hit during the country's recent economic troubles; however, it has emerged intact and appears ready to take full advantage of the country's improving economy. Together with Wal-Mart, Cifra has already invested just under $1.5 billion in opening new stores and improving its systems along the lines of the very successful Wal-Mart model. As in the rest of Latin America, the retail market is dominated by relatively small operations; in Mexico only 23% of sales are generated by the large retailers, compared with 95% in the United States. As consumers gradually recover their spending power and increase their purchases, there is tremendous potential for growth. Even compared to their Latin American neighbors, Mexican retailers lag in terms of revenue per square foot.

Although the country has begun to recover from the 1994 peso devaluation, analysts say that retailers in Mexico generate an average of just $200 of revenue per square foot of retail space, compared with $800 in Brazil, $1,000 in Argentina and $600 in Chile. When spending recovers, Cifra and Wal-Mart will be ready. Going into 1997, Cifra had a pile of cash, no debt, a large land bank ready for new store development, and the country's most successful retailing systems and management. It also has Wal-Mart.

COMPANY STATEMENT (from the 1996 annual report)

"At the close of this fiscal year our company has no debt, either in pesos or dollars. It also has the necessary liquidity to face adverse situations, such as the ones we have had to contend with in the past. We have sufficient reserves and resources that will allow us to continue growing at whatever pace is necessary, not only to maintain but also to increase our market share. Cifra's capital structure and reserves, at the present time, are substantial and we will endeavor to strengthen them even more. . . .

"We are optimistic about the future, since we operate in a dynamic market whose composition and demographic trends are very favorable for our business. Mexico's population continues to grow and 57% of the people are under 25 years of age. These young men and women will soon have families of their own, and this will greatly expand the need for the goods and services that we offer at the lowest prices."

PERFORMANCE

That Cifra weathered the recent Mexican recession as well as it did is testament to the quality of this company's management. Its score of 95 in our grading system reflects the strength of this firm and its fine performance over time despite the last few difficult years in Mexico. Cifra received top marks for all growth categories, even though operating results in dollars generally were down during 1994–1995, following the peso devaluation. Revenues and EBDIT in dollars recorded compound annual growth of 22% and 17%, respectively. EP/ADR increased by 18% per annum. Cifra also has no long-term debt, lowering the risk for investors. ROE has fallen steadily but still averaged 18% over the nine-year history. The share price rose at a compound annual rate of 22% in dollars, despite closing 1996 about 60% below its all-time high, recorded in 1993. Dividend payments have been sporadic during the period.

If you had invested $10,000 in Cifra at the end of July 1987, you would have bought about 6,250 ADRs (or ADR equivalents) at around $1.50 each (excluding commissions). During the following nine years, there was a two-for-one bonus issue in 1988, a one-for-three bonus issue in October 1990, and a two-for-one stock split in October 1990. By the end of 1996, you would have had around 50,000 ADRs worth $61,000. You would also have received $9,000 in dividends through 1994 (Cifra did not pay a dividend in 1988, 1995 and 1996).

CIFRA

Ticker Symbol and Exchange: CFRAY—OTC   **CUSIP No.: 171785207**

OPERATING AND PER SHARE DATA
(in millions of nominal Mexican pesos and pesos per share)

	Jul 86	Jul 87	Jul 88	Jul 89	Dec 90	Dec 91	Dec 92	Dec 93	Dec 94	Dec 95	Dec 96	CAGR
Sales	N/A	706	2,003	3,056	6,377	8,509	11,496	14,231	15,637	20,172	23,251	47.4%
EBDIT	N/A	115	231	345	735	892	1,183	1,344	1,526	2,383	2,670	41.8%
Net Profit	N/A	61	112	161	447	541	713	798	872	1,431	1,593	43.7%
EPS	N/A	0.02	0.04	0.05	0.14	0.17	0.22	0.25	0.27	0.45	0.50	43.0%
DPS	N/A	0.06	—	0.06	0.16	0.07	0.10	0.13	0.08	—	—	N/M

OPERATING AND PER SHARE DATA
(in millions of U.S. dollars and dollars per ADR)

	Jul 86	Jul 87	Jul 88	Jul 89	Dec 90	Dec 91	Dec 92	Dec 93	Dec 94	Dec 95	Dec 96	CAGR
Sales	N/A	495	860	1,203	2,162	2,766	3,691	4,580	3,165	2,623	2,947	21.9%
EBDIT	N/A	80.7	99.1	135.8	249.2	290.0	379.8	432.6	308.9	309.9	338.4	17.3%
Net Profit	N/A	42.8	48.1	63.3	151.7	176.0	228.9	256.8	176.5	186.0	201.9	18.8%
EP/ADR	N/A	0.01	0.02	0.02	0.05	0.06	0.07	0.08	0.05	0.06	0.06	18.2%
DP/ADR	N/A	0.04	—	0.02	0.05	0.02	0.03	0.04	0.02	—	—	N/M

KEY RATIOS

	Jul 86	Jul 87	Jul 88	Jul 89	Dec 90	Dec 91	Dec 92	Dec 93	Dec 94	Dec 95	Dec 96	AVG
EBDIT Margin	N/A	16.3%	11.5%	11.3%	11.5%	10.5%	10.3%	9.4%	9.8%	11.8%	11.5%	11.4%
ROE	N/A	28.2%	20.5%	18.7%	24.4%	20.7%	19.0%	14.8%	10.9%	11.6%	10.4%	17.9%
LT Debt/Total Cap	N/A	0.0%	0.0%	0.0%	0.0%	0.0%	0.0%	0.0%	0.0%	0.0%	0.0%	0.0%
P/E (Projected)	N/A	11.9	10.7	3.5	10.1	17.5	25.4	59.2	35.0	16.6	20.7	21.1

STOCK PRICE CHART
(fiscal year-end closing price, in U.S. dollars, adjusted for capital changes)

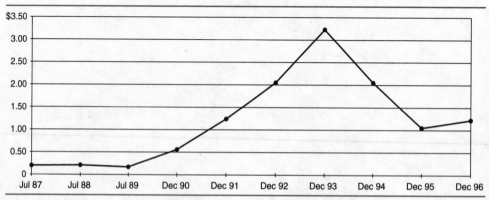

Note: Figures in U.S. dollars are translated from local currency using year-end exchange rates.

CITIC PACIFIC (CTPCF—OTC)

Address: Level 35, Two Pacific Place / 88 Queensway / Hong Kong
Tel.: (011) 852 2820 2111   **Fax:** (011) 852 2877 2771   **Web site:** http://www.citicpacific.com

BASIC INFORMATION

Country: Hong Kong
Industry: Multi-industry
Investment thesis: Investment arm of the Chinese government; property and infrastructure in Hong Kong, China

Market capitalization: $10 billion
Share status: Foreign shares trade OTC

COMPANY GRADING BOX

Growth Categories		Quality of Management	
Revenue Growth	15	Return on Equity	5
Operating Income Growth	20	**Risk**	
Earnings per Share Growth	20	Long-Term Debt/Total Capital	10
Share Price Growth	15	**Total QM&R (maximum 20)**	15
Total Growth (maximum 80)	70	**FINAL GRADE**	85

BACKGROUND

How would you like to invest alongside the government of the People's Republic of China in the future of Hong Kong and the mainland? Citic Pacific is known as the blue chip of the "red chips," Chinese companies listed on the Hong Kong Stock Exchange and subject to Hong Kong accounting practices. It is the oldest, largest, and best-managed company of this group, and it has investments in most of Hong Kong's key industries, as well as investments in mainland China.

Citic's specialty? Investments in Hong Kong and China's infrastructure. Twenty-seven percent of revenue comes from the aviation industry, including major holdings in Cathay Pacific and Dragonair (the leading airline for flights between Hong Kong and mainland China); 17% comes from telecommunications, including an 8% stake in Hong Kong's main telecommunications company, Hong Kong Telecom; 5% comes from power generation, an area in which management is aggressively expanding in Hong Kong and on the mainland (in March 1997 Citic Pacific bought China Power and Light, Hong Kong's largest power company); and 19% comes from "civil facilities," including bridge and tunnel construction and management.

Citic is also heavily invested in property development, with 16% of revenue derived from its involvement in real estate, as well as in various trading operations and credit and distribution activities, accounting for 10% of revenue. Then there are Citic Pacific's steel plants and a cable-manufacturing company. Finally, a Citic Pacific subsidiary is the Hong Kong distributor for Acura, Honda, Isuzu, Nissan, and Audi (together representing 25% of the Hong Kong market). Citic also trades in everything from foodstuffs to building materials to audiovisual equipment, and it supplies food to hotels, restaurants, and the catering industry in Hong Kong and mainland China. Our conclusion? So far, Citic has made some pretty good investment decisions.

Citic Pacific's performance suffered in 1997 as a result of the "Asian Contagion," but this company has lived through crises before. As Asian earnings begin to recover and China resumes strong growth, Citic Pacific is uniquely positioned to prosper.

COMPANY STATEMENT (from the 1996 annual report)

"Citic concentrates its business interests in infrastructure in its broadest sense, trading and distribution and property, mainly in Hong Kong, Macau and the Mainland of China. Citic Pacific's shares are listed on the Hong Kong Stock Exchange and Group companies employ over 11,750 people.

"1997 marks the seventh anniversary of the founding of Citic Pacific and it is pleasing to see what has been achieved. Your company has developed from a small listed company into one of the largest in Hong Kong. A solid base of recurrent income has been built and extensive program of developments are in progress which will take us well into the next century. 1997 is also a historical year for Hong Kong with the change in sovereignty. I remain very confident for the future prosperity of both Hong Kong and Mainland China. Your Company will continue to focus its businesses in Hong Kong and Mainland China in those sectors in which we have expertise. In addition to organic growth, the Company's policy of expansion will also seek out for acquisition business that meets its operational and financial criteria."—Lung Yung Chikin, Chairman

---

PERFORMANCE

Citic Pacific received a total score of 85 points in our grading system, garnering particularly high marks for growth in EBDIT and EPS (both in dollar terms). EBDIT and EPS increased in each of the last four years (we are using numbers only back to 1992, since that is when Citic became the company it is today), with compound annual growth of 32% and 39% respectively. EPS more than doubled from 1995 to 1996. Revenues in dollars increased in three of the last four years, with compound annual growth of 11%. ROE averaged a respectable 12% and reached an impressive 19% in 1996. At the same time, the long-term debt to total capital ratio has remained moderate, averaging 18%. Share price performance has been somewhat inconsistent, due in large part to the vagaries of the Hong Kong economy and equity market; however, growth has been impressive, increasing at a compound annual rate of 35%. Dividends per share increased in each of the last four years, showing compound annual growth of 32%.

If you had invested $10,000 in Citic Pacific in 1992, you would have purchased 5,650 shares at around $1.75 each (excluding commissions). During the next four years, there were no significant capital changes. By 1996, your shares would have been worth an estimated $32,800. You would also have received total dividend payments of around $2,100.

CITIC PACIFIC

Ticker Symbol and Exchange: CTPCF—OTC   **SEDOL Code: 6196152**

OPERATING AND PER SHARE DATA
(in millions of Hong Kong dollars and dollars per share)

	1986	1987	1988	1989	1990	1991	1992	1993	1994	1995	1996	CAGR
Sales	N/M	N/M	N/M	N/M	N/M	N/M	7,834	10,780	12,123	10,836	12,756	13.0%
EBDIT	N/M	N/M	N/M	N/M	N/M	N/M	1,414	2,285	3,468	4,125	4,261	31.8%
Net Profit	N/M	N/M	N/M	N/M	N/M	N/M	1,040	1,887	2,570	3,073	6,860	60.3%
EPS	N/M	N/M	N/M	N/M	N/M	N/M	0.87	1.08	1.32	1.53	3.22	38.7%
DPS	N/M	N/M	N/M	N/M	N/M	N/M	0.30	0.38	0.48	0.55	0.92	32.3%

OPERATING AND PER SHARE DATA
(in millions of U.S. dollars and dollars per share)

	1986	1987	1988	1989	1990	1991	1992	1993	1994	1995	1996	CAGR
Sales	N/M	N/M	N/M	N/M	N/M	N/M	1,012	1,395	1,566	1,402	1,650	13.0%
EBDIT	N/M	N/M	N/M	N/M	N/M	N/M	183	296	448	534	551	31.8%
Net Profit	N/M	N/M	N/M	N/M	N/M	N/M	134	244	332	398	887	60.3%
EPS	N/M	N/M	N/M	N/M	N/M	N/M	0.11	0.14	0.17	0.20	0.42	38.7%
DPS	N/M	N/M	N/M	N/M	N/M	N/M	0.04	0.05	0.06	0.07	0.12	32.4%

KEY RATIOS

	1986	1987	1988	1989	1990	1991	1992	1993	1994	1995	1996	AVG
EBDIT Margin	N/M	N/M	N/M	N/M	N/M	N/M	18.0%	21.2%	28.6%	38.1%	33.4%	27.9%
ROE	N/M	N/M	N/M	N/M	N/M	N/M	10.3%	8.8%	10.2%	11.5%	18.8%	11.9%
LT Debt/Total Cap	N/M	N/M	N/M	N/M	N/M	N/M	3.5%	11.7%	25.3%	25.2%	15.8%	16.3%
P/E (Projected)	N/M	N/M	N/M	N/M	N/M	N/M	12.7	19.3	12.2	8.2	20.9	14.6

STOCK PRICE CHART
(fiscal year-end closing price, in U.S. dollars, adjusted for capital changes)

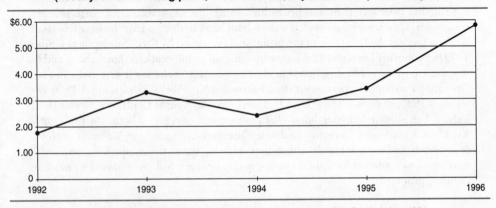

Notes: Results prior to 1992 are not comparable, as company was changed into Citic Pacific in late 1991.
Figures in U.S. dollars are translated from local currency using year-end exchange rates.

CITY DEVELOPMENTS (CDEVY—OTC)

Address: 36 Robinson Road / 20-01 City House / 0106 Singapore
Tel.: (011) 65 221 2266   **Fax:** (011) 65 223 2746

BASIC INFORMATION

Country: Singapore
Industry: Property
Investment thesis: Largest property developer in Singapore; aggressively diversifying into hotels

Market capitalization: $7.3 billion
Share status: ADRs trade OTC

COMPANY GRADING BOX

Growth Categories		Quality of Management	
Revenue Growth	20	Return on Equity	0
Operating Income Growth	20	**Risk**	
Earnings per Share Growth	20	Long-Term Debt/Total Capital	0
Share Price Growth	20	**Total QM&R (maximum 20)**	0
Total Growth (maximum 80)	**80**	**FINAL GRADE**	**80**

BACKGROUND

City Developments is the largest property firm in Singapore, an island city-state that has had a thriving property market. It is one of the biggest commercial landlords in Singapore, operates in thirteen countries, and employs more than 10,000 people. Today, more than 60% of its revenues comes from its property development business, just over 30% from its hotel business, and around 6% from rental income. The sixth largest company traded on the Singapore stock exchange, it counts HSBC Holdings (see page 183), with just under 12%, and U.S. banking giant Chase Manhattan, with just over 7%, among its major shareholders.

Although hard hit by the 1997 "Asian contagion," like all companies in the region, it could be another interesting investment when those economies turn around.

The company's operations are divided into four divisions: residential property development, industrial property development, investment properties (for which City Developments acts as landlord), and hotels. The property side of the business is booming, with overseas buyers from all over Asia helping to fuel demand. In Singapore the government keeps a tight control over the amount of residential real estate that is developed, keeping supplies relatively tight and prices high. And, like most successful Asian property companies, City Developments has a large land bank to draw on for the next few years.

Then there is the hotel side of the business, 51% owned by City Developments. Since 1989 the company has spent $2.5 billion building up an international hotel chain, and today the group owns fifty-five hotels in eleven countries, including a 42% stake in Plaza Operating Partners, the partnership that has owned New York City's landmark Plaza Hotel since 1995. Even more recently, City Developments bought Copthorne Hotels Holdings, a U.K.-based four-star hotel chain comprising seventeen hotels in the United Kingdom, France, and Germany. Last year, the company created the Millennium Hotels & Resorts brand name for itself. Although on a buying spree, the company's chairman has developed a reputation for not overpaying and is believed to have amassed a promising group of properties.

"The residential property market remained resilient in 1995 with the private property price index rising by about 10.3 percent compared to 42 percent in 1994. During the year under review we launched four residential projects . . . comprising a total of 1,129 units, of which about 95 percent have been sold to date.

"The investment sentiment in industrial space in 1995 was bullish, supported by the strong performance of the manufacturing sector. Capital values for industrial property surged by over twenty percent in 1995 while that of prime industrial space went up by as much as 39 percent. The strong demand was evident when one block of Citilink Warehouse Complex comprising 15,000 square meters was sold within a day of its launch. . . .

"Demand for office space was also strong with an island-wide occupancy rate of about 93 percent and 98 percent for prime grade-A office space in the Raffles Places area. . . .

"CDL Hotels International achieved yet another year of significant growth in performance and portfolio. . . . During the year we launched our new hotel brand, Millennium Hotels & Resorts, reinforcing our aim to become a major player in the international hotel industry. The unveiling of the new brand is part of a global strategy aligning hotels under strategic brands."

PERFORMANCE

City Developments gets the highest possible scores for growth and an overall score of 80 in our grading system. EBDIT in dollars and EP/ADR increased in every one of the last ten years, with compound annual growth of 39% and 59%, respectively. Revenues in dollars increased in eight of the last ten years, with compound annual growth of 35%. The share price kept pace, increasing at a compound annual rate of nearly 32%. ROE increased from a low of 3.5% in 1988 to 20% in 1996, though the 9% average for the decade was lower than that of most of the companies on our list. As for risk, the ratio of long-term debt to total capital is a little higher than for most of our companies, averaging 37% for the decade.

If you had invested $10,000 in City Developments at the end of 1986, you would have purchased around 2,300 ADRs (or ADR equivalents) at $4.25 each (excluding commissions). During the next ten years, there were a one-for-four rights issue in June 1987, a one-for-five rights issue in July 1988, a one-for-ten rights issue in January 1992, and a one-for-five rights issue in June 1994. By the end of 1996, you would have had around 17,200 ADRs worth an estimated $155,200. You would also have received dividend payments of around $5,000.

CITY DEVELOPMENTS

Ticker Symbol and Exchange: CDEVY—OTC

CUSIP No.: 177797305

OPERATING AND PER SHARE DATA
(in millions of Singaporean dollars and dollars per share)

	1986	1987	1988	1989	1990	1991	1992	1993	1994	1995	1996	CAGR
Sales	205	165	314	307	432	544	506	752	1,139	1,972	2,644	29.1%
EBDIT	64	63	72	118	160	197	215	295	468	789	1,076	32.7%
Net Profit	26	24	25	37	44	51	73	115	201	400	535	35.5%
EPS	0.01	0.02	0.03	0.05	0.06	0.07	0.13	0.17	0.27	0.51	0.68	52.5%
DPS	0.01	0.02	0.03	0.03	0.03	0.03	0.04	0.06	0.05	0.06	0.08	23.1%

OPERATING AND PER SHARE DATA
(in millions of U.S. dollars and dollars per ADR)

	1986	1987	1988	1989	1990	1991	1992	1993	1994	1995	1996	CAGR
Sales	94	83	161	162	248	336	309	467	780	1,399	1,889	34.9%
EBDIT	29.4	31.7	36.9	62.3	91.7	121.5	131.1	183.1	320.3	559.5	768.8	38.6%
Net Profit	11.8	12.0	12.8	19.2	25.3	31.7	44.7	71.3	137.4	283.8	382.1	41.6%
EP/ADR	0.00	0.01	0.02	0.03	0.03	0.04	0.08	0.11	0.18	0.36	0.49	59.3%
DP/ADR	0.00	0.01	0.02	0.02	0.02	0.02	0.02	0.04	0.03	0.04	0.06	28.6%

KEY RATIOS

	1986	1987	1988	1989	1990	1991	1992	1993	1994	1995	1996	AVG
EBDIT Margin	31.1%	38.4%	22.9%	38.6%	36.9%	36.2%	42.5%	39.2%	41.1%	40.0%	40.7%	37.1%
ROE	5.9%	4.4%	3.5%	5.0%	5.8%	6.5%	7.4%	10.3%	11.4%	18.8%	20.1%	9.0%
LT Debt/Total Cap	6.0%	26.0%	28.9%	38.5%	44.4%	41.1%	43.3%	49.6%	44.5%	46.0%	39.9%	37.1%
P/E (Projected)	63.0	46.7	40.0	46.7	25.7	23.0	17.6	25.9	15.9	15.1	18.0	30.7

STOCK PRICE CHART
(fiscal year-end closing price, in U.S. dollars, adjusted for capital changes)

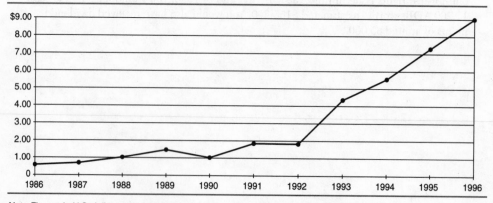

Note: Figures in U.S. dollars are translated from local currency using year-end exchange rates.

COCA-COLA AMATIL (CCLAY—OTC)

Address: 71 Macquarie Street / Sydney, NSW 2000 / Australia
Tel.: (011) 61 2 259 6666   **Fax:** (011) 61 2 259 6623   **Web site:** http://www.ccamatil.com

BASIC INFORMATION

Country: Australia
Industry: Food and beverages
Market capitalization: $4.6 billion
Share status: ADRs trade OTC
Investment thesis: Largest Coke bottler based outside the United States; operates in seventeen countries

COMPANY GRADING BOX

Growth Categories		Quality of Management	
Revenue Growth	15	Return on Equity	5
Operating Income Growth	15	**Risk**	
Earnings per Share Growth	5	Long-Term Debt/Total Capital	5
Share Price Growth	20	**Total QM&R (maximum 20)**	10
Total Growth (maximum 80)	**55**	**FINAL GRADE**	**65**

BACKGROUND

Most of us think of Coca-Cola as a well-run company with a fantastic brand name. That's a big part of the reason that Coke's "anchor bottlers" look so attractive. Worldwide, there are ten of them (two were designated in 1997). And Coca-Cola Amatil (CCA) is one of our favorites. Based in Australia, CCA bottles the great American soft drink throughout Asia. In 1998 Coke Amatil announced that it will spin off its European assets into a separate company to be listed on the London Stock Exchange, allowing the company (CCA) to concentrate on Asia.

In 1997, Coca-Cola Amatil announced plans to buy the soft drink bottling unit of the Philippines-based San Miguel Corporation, in a deal valued at $2.7 billion. Between them, CCA and the Philippine bottler had revenues of $3.7 billion in 1996. In a statement made shortly after the transaction was announced, Coca-Cola's late CEO, Roberto Goizueta, spoke of "the beginning of a new era for the Coca-Cola business in Asia." In 1998, CCA announced it would buy the franchise for South Korea.

Coca-Cola established its first Australian office in 1937, long before it put its anchor bottling system into place. Over the years, bottlers sprang up around the country. Then, in 1989, Amatil Limited, one of Australia's oldest corporations, started selling off its other interests to focus on its beverage investments, including a number of Coca-Cola bottlers within Australia as well as overseas. Coca-Cola Amatil has been on the go ever since. An aggressive expansion policy—through marketing and sales as well as acquisitions—put this company onto our list. Between 1992 and 1995 CCA spent close to $1 billion on acquisitions and invested almost $900 million in marketing and production infrastructure. The spending picked up again after Kerry Group, owned by Chinese billionaire Robert Kuok, bought 8.3 percent of CCA in 1996 for $667 million (Australian). CCA and Kerry Group, which has Coke interests in China, now have a "strategic alliance."

COMPANY STATEMENT (from the 1996 annual report)

"Global Strategies

- Market leadership in every territory: CCA aims to achieve market leadership in every territory in which it operates.

- Operational development: CCA seeks to develop operations by the rapid establishment of effective business infrastructure.
- Employee development: A competent and committed workforce is an essential requirement for CCA to achieve its growth opportunity.
- Geographic expansion: Single country markets are CCA's preferred economic unit.

"The company's core growth strategies remain in place and the Company will continue to invest in market development through expanding production capacity, enhancing distribution efficiencies and building marketing programs to meet escalating consumer demand across all three of our regions."

PERFORMANCE

Over the last ten years, Coca-Cola Amatil performed admirably in revenue growth and excellently in share price performance, but its overall score of 65 points was pulled down by the years before the company finished its restructuring. Revenues in dollars recorded compound annual growth of almost 9%, though they have doubled since 1990. After taking a turn for the worse in 1989–1990, as the company completed selling off its noncore businesses, EP/ADR resumed growing, though the compound growth rate was just about 6% for the decade. This company did receive points for quality of management and risk. ROE averaged a respectable 13% for the decade, and the long-term debt to total capital ratio was maintained at a reasonable level, averaging 33% for the decade.

If you had invested $10,000 in Coca-Cola Amatil at the end of 1986, you would have purchased around 850 ADRs (or ADR equivalents) at about $11.75 each (excluding commissions). During the following ten years, there were a two-for-five bonus issue in 1987, a two-for-one stock split in 1991, a one-for-four bonus issue in 1993, a one-for-four bonus issue in 1994, and a one-for-four bonus issue in 1995. By the end of 1996, you would have had around 3,850 ADRs worth an estimated $82,200. You would also have received around $7,100 in dividend payments.

COCA-COLA AMATIL

Ticker Symbol and Exchange: CCLAY—OTC   **CUSIP No.: 191085208**

OPERATING AND PER SHARE DATA
(in millions of Australian dollars and dollars per share)

	1986	1987	1988	1989	1990	1991	1992	1993	1994	1995	1996	CAGR
Sales	1,919	2,103	2,187	2,535	1,537	1,792	2,108	1,951	2,239	2,968	3,705	6.8%
EBDIT	194.0	222.4	217.7	264.7	234.2	243.4	266.6	277.4	325.0	449.2	488.0	9.7%
Net Profit	77.3	85.2	88.7	81.2	56.9	68.0	65.9	87.7	110.8	138.6	142.1	6.3%
EPS	0.18	0.19	0.20	0.18	0.11	0.13	0.14	0.23	0.28	0.31	0.27	4.3%
DPS	0.06	0.07	0.09	0.04	0.09	0.10	0.09	0.14	0.17	0.19	0.19	12.2%

OPERATING AND PER SHARE DATA
(in millions of U.S. dollars and dollars per ADR)

	1986	1987	1988	1989	1990	1991	1992	1993	1994	1995	1996	CAGR
Sales	1,279	1,519	1,869	1,996	1,182	1,358	1,454	1,327	1,736	2,204	2,943	8.7%
EBDIT	129.3	160.6	186.1	208.4	180.2	184.4	183.9	188.7	251.9	333.5	387.6	11.6%
Net Profit	51.5	61.5	75.8	63.9	43.8	51.5	45.4	59.7	85.9	102.9	112.9	8.2%
EP/ADR	0.24	0.27	0.34	0.28	0.17	0.20	0.19	0.31	0.43	0.46	0.44	6.1%
DP/ADR	0.08	0.10	0.15	0.06	0.14	0.15	0.12	0.19	0.26	0.28	0.30	14.2%

KEY RATIOS

	1986	1987	1988	1989	1990	1991	1992	1993	1994	1995	1996	AVG
EBDIT Margin	10.1%	10.6%	10.0%	10.4%	15.2%	13.6%	12.6%	14.2%	14.5%	15.1%	13.2%	12.6%
ROE	15.0%	14.8%	12.3%	32.3%	9.0%	9.9%	8.4%	7.5%	9.1%	7.9%	5.4%	12.6%
LT Debt/Total Cap	23.9%	25.6%	23.5%	44.6%	37.2%	36.2%	30.9%	40.1%	38.5%	33.0%	29.4%	33.4%
P/E (Projected)	10.3	10.2	14.7	35.4	24.8	38.6	20.3	31.9	25.7	39.2	43.4	25.1

STOCK PRICE CHART
(fiscal year-end closing price, in U.S. dollars, adjusted for capital changes)

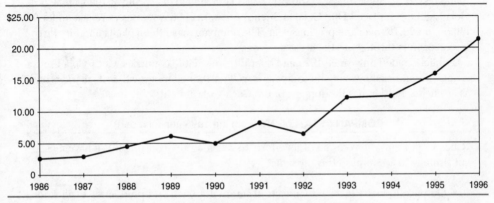

Note: Figures in U.S. dollars are translated from local currency using year-end exchange rates.

COCA-COLA FEMSA (KOF—NYSE)

Address: Rio Amazonas No. 43 / Colonia Cuauhtémoc / 06500 Mexico D.F.
Tel.: (011) 525 209 09 09   **Fax:** (011) 525 705 71 26

BASIC INFORMATION

Country: Mexico

Industry: Food and beverages

Investment thesis: Coca-Cola anchor bottler in parts of Mexico and Argentina

Market capitalization: $1.37 billion

Share status: ADRs trade on NYSE

COMPANY GRADING BOX

Growth Categories		Quality of Management	
Revenue Growth	20	Return on Equity	5
Operating Income Growth	20	**Risk**	
Earnings per Share Growth	10	Long-Term Debt/Total Capital	5
Share Price Growth	0	**Total QM&R (maximum 20)**	10
Total Growth (maximum 80)	50	**FINAL GRADE**	60

BACKGROUND

Coca-Cola Femsa is a Mexican joint venture between Fomento Económico Mexicano, which owns 51% of its capital stock, and a subsidiary of Atlanta-based Coca-Cola, which owns 30% of the company. The remaining 19% is publicly traded. Like Coca-Cola Amatil (page 111) and Panamco (page 243), it is one of Coca-Cola's ten anchor bottlers. In 1997 Coca-Cola Femsa bought out the Coca-Cola Export Corporation to take full ownership of Coca-Cola Femsa Buenos Aires (it had been the majority owner since 1994). Although Coca-Cola Femsa's numbers have been hurt by Mexico and Argentina's recent economic woes, in 1995 the company managed to increase its already dominant position in a number of its markets. It not only survived the recession, it made itself stronger. In Mexico City and its environs, Coca-Cola Femsa increased its share of the cola market by 5%, to 62.2%, while in the southeast part of Mexico the company's market share increased by 1%, to 74.6%. In Buenos Aires, Coca-Cola Femsa gained an additional 3.4% of the cola market, for a total of 77.1%.

Coca-Cola Femsa offers customers a full range of Coca-Cola products, including Coke, Diet Coke, Fresca, Sprite, and Fanta. It has also added beverages tailored to its markets: Lift, an apple-flavored soft drink, was launched in the spring of 1995, and Coca-Cola Light has replaced Diet Coke in Buenos Aires. In 1996 revenues were just under $1 billion, up 22.7% over the previous year. The company has fifteen plants and fifty distribution centers throughout the areas it covers.

Publicly traded only since 1994 and operating in volatile countries, Coca-Cola Femsa is not without risk; however, the company is well positioned for growth in its markets and, as an anchor bottler, has the support of the Coca-Cola system.

COMPANY STATEMENT (from the 1996 annual report)

"Coca-Cola Femsa devotes all of its efforts to reaching the consumer. We have a clear-cut strategy to accomplish this mission:

- Outpace industry growth by means of internal growth and product diversification;
- Undertake continuous improvements in operating efficiencies at our facilities;

- Stimulate higher per capita beverage consumption through product innovation, channel marketing, sales force restructuring and continuous promotions;
- Update and improve information and administrative systems; and
- Align financial strategy with Coca-Cola Femsa's growth objectives.

"Our Corporate Strengths:

- We are only one of two Coca-Cola "anchor bottlers" in Latin America and are directly responsible for almost three percent of The Coca-Cola Company's sales volume worldwide.
- Our beverage brands are highly regarded by consumers; and
- We have favorable relations with our employees, their families and their labor unions, contributing to our growth and profitability.

PERFORMANCE

Coca-Cola Femsa gets high marks for growth and an overall score of 60 in our grading system. Over the last eight years, this company's revenues in dollar terms have grown every year, with compound annual growth of 22%. EBDIT showed compound annual growth of 53% and increased in six out of the last eight years. EP/ADR have been inconsistent and less impressive but still rose at a compound annual rate of 16%. ROE was 14.4% in 1996, up from 13.3% in 1995 and 13.5% in 1994. On the other hand, Coca-Cola Femsa's ADR price performance in the three years since the company went public suffered with the rest of the Mexican equity market in 1994 and did not recover completely by the end of 1996. As for risk, the long-term debt to total capital ratio increased from 15.8% in 1994 to 35.7% in 1996.

Coca-Cola Femsa has been publicly traded only since 1993 and is a relatively young company. Unfortunately, the Mexican peso devalued sharply in 1994, interrupting the first few years of share price performance. If you had invested $10,000 in Coca-Cola Femsa at the end of 1993, you would have purchased around 300 ADRs at about $32.75 each. By the end of 1996, your ADRs would have been worth only an estimated $8,800. We think this stock is a "keeper," however, because the operating performance of the company has been positive, and, as the Mexican economy recovers, we believe shareholders will be rewarded.

COCA-COLA FEMSA

Ticker Symbol and Exchange: KOF—NYSE   **CUSIP No.: 191241108**

OPERATING AND PER SHARE DATA
(in millions of nominal Mexican pesos and pesos per share)

	1986	1987	1988	1989	1990	1991	1992	1993	1994	1995	1996	CAGR
Sales	N/A	N/A	446	578	867	1,256	1,533	1,915	3,108	6,145	7,628	42.6%
EBDIT	N/A	N/A	12	30	88	199	229	313	439	606	1,223	78.6%
Net Profit	N/A	N/A	10	32	79	130	103	161	212	316	499	63.6%
EPS	N/A	N/A	N/M	0.13	0.30	0.50	0.32	0.34	0.45	0.67	1.05	34.8%
DPS	N/A	N/A	N/A	N/A	N/A	N/A	N/A	N/A	0.07	0.08	0.10	15.2%

OPERATING AND PER SHARE DATA
(in millions of U.S. dollars and dollars per ADR)

	1986	1987	1988	1989	1990	1991	1992	1993	1994	1995	1996	CAGR
Sales	N/A	N/A	196	216	294	409	491	616	634	800	970	22.2%
EBDIT	N/A	N/A	5.2	11.2	29.9	64.7	73.5	100.6	89.5	78.9	155.5	53.0%
Net Profit	N/A	N/A	4.3	11.9	26.6	42.4	33.1	51.6	43.2	41.1	63.4	40.2%
EP/ADR	N/A	N/A	N/M	0.49	1.02	1.63	1.03	1.09	0.92	0.87	1.34	15.6%
DP/ADR	N/A	N/A	N/A	N/A	N/A	N/A	N/A	0.15	0.15	0.11	0.12	−6.1%

KEY RATIOS

	1986	1987	1988	1989	1990	1991	1992	1993	1994	1995	1996	AVG
EBDIT Margin	N/A	N/A	N/A	N/A	N/A	N/A	N/A	N/A	14.1%	9.9%	16.0%	13.3%
ROE	N/A	N/A	N/A	N/A	N/A	N/A	N/A	N/A	13.5%	13.3%	16.4%	14.4%
LT Debt/Total Cap	N/A	N/A	N/A	N/A	N/A	N/A	N/A	N/A	15.8%	36.1%	35.7%	29.2%
P/E (Projected)	N/A	N/A	N/A	N/A	N/A	N/A	N/A	35.7	28.2	13.8	18.6	24.1

STOCK PRICE CHART
(fiscal year-end closing price, in U.S. dollars, adjusted for capital changes)

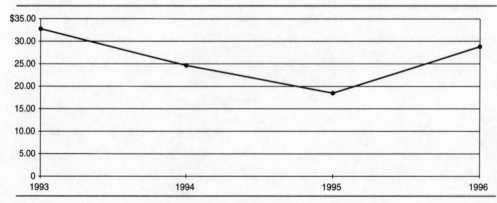

Note: Figures in U.S. dollars are translated from local currency using year-end exchange rates.

COLRUYT (COYTF—OTC)

Address: Wilgenveld / Edingensesteenweg 196 / Halle / Belgium
Tel.: (011) 32 2 360 1040 **Fax:** (011) 32 2 360 0207

BASIC INFORMATION

Country: Belgium **Market capitalization:** $1.6 billion
Industry: Retailing, food **Share status:** Foreign shares trade OTC
Investment thesis: Leading food retailer in Belgium, expanding elsewhere in Europe

COMPANY GRADING BOX

Growth Categories		Quality of Management	
Revenue Growth	20	Return on Equity	10
Operating Income Growth	20	**Risk**	
Earnings per Share Growth	20	Long-Term Debt/Total Capital	0
Share Price Growth	20	**Total QM&R (maximum 20)**	10
Total Growth (maximum 80)	**80**	**FINAL GRADE**	**90**

BACKGROUND

Belgium's Colruyt has been described as a combination quality food retailer and discount store, a formula that has allowed it to steadily take market share from some of its largest Belgian competitors and become the country's dominant discount supermarket. It has done what it has by offering an extensive selection of branded and private-label goods and high-quality fresh food in basic no-frills stores. Taking its cue from U.S. discounters, Colruyt says it guarantees the best prices on many of the Belgian staples. According to company literature, employees regularly comb through published ads of their competitors' prices, then adjust Colruyt's prices before the store opens. The company's motto insists that it offers "the certainty of the best prices."

The business was founded in 1925 by a baker, Franz Colruyt, in a town near the current headquarters. It was originally a wholesaler that sold mostly foods imported from overseas to retail stores throughout the country. In 1965, as the first supermarkets started appearing in Belgium, the company went into discount retailing. And its discount strategy caught on. The chain now employs an estimated 5,000 people, reported more than $2 billion in 1996 revenues, and comprises more than 120 stores throughout Belgium.

Colruyt is also beginning to export its strategy, though analysts continue to see room for growth in its Belgian business. In the mid-1990s Colruyt bought a French supermarket chain called Ripotot and invested in the distribution arm of a Portuguese supermarket and hypermarket company. Chairman Jef Colruyt, whose family still holds a majority of the shares outstanding, has said the company is looking for synergies with its existing businesses.

Within Colruyt the supermarket chain is by far the most important division; however, the company does operate in three other businesses: Dolmen Computer Applications offers its services to companies looking to outsource computer operations (on-site consultants to computer maintenance); Druco is a graphics service center; and Droomland is a small chain of toy stores.

COMPANY STATEMENT (from a company-provided profile)

"When Colruyt started in distribution it was a little like Tom Thumb, having very few resources (whether capital or people) at its disposal. Colruyt thus needed to come up with a few aces which had not been played by anyone before.

"Colruyt found these aces in a unique sales system situated in a 'different' kind of building, organized in a simple, rational and effective manner. And right from the start there were the famous punch cards and the computer, which enabled daily supervision of stocks and sales figures, all in the interest of ensuring the lowest food prices.

"The growth in turnover has been truly astonishing: 300 million BEF at the end of the first financial year (1965–66), 1.2 billion in 1970, 13.6 billion in 1980, 27.3 billion in 1990 and 41.5 billion in 1993.

"The increase in personnel has been equally impressive: 180 people in 1965, 629 in 1970, 2,131 in 1980, 2,920 in 1990 and 4,729 in 1993.

"Colruyt's main goal has always been to guarantee customers the lowest food prices. That's why the Colruyt formula has been identified from the beginning with the term discount. Today more than ever, Colruyt remains true to its discount image. Not at the cost of neglecting its many other advantages, however. In addition to guaranteeing the lowest prices, Colruyt offers its customers an enormous choice (an assortment of 6,000 food products) and a strong emphasis on quality."

PERFORMANCE

Colruyt received an overall score of 90 points, performing strongly in terms of consistency and growth. The company also rewarded investors with tremendous returns over the years and excellent growth numbers. Over the ten years from 1987, revenues in dollars grew every year, with compound annual growth of almost 14%. EBDIT increased in eight of the last ten years, showing compound annual growth of more than 16%, while EPS in dollars increased from $2.13 to $18.98. The share price has set a new high every year since 1986 and shown a compound annual growth of 33%. Colruyt also got top marks for its ROE, which averaged just over 20%. It lost points only in the risk category, with a high long-term debt to total capital ratio, averaging 41% during the ten-year period. However, it is worth noting that by 1997 the company had brought its debt down to a comfortable 15% from a high of 75% in 1987.

Dividends per share increased in eight of the last nine years (the company began issuing dividends in 1987), with compound annual growth of 30%. The dividend per share in dollars reached $4.26 in 1997, up from $0.30 in 1987.

If you had invested $10,000 in Colruyt in March 1987, you would have purchased around 50 shares at $190 each (excluding commissions). During the following ten years, there was a ten-for-one stock split. By March 1997, you would have had around 525 shares, worth $170,000. You would also have received around $11,300 in dividend payments.

COLRUYT

Ticker Symbol and Exchange: COYTF—OTC   **SEDOL Code: 4211853**

OPERATING AND PER SHARE DATA
(in millions of Belgian francs and francs per share)

	Mar 87	Mar 88	Mar 89	Mar 90	Mar 91	Mar 92	Mar 93	Mar 94	Mar 95	Mar 96	Mar 97	CAGR
Sales	22,149	21,536	24,042	27,354	32,334	37,481	41,461	46,162	52,861	59,453	68,446	11.9%
EBDIT	1,832	1,831	2,013	2,185	3,055	3,082	3,461	3,857	3,912	4,701	6,070	12.7%
Net Profit	218	320	459	683	1,093	1,304	1,527	1,564	1,780	1,932	2,164	25.8%
EPS	79.71	92.35	131.35	191.19	295.56	347.10	400.37	407.19	460.47	518.00	575.00	21.8%
DPS	11.25	18.75	26.25	3.38	45.00	60.00	74.25	89.10	98.75	112.50	129.00	27.6%

OPERATING AND PER SHARE DATA
(in millions of U.S. dollars and dollars per share)

	Mar 87	Mar 88	Mar 89	Mar 90	Mar 91	Mar 92	Mar 93	Mar 94	Mar 95	Mar 96	Mar 97	CAGR
Sales	593	619	607	782	924	1,109	1,253	1,395	1,537	2,108	2,259	14.3%
EBDIT	49.0	52.6	50.8	62.4	87.3	91.2	104.6	116.5	113.7	166.7	200.3	15.1%
Net Profit	5.8	9.2	11.6	19.5	31.2	38.6	46.1	47.2	51.7	68.5	71.4	28.5%
EPS	2.13	2.65	3.32	5.46	8.44	10.27	12.10	12.30	13.39	18.37	18.98	24.4%
DPS	0.30	0.54	0.66	0.10	1.29	1.78	2.24	2.69	2.87	3.99	4.26	30.3%

KEY RATIOS

	Mar 87	Mar 88	Mar 89	Mar 90	Mar 91	Mar 92	Mar 93	Mar 94	Mar 95	Mar 96	Mar 97	AVG
EBDIT Margin	8.3%	8.5%	8.4%	8.0%	9.4%	8.2%	8.3%	8.4%	7.4%	7.9%	8.9%	8.3%
ROE	10.9%	11.4%	15.3%	20.6%	27.5%	29.0%	27.6%	21.8%	21.2%	21.5%	18.8%	20.5%
LT Debt/Total Cap	75.5%	67.6%	65.8%	55.8%	48.3%	23.0%	25.0%	21.0%	18.0%	26.3%	21.4%	40.7%
P/E (Projected)	7.7	7.0	4.0	4.8	6.4	7.7	11.7	12.6	15.1	11.6	14.7	9.4

STOCK PRICE CHART
(fiscal year-end closing price, in U.S. dollars, adjusted for capital changes)

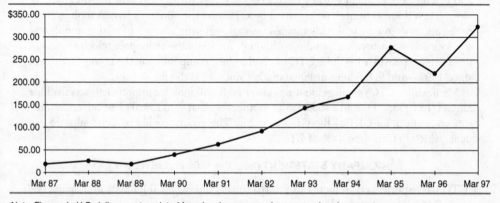

Note: Figures in U.S. dollars are translated from local currency using year-end exchange rates.

COMPAÑÍA DE TELECOMUNICACIONES DE CHILE (CTC—NYSE)

Address: Providencia #111, 2nd Floor / Santiago / Chile
Tel.: (011) 56 2 691 3867 or (800) 814-0282 **Fax:** (011) 56 2 696 1419 **Web site:** http://www.ctc.cl
or
Address: Dewe Rogerson Inc. / 850 Third Avenue, 20th Floor / New York, NY 10022
Tel.: (212) 688-6840   **Fax:** (212) 838-3393

BASIC INFORMATION

Country: Chile
Industry: Telecommunications services
Investment thesis: Dominant provider of telecommunications services in Chile

Market capitalization: $6 billion
Share status: ADRs trade on NYSE

COMPANY GRADING BOX

Growth Categories		Quality of Management	
Revenue Growth	20	Return on Equity	5
Operating Income Growth	20	**Risk**	
Earnings per Share Growth	20	Long-Term Debt/Total Capital	0
Share Price Growth	20	**Total QM&R (maximum 20)**	5
Total Growth (maximum 80)	**80**	**FINAL GRADE**	**85**

BACKGROUND

The growth story of CTC, Compañía de Telecomunicaciones de Chile, is intricately tied to the growth story of the Chilean economy, which has been expanding for more than ten years. From 1992 to 1995, the economy grew at an average rate of 7.2% per annum. CTC, founded as a private company in 1930 and government controlled from 1971 to 1989, is the country's largest telecommunications company. It is also reputed to be Latin America's most efficient.

At the end of 1996, CTC had more than 2 million lines in service, 14.3 lines for every 100 people. CTC also extended its fiber-optic network in 1996 to more than 3,100 kilometers, the most extensive fiber-optic network in the country; created the first interactive cable TV channel in Chile; added more advanced voice, data, and transmission services (including tele-education, telemedicine and voice conferencing capabilities); and established an alliance to expand access services to Internet and information services. Then there is Startel, 55% owned by CTC and the country's largest mobile communications company with nationwide coverage, offering a range of analog and digital services and aggressively expanding. Although for years the monopoly telecommunications service provider in Chile, CTC has had to face competition in the domestic market since 1992—and in the long-distance market since 1994. So far, so good.

Meanwhile, CTC's management has also said it will look for appropriate acquisitions abroad. In 1996, CTC had a stake in the partnership that won Brazil's first telecommunications auction, for CRT of Rio Grande do Sul. The group was led by Telefónica de España, which in turn owns 44% of CTC.

COMPANY STATEMENT (from the 1996 annual report)

"CTC has experienced tremendous growth since 1990, when Telefónica de España became CTC's main shareholder.

- Average annual investment for the period 1990–1996 reached $509 million.
- The number of lines in service increased by 153%, and domestic line density grew from 6.6 lines per 100 people in 1990 to 14.3 lines in 1996.
- In 1993, CTC became one of the first companies in the world to have a full digital network.
- The company's market capitalization grew from $741 in 1990 to $4,916 in 1996.

"To deal with the rapid changes in the telecommunications market, CTC has introduced new businesses, such as mobile communications, long distance, cable television, telecommunications equipment marketing, and other businesses that enhance the use of its network. CTC, once a domestic local service operator, is now a telecommunications corporation that supplies a full range of services."

PERFORMANCE

Consistency has been a hallmark of CTC, despite the tumult caused by the deregulation of the long-distance market in Chile. EBDIT in dollars increased every year over the last eight years, with compound annual growth of around 25%. EP/ADR increased in seven of the last eight years, with compound annual growth of 17%. ROE averaged 16%, good for a telephone company but a little lower than that of some of the other companies in this book. As for risk, the ratio of long-term debt to total capital averaged 36%, a little higher than many of the companies in this book but reasonable for a telephone company, which requires large capital expenditures but is supported by steady cash flows.

CTC's ADR price performance in recent years reflects investors' concerns about the impact of competition in Chile's telephone market on CTC's earnings. During 1994–1995, the ADR price closed the year at lower levels than recorded at the end of 1993. Despite this setback, the ADR price increased at a compound annual rate of 44% during the period. Shareholders also received a strong income stream from CTC, with the company maintaining a dividend payout ratio of 50 to 60% during the last five years.

If you had invested $10,000 in CTC at the end of 1989, you would have bought around 5,750 ADRs (or ADR equivalents) at about $1.75 each (excluding commissions). During the following seven years, CTC had no changes in capital structure. By the end of 1996, you would have had 5,750 ADRs worth an estimated $130,900. You would also have received dividend payments of around $29,300.

COMPAÑÍA DE TELECOMUNICACIONES DE CHILE

Ticker Symbol and Exchange: CTC—NYSE   **CUSIP No.: 204449300**

OPERATING AND PER SHARE DATA
(in billions of nominal Chilean pesos and pesos per share)

	1986	1987	1988	1989	1990	1991	1992	1993	1994	1995	1996	CAGR
Sales	N/A	N/A	52	80	126	180	246	291	333	421	541	34.0%
EBDIT	N/A	N/A	30	43	67	96	133	196	219	237	316	34.2%
Net Profit	N/A	N/A	19	29	36	52	69	90	91	109	151	29.4%
EPS	N/A	N/A	29.27	41.88	47.20	60.40	80.09	104.54	105.70	·126.89	175.20	25.1%
DPS	N/A	N/A	N/A	35.45	37.74	38.04	45.87	55.20	63.74	67.30	87.60	13.8%

OPERATING AND PER SHARE DATA
(in millions of U.S. dollars and dollars per ADR)

	1986	1987	1988	1989	1990	1991	1992	1993	1994	1995	1996	CAGR
Sales	N/A	N/A	213	272	376	484	647	684	824	1,034	1,272	25.1%
EBDIT	N/A	N/A	122.6	146.6	201.2	258.4	350.1	461.3	542.5	581.6	743.2	25.3%
Net Profit	N/A	N/A	78.5	99.8	108.4	139.0	180.9	210.9	224.7	267.7	353.9	20.7%
EP/ADR	N/A	N/A	0.48	0.57	0.56	0.65	0.84	0.98	1.05	1.25	1.65	16.7%
DP/ADR	N/A	N/A	N/A	0.48	0.45	0.41	0.48	0.52	0.63	0.66	0.82	8.0%

KEY RATIOS

	1986	1987	1988	1989	1990	1991	1992	1993	1994	1995	1996	AVG
EBDIT Margin	N/A	N/A	57.7%	54.0%	53.5%	53.4%	54.1%	67.5%	65.8%	56.2%	58.4%	57.9%
ROE	N/A	N/A	15.6%	18.3%	13.4%	15.0%	16.3%	17.5%	15.3%	16.0%	18.4%	16.2%
LT Debt/Total Cap	N/A	N/A	20.2%	28.0%	32.0%	37.3%	39.4%	36.8%	40.9%	44.9%	46.2%	36.2%
P/E (Projected)	N/A	N/A	N/A	3.1	4.2	8.7	12.3	20.6	13.7	10.7	13.6	10.9

STOCK PRICE CHART
(fiscal year-end closing price, in U.S. dollars, adjusted for capital changes)

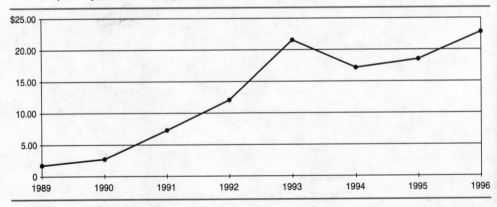

Notes: 1996 dividend is estimated. Figures in U.S. dollars are translated from local currency using year-end exchange rates.

COMPASS GROUP (CMSGY—OTC)

Address: Cowley House / Guildford Street / Chertsey, Surrey KT16 9BA / United Kingdom
Tel.: (011) 44 1932 573 000 **Fax:** (011) 44 1932 569 956 **U.S. Web site:** http://compassusa.com

BASIC INFORMATION

Country: United Kingdom
Industry: Industrial service
Investment thesis: One of the largest contract catering companies in the world

Market capitalization: $3.26 billion
Share status: ADRs trade OTC

COMPANY GRADING BOX

Growth Categories		Quality of Management	
Revenue Growth	20	Return on Equity	0
Operating Income Growth	20	**Risk**	
Earnings per Share Growth	20	EBDIT/Interest Expense	10
Share Price Growth	20	**Total QM&R (maximum 20)**	10
Total Growth (maximum 80)	**80**	**FINAL GRADE**	**90**

BACKGROUND

Throughout Europe and the United States, U.K.-based Compass Group is feeding patients and staff at hospitals, passengers on airlines, workers in factories, students at school, and sports fans at sporting events. In the United States, Compass Group is even feeding prisoners behind bars (Compass Group provides all "commissary services" to the Utah and Kansas Departments of Correction). The company's expertise runs the gamut from vending machines to executive catering, anything under the heading of contracted-out food services.

Compass Group, now one of the largest food service companies in the world, has been a beneficiary of one of our favorite trends, the "outsourcing" of noncore business activities. There is no reason to think that trend won't continue. Today Compass Group has more than 120,000 employees. And management has been actively buying up competitors (in mid-1996 the company made a major purchase, buying a majority stake in Eurest, the third largest caterer in France). Compass Group has also been developing business in South America and the Far East and developing new lines of its business, such as branded outlets, in its larger markets.

The branded outlets include names with worldwide recognition such as Burger King and Kentucky Fried Chicken, as well as Compass Group's own more recently created brands, such as Upper Crust and Not Just Donuts. This is not a company that sits still.

Next on the agenda: Compass Group is hoping to use its international presence to win global contracts. It could be on its way. In late 1995 the company was awarded a $250 million contract by IBM to serve more than 100,000 employees at twenty-nine U.S. sites (including staff restaurants, customer briefing centers, sundry shops, executive dining facilities, and vending machines). A Compass Group subsidiary already serves forty IBM sites in Europe and South America.

COMPANY STATEMENT (from the 1996 annual report)

"Our aim is to be the most profitable and highest quality operator of the world's top food-service brands. In practice, this means that we have a clear mission—to achieve leadership in our chosen specialist markets.

- We are a service company;
- Providing food and beverages is at the core of what we do;
- We choose to operate in market sectors which are big enough for us to specialize in;
- We provide these services in chosen geographical markets to an international client base;

"By following this strategy we start our 1997 year in a very strong position;

- We are very well represented in more than 40 countries worldwide;
- We have a strong portfolio of in-house and franchised brands;
- We are well placed to take advantage of outsourcing opportunities, particularly in healthcare catering and education catering markets world wide, creating significant organic growth opportunities;
- We are able to maximize our purchasing power, both nationally and internationally;
- We are able to focus on our core market—food service provision.

"Having built a strong, focused foodservice organization in the major geographical markets, the Group is now well placed to take advantage of the opportunities for organic growth. This will be further supported by the benefits of our size, enabling the use of our purchasing power to improve the quality and cost effectiveness of our service. We are able to derive many other benefits from the effective use of economies of scale; systems development, marketing, quality and training programs as well as management development and the ability to offer a service to international clients."

PERFORMANCE

Compass came out well with a score of 90 in our grading system and the highest possible marks for growth. In dollars, EBDIT increased in nine of the last ten years, with compound annual growth of 29% and 34%, respectively. EP/ADR (or ADR equivalent) in dollars increased in eight of the last ten years, with compound annual growth of 22%. ADR price performance was in line with EP/ADR growth, the ADR price in dollars increasing at a compound annual rate of 20%. ROE was high but moved up and down dramatically as Compass made a series of acquisitions, fully reflected in each year's balance sheets (as demanded by U.K. accounting practices) and rendering the ROE numbers N/M (or not meaningful). For the same reason, we chose to include the ratio of EBDIT to interest expense, which averaged a comfortable 6%, rather than long-term debt to total capital (which is misleadingly high due to the same U.K. accounting practice).

If you had invested $10,000 in Compass in September 1989, you would have purchased around 1,630 ADRs (or ADR equivalents) at about $6 each (excluding commissions). During the following seven years, there were a six-for-nineteen rights issue in May 1993, a one-for-one bonus issue in March 1994, and a six-for-nineteen rights issue in May 1994. By September 1996, you would have had around 4,170 ADRs worth an estimated $36,500. You would also have received dividend payments of around $3,000.

COMPASS GROUP

Ticker Symbol and Exchange: CMSGY—OTC **CUSIP No.: 20449X104**

OPERATING AND PER SHARE DATA
(in millions of British pounds and pounds per share)

	Sep 86	Sep 87	Sep 88	Sep 89	Sep 90	Sep 91	Sep 92	Sep 93	Sep 94	Sep 95	Sep 96	CAGR
Sales	229	261	277	343	353	321	345	497	918	1,506	2,652	27.8%
EBDIT	11.7	20.6	27.7	35.4	42.1	42.6	45.0	56.0	84.7	129.9	202.9	33.0%
Net Profit	8.5	10.6	8.7	16.2	19.2	21.4	23.5	27.9	39.4	54.0	99.4	27.9%
EPS	0.05	0.06	0.05	0.10	0.11	0.12	0.14	0.15	0.19	0.23	0.32	20.5%
DPS	N/M	N/M	N/M	0.04	0.04	0.04	0.05	0.05	0.07	0.08	0.09	13.6%

OPERATING AND PER SHARE DATA
(in millions of U.S. dollars and dollars per ADR)

	Sep 86	Sep 87	Sep 88	Sep 89	Sep 90	Sep 91	Sep 92	Sep 93	Sep 94	Sep 95	Sep 96	CAGR
Sales	332	424	468	555	662	561	615	743	1,448	2,384	4,150	28.8%
EBDIT	17	33	47	57	79	74	80	84	134	206	318	34.1%
Net Profit	12	17	15	26	36	37	42	42	62	85	156	28.9%
EP/ADR	0.07	0.10	0.09	0.16	0.21	0.22	0.24	0.22	0.30	0.36	0.50	21.5%
DP/ADR	N/M	N/M	N/M	0.06	0.08	0.08	0.09	0.08	0.11	0.12	0.13	13.1%

KEY RATIOS

	Sep 86	Sep 87	Sep 88	Sep 89	Sep 90	Sep 91	Sep 92	Sep 93	Sep 94	Sep 95	Sep 96	AVG
EBDIT Margin	5.1%	7.9%	10.0%	10.3%	11.9%	13.3%	13.0%	11.3%	9.2%	8.6%	7.7%	9.8%
ROE	N/M	N/M	N/M	N/M	N/M	N/M	N/M	N/M	N/M	N/M	N/M	N/M
EBDIT/Interest Expense	3.5	4.7	2.3	5.1	4.5	6.2	8.3	8.6	10.2	6.8	5.5	6.0
P/E (Projected)	N/A	N/M	N/M	13.2	10.1	12.8	13.1	12.1	14.1	13.2	16.0	13.1

STOCK PRICE CHART
(fiscal year-end closing price, in U.S. dollars, adjusted for capital changes)

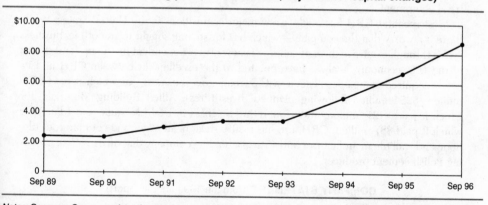

Notes: Compass Group consistently reports negative shareholders' equity because according to U.K. GAAP it must write off the goodwill on any acquisitions from shareholders' equity immediately. Under U.S. GAAP, a U.S. company could write off goodwill over a forty-year period. To measure risk for Compass Group, we therefore analyzed interest payment coverage, that is, EBDIT divided by interest expense.

CRH (CRHCY—NASDAQ)

Address: Belgard Castle / Clondalkin / Dublin 22 / Ireland
Tel.: (011) 353 1 404 1000   **Fax:** (011) 353 1 404 1010   **Web site:** http://www.crh.ie/crh

BASIC INFORMATION

Country: Ireland
Industry: Building materials
Investment thesis: One of the world's largest manufacturers and suppliers of building materials

Market capitalization: $3.47 billion
Share status: ADRs trade on NASDAQ

COMPANY GRADING BOX

Growth Categories		Quality of Management	
Revenue Growth	20	Return on Equity	5
Operating Income Growth	20	**Risk**	
Earnings per Share Growth	20	Long-Term Debt/Total Capital	0
Share Price Growth	10	**Total QM&R (maximum 20)**	5
Total Growth (maximum 80)	70	**FINAL GRADE**	75

BACKGROUND

The name may not ring any bells, but CRH, a Dublin-based building materials supplier, is making inroads. A *Fortune* magazine writer recently even used CRH to talk about the global marketplace; he wrote about how he had discovered this great company in Ireland, only to find out that the company paves American freeways. CRH corporate headquarters may be a stunning historic castle, but this company is very much of the present.

By its twenty-sixth birthday, in 1996, more than two thirds of CRH's $4 billion–plus of revenues came from outside Ireland and the United Kingdom, it employed more than 19,000 people in twelve countries, and it had grown sales an average of 15.7% annually over the last ten years. Among its businesses: the production and supply of building products to the building and construction industry, including cement, ready-mix concrete, and asphalt road products; the production of materials used in the steel, cement, and glass manufacturing industries; civil engineering contracting; property development; do-it-yourself retailing; even precast concrete enclosures for telecommunications and electrical equipment.

Most recently, CRH has made a few major acquisitions in the United States. While there is a worry that the company—which has for so long sought to smooth its business cycles through extensive diversification—is now overly dependent on the ups and downs of the U.S. economy, analysts have pointed to the excellent fit between CRH and its newly acquired companies: Tilcon, a U.S. road-stone business, for which it paid $329 million ($254 million following planned divestitures); Allied Building Materials, for which it paid $121 million; and a quarrying business in Utah, Nevada, and Idaho, for which it paid $87 million. CRH also has a 20% stake in an Argentine ceramic roof tile, floor, and wall tile manufacturer and 45% in a holding company that owns 75% of a leading Polish cement producer.

COMPANY STATEMENT (from the 1996 annual report)

"CRH strategic vision: be an international leader in building products and materials and deliver sustained and superior returns for all stakeholders. The consistent strategy that makes this possible includes:

- Growth platforms: a presence across the building and construction industry supply chain, from the manufacturing of primary materials to building products and distribution in 12 countries, provides a unique exposure to opportunities and platforms for future growth.
- Devolved development: by pushing the entrepreneurial development function down into regions and product groups, we can create opportunities for a continuing flow of value-adding mid-sized acquisitions and projects.
- Unique balance: across regions and products and all sectors of building and construction, new build and improvement helps to smooth the effect of industry and economic cycles.
- Leadership positions: we patiently build leadership positions in the markets we enter by paying fair prices for good companies through negotiated deals that meet sellers' diverse needs and then seamlessly integrating and developing, rather than overpaying for major market positions which can destroy shareholder value. . . .
- People: there is a depth of management in our core businesses. It is enhanced by the monthly addition of new companies that keep the Group young and vital and bring a healthy mix of management from three very different streams: owner-entrepreneurs who join with their companies, internally developed managers and highly qualified development professionals. . . .
- Financial strength: conservative accounting, a very healthy balance sheet, an exceptionally low tax charge and strong cash flow enable the Group to take advantage of investment opportunities. . . .
- Deliver TSR: Total shareholder returns is a key overall objective. CRH has consistently delivered superior long-term returns and has the strategy, structure, people and exposure to opportunities to ensure continued growth."

PERFORMANCE

CRH received top scores for growth in revenues, EP/ADR, and EBDIT and a total of 75 points in our grading system. In dollars, revenues and EBDIT have grown in eight of the last ten years, with compound annual growth of 18% and 19% respectively. EP/ADR increased in eight of the last ten years, with compound annual growth of 15%. And the ADR price increased at a compound annual rate of 17%. ROE was 18% in 1996, up from 11% in 1986 (though down from a high for this period of 20% in 1990). As for risk, the company did not score as well as some of the others on our list, with the long-term debt to total capital ratio rising from 26% in 1986 to 54% in 1996.

If you had invested $10,000 in CRH at the end of 1986, you would have purchased around 930 ADRs (or ADR equivalents) at about $10.75 each (excluding commissions). During the following ten years, there was a one-for-five rights issue in September 1993. By the end of 1996, you would have owned around 960 shares worth an estimated $50,000. You would also have received around $5,300 in dividend payments.

CRH

Ticker Symbol and Exchange: CRHCY—NASDAQ   **CUSIP No.: 12626K203**

OPERATING AND PER SHARE DATA
(in millions of Irish punts and punts per share)

	1986	1987	1988	1989	1990	1991	1992	1993	1994	1995	1996	CAGR
Sales	567	707	914	1,022	1,216	1,146	1,114	1,427	1,612	1,911	2,428	15.7%
EBDIT	62.7	80.4	107.2	127.2	147.3	125.4	115.1	147.0	189.6	243.4	295.8	16.8%
Net Profit	29.6	36.0	48.8	62.9	70.5	50.4	46.6	62.0	92.9	126.2	148.7	17.5%
EPS	0.12	0.13	0.17	0.22	0.25	0.17	0.16	0.20	0.26	0.36	0.41	13.1%
DPS	0.04	0.04	0.04	0.05	0.06	0.06	0.07	0.07	0.08	0.09	0.10	10.9%

OPERATING AND PER SHARE DATA
(in millions of U.S. dollars and dollars per ADR)

	1986	1987	1988	1989	1990	1991	1992	1993	1994	1995	1996	CAGR
Sales	794	1,185	1,377	1,591	2,158	2,001	1,810	2,007	2,496	3,059	4,108	17.9%
EBDIT	88	135	161	198	261	219	187	207	294	390	501	19.0%
Net Profit	41	60	74	98	125	88	76	87	144	202	252	19.8%
EP/ADR	0.83	1.12	1.27	1.68	2.22	1.51	1.27	1.41	2.04	2.85	3.43	15.3%
DP/ADR	0.25	0.33	0.33	0.40	0.52	0.55	0.53	0.51	0.63	0.73	0.86	13.1%

KEY RATIOS

	1986	1987	1988	1989	1990	1991	1992	1993	1994	1995	1996	AVG
EBDIT Margin	11.1%	11.4%	11.7%	12.4%	12.1%	10.9%	10.3%	10.3%	11.8%	12.7%	12.2%	11.5%
ROE	10.7%	11.0%	14.0%	18.0%	20.0%	13.0%	13.0%	10.9%	15.6%	18.4%	17.9%	14.8%
LT Debt/Total Cap	28.0%	35.9%	39.5%	42.4%	56.4%	55.3%	57.5%	50.8%	41.6%	41.1%	54.1%	45.7%
P/E (Projected)	11.1	7.0	7.1	10.2	12.6	13.7	9.3	14.2	10.1	11.6	13.2	10.9

STOCK PRICE CHART
(fiscal year-end closing price, in U.S. dollars, adjusted for capital changes)

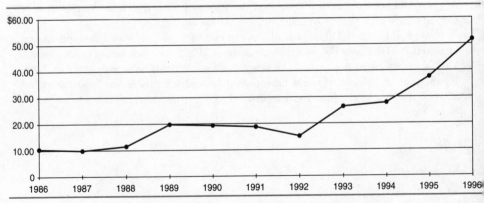

Note: Figures in U.S. dollars are translated from local currency using year-end exchange rates.

CYCLE & CARRIAGE (CYCRY—OTC)

Address: 239 Alexandra Road / Singapore 159930
Tel.: (011) 65 473 3122   **Fax:** (011) 65 475 7088

BASIC INFORMATION

Country: Singapore
Industry: Auto equipment
Investment thesis: Mercedes-Benz and Mitsubishi franchises in Singapore; expanding in Asia

Market capitalization: $2.44 billion
Share status: ADRs trade OTC

COMPANY GRADING BOX

Growth Categories		Quality of Management	
Revenue Growth	20	Return on Equity	5
Operating Income Growth	20	**Risk**	
Earnings per Share Growth	20	Long-Term Debt/Total Capital	10
Share Price Growth	20	**Total QM&R (maximum 20)**	15
Total Growth (maximum 80)	**80**	**FINAL GRADE**	**95**

BACKGROUND

Until pretty recently, whenever you read about foreign markets, you were bound to run into stories about the economic growth in Asia. And undoubtedly you have seen that people (whether they're in the United States, Singapore, or France) who make money, spend money. So it makes sense that Cycle & Carriage, the company with the Mercedes-Benz franchise in Singapore, has done pretty well over the last eight years. And that's just one of Cycle & Carriage's businesses. In Singapore, where it generates about 60% of its revenues, Cycle & Carriage also has the franchises for Mitsubishi and Proton, as well as a sizable property business. Overall, an estimated 86% of revenues come from the car side of the business and 6% from property. Total 1996 revenues: $1 billion. While the 1997 collapse of Asian markets took its inevitable toll on Cycle & Carriage, the company's strong management history should help it survive and—eventually—again prosper.

There are also Cycle & Carriage's overseas auto businesses. As the Singapore market has become more and more competitive, Cycle & Carriage has gone elsewhere, looking for higher returns. In Malaysia, Cycle & Carriage Bintang, which is 49% owned by Cycle & Carriage, holds the franchise for Mercedes-Benz, Mazda, and Kia, the Korean auto company, and is aggressively expanding in after-sales auto servicing. Cycle & Carriage also owns 85% of Cycle & Carriage (Malaysia), an authorized dealer for Proton and Mazda passenger cars and Mazda and Isuzu commercial vehicles. Then there is the group's 49%-owned associate company Astre in Australia, which holds the Audi, Chrysler, and Hyundai franchises and has a stake in a joint-venture vehicle finance company. Finally, in New Zealand, Cycle & Carriage has Mazda, Chrysler Jeep, and Mitsubishi dealerships; in Thailand it has Ford dealerships; and in Vietnam it has Mercedes-Benz dealerships, a car rental agency, and a vehicle workshop. Most recently, Cycle & Carriage has entered into a joint venture to sell imported cars in Myanmar.

Although it generates a relatively small percentage of Cycle & Carriage's overall revenues, property development and investment have been very profitable for the company. Rental income is one source of recurring revenues. Other Cycle & Carriage investments include stakes in a chain of pharmacies, a wholesale health care business, a hotel in Malaysia, and—in Singapore—a vehicle-financing company, a manufacturer of high-performance engines, and a maritime business involved with shipbuilding and ship repair.

COMPANY STATEMENT (from the 1996 annual report)

"Cycle & Carriage is a diversified group ranked among Singapore's top 20 listed companies. Its core businesses are concentrated on motor vehicles and property.

"Its success as a leading regional motor vehicle group is driven by a mission to provide the highest quality of customer service in all markets. With strong professional management at its helm, the Group strives to capitalize on further regional expansion opportunities to achieve a broad earnings base.

"The Group today comprises more than 90 subsidiaries and associates, staffed by close to 5,000 dedicated employees throughout its operations in Singapore, Malaysia, Australia, New Zealand, Thailand, Vietnam and Myanmar."

PERFORMANCE

Cycle & Carriage received the highest possible score for growth and an overall score of 95 in our grading system. In dollars, revenues and EBDIT increased in every one of the last nine years, with compound annual growth of 39% and 41%, respectively. EP/ADR also increased in every one of the last nine years, with compound annual growth of 38%. Shareholders did well; the ADR price increased at a compound annual rate of 36% over the nine years. Although the 12% average ROE was lower than for many of the companies on our list, ROE increased steadily through the decade and was 16% in 1996. As for risk, the long-term debt to total capital ratio averaged a very comfortable 6%.

If you had invested $10,000 in Cycle & Carriage in September 1987, you would have purchased around 4,060 ADRs (or ADR equivalents) at about $2.25 each (excluding commissions). During the following ten years, there was a two-for-five rights issue in February 1990. By December 1996, you would have had around 6,500 shares worth an estimated $160,000. You would also have received dividend payments of around $5,800.

CYCLE & CARRIAGE

Ticker Symbol and Exchange: CYCRY—OTC   **CUSIP No.: 232903302**

OPERATING AND PER SHARE DATA
(in millions of Singaporean dollars and dollars per share)

	Sep 86	Sep 87	Sep 88	Sep 89	Sep 90	Sep 91	Sep 92	Dec 93	Dec 94	Dec 95	Dec 96	CAGR
Sales	N/A	230	261	406	723	941	1,244	1,910	2,082	2,938	3,011	33.1%
EBDIT	N/A	22	35	57	84	103	98	189	217	298	323	34.6%
Net Profit	N/A	15	20	35	54	72	66	112	124	182	200	33.5%
EPS	N/A	0.07	0.10	0.17	0.33	0.41	0.34	0.40	0.53	0.78	0.86	32.1%
DPS	N/A	0.03	0.04	0.06	0.10	0.17	0.17	0.18	0.23	0.32	0.36	31.8%

OPERATING AND PER SHARE DATA
(in millions of U.S. dollars and dollars per ADR)

	Sep 86	Sep 87	Sep 88	Sep 89	Sep 90	Sep 91	Sep 92	Dec 93	Dec 94	Dec 95	Dec 96	CAGR
Sales	N/A	110	128	207	411	560	782	1,186	1,426	2,084	2,151	39.1%
EBDIT	N/A	10.6	17.1	29.1	47.8	61.4	61.8	117.2	148.7	211.0	230.4	40.8%
Net Profit	N/A	7.1	9.7	17.7	30.6	42.9	41.4	69.6	84.7	128.8	142.9	39.6%
EP/ADR	N/A	0.03	0.05	0.09	0.19	0.24	0.21	0.25	0.36	0.55	0.61	38.2%
DP/ADR	N/A	0.01	0.02	0.03	0.06	0.10	0.11	0.11	0.16	0.23	0.26	37.8%

KEY RATIOS

	Sep 86	Sep 87	Sep 88	Sep 89	Sep 90	Sep 91	Sep 92	Dec 93	Dec 94	Dec 95	Dec 96	AVG
EBDIT Margin	N/A	9.7%	13.4%	14.1%	11.6%	11.0%	7.9%	9.9%	10.4%	10.1%	10.7%	10.9%
ROE	N/A	5.4%	7.1%	11.2%	12.0%	14.8%	10.7%	11.0%	12.9%	16.5%	15.9%	11.7%
LT Debt/Total Cap	N/A	0.0%	0.0%	0.0%	9.8%	10.3%	8.0%	11.3%	8.0%	5.4%	5.3%	5.8%
P/E (Projected)	N/A	16.0	12.0	9.6	8.5	14.6	14.8	16.0	16.8	16.4	17.8	14.3

STOCK PRICE CHART
(fiscal year-end closing price, in U.S. dollars, adjusted for capital changes)

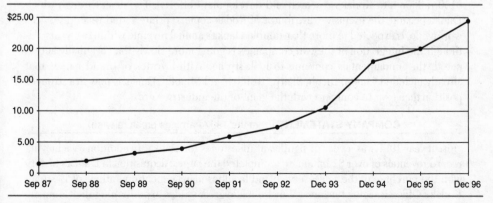

Note: Figures in U.S. dollars are translated from local currency using year-end exchange rates.

DANKA BUSINESS SYSTEMS (DANKY—NASDAQ)

Address: Masters House / 107 Hammersmith Road / London W14 0QH / United Kingdom
or
Address: 11201 Danka Circle North / St. Petersburg / Florida 33716
Tel.: (813) 579-2797   **Fax:** (813) 577-4802   **Web site:** http://www.danka.com

BASIC INFORMATION

Country: United Kingdom   **Market capitalization:** $1.72 billion
Industry: Office equipment   **Share status:** ADRs trade on NASDAQ
Investment thesis: World's largest independent supplier and service provider for copiers, facsimiles

COMPANY GRADING BOX

Growth Categories		Quality of Management	
Revenue Growth	20	Return on Equity	5
Operating Income Growth	20	**Risk**	
Earnings per Share Growth	20	Long-Term Debt/Total Capital	0
Share Price Growth	20	**Total QM&R (maximum 20)**	5
Total Growth (maximum 80)	**80**	**FINAL GRADE**	**85**

BACKGROUND

Danka distributes, sells and services fax and copier machines to companies in more than 30 countries from more than 700 offices, setting the pace in a business that is booming as more and more companies choose to contract out noncore functions. In other words, Danka is a successful outsourcing company, and it looks as though well-run outsourcing companies have a lot of room for growth. Danka's contracts and service contract renewals are the most profitable part of its business, providing a steady stream of revenue. This company is not a high-technology play; it's a mundane but profitable service business in which Danka, with more than 20,000 employees, is one of the largest players.

This U.K.-owned company was actually founded in St. Petersburg, Florida, in 1977, then bought by a London-based group in 1986 (hence the two addresses noted above). The U.K. owners haven't missed a beat. Most recently, at the end of 1996, Danka paid Eastman Kodak $688 million for its Office Imaging sales, marketing, and equipment service operations, as well as its facilities management business (Danka will put more than $150 million into Kodak's research and development efforts). The deal, through which Danka became the exclusive distributor of Kodak copiers, printers, and related services worldwide, is expected to more than double Danka's annual revenue within two years. Although the integration of the two companies is going more slowly than originally anticipated, the fundamentals continue to look strong. With a roster of brand names that already included Canon, Ricoh, Sharp, Toshiba, and Minolta, Danka is now in a stronger position than ever to compete with the giant of the industry, Xerox.

COMPANY STATEMENT (from the 1997 earnings press release)

"Fiscal year 1997 was a year of significant milestones for Danka. In addition to achieving record revenues of over $2 billion, we completed the largest acquisition in Danka's history with the purchase of the sales, service and facilities management operations of Eastman Kodak's Office Imaging business. We also made great strides in positioning the Company to capitalize on the changing market demands and to better support our customers.

"With Danka's purchase of Kodak's facilities management business, management believes it has gained an important gateway to the rapidly growing outsourcing industry. In addition to traditional facilities management, Danka Imaging Services also provides strategic consulting to customers on how to manage their document systems and which products best suit their needs."

PERFORMANCE

Danka received high marks for growth and an overall score of 85 points in our grading system. Revenues in dollars increased in eight of the last nine years, with compound annual growth of 45%. EBDIT and EP/ADR increased in seven of the last nine years, with compound annual growth of 39% and 24%, respectively. Not bad. The ADR (and ADR equivalent) price set a new high in each of the last seven years and increased from a low of $1.03 in 1987 to a high of $51.00 in 1997, with compound annual growth of 40%. ROE, which averaged 15% over the nine years, was 10.2% in 1996, up from 3.8% in 1987. As for risk, the long-term debt to total capital ratio shot up to 70% in 1997 as a result of the Kodak acquisition; however, it averaged 50% and was 42% in 1996. It is worth noting that Danka reports its results separately in U.S. dollars and British pounds, reflecting the accounting principles of both countries; the company actually publishes two annual reports.

If you had invested $10,000 in Danka in March 1988, you would have purchased around 1,660 ADRs (or ADR equivalents) at about $6 each (excluding commissions). There was a four-for-one stock split in July 1993. By March 1997, you would have had around 6,620 ADRs worth an estimated $207,900. You would also have received dividend payments of around $4,600.

DANKA BUSINESS SYSTEMS

Ticker Symbol and Exchange: DANKY—NASDAQ **CUSIP No.: 236277109**

OPERATING AND PER SHARE DATA
(in millions of British pounds and pounds per share)

	Mar 87	Mar 88	Mar 89	Mar 90	Mar 91	Mar 92	Mar 93	Mar 94	Mar 95	Mar 96	Mar 97	CAGR
Sales	N/A	35.0	53.0	89.0	94.0	115.0	186.0	347.0	516.0	793.0	1,324	49.5%
EBIT	N/A	4.0	6.1	9.7	10.9	12.2	18.8	34.4	50.3	69.2	51.0	30.4%
Net Profit	N/A	3.8	5.1	7.8	8.7	10.2	16.2	20.4	31.8	37.7	20.6	19.1%
EPS	N/A	0.03	0.03	0.05	0.06	0.07	0.11	0.12	0.17	0.22	0.26	29.0%
DPS	N/A	0.004	0.005	0.006	0.008	0.009	0.011	0.015	0.018	0.022	0.026	23.1%

OPERATING AND PER SHARE DATA
(in millions of U.S. dollars and dollars per ADR)

	Mar 87	Mar 88	Mar 89	Mar 90	Mar 91	Mar 92	Mar 93	Mar 94	Mar 95	Mar 96	Mar 97	CAGR
Sales	N/A	58	105	163	204	236	353	531	802	1,240	2,101	45.4%
EBIT	N/A	7.5	7.5	11.5	7.8	9.6	30.4	47.9	71.6	96.2	101.9	38.6%
Net Profit	N/A	7.2	5.1	8.1	0.8	4.6	21.2	26.5	39.0	46.3	41.8	30.1%
EP/ADR	N/A	0.10	0.13	0.21	0.02	0.11	0.51	0.59	0.80	0.88	0.72	23.9%
DP/ADR	N/A	0.03	0.03	0.04	0.05	0.06	0.07	0.09	0.11	0.13	0.13	17.6%

KEY RATIOS

	Mar 87	Mar 88	Mar 89	Mar 90	Mar 91	Mar 92	Mar 93	Mar 94	Mar 95	Mar 96	Mar 97	AVG
EBDIT Margin	N/A	13.0%	7.1%	7.1%	3.8%	4.1%	8.6%	9.0%	8.9%	7.8%	4.9%	7.4%
ROE	N/A	5.6%	17.6%	21.1%	10.5%	10.6%	34.1%	15.6%	18.9%	10.5%	9.0%	15.3%
LT Debt/Total Cap	N/A	22.5%	71.3%	71.3%	74.6%	32.1%	24.3%	28.4%	53.1%	41.9%	69.5%	48.9%
P/E (Projected)	N/A	5.9	6.4	7.1	5.7	4.2	13.7	19.3	18.6	26.3	14.9	12.2

STOCK PRICE CHART
(fiscal year-end closing price, in U.S. dollars, adjusted for capital changes)

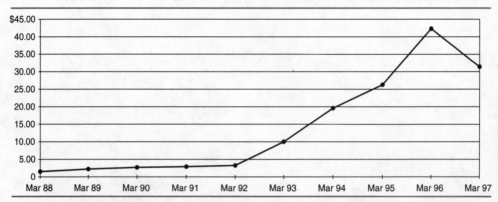

Notes: Danka reports results in both U.S. dollars and British pounds sterling using different accounting principles. Accordingly, the figures shown above in dollars and pounds were entered separately and are not strictly comparable. ADR prices prior to 1992 are estimated based on local share prices and year-end exchange rates.

DIMENSION DATA (DDTJ.J—JOHANNESBURG)

Address: Corner Sloane Street and Meadowbrook Lane / Epsom Downs / Sandton 2125 / South Africa
Tel.: (011) 27 11 709 1000   **Fax:** (011) 27 11 709 1626   **Web site:** http://didata.co.za

BASIC INFORMATION

Country: South Africa   **Market capitalization:** $1.3 billion
Industry: Business services   **Share status:** Foreign shares trade on Johannesburg Exchange
Investment thesis: Leading information technology company in South Africa

COMPANY GRADING BOX

Growth Categories		Quality of Management	
Revenue Growth	20	Return on Equity	10
Operating Income Growth	20	**Risk**	
Earnings per Share Growth	20	Long-Term Debt/Total Capital	10
Share Price Growth	20	**Total QM&R (maximum 20)**	**20**
Total Growth (maximum 80)	**80**	**FINAL GRADE**	**100**

BACKGROUND

Talk about high growth! South Africa–based Dimension Data is off the charts. Dimension Data has been leading the charge for a high-tech revolution in South Africa, taking advantage of an incredible pent-up demand in a country that for years was ostracized from the international community. Like many U.S. high-tech companies, it has traded at a premium to its local market for years, but it's a premium that appears to be justified by an outstanding track record. Over the last eight years, Dimension Data has increased its revenues in dollars 53.4% annually and earnings per share 26.7% per annum. Its three key operations are communications, software, and services—though to date communications has accounted for the largest percentage of revenues (62%) and operating profits (51%).

The communications unit has put in networking systems for some of South Africa's largest companies, and analysts have estimated that Dimension Data is responsible for around 55% of U.S.-based Cisco's revenues in South Africa. Recently, the division has shifted its focus from product sales to higher-margin systems integration and "value-added" services. Consulting accounts for 19% of the communications division's revenues. And in February 1997 Dimension Data bought the Merchants Group, based in the United Kingdom, a company specializing in outsourcing and call center consulting. Dimension Data Interactive has taken on the company's call center business.

Dimension Data's software division (which recently sold Computer Associates Africa back to the parent company) focuses on advisory services and project development, particularly data warehousing and outsourcing. It has been steadily reducing its exposure to the mainframe market. Then there is Dimension Data's services division, dominated by a joint venture with U.S.-based EDS. Analysts are projecting that this relatively new unit, EDS Africa, will be the fastest growing within Dimension Data. Outsourcing contracts from major South African companies have been streaming in.

Dimension Data has also been making acquisitions. Domestically, Dimension Data bought 25% of Internet Solutions, a leading South African Internet company, with an option to increase its stake to 50% by the end of 1997. Overseas, in addition to the Merchants Group, Dimension Data bought a 70% stake in an Australian company with similar areas of expertise, Com Tech, giving it a start in the Pacific Rim. And at the end of October 1997, Dimension Data completed its acquisition of a Com Tech competitor in Australia, Datacraft (including a 55% stake in Datacraft Asia).

COMPANY STATEMENT (from the 1996 annual report)

"In the late 1970s, IT was the domain of technocrats; few business people had begun to appreciate what it could do for them. Entering the 1980s, businesses began to make technology work for them as they learned to get more out of it and, then, to get more for less. Now, technology pervades every facet of business and companies realize the challenge is not simply to use it more effectively, but that its intelligent use will be the difference between success and failure. This change is being driven from the chief executive's office and it is profound. Supporting this advancement, new entrants to the workplace are comfortable with and eager to use IT to its full potential.

"The sanctions era resulted in the accelerated development of systems' integration companies in South Africa because there were few multinational technology corporations serving our market. As a result, groups of the size, breadth and diversity of Dimension Data are a rarity in the world market and we believe that the experience and success enjoyed in South Africa will offer value to international partners.

"As companies increasingly use technology to their own advantage, one might expect customers to become less reliant on outside suppliers. We are finding that the opposite is true."

PERFORMANCE

Dimension Data is one of the few companies in this book to receive a perfect score of 100 in our grading system. In terms of growth, consistency, management, and risk levels, it came through with flying colors. And the share price performance in the eight years since it went public has been unbelievable, increasing at a compound annual rate of 60%. It is worth pointing out, however, that the exercise of calculating shareholder returns since inception may be somewhat misleading. Eight years ago the market capitalization of this company was so small, the political constraints on South Africa so great, and the volume of shares traded so little that only a very few lucky investors profited from Dimension Data's great success. Still, the company's shares have traded liquidly enough over the last two years or so and performance has continued to be excellent. Investors can at least take comfort that this is a management team that knows how to run a successful and profitable business.

Revenues in dollars have increased at a compound annual rate of 49% since 1991, rising every year (we have sales figures dating back only six years). EBDIT rose in seven out of eight years (it was flat one year), with growth of 38%. EPS increased every year during the last eight, rising by 27% per annum. ROE averaged a high 29% during the period, while the company had no long-term debt and thus got a perfect score on our risk measure.

If you had been one of those lucky investors who put $10,000 into Dimension Data in September 1988, you would have purchased around 19,800 shares at about $0.50 a share (excluding commissions). In 1995 the company issued a 1.5-for-100 stock dividend, and in 1996 it had a ten-for-one stock split. By September 1996, you would have had around 200,000 shares worth an estimated $398,000. The company did not pay significant dividends during the period. Incidentally, even if you had not invested until September 1994, you would still have made four times your initial investment.

DIMENSION DATA

Ticker Symbol and Exchange: DIDHF—OTC **SEDOL Code: 6260035**

OPERATING AND PER SHARE DATA
(in millions of South African rand and rand per share)

	Sep 86	Sep 87	Sep 88	Sep 89	Sep 90	Sep 91	Sep 92	Sep 93	Sep 94	Sep 95	Sep 96	CAGR
Sales	N/A	N/A	N/A	N/A	N/A	87.1	113.4	147.7	218.4	719.8	1,019.0	63.6%
EBDIT	N/A	N/A	6.7	10.7	14.0	17.9	23.8	29.0	42.1	110.7	164.1	49.0%
Net Profit	N/A	N/A	3.5	5.4	6.7	8.7	11.5	18.0	25.0	51.0	84.2	49.0%
EPS	N/A	N/A	0.02	0.03	0.03	0.04	0.05	0.07	0.09	0.13	0.21	36.5%
DPS	N/A	N/A	0.01	0.01	0.01	0.02	0.02	0.03	N/M	N/M	N/M	N/M

OPERATING AND PER SHARE DATA
(in millions of U.S. dollars and dollars per share)

	Sep 86	Sep 87	Sep 88	Sep 89	Sep 90	Sep 91	Sep 92	Sep 93	Sep 94	Sep 95	Sep 96	CAGR
Sales	N/A	N/A	N/A	N/A	N/A	31.1	40.5	43.1	61.3	197.2	224.4	48.5%
EBDIT	N/A	N/A	2.7	4.0	5.5	6.4	8.5	8.4	11.8	30.3	36.1	38.3%
Net Profit	N/A	N/A	1.4	2.0	2.6	3.1	4.1	5.3	7.0	14.0	18.5	38.2%
EPS	N/A	N/A	0.01	0.01	0.01	0.01	0.02	0.02	0.02	0.04	0.05	26.7%
DPS	N/A	N/A	0.00	0.00	0.01	0.01	0.01	0.01	N/M	N/M	N/M	N/M

KEY RATIOS

	Sep 86	Sep 87	Sep 88	Sep 89	Sep 90	Sep 91	Sep 92	Sep 93	Sep 94	Sep 95	Sep 96	AVG
EBDIT Margin	N/A	N/A	N/A	N/A	N/A	20.6%	21.0%	19.6%	19.3%	15.4%	16.1%	18.7%
ROE	N/A	N/A	31.0%	33.0%	35.0%	33.0%	35.0%	20.0%	22.0%	22.0%	27.0%	28.7%
LT Debt/Total Cap	N/A	N/A	0.0%	0.0%	0.0%	0.0%	0.0%	0.0%	0.0%	0.0%	0.0%	0.0%
P/E (Projected)	N/A	N/A	4.4	6.1	5.9	8.1	14.1	14.1	14.0	14.9	22.1	11.5

STOCK PRICE CHART
(fiscal year-end closing price, in U.S. dollars, adjusted for capital changes)

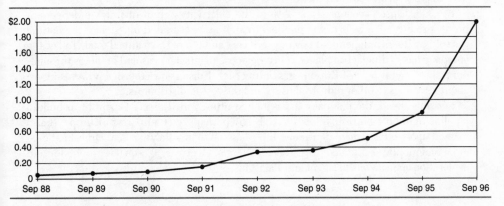

Note: Figures in U.S. dollars are translated from local currency using year-end exchange rates.

EDISON (SELI.MI—MILAN)

Address: Foro Buonaparte 31 / 20121 Milan / Italy
Tel.: (011) 39 2 6222 1   **Fax:** (011) 39 2 6222 8572

BASIC INFORMATION

Country: Italy   **Market capitalization:** $3.36 billion
Industry: Natural gas   **Share status:** Foreign shares trade on Milan Exchange
Investment thesis: Leading independent Italian power producer; electric power and natural gas

COMPANY GRADING BOX

Growth Categories		Quality of Management	
Revenue Growth	20	Return on Equity	0
Operating Income Growth	20	**Risk**	
Earnings per Share Growth	10	Long-Term Debt/Total Capital	10
Share Price Growth	10	**Total QM&R (maximum 20)**	10
Total Growth (maximum 80)	60	**FINAL GRADE**	70

BACKGROUND

Edison has quite an illustrious history. Founded in Milan in 1881, Edison built the first thermoelectric power station in Europe, the second in the world (Thomas Edison built the first one, in New York, earlier that same year). By 1962 Edison was the largest non-government-owned industrial company in Italy, employing more than 28,000 people. Then Italy nationalized most of the country's electricity industry, and Edison went into something of a holding pattern, reduced to supplying electricity (mostly through hydro-electric plants) for a group of industrial plants, while the state-run monopoly controlled most of the country's power.

That all began to change again in the early 1980s, when Italy banned nuclear power. The country was faced with a large deficit in energy capacity and needed companies such as Edison to fill the gap. In 1992 the Italian state again allowed independent power producers to sell electricity to the national network and established fixed—profitable—prices, in order to encourage independent producers to step in, build new plants, and bring more power on line. In response, Edison launched a massive investment campaign, nearly tripling its electricity sales, and bought major Italian natural gas reserves, making natural gas a second core business.

In 1996, Edison accounted for 37% of the electricity output of Italy's independent power producers and 7% of the national total; it also accounted for 81% of the natural gas sold by Italy's independent power producers and 8% of the national total. Today, the company has hydroelectric plants, thermoelectric plants, and gas and oil fields throughout Italy. Roughly 50% of Edison's gas output fuels Edison's own thermal power stations; about 29% goes to other industrial users and the rest to distributors.

Looking ahead, the company has a joint venture with Russia's Gazprom to build a pipeline to import gas from Siberia to Italy and perhaps to other parts of Europe. It also teamed up with Électricité de France International to buy Italy's second largest national independent power producer, Ilva Servizi Energie. Overseas, Edison has production and exploration concessions in Egypt and Pakistan.

COMPANY STATEMENT (from the 1995 annual report, figures updated for 1996)

"Today Edison is the most important private Italian utility company, active in both production and transport of electricity and natural gas. Electric energy is produced in thermoelectric plants fueled by natural gas and in hydroelectric plants which are highly compatible with environment preservation guidelines and with the safety and health of employees and surrounding communities.

"The Company today has 3,400 megawatts capacity and plans to reach 3,600 megawatts by 1998. Edison has become a valuable partner for leading international utility companies as is shown by the two recent joint ventures it has undertaken. . . .

"The outlook for the future is encouraging: the growth rate for overall energy demand, in particular for electricity, is higher than the GDP rate. This is a trend that can be found in many industrialized countries, thanks to the increasing role played by high technology services. Greater quantities of energy must be produced by means of low environment impact, environment-friendly and highly efficient systems.

"Edison is ready to face these challenges, not only in the field of electric energy, but also in that of natural gas. Thanks to this upstream integration Edison can maintain its demanding growth course, compatibly with the environment."

PERFORMANCE

Edison, which received 70 points overall in our grading system, stands out for its revenue growth. Revenues in dollars increased in each of the last seven years, showing compound annual growth of 19%. EBDIT increased in six of the last seven years, showing compound annual growth of 15%. The less-than-stellar EPS in dollars reflect the fact that this is a company that invested heavily in future growth, particularly in the early 1990s. EPS increased in five of the last seven years (and each of the last four years), with compound annual growth of 10%. ROE has steadily improved in the years since this company went public, from a low of 5.4% in 1990 to a high of 14.6% in 1996. The long-term debt to total capital ratio remained reasonable, averaging 21% over the last seven years. The share price increased in each of the last four years, after declining in 1992, and recorded compound annual growth of 17%.

If you had invested $10,000 in Edison at the end of 1989, you would have purchased around 4,950 shares at about $2 each (excluding commissions). There were no capital changes in the stock during the next seven years. By the end of 1996, your 4,950 shares would have been worth an estimated $30,700. You would also have received dividend payments of around $3,700.

EDISON

Ticker Symbol and Exchange: SELI.MI—Milan **SEDOL Code: 4764465**

OPERATING AND PER SHARE DATA
(in billions of Italian lire and lire per share)

	1986	1987	1988	1989	1990	1991	1992	1993	1994	1995	1996	CAGR
Sales	N/A	N/A	N/A	463	486	532	572	832	1,020	1,174	1,887	22.2%
EBDIT	N/A	N/A	N/A	241	265	303	306	481	511	526	796	18.6%
Net Profit	N/A	N/A	N/A	133	92	122	120	194	224	268	370	15.8%
EPS	N/A	N/A	N/A	211	147	194	190	306	353	423	505	13.3%
DPS	N/A	N/A	N/A	70	70	75	80	90	190	190	200	16.2%

OPERATING AND PER SHARE DATA
(in millions of U.S. dollars and dollars per share)

	1986	1987	1988	1989	1990	1991	1992	1993	1994	1995	1996	CAGR
Sales	N/A	N/A	N/A	365	432	463	389	485	633	739	1,231	18.9%
EBDIT	N/A	N/A	N/A	191	235	263	208	280	317	331	519	15.4%
Net Profit	N/A	N/A	N/A	105	82	107	82	113	139	169	241	12.7%
EPS	N/A	N/A	N/A	0.17	0.13	0.17	0.13	0.18	0.22	0.27	0.33	10.3%
DPS	N/A	N/A	N/A	0.055	0.06	0.07	0.05	0.05	0.12	0.12	0.130	13.1%

KEY RATIOS

	1986	1987	1988	1989	1990	1991	1992	1993	1994	1995	1996	AVG
EBDIT Margin	N/A	N/A	N/A	52.1%	54.4%	56.9%	53.5%	57.8%	50.1%	44.8%	42.2%	51.5%
ROE	N/A	N/A	N/A	7.8%	5.4%	6.8%	6.2%	9.4%	10.4%	10.6%	14.6%	8.9%
LT Debt/Total Cap	N/A	N/A	N/A	24.5%	25.0%	20.1%	18.1%	20.0%	19.0%	24.6%	19.6%	21.4%
P/E (Projected)	N/A	N/A	N/A	17.6	12.7	18.5	13.2	20.9	16.8	13.5	15.8	16.1

STOCK PRICE CHART
(fiscal year-end closing price, in U.S. dollars, adjusted for capital changes)

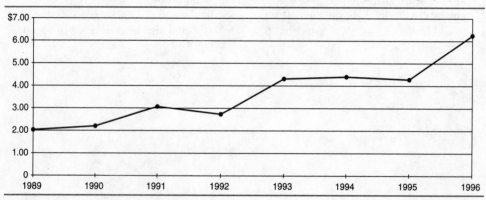

Note: Figures prior to 1989 are available but not comparable. Figures in U.S. dollars are translated from local currency using year-end exchange rates.

ENDESA (ELE—NYSE)

Address: Principe de Vergara / 187-28002 Madrid / Spain
Tel.: (011) 34 1 566 88 00   **Fax:** (011) 34 1 563 81 81   **Web site:** http://endesa.sa.com
or
Address: 745 Fifth Avenue, Suite 1610 / New York, NY 10151-0061
Tel.: (212) 750-7200   **Fax:** (212) 750-7433

BASIC INFORMATION

Country: Spain   **Market capitalization:** $16.59 billion
Industry: Electric utility   **Share status:** ADRs trade on NYSE
Investment thesis: Leading electric utility in Spain, expanding at home and abroad

COMPANY GRADING BOX

Growth Categories		Quality of Management	
Revenue Growth	20	Return on Equity	5
Operating Income Growth	20	**Risk**	
Earnings per Share Growth	20	Long-Term Debt/Total Capital	0
Share Price Growth	20	**Total QM&R (maximum 20)**	**5**
Total Growth (maximum 80)	**80**	**FINAL GRADE**	**85**

BACKGROUND

Endesa (Empresa Nacional de Electricidad) is a government-controlled electric utility powerhouse with 53% of the electricity market in Spain—and it has been expanding around the globe. Now privatization is on the horizon. The Spanish government began by offering between 25% and 30% of the company to the public in late 1997 and has said the company will be fully privatized by the end of 1999.

Ahead of the sale, Endesa has been expanding aggressively, both domestically and internationally. Management is preparing itself to face Spain's new regulatory environment, characterized by lower rates and greater competition. The company has restructured its core operations, creating greater economies of scale, and increased its efforts to diversify. Within Spain, Endesa spent $1.56 billion to raise its stakes in two Spanish regional electric utilities to 75%, up from 39% in one and 49% in the other. Those two deals have helped turn Endesa into the fourth largest electric utility in Europe in terms of installed capacity and the third largest worldwide in terms of market capitalization.

In August 1997 Endesa announced it would acquire a large stake in Chile's Enersis (see page 144), creating a powerhouse in the Latin American electricity industry. However, even before that deal, Endesa held sizable stakes in electricity companies in Argentina, Brazil, Chile, Venezuela, Peru, and Santo Domingo. Going forward, Endesa and Enersis will join forces to buy up Latin American electricity assets. Already the two are cooperating on one of the biggest privatizations in history: approximately $50 billion worth of electricity generation, transmission, and distribution assets in Brazil.

Endesa also owns interests in natural gas and hydroelectric production facilities in Spain, cable television throughout Spain and France, and nearly 8% of Spain's second largest digital mobile telephone operator; it is also part of a consortium with the winning bid for 70% of Spain's second largest basic telephone operator and has interests in two Spanish companies that specialize in the treatment of solid waste.

At the end of 1996, Endesa's overseas operations generated just 6% of total revenues; however, Endesa—which has a tremendous cash flow—has said it would like its overseas operations to generate 20 to 25% of revenues by the year 2001. Management has also said it now is interested primarily in controlling businesses overseas, rather than in being a passive investor.

COMPANY STATEMENT (from the 1995 annual report)

"The electricity industry, like other industries, is undergoing a profound transformation, driven by customer and government insistence on greater efficiency and lower prices.

"These pressures are being addressed, first, by the process towards industry globalization, whereby electric utilities are seeking new competitive niches by taking advantage of business opportunities in other countries and markets; second, by gas-fired electricity generation using low-cost, combined-cycle technologies; and thirdly, by the appearance of new players in an industry which is lowering its entry barriers. The regulatory frameworks call for a greater presence of market forces, so as to guarantee more competitive prices, the development of mechanisms to gradually pass on the greater efficiency to the consumer, and the establishment of measures through which the costs of the transitional process can be recovered.

"To compete successfully in the future will require a global enterprise with a sound command of technological and commercial factors and which has an appropriate size to enable it to operate in the international arena, optimizing its skills in the creation of value in all the facets of the electricity business, including primary fuels and in other business areas—water, gas and telecommunications—taking advantage of its existing relationships with customers."

PERFORMANCE

Endesa scores highly on both consistency and growth and places well with an overall score of 85 points. The company gets top marks for revenues (increasing in nine of the ten years, with a compound annual growth rate of 18%), EBDIT (up in eight of the ten years with a growth rate of about 15% per annum), EP/ADR (up in eight of the ten years, with a growth rate of 21% per annum), and share price performance (up in nine of the ten years and posting compound growth of 25% per annum). The company lost a few points with an ROE of 16%, as many other companies on our list show a higher average return, and scored no points in our risk category, with long-term debt averaging 45% of total capital. However, it is worth noting that compared with other electric utilities, 16% ROE is quite high while a 45% debt to total capital ratio is very reasonable. Adjusted for the industry in which it operates, Endesa would be among our top finishers.

Endesa's ADR price increased from a low of $4.23 in 1986 to a high of $71.55 in 1996. Dividends were strong during the period, rising eight out of ten years and averaging 38% of earnings. The dividend per ADR reached $1.64 in 1996, up from $0.50 in 1986.

If you had invested $10,000 in Endesa at the end of 1986, you would have purchased around 1,160 ADRs (or ADR equivalents) at about $8.50 each (excluding commissions). In April 1988 Endesa had a one-for-seven bonus issue. By the end of 1996, you would have had around 1,320 ADRs worth an estimated $93,350. You would also have received around $14,000 in dividend payments.

ENDESA

Ticker Symbol and Exchange: ELE—NYSE　　　　　　**CUSIP No.: 292447208**

OPERATING AND PER SHARE DATA
(in billions of Spanish pesetas and pesetas per share)

	1986	1987	1988	1989	1990	1991	1992	1993	1994	1995	1996	CAGR
Sales	239	268	467	549	568	685	701	737	795	862	1,260	18.1%
EBDIT	134	160	247	281	285	341	348	356	368	397	566	15.5%
Net Profit	28	45	62	72	80	105	115	117	133	150	168	19.5%
EPS	95.6	151.9	238.1	276.5	306.5	404.6	440.4	449.2	510.4	576.5	646.8	21.1%
DPS	64.8	69.0	90.0	109.0	109.0	120.0	132.0	143.0	158.0	186.0	214.4	12.7%

OPERATING AND PER SHARE DATA
(in millions of U.S. dollars and dollars per ADR)

	1986	1987	1988	1989	1990	1991	1992	1993	1994	1995	1996	CAGR
Sales	1,822	2,493	4,122	5,016	5,948	7,076	6,088	5,154	6,039	7,089	9,611	18.1%
EBDIT	1,023	1,485	2,180	2,566	2,988	3,518	3,021	2,491	2,795	3,262	4,317	15.5%
Net Profit	216	420	546	657	835	1,087	994	817	1,008	1,233	1,283	19.5%
EP/ADR	0.73	1.41	2.10	2.53	3.21	4.18	3.82	3.14	3.88	4.74	4.93	21.1%
DP/ADR	0.49	0.64	0.79	1.00	1.14	1.24	1.15	1.00	1.20	1.53	1.64	12.7%

KEY RATIOS

	1986	1987	1988	1989	1990	1991	1992	1993	1994	1995	1996	AVG
EBDIT Margin	56.2%	59.6%	52.9%	51.1%	50.2%	49.7%	49.6%	48.3%	46.3%	46.0%	44.9%	50.4%
ROE	11.0%	16.1%	16.2%	16.8%	17.7%	19.1%	18.3%	16.5%	16.7%	17.1%	14.0%	16.3%
LT Debt/Total Cap	70.9%	67.7%	55.5%	52.6%	47.9%	38.7%	33.1%	25.2%	29.0%	25.5%	43.0%	44.5%
P/E (Projected)	6.5	4.3	5.8	7.5	5.4	6.6	8.2	13.3	9.3	10.6	13.4	8.3

STOCK PRICE CHART
(fiscal year-end closing price, in U.S. dollars, adjusted for capital changes)

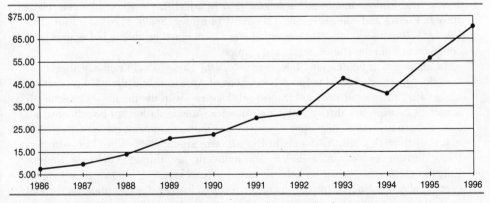

Note: Figures in U.S. dollars are translated from local currency using year-end exchange rates.

ENERSIS (ENI—NYSE)

Address: Santo Domingo 789 / Santiago / Chile
Tel.: (011) 56 2 632 1491   **Fax:** (011) 56 2 632 4832
or
Address: Dewe Rogerson / 850 Third Avenue, 20th Floor / New York, NY 10022
Tel.: (212) 688-6840   **Fax:** (212) 838-3393

BASIC INFORMATION

Country: Chile   **Market capitalization:** $4 billion
Industry: Electric utility   **Share status:** ADRs trade on NYSE
Investment thesis: Largest publicly held electric power conglomerate in Latin America

COMPANY GRADING BOX

Growth Categories		Quality of Management	
Revenue Growth	20	Return on Equity	10
Operating Income Growth	20	**Risk**	
Earnings per Share Growth	20	Long-Term Debt/Total Capital	10
Share Price Growth	15	**Total QM&R (maximum 20)**	**20**
Total Growth (maximum 80)	**75**	**FINAL GRADE**	**95**

BACKGROUND

We have not included many electric utilities in this book, but Enersis's track record—as the largest publicly held electric power conglomerate in Latin America—fits the profile of a growth company. Privatized in 1982, this $4 billion market capitalization company had revenues of $2.7 billion in 1996. Since the company went public in 1990, revenues in dollars have been increasing at a compound annual rate of 39%. Among Enersis's key investments in Chile are its 75% stake in Chilectra, the largest electric distribution company in Chile; its 25% stake in Endesa, Chile's largest (and lowest-cost) electricity generation company; and its 85% stake in Chile's fourth largest electricity distribution company.

Now Enersis and Spain's Endesa (see page 141) are joining forces to participate in buying Latin American electricity assets, beginning with one of the biggest privatizations in history: approximately $50 billion worth of electricity generation, transmission, and distribution assets in Brazil. The joint venture is part of a broader agreement between Enersis and Endesa announced in August 1997 by which Endesa bought a controlling stake in Enersis and Enersis received about 5% of Endesa Spain. The deal ensures that Enersis will remain a dominant player in Latin America and be able to bid against giant competitors from the United States and Europe.

In addition to its holdings in Chile, even before the Endesa deal Enersis, with its huge cash flow, had participated in the privatizations of Argentine and Peruvian companies, along with strategic partners and its own subsidiaries—with the intention of selectively exporting its expertise throughout Latin America. Among its foreign investments is a 51% stake in Edesur, an Argentine electricity distribution company, owned directly and indirectly through Chilectra. Similarly, Enersis owns around 29% of two Peruvian electricity distribution companies, directly and indirectly, also through Chilectra. Endesa, Enersis's electricity generation holding, has also been investing abroad, mostly in Argentina, allowing Enersis to participate indirectly in further diversification throughout the region.

COMPANY STATEMENT (from a February 1996 offering prospectus)

"The Company's business strategy is to use its accumulated utility experience and expertise to improve the profitability of its existing businesses in Chile, Argentina and Peru and to enhance the value of other businesses it may acquire in Latin America. The Company believes it has proven expertise in managing privatized utilities, including experience in reducing energy losses, implementing proprietary billing and accounts receivable management systems, improving labor relations, increasing work-force productivity, streamlining information systems, and operating under tariff and regulatory frameworks that reward efficient operations.

"As part of its strategy to expand its utility business in Latin America, the Company intends to continue to participate in privatizations of state-owned electric distribution and generation businesses. Management continually evaluates investment opportunities in Latin American countries where management perceives the existence of acceptable political and economic conditions and the prospect of an appropriate regulatory framework. . . .

"The Company has invested and may continue to invest in new businesses through majority or minority participations in partnership with domestic and international companies, including related companies. In all of its operations, whether or not majority controlled, the Company seeks to exert the highest possible degree of managerial influence and has a policy of long-term ownership linked with operational control. The Company does not approach its minority participations as passive investments."

PERFORMANCE

Enersis received a total of 95 points in our grading system, remarkable considering the turmoil in the Latin American markets over the last few years. Revenues, EBITDA in dollars, and EP/ADR increased in each of the last six years, recording compound annual growth of 39%, 53% and 17%, respectively. Shareholders did well by this company; with the ADR price increasing at a compound annual rate of 43% over the last six years, although the shares have been flat for the last few years. The EBITDA margin averaged 40% over the last two years. ROE averaged 25% over the last six years, very high for an electric utility. And the long-term debt to total capital ratio averaged around 20%—though it jumped to 26% in 1996, as the company pursued acquisitions abroad.

If you had invested $10,000 in Enersis at the end of 1990, you would have purchased around 100 ADRs (or ADR equivalents) at about $99.50 each (excluding commissions). During the following six years, there were a thirty-for-one stock split in July 1991, a 1-for-8.6 rights issue in August 1993, and a 1-for-12.1 rights issue in December 1995. By the end of 1996, you would have had around 3,050 shares worth an estimated $85,300. You would also have received dividend payments of around $16,900.

ENERSIS

Ticker Symbol and Exchange: ENI—NYSE   **CUSIP No.: 29274F104**

OPERATING AND PER SHARE DATA
(in billions of nominal Chilean pesos and pesos per share)

	1986	1987	1988	1989	1990	1991	1992	1993	1994	1995	1996	CAGR
Sales	N/A	N/A	N/A	N/A	126	147	170	211	343	736	1,161	44.8%
EBITDA	N/A	N/A	N/A	N/A	33	55	71	61	99	210	537	59.2%
Net Profit	N/A	N/A	N/A	N/A	32	49	65	48	69	98	106	22.1%
EPS	N/A	N/A	N/A	N/A	4.71	7.21	9.56	7.06	10.12	14.41	15.59	22.1%
DPS	N/A	N/A	N/A	N/A	3.19	4.00	3.98	4.07	6.45	8.32	10.21	21.4%

OPERATING AND PER SHARE DATA
(in millions of U.S. dollars and dollars per ADR)

	1986	1987	1988	1989	1990	1991	1992	1993	1994	1995	1996	CAGR
Sales	N/A	N/A	N/A	N/A	376	395	447	496	849	1,808	2,730	39.1%
EBITDA	N/A	N/A	N/A	N/A	99	148	187	143	245	516	1,263	53.0%
Net Profit	N/A	N/A	N/A	N/A	95.5	131.7	171.0	112.7	170.3	240.7	249.2	17.3%
EP/ADR	N/A	N/A	N/A	N/A	0.70	0.97	1.26	0.83	1.25	1.77	1.83	17.3%
DP/ADR	N/A	N/A	N/A	N/A	0.48	0.54	0.52	0.48	0.80	1.02	1.20	16.7%

KEY RATIOS

	1986	1987	1988	1989	1990	1991	1992	1993	1994	1995	1996	AVG
EBITDA Margin	N/A	N/A	N/A	N/A	26.2%	37.4%	41.8%	28.9%	28.9%	28.5%	46.3%	34.0%
ROE	N/A	N/A	N/A	N/A	28.3%	36.4%	35.7%	17.5%	18.4%	21.1%	18.4%	25.1%
LT Debt/Total Cap	N/A	N/A	N/A	N/A	17.7%	8.7%	15.1%	17.6%	11.9%	41.4%	26.0%	19.8%
P/E (Projected)	N/A	N/A	N/A	N/A	3.4	10.4	15.5	18.8	15.8	15.8	12.5	14.7

STOCK PRICE CHART
(fiscal year-end closing price, in U.S. dollars, adjusted for capital changes)

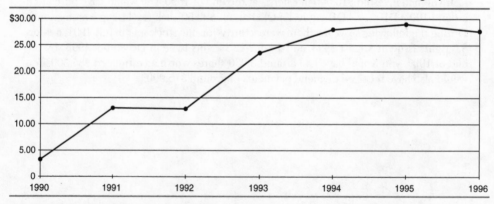

Note: Figures in U.S. dollars are translated from local currency using year-end exchange rates.

ERICSSON (ERICY—NASDAQ)

Address: Telefonaktiebolaget LM Ericsson / 126 25 Stockholm / Sweden
Tel.: (011) 46 8 719 5340   **Fax:** (011) 46 8 719 1976   **Web site:** http://www.ericsson.com
or
Address: 100 Park Avenue, 27th Floor / New York, NY 10017
Tel.: (212) 685-4030   **Fax:** (212) 213-0159

BASIC INFORMATION

Country: Sweden   **Market capitalization:** $30.97 billion
Industry: Telecommunications equipment   **Share status:** ADRs trade on NASDAQ
Investment thesis: A leading manufacturer of telecommunications equipment

COMPANY GRADING BOX

Growth Categories		Quality of Management	
Revenue Growth	20	Return on Equity	5
Operating Income Growth	20	**Risk**	
Earnings per Share Growth	20	Long-Term Debt/Total Capital	0
Share Price Growth	20	**Total QM&R (maximum 20)**	5
Total Growth (maximum 80)	**80**	**FINAL GRADE**	**85**

BACKGROUND

This 120-year-old Swedish firm, a manufacturer of systems and products for wired and mobile telecommunications, has been doing business in the United States since around 1900. Today, the United States represents Ericsson's largest single market. All told, Ericsson is active in more than 100 countries and has joint ventures with companies such as Texas Instruments and Hewlett-Packard and cooperation agreements with companies such as Microsoft and IBM. In addition to the United States, Ericsson has a major presence throughout the European Union and is aggressively expanding in Asia.

Worldwide, the company has slightly more than 40% of the market for mobile telecommunications, serving about 54 million subscribers in 78 countries—and an even higher percentage of the market for digital systems (the number of digital systems is growing considerably faster than that of analog systems). At the end of 1996, AXE, Ericsson's digital system for wired and mobile networks, was the most sold digital system. At the beginning of 1997, 118 million AXE systems had been installed or were on order in 117 countries.

The telecommunications industry is booming throughout the world, with deregulation and the rise of mobile telephony powering the surge. At year-end 1995 there were 85 million mobile telephone subscribers worldwide. Ericsson sees that number coming close to 350 million by the year 2000. To maintain its standing as a leader in its core industries, the company spends about 20% of its annual sales revenue on technical development and has about 18,000 employees active in its research and development program.

Among Ericsson's key products: the AXE digital exchange system; ETNA transport network products; TMOS operating support systems for telecommunications networks; radio base stations; mobile telephones; and Consono and business phone digital systems for business communications.

COMPANY STATEMENT (from the 1996 annual report)

"After extensive deliberations during the spring and summer of 1996, Ericsson's corporate management took a decision on a long term vision and strategies toward the year 2005. Some of the principal points are described below.

"Ericsson believes in a world in which communication using speech, data, images and video (multi-media) will be available and affordable for most of the world's population. This will be made possible by many different types of networks and systems and by a variety of communication and service suppliers in an increasingly deregulated and competitive market. Wireless communication will to an increasing extent be viewed as a fully equivalent alternative to wireline connections. Ericsson views itself as one of the most important and progressive global players in making these forms of mass communication possible. Ericsson will thus make a tangible positive contribution to economic, industrial and social development in the world, an achievement in which we take pride.

"Ericsson's vision for the year 2005 is to be the leading global supplier in this new world. We wish to be regarded as the best innovators and as entrepreneurs collaborating in global teams. Ericsson should be viewed as a model for global networked organizations."

PERFORMANCE

Ericsson received 85 points in our grading system, with the highest possible points for growth. EP/ADR increased at a compound annual rate of 31%—far outstripping revenue growth, 15%, and growth in operating income plus depreciation, 16%. Talk about creating value for shareholders! ADR price performance followed EP/ADR growth, with the ADR price rising at a compound annual rate of 35%. Dividend per ADR growth was also strong, increasing at a compound annual rate of 19%. ROE has been on the rise since 1992, moving from a low of 3% in that year to 18.6% in 1996, but the 13% average rate is still a bit low when compared with some of the other companies on this list. As for risk, the long-term debt to total capital ratio declined to 24% in 1996, from 33.4% in 1986.

If you had invested $10,000 in Ericsson at the end of 1986, you would have purchased around 265 ADRs (or ADR equivalents) at about $37.75 each (excluding commissions). During the following ten years, there were a five-for-one stock subdivision in September 1990, a four-for-one stock split in June 1995, and a one-for-ten rights issue in September 1995. By the end of 1996, you would have had around 6,620 ADRs worth an estimated $203,700. You would also have received around $12,500 in dividend payments.

ERICSSON

Ticker Symbol and Exchange: ERICY—NASDAQ　　　　　**CUSIP No.: 294821400**

OPERATING AND PER SHARE DATA
(in millions of Swedish kronor and kronor per share)

	1986	1987	1988	1989	1990	1991	1992	1993	1994	1995	1996	CAGR
Sales	31,644	32,400	31,297	39,549	45,702	45,793	47,020	62,954	82,554	98,780	124,266	14.7%
EBDIT	3,438	3,398	3,649	5,851	7,266	4,145	3,947	6,181	9,557	11,778	14,974	15.9%
Net Profit	388	518	1,033	2,335	3,450	886	479	2,835	3,949	5,439	7,110	33.8%
EPS	0.49	0.92	1.34	2.46	3.42	1.04	0.56	3.07	4.30	5.83	7.27	31.0%
DPS	0.43	0.45	0.53	0.70	0.88	0.88	0.88	1.13	1.38	1.75	2.50	19.2%

OPERATING AND PER SHARE DATA
(in millions of U.S. dollars and dollars per ADR)

	1986	1987	1988	1989	1990	1991	1992	1993	1994	1995	1996	CAGR
Sales	4,640	5,606	5,122	6,379	8,118	8,251	6,641	7,548	11,111	14,877	18,115	14.6%
EBDIT	504	588	597	944	1,291	747	557	741	1,286	1,774	2,183	15.8%
Net Profit	57	90	169	377	613	160	68	340	531	819	1,036	33.7%
EP/ADR	0.07	0.16	0.22	0.40	0.61	0.19	0.08	0.37	0.58	0.88	1.06	30.9%
DP/ADR	0.06	0.08	0.09	0.11	0.16	0.16	0.12	0.14	0.19	0.26	0.36	19.2%

KEY RATIOS

	1986	1987	1988	1989	1990	1991	1992	1993	1994	1995	1996	AVG
EBDIT Margin	10.9%	10.5%	11.7%	14.8%	15.9%	9.1%	8.4%	9.8%	11.6%	11.9%	12.0%	11.5%
ROE	3.8%	7.5%	11.5%	17.5%	20.4%	5.3%	2.8%	14.5%	17.7%	18.9%	19.0%	12.6%
LT Debt/Total Cap	33.4%	48.7%	44.3%	38.0%	33.6%	38.8%	41.0%	38.2%	36.6%	25.6%	24.1%	36.6%
P/E (Projected)	11.2	5.4	7.2	12.3	42.4	46.1	14.5	19.0	16.9	17.9	24.6	19.8

STOCK PRICE CHART
(fiscal year-end closing price, in U.S. dollars, adjusted for capital changes)

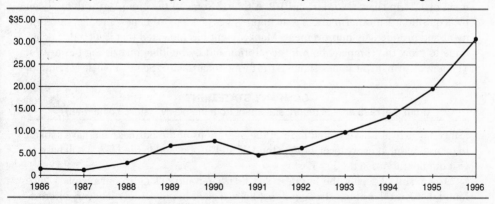

Note: Figures in U.S. dollars are translated from local currency using year-end exchange rates.

EUROTHERM (ETHIF—OTC)

Address: Leonardslee / Lower Beeding / Horsham, West Sussex RH13 6PP / United Kingdom
Tel.: (011) 44 1403 892 000   **Fax:** (011) 44 1403 892 011

BASIC INFORMATION

Country: United Kingdom
Industry: Electrical and electronic
Investment thesis: One of the world's largest manufacturers of industrial control equipment

Market capitalization: $679 million
Share status: Foreign shares trade OTC

COMPANY GRADING BOX

Growth Categories		Quality of Management	
Revenue Growth	10	Return on Equity	10
Operating Income Growth	15	**Risk**	
Earnings per Share Growth	20	Long-Term Debt/Total Capital	10
Share Price Growth	20	**Total QM&R (maximum 20)**	**20**
Total Growth (maximum 80)	**65**	**FINAL GRADE**	**85**

BACKGROUND

After a boardroom battle closely followed in the British business press, this industrial controls manufacturer has gone back to the business at hand—and shareholders have been declared the winners. A new chairman has been installed (see statement below), and the man credited with turning Eurotherm around in the six years since he arrived, Claes Hultman, has been reinstated as chief executive, reportedly in large part due to pressure exerted by institutional shareholders.

So what does this company do? The business, which had 1996 revenues of $336 million, is divided into three main operating units: the Controls and Instrumentation Division, which manufactures temperature, power, and humidity controls, as well as process controls, for a range of industries; the Drives Division, which manufactures electronic motor speed controllers and integrated drives systems; and the Gauging Division, which manufactures products that gauge and control product thickness for the paper, plastics, rubber, and film industries.

Founded in 1965 to make a new type of temperature controller for industrial machinery, Eurotherm has been adding technologies since the founders sponsored the development of a "strip chart recorder" in 1972. Although some of the group's growth has been by acquisition, Eurotherm also has an impressive track record in new product development and productivity improvement. Management has indicated that it intends to continue to grow the company both by acquisition and by building on existing businesses. The new chairman, Sir James Hann, is the former chairman of Scottish Nuclear Limited.

COMPANY STATEMENT
(from the 1996 annual report; statement from the newly installed chairman)

"Since my arrival I have visited most of the operations of the business and have spoken to management at every level, here in the UK, in Europe, and in the USA. I still have to visit our operations in the Far East.

"As a result of seeing the businesses at first hand and talking to our people I have found that Eurotherm has strong product lines, a good brand name, some very interesting niche markets, high quality production facilities and a blue chip customer base. At the headquarters I found that management has a high standard of internal control throughout their worldwide operations which ensures that the Group's internal financial procedures and reporting standards are working as expected. There is also a well advanced program of corporate governance designed to meet the most stringent rules currently imposed.

"Eurotherm's successful growth since 1991 has been mainly driven by productivity improvements, by margin enhancement and new product development.

"Since August we have carried out a comprehensive strategic review which certainly reinforces this strategy. We therefore propose to seek further organic growth in new markets and by greater penetration into geographic regions in which the company already operates. We shall also continue to introduce new products, many home grown but some acquired. The four recent small acquisitions are examples of this and should contribute over coming years to Eurotherm's growth and profits."

PERFORMANCE

Eurotherm has a low long-term debt to total capital ratio, a high ROE, and excellent EPS growth, all factors in its overall score of 85 points in our grading system. EPS and share price in dollars increased in nine of the last ten years, rising at a compound annual rate of 21% and 23%, respectively. EBDIT, also up in nine of the last ten years, increased at a compound annual rate of 12%. On the other hand, revenues in dollars increased at a compound annual rate just short of 9%—lower than most of the companies in our book. ROE increased every year in each of the last five years, averaging 19% over the last ten years. As for risk, the long-term debt to total capital ratio declined to 1.3% in 1996 from 21.5% in 1986.

If you had invested $10,000 in Eurotherm in October 1986, you would have purchased around 1,800 shares at about $5.50 each (excluding commissions). During the following ten years, there were a one-for-two bonus issue in April 1989, a one-for-two bonus issue in April 1990, and a one-for-one bonus issue in March 1994. By October 1996, you would have had around 8,100 shares worth an estimated $80,700. You would also have received dividend payments of around $5,900.

EUROTHERM

Ticker Symbol and Exchange: ETHIF—OTC   **SEDOL Code: 323116**

OPERATING AND PER SHARE DATA
(in millions of British pounds and pounds per share)

	Oct 86	Oct 87	Oct 88	Oct 89	Oct 90	Oct 91	Oct 92	Oct 93	Oct 94	Oct 95	Oct 96	CAGR
Sales	99.0	112.0	129.0	149.0	164.0	158.0	155.0	158.0	168.0	195.0	206.5	7.6%
EBDIT	14.3	18.2	21.6	23.9	20.8	14.0	20.9	25.1	30.2	38.0	42.2	11.4%
Net Profit	5.3	7.8	10.0	11.3	8.5	4.5	9.7	13.3	17.2	22.4	24.8	16.7%
EPS	0.04	0.06	0.08	0.09	0.10	0.05	0.11	0.15	0.19	0.25	0.28	20.3%
DPS	0.01	0.01	0.02	0.02	0.04	0.04	0.04	0.05	0.06	0.08	0.09	23.3%

OPERATING AND PER SHARE DATA
(in millions of U.S. dollars and dollars per share)

	Oct 86	Oct 87	Oct 88	Oct 89	Oct 90	Oct 91	Oct 92	Oct 93	Oct 94	Oct 95	Oct 96	CAGR
Sales	147	182	217	235	319	275	241	234	275	308	336	8.6%
EBDIT	21	30	36	38	40	24	33	37	49	60	69	12.4%
Net Profit	8	13	17	18	17	8	15	20	28	35	40	17.7%
EPS	0.06	0.10	0.13	0.14	0.19	0.09	0.17	0.22	0.32	0.40	0.45	21.4%
DPS	0.02	0.02	0.03	0.03	0.07	0.06	0.06	0.07	0.09	0.12	0.15	24.4%

KEY RATIOS

	Oct 86	Oct 87	Oct 88	Oct 89	Oct 90	Oct 91	Oct 92	Oct 93	Oct 94	Oct 95	Oct 96	AVG
EBDIT Margin	14.4%	16.2%	16.7%	16.0%	13.7%	8.9%	13.5%	15.9%	18.0%	19.5%	20.4%	15.7%
ROE	15.7%	20.4%	20.9%	19.5%	17.1%	8.7%	16.9%	20.5%	23.0%	25.1%	25.6%	19.4%
LT Debt/Total Cap	21.5%	18.4%	13.9%	14.4%	19.2%	17.8%	13.1%	7.6%	3.7%	2.5%	1.3%	12.1%
P/E (Projected)	13.1	12.9	15.2	9.5	18.0	13.4	13.2	16.3	15.1	20.4	20.1	15.2

STOCK PRICE CHART
(fiscal year-end closing price, in U.S. dollars, adjusted for capital changes)

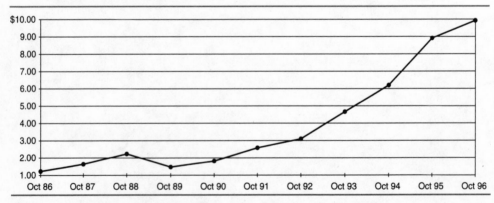

Note: Figures in U.S. dollars are translated from local currency using year-end exchange rates.

FAIREY GROUP (FARRF—OTC)

Address: Station Road / Egham, Surrey TW20 9NP/United Kingdom
Tel.: (011) 44 1784 470 470   **Fax:** (011) 44 1784 470 848

BASIC INFORMATION

Country: United Kingdom
Industry: Electrical and electronic
Market capitalization: $793 million
Share status: Foreign shares trade OTC
Investment thesis: Manufactures and distributes specialized components for industrial use

COMPANY GRADING BOX

Growth Categories		Quality of Management	
Revenue Growth	10	Return on Equity	10
Operating Income Growth	20	**Risk**	
Earnings per Share Growth	20	Long-Term Debt/Total Capital	5
Share Price Growth	20	**Total QM&R (maximum 20)**	15
Total Growth (maximum 80)	70	**FINAL GRADE**	85

BACKGROUND

Fairey Group is a holding company for nineteen relatively autonomous businesses involved in everything from the design and manufacture of control products for industrial applications to porcelain insulators for high-voltage electricity distribution to aerospace and defense products. Their products are used in aircraft, car headlights, and high-speed printing. The emphasis is on proprietary technology, which is used in products all over the world. One of its companies produces metal detectors that check for metal in ice-cream products. Another manufactures an "in-line beer analyzer" to help breweries keep track of their brews.

And Fairey is still buying companies. In September 1996 Fairey, which had 1996 revenues of $423 million, bought Fusion UV Systems of the United States for $126 million. Fusion supplies a type of patented ultraviolet lamp to companies involved with fiber optics, electronics, and automobiles. And in early 1997 Fairey bought Burnfield PLC, an industrial electronics manufacturer with clients in the food and cement sectors as well as the semiconductor and disc drive industries. Today by far the largest share of Fairey's revenues, more than 58%, comes from the companies involved in electronics and electrical power. And its largest market is the United States, followed by the United Kingdom.

Fairey gives its companies the benefits of autonomy and of a large organization. It has the resources to stand behind growth through capital investments in research and equipment and the management experience to let the individual companies do what they do best.

COMPANY STATEMENT (from the 1996 annual report)

"Fairey Group, with its long and successful tradition in high technology engineering, brings together companies with expertise in industrial electronics, process technology and specialist engineering.

"Fairey's strength is in managing autonomous companies so as to encourage them to develop their business within the supporting framework of the group. We maintain constructive relationships with and between our operating companies, helping them to define and meet their individual development and growth objectives. The focus is on markets with potential for growth and on technologies that provide a foundation for continuing product development.

"Three-quarters of group sales are represented by products which control or enhance manufacturing processes to improve productivity, yield and product quality. They are supplied from facilities in the US and Europe to diverse markets such as semi-conductors, food, pharmaceuticals, telecommunications, automotive, material converting and printing.

"The specialist engineering companies serve an equivalent diversity of markets, providing critical components for system performance in aerospace, electricity generation and supply and fluid power."

PERFORMANCE

Fairey, which received a total of 85 points in our grading system, shines in EPS and share price performance (both in dollars). EPS increased in seven of the last nine years, with compound annual growth of 24%. The share price set a new high in each of the eight years since Fairey went public, increasing at a compound rate of 28%. In dollars, revenue growth—inconsistent in the late 1980s—averaged just 11% for the nine-year period. However, revenues did increase in each of the last four years. ROE, on the other hand, averaged an impressive 34% for the whole nine years. As for risk, the ratio of long-term debt to total capital averaged an acceptable 27%. However, a series of acquisitions in 1996 drove that ratio much higher and ROE much lower. Those numbers are assumed to be a temporary distortion and therefore not material (N/M in the table) to this company's long-term prospects. Even so, investors should be aware of the situation.

If you had invested $10,000 in Fairey at the end of 1988, you would have purchased around 3,650 shares at about $2.75 each (excluding commissions). In June 1994 there was a one-for-one bonus issue. By the end of 1996, you would have had around 7,300 shares worth an estimated $72,700. You would also have received dividend payments of around $6,000.

FAIREY GROUP

Ticker Symbol and Exchange: FARRF—OTC   **SEDOL Code: 330860**

OPERATING AND PER SHARE DATA
(in millions of British pounds and pounds per share)

	1986	1987	1988	1989	1990	1991	1992	1993	1994	1995	1996	CAGR
Sales	N/A	85.0	82.0	83.0	86.0	89.0	104.0	130.0	145.0	196.0	247.0	12.6%
EBDIT	N/A	10.3	13.1	14.4	15.3	28.8	50.7	25.0	29.0	39.8	52.7	19.9%
Net Profit	N/A	2.7	5.6	8.2	9.1	9.4	11.4	14.1	17.2	22.3	28.6	30.0%
EPS	N/A	0.04	0.08	0.12	0.14	0.14	0.16	0.19	0.23	0.27	0.32	25.7%
DPS	N/A	0.00	0.00	0.04	0.04	0.05	0.05	0.06	0.07	0.08	0.09	13.5%

OPERATING AND PER SHARE DATA
(in millions of U.S. dollars and dollars per share)

	1986	1987	1988	1989	1990	1991	1992	1993	1994	1995	1996	CAGR
Sales	N/A	160	148	134	166	166	157	192	227	304	423	11.4%
EBDIT	N/A	19	24	23	30	54	77	37	45	62	90	18.6%
Net Profit	N/A	5	10	13	18	18	17	21	27	35	49	28.6%
EPS	N/A	0.08	0.15	0.20	0.27	0.26	0.24	0.28	0.36	0.42	0.55	24.3%
DPS	N/A	—	—	0.06	0.08	0.08	0.08	0.09	0.11	0.12	0.15	14.5%

KEY RATIOS

	1986	1987	1988	1989	1990	1991	1992	1993	1994	1995	1996	AVG
EBDIT Margin	N/A	12.1%	16.0%	17.3%	17.8%	32.4%	48.8%	19.2%	20.0%	20.3%	21.3%	22.5%
ROE	N/A	39.1%	17.8%	22.1%	21.3%	23.5%	29.2%	32.3%	55.0%	66.8%	N/M	34.1%
LT Debt/Total Cap	N/A	65.9%	9.5%	10.4%	7.7%	13.1%	25.8%	23.8%	42.9%	40.8%	N/M	26.7%
P/E (Projected)	N/A	N/M	6.0	7.1	7.6	9.4	13.2	14.7	14.8	16.7	15.8	12.4

STOCK PRICE CHART
(fiscal year-end closing price, in U.S. dollars, adjusted for capital changes)

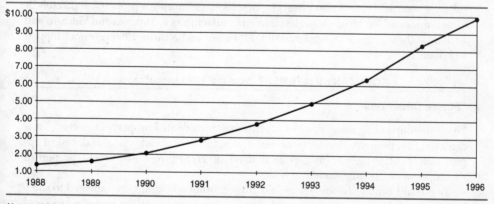

Notes: 1988 year-end price is average of high and low. Figures in U.S. dollars are translated from local currency using year-end exchange rates.

FRASER AND NEAVE (FRNVF—OTC)

Address: 21-00 Alexandra Point / 438 Alexandra Road / Singapore 119958
Tel.: (011) 65 272 9488   **Fax:** (011) 65 271 0811

BASIC INFORMATION

Country: Singapore
Industry: Food and beverages
Market capitalization: $2.47 billion
Share status: Foreign shares trade OTC
Investment thesis: Coca-Cola anchor bottler in Asia; manages seventeen soft drink plants in eight countries

COMPANY GRADING BOX

Growth Categories		Quality of Management	
Revenue Growth	20	Return on Equity	0
Operating Income Growth	20	**Risk**	
Earnings per Share Growth	20	Long-Term Debt/Total Capital	10
Share Price Growth	10	**Total QM&R (maximum 20)**	**10**
Total Growth (maximum 80)	**70**	**FINAL GRADE**	**80**

BACKGROUND

Fraser and Neave is another one of our anchor Coca-Cola bottlers. Through a 75%-owned subsidiary formed in a joint venture with Coca-Cola in 1992, Fraser and Neave manages seventeen soft drink factories in eight countries, including Singapore, Malaysia, Brunei, Cambodia, and Vietnam. Although 1996 earnings did not keep pace with the company's past stellar performance, management has said it is investing heavily in new facilities and distribution infrastructure. Over the last few years this company (along with Coca-Cola) has broadened its reach in the region from 23.6 million people to 264.6 million people. That's a lot of potential demand. And Fraser and Neave wants to meet it. This 113-year-old company is not afraid to invest in the future. Of course, the 1997 "Asian contagion" has been tough, but Fraser and Neave has relatively recession-proof products—and a strong history—which should help it weather the crisis and prosper.

There is more to Fraser and Neave than soft drinks. Its joint venture with Heineken (see page 174), Asia Pacific Breweries, operates fifteen breweries throughout the region (and is aggressively pushing into China). Through a majority-owned real estate subsidiary, Fraser and Neave also invests in, develops, and manages property; separately, it owns dairies and has interests in glass bottle manufacturers in Malaysia and Vietnam and a Chinese theme park in Singapore. All told, Fraser and Neave's 1996 revenues topped $2 billion.

COMPANY STATEMENT (from the 1996 annual report)

"Future Directions

"With the impending completion of . . . two major residential property projects . . . it is expected that property development earnings in the year ahead will be reduced to approximately $120 million [Singapore dollars]. Earnings from investment properties should, however, be maintained, at least.

"In the soft drinks division, the results from existing operations are expected to show improvement. However, if on-going efforts to seek new opportunities to expand regional activities are successful, it may be that start-up investment in new ventures will, in the shorter term, absorb the gains before they reach our bottom line.

"The breweries division faces a similar dilemma and in the interest of building strength for the future, it may have to absorb start-up losses to the detriment of current profitability.

"We are fortunate that the group starts from a sound financial base (shareholders' funds increased by 26% last year to $2.5 billion) with a spread of solid core businesses. Otherwise we could not undertake this enormous regional expansion strategy with its initial strain on capital resources (both financial and human) but which will be the basis on which we can look ahead with confidence to growth as we approach the turn of the century."

PERFORMANCE

Fraser and Neave gets high marks for growth and an overall score of 80 points in our grading system. Over the last ten years, revenues in dollars and EBDIT increased every year, with compound annual growth of 33% and 30%, respectively. EPS in dollars increased in nine of the last ten years, with compound annual growth of just under 22%. The share price in dollars increased at a compound annual rate of 17%. ROE averaged a less impressive 9% during the ten years. And the long-term debt to total capital ratio averaged 18% (though it jumped to 44% in 1996, when the company invested heavily in its own infrastructure).

If you had invested $10,000 in Fraser and Neave in September 1986, you would have purchased around 1,900 shares at about $5.25 each (excluding commissions). During the following ten years, there were a two-for-five rights issue in September 1988, a one-for-five rights issue in April 1993, and a one-for-five bonus issue in March 1996. By September 1996, you would have had around 4,800 shares worth an estimated $49,500. You would also have received dividend payments of around $3,600.

FRASER AND NEAVE

Ticker Symbol and Exchange: FRNVF—OTC   **SEDOL Code: 6350602**

OPERATING AND PER SHARE DATA
(in millions of Singaporean dollars and dollars per share)

	Sep 86	Sep 87	Sep 88	Sep 89	Sep 90	Sep 91	Sep 92	Sep 93	Sep 94	Sep 95	Sep 96	CAGR
Sales	246	811	1,002	1,163	1,080	1,169	1,248	1,302	2,087	2,533	2,811	27.6%
EBDIT	63.0	140.0	167.0	189.0	176.0	233.0	252.0	274.0	398.0	498.0	546.0	24.1%
Net Profit	31.0	41.0	50.0	63.0	53.0	57.0	72.0	83.0	134.0	185.0	218.0	21.5%
EPS	0.15	0.20	0.24	0.27	0.23	0.25	0.31	0.34	0.50	0.65	0.75	17.2%
DPS	0.07	0.07	0.07	0.09	0.09	0.10	0.10	0.11	0.13	0.14	0.18	9.9%

OPERATING AND PER SHARE DATA
(in millions of U.S. dollars and dollars per share)

	Sep 86	Sep 87	Sep 88	Sep 89	Sep 90	Sep 91	Sep 92	Sep 93	Sep 94	Sep 95	Sep 96	CAGR
Sales	113	388	491	593	614	696	785	824	1,410	1,784	2,008	33.3%
EBDIT	29.0	67.0	81.9	96.4	100.0	138.7	158.5	173.4	268.9	350.7	390.0	29.7%
Net Profit	14.3	19.6	24.5	32.1	30.1	33.9	45.3	52.5	90.5	130.3	155.7	27.0%
EPS	0.07	0.10	0.12	0.14	0.13	0.15	0.19	0.22	0.34	0.46	0.53	22.4%
DPS	0.03	0.03	0.04	0.05	0.05	0.06	0.06	0.07	0.08	0.10	0.13	14.8%

KEY RATIOS

	Sep 86	Sep 87	Sep 88	Sep 89	Sep 90	Sep 91	Sep 92	Sep 93	Sep 94	Sep 95	Sep 96	AVG
EBDIT Margin	25.6%	17.3%	16.7%	16.3%	16.3%	19.9%	20.2%	21.0%	19.1%	19.7%	19.4%	19%
ROE	9.0%	10.0%	11.0%	11.0%	8.0%	8.0%	8.0%	7.0%	8.0%	10.0%	10.0%	9%
LT Debt/Total Cap	2.0%	−9.0%	10.0%	−11.0%	−5.0%	51.0%	52.0%	31.0%	13.0%	20.0%	44.0%	18%
P/E (Projected)	22.8	17.9	14.6	28.5	20.0	21.3	25.1	29.7	19.6	19.6	23.0	22.0

STOCK PRICE CHART
(fiscal year-end closing price, in U.S. dollars, adjusted for capital changes)

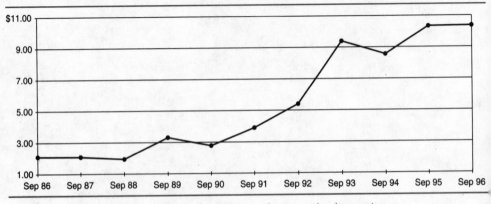

Note: Figures in U.S. dollars are translated from local currency using year-end exchange rates.

FRESENIUS MEDICAL CARE (FMS—NYSE)

Address: 61343 Bad Homburg v.d.H. / Germany
Tel.: (011) 49 61 71 67 0   **Fax:** (011) 49 61 71 60 24 88

BASIC INFORMATION

Country: Germany
Industry: Health care
Investment thesis: The largest fully integrated provider of dialysis services in the world

Market capitalization: $4.15 billion
Share status: ADRs trade on NYSE

COMPANY GRADING BOX

Growth Categories		Quality of Management	
Revenue Growth	20	Return on Equity	0
Operating Income Growth	20	**Risk**	
Earnings per Share Growth	20	Long-Term Debt/Total Capital	10
Share Price Growth	15	**Total QM&R (maximum 20)**	**10**
Total Growth (maximum 80)	**75**	**FINAL GRADE**	**85**

BACKGROUND

Fresenius Medical Care is a leading manufacturer, distributor, and service provider of medical products and systems used in the treatment of kidney failure. Its products do what the kidneys are supposed to do, cleansing a patient's blood of waste products and fluids. With the company's 1996 merger with National Medical Care—the largest provider of dialysis services in the world—Fresenius consolidated its position in the U.S. market and gave itself a platform for further growth. Today it is the largest vertically integrated dialysis company worldwide, with more than 32,521 employees (80% outside Germany), operations in more than twenty-four countries, and 1996 revenues of $3 billion. The company treats more than 56,000 dialysis patients in around 770 centers all over the world.

Fresenius's extensive research efforts are focused on advancing all aspects of the treatment of kidney failure—everything from decreasing the risk from blood donations to increasing its own manufacturing capabilities, improving the feeds used as supplementary nutrition for patients who have lost their appetites, and lowering costs without compromising quality. Fresenius, which began eighty years ago as a Frankfurt pharmacy, is also still actively expanding all over the world; in 1996 the company bought a Mexican infusions and medical business and signed a tentative collaboration with a British company to expand one part of its dialysis business.

COMPANY STATEMENT (from the 1996 annual report)

"Today, Fresenius is a health care company operating worldwide with products and services for dialysis, the hospital and home care, i.e. the care of patients who are discharged from the hospital and still require medical care at home.

"In the Project Business, Fresenius offers engineering, management and other services for hospitals and the pharmaceutical and medical disposables industry worldwide. We consider these fields to be our core competencies.

"Our target is to grow through the continued expansion of the basis for international operations, through alliances, through an innovative product range and through excellent services. The markets in which we operate are mainly managed locally by our entrepreneurs within the company. This ensures closer customer relations and secures the flexibility of the company."

PERFORMANCE

Fresenius's restated numbers (reflecting the 1996 merger of Fresenius and National Care) go back only as far as 1992; thus our pre-1992 figures are for the old Fresenius only and are not strictly comparable. Even so, we included them to give some illustration of the quality of this company's management and the longevity of its track record. That said, Fresenius Medical Care received an overall score of 85 points with top marks for revenue, EBDIT, and EPS growth and a low long-term debt to total capital ratio.

In dollars, revenues and EBDIT increased in every one of the last ten years, with compound annual growth of 25% and 24%, respectively. EP/ADR in dollars increased in nine of the last ten years, with compound annual growth of 16%. The ADR price in dollars increased at a compound annual rate of 23%—not doing a whole lot for a number of years, then increasing sixfold since 1993. Fresenius lost points with an average ROE of 11%; however, ROE increased from 4% in 1989 to 18% in 1996. The long-term debt to total capital ratio averaged a very comfortable 15%.

If you had invested $10,000 in Fresenius at the end of 1986, you would have purchased around 95 ADRs (or ADR equivalents) at about $105 each (excluding commissions). Among the capital changes over the next ten years, there were a one-for-three rights issue in July 1992, a one-for-eight bonus issue in May 1994, and a ten-for-one stock split in December 1995. At the end of 1996, you would have had around 1,170 ADRs worth an estimated $79,600. You would also have received dividend payments of around $2,800.

FRESENIUS MEDICAL CARE

Ticker Symbol and Exchange: FMS—NYSE **CUSIP No.: 358029106**

OPERATING AND PER SHARE DATA
(in millions of German marks and marks per share)

	1986	1987	1988	1989	1990	1991	1992	1993	1994	1995	1996	CAGR
Sales	465	523	615	674	1,030	1,228	1,552	1,749	2,045	2,236	3,635	22.8%
EBDIT	56.5	62.9	71.2	67.3	105.9	120.0	139.3	162.3	200.7	259.0	404.0	21.7%
Net Profit	21.0	22.9	23.0	13.4	18.2	23.1	24.0	45.0	71.0	91.0	132.0	20.2%
EPS	1.91	2.09	2.10	0.98	1.33	1.69	1.90	2.85	3.90	5.17	7.05	14.0%
DPS	0.62	0.62	0.62	0.66	0.66	0.75	0.76	1.65	1.30	1.50	1.79	12.5%

OPERATING AND PER SHARE DATA
(in millions of U.S. dollars and dollars per ADR)

	1986	1987	1988	1989	1990	1991	1992	1993	1994	1995	1996	CAGR
Sales	242	333	347	399	691	808	958	1,005	1,319	1,553	2,330	25.4%
EBDIT	29.4	40.1	40.2	39.8	71.1	78.9	86.0	93.3	129.5	179.9	259.0	24.3%
Net Profit	10.9	14.6	13.0	7.9	12.2	15.2	14.8	25.9	45.8	63.2	84.6	22.7%
EP/ADR	0.33	0.44	0.40	0.19	0.30	0.37	0.39	0.55	0.84	1.20	1.51	16.3%
DP/ADR	0.11	0.13	0.12	0.13	0.15	0.16	0.16	0.32	0.28	0.35	0.38	12.6%

KEY RATIOS

	1986	1987	1988	1989	1990	1991	1992	1993	1994	1995	1996	AVG
EBDIT Margin	12.2%	12.0%	11.6%	10.0%	10.3%	9.8%	9.0%	9.3%	9.8%	11.6%	11.1%	10.6%
ROE	11.5%	12.3%	11.7%	4.0%	6.1%	7.8%	5.8%	10.5%	13.3%	15.5%	18.2%	10.6%
LT Debt/Total Cap	15.7%	13.6%	6.8%	9.7%	13.3%	14.4%	13.1%	20.3%	12.5%	11.6%	36.0%	15.2%
P/E (Projected)	23.6	19.3	41.4	32.3	19.5	19.3	12.1	13.6	14.5	19.4	27.9	22.1

STOCK PRICE CHART
(fiscal year-end closing price, in U.S. dollars, adjusted for capital changes)

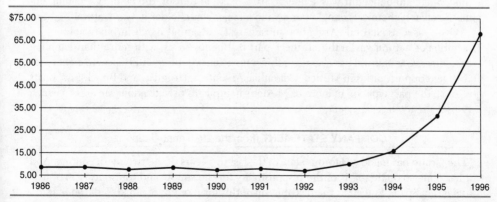

Note: Figures in U.S. dollars are translated from local currency using year-end exchange rates.

GAS NATURAL (CDGSF—OTC)

Address: Avenida Portal de l'Angel 22 / 08002 Barcelona / Spain
Tel.: (011) 34 402 51 00   **Fax:** (011) 34 402 58 70

BASIC INFORMATION

Country: Spain
Industry: Natural gas
Investment thesis: Leading supplier and distributor of natural gas in Spain

Market capitalization: $7.92 billion
Share status: Foreign shares trade OTC

COMPANY GRADING BOX

Growth Categories		Quality of Management	
Revenue Growth	20	Return on Equity	5
Operating Income Growth	20	**Risk**	
Earnings per Share Growth	20	Long-Term Debt/Total Capital	10
Share Price Growth	20	**Total QM&R (maximum 20)**	15
Total Growth (maximum 80)	80	**FINAL GRADE**	95

BACKGROUND

Natural gas is hardly a glamour industry, but for Spain's Gas Natural it has been very profitable. This company, with a market capitalization of $7.9 billion and $2.5 billion in sales in 1996, is the leading supplier and distributor of natural gas in Spain. And demand for natural gas—as a cleaner, more economical form of energy—continues to rise, particularly in Spain's industrial sector. In 1995 alone, Spanish consumption of natural gas rose 16%. And in all of western Europe, natural gas now represents more than 20% of energy consumption (although that percentage is much lower in Spain). To meet that growing demand and extend its reach, Gas Natural recently completed the Maghreb–Europe gas pipeline, running through the Iberian Peninsula. Gas Natural's gas distribution network is expected to cover 90% of the Spanish mainland by the year 2000 as opposed to 60% today.

Partially state owned into the mid-1990s, the Spanish government's public sector holding company sold off its remaining 3.8% stake in the company at the end of 1996. Forty percent of the shares were placed abroad and another 60% domestically (the first time a Spanish privatization was weighted toward the domestic market). At the same time, Spain announced it was selling its 10% stake in Repsol, the country's leading domestic oil and chemicals conglomerate and a major shareholder in Gas Natural.

Overseas, Gas Natural's Argentine subsidiary, Gas Natural Ban, is in charge of the distribution of natural gas in the northern part of Buenos Aires, with more than 1 million customers. Gas Natural has also recently set up a joint venture with Repsol to explore investment opportunities in Mexico, Colombia, Argentina, Uruguay, and Brazil. First on its agenda: the participation in more of Mexico's natural gas privatizations, an area in which Repsol already has experience.

COMPANY STATEMENT (from the 1995 annual report)

"The Group has made a vigorous start to the last five years of the twentieth century. And it has done so on the basis of the responsibility for the supply and transportation of natural gas in Spain, as well as the distribution of this form of energy to 90% of the market.

As you know, this means we rank fourth in Europe in terms of customers, second in terms of market capitalization and first in terms of growth rate. . . .

"The Gas Natural Group has a considerable market which is far from being saturated. We should also take into account the objectives laid down for natural gas in the National Energy Plan, 1991–2000 (PEN), revised at the end of 1995, and which foresee it enjoying a 12% share in primary-energy consumption in Spain by the end of the century.

"In order to cover the steady rise in demand for natural gas in the domestic-commercial and industrial markets, which in the revised PEN involves an increase of 12.6% in the level of consumption initially envisaged for the year 2000, we need an extensive transport infrastructure which, supplementing the already existing one, will be able to satisfy the growing demands of the market, in terms of both quantity and quality."

PERFORMANCE

Gas Natural is one of our top scorers, receiving 95 points in our grading system. EBDIT in dollars increased in each of the last ten years, with compound annual growth of 33%. Revenues and EPS in dollars increased in nine of the last ten years, with compound annual growth of 24% and 31%, respectively. Investors have been well rewarded: since 1987, the share price has increased at a compound annual rate of 32% and dividends have risen at a compound rate of 20%. The company also maintained an average dividend payout ratio of 27%, providing handsome income returns. The ratio of long-term debt to total capital was comfortable, averaging 24% for the ten-year period, although it moved up to 43% in 1996 as the company stepped up its expansion. On the other hand, ROE improved in the 1990s, hitting 18% in 1996, although it averaged 13% for the ten-year period.

If you had invested $10,000 in Gas Natural at the end of 1987, you would have purchased around 410 shares at about $24.25 each (excluding commissions). During the following nine-year period, there were a one-for-eight rights issue in April 1988 and a one-for-eight rights issue in June 1989. By the end of 1996, you would have had around 530 shares worth an estimated $121,000. You would also have received dividend payments of around $5,200.

GAS NATURAL

Ticker Symbol and Exchange: CDGSF—OTC   **SEDOL Code: 4179865**

OPERATING AND PER SHARE DATA
(in billions of Spanish pesetas and pesetas per share)

	1986	1987	1988	1989	1990	1991	1992	1993	1994	1995	1996	CAGR
Sales	37.1	38.5	42.5	44.9	56.0	86.1	100.6	155.3	213.2	290.1	328.4	24.4%
EBDIT	6.7	9.3	11.3	12.4	15.6	24.8	30.2	48.5	65.3	92.0	112.1	32.6%
Net Profit	1.5	3.2	4.4	7.6	9.0	9.9	14.2	21.5	23.9	35.8	47.3	40.8%
EPS	83.2	174.1	222.4	288.0	341.2	265.6	379.9	576.3	639.2	960.4	1,267.4	31.3%
DPS	38.7	47.4	57.8	65.0	98.0	98.0	108.0	128.0	150.0	200.0	238.6	20.0%

OPERATING AND PER SHARE DATA
(in millions of U.S. dollars and dollars per share)

	1986	1987	1988	1989	1990	1991	1992	1993	1994	1995	1996	CAGR
Sales	283	358	375	410	587	889	874	1,086	1,620	2,386	2,505	24.4%
EBDIT	51	86	100	113	164	256	263	339	496	757	855	32.6%
Net Profit	12	30	39	69	94	102	123	150	181	295	361	40.8%
EPS	0.63	1.62	1.96	2.63	3.57	2.74	3.30	4.03	4.86	7.90	9.67	31.3%
DPS	0.29	0.44	0.51	0.59	1.03	1.01	0.94	0.90	1.14	1.64	1.82	17.1%

KEY RATIOS

	1986	1987	1988	1989	1990	1991	1992	1993	1994	1995	1996	AVG
EBDIT Margin	18.0%	24.1%	26.6%	27.6%	27.9%	28.8%	30.1%	31.2%	30.6%	31.7%	34.1%	28.2%
ROE	6.2%	11.0%	12.6%	13.6%	15.1%	8.4%	11.3%	15.7%	12.1%	15.9%	18.3%	12.7%
LT Debt/Total Cap	22.9%	28.0%	33.6%	17.2%	9.2%	7.5%	6.7%	14.5%	39.7%	41.7%	43.3%	24.0%
P/E (Projected)	N/M	9.4	10.5	16.2	15.8	16.2	10.2	13.3	11.8	14.9	20.4	13.9

STOCK PRICE CHART
(fiscal year-end closing price, in U.S. dollars, adjusted for capital changes)

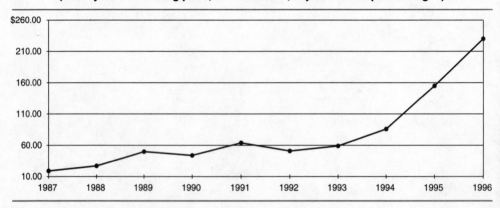

Note: Figures in U.S. dollars are translated from local currency using year-end exchange rates.

GEHE (GEHG.F—FRANKFURT)

Address: Neckartalstrasse 155 / 70376 Stuttgart / Germany
Tel.: (011) 49 71 1 50 01 00   **Fax:** (011) 49 71 1 50 01 500

BASIC INFORMATION

Country: Germany   **Market capitalization:** $5.03 billion
Industry: Health and personal care **Share status:** Foreign shares trade on Frankfurt Exchange
Investment thesis: One of the world's leading pharmaceutical wholesalers

COMPANY GRADING BOX

Growth Categories		Quality of Management	
Revenue Growth	20	Return on Equity	5
Pretax Profit Growth	20	**Risk**	
Earnings per Share Growth	20	Long-Term Debt/Total Capital	5
Share Price Growth	20	**Total QM&R (maximum 20)**	10
Total Growth (maximum 80)	80	**FINAL GRADE**	90

BACKGROUND

GEHE is a leading German pharmaceutical wholesale company with an interest in the mail-order business (specializing in office and warehouse equipment) as well as in health care services. Although the company is based in Stuttgart, about 73% of 1996 sales were generated outside Germany through operations in sixteen countries, primarily elsewhere in continental Europe and the U.K.

Most recently, GEHE has been building up its position in the United Kingdom, positioning itself to serve an aging population. GEHE's 1995 purchase of U.K.-based pharmaceutical wholesaler AAH gave it 30% of the British wholesale market and consolidated its role as a leading pharmaceutical wholesaler. In early 1997, GEHE also completed the purchase of U.K.-based Lloyd's Chemists, adding another 920 pharmacies and consolidating its role in the British pharmaceutical market (in the early 1990s, GEHE bought OCP Group in France, giving it a 41% share of the French market).

GEHE has continued to report impressive numbers despite pricing pressures all over Europe. Developing economies of scale within key markets, rationalizing businesses, developing new customer bases, and constantly improving service to existing customers are all elements of GEHE's so far successful business plan.

Although only a small percentage of GEHE's revenues come from the Healthcare Services Division, focusing on home care, the sector represents potential for growth. This two-year-old division is at the cusp of a new movement in international health care, the trend toward treating patients at home. Home care is considered a more caring and less expensive alternative to hospitals. And it is just catching on.

COMPANY STATEMENT (from the 1996 annual report)

"Pharmaceutical distribution has gained even more importance for GEHE than in the past. It is therefore more important than ever for us as market leader in Europe to understand the various structures of the health systems and the resulting market characteristics in the main countries of Europe, and take an active role in shaping changes, ensuring an exchange of experience thus gained among our subsidiaries and, where possible, utilizing this information for the good of our customers.

"Change is the order of the day in the healthcare markets in Central and Western European countries as it is in the large industrial nations, Japan and the USA. Here an interesting phenomenon can be observed: the cost of healthcare services has been increasing over the years in these countries to an extent that the statutory health insurance schemes, with the exception of the USA, are continually being plunged into new funding crises. Then, the most diverse government measures are introduced to curb costs (usually at the expense of the service supplier). In the short term this helps to close funding gaps but cannot solve the basic problem of the diverging income and expenditure of the statutory health insurers. . . .

"Apart from the less pleasant conclusion that we will all in future have to spend a higher proportion of our income on 'our most prized possession' (health) than in the past, you as a shareholder will also notice that GEHE is active in a market which, despite occasional turbulence, is likely to experience continuous growth in the long term."

PERFORMANCE

GEHE received top marks for both consistency and growth, scoring 90 points on our grading system. Revenues in dollars rose every year during the last ten and recorded compound growth of 28%. Pretax profit (operating income data for GEHE were incomplete) increased in eight of the ten years but grew faster than revenues, at 48% per annum. EPS increased in nine of the ten years and recorded compound growth of 26%, which is impressive but around half the rate recorded for pretax and net income growth owing to several rights issues that diluted EPS. GEHE lost a few points on ROE, which averaged a moderate 12.3% during the decade. It also scored low points for risk, where the firm had a long-term debt to total capital ratio averaging 35%.

Share price performance was particularly impressive, rising at a compound rate of 31% per annum during the ten-year period. The dividend payout ratio was also positive, averaging 30 to 40% of earnings and growing by about 18% per annum.

If you had invested $10,000 in GEHE in 1986, you would have purchased around 90 shares at about $110 each (excluding commissions). During the next ten years, GEHE had many corporate actions. The company had a one-for-five rights issue in 1987, a one-for-three rights issue in 1989, a one-for-ten rights issue in 1990, a one-for-one bonus issue in 1992, a one-for-five rights issue in 1993, a one-for-four rights issue in 1995, and a ten-for-one stock split in 1996. By the end of 1996, you would have had around 2,400 shares worth an estimated $152,000. You would also have received dividend payments of around $12,000.

GEHE

Ticker Symbol and Exchange: GEHG.F—Frankfurt   **SEDOL Code: 5105182**

OPERATING AND PER SHARE DATA
(in millions of German marks and marks per share)

	1986	1987	1988	1989	1990	1991	1992	1993	1994	1995	1996	CAGR
Sales	2,223	2,511	2,878	3,291	3,786	5,037	5,435	10,176	15,200	19,156	21,425	25.4%
Pretax Profit	21	34	65	90	109	175	175	184	235	335	847	44.9%
Net Profit	13	18	29	46	59	76	90	93	140	211	440	42.7%
EPS	0.69	0.80	1.06	1.19	1.38	1.78	1.86	1.90	2.49	3.26	3.75	18.4%
DPS	0.40	0.45	0.50	0.60	0.60	0.70	0.70	0.70	1.00	1.00	1.30	12.5%

OPERATING AND PER SHARE DATA
(in millions of U.S. dollars and dollars per share)

	1986	1987	1988	1989	1990	1991	1992	1993	1994	1995	1996	CAGR
Sales	1,158	1,599	1,626	1,947	2,541	3,314	3,355	5,848	9,806	13,303	13,734	28.1%
Pretax Profit	10.8	21.7	36.7	53.3	73.2	115.1	108.0	105.7	151.6	232.6	542.9	48.0%
Net Profit	6.6	11.5	16.4	27.2	39.6	50.0	55.6	53.4	90.3	146.5	282.1	45.7%
EPS	0.36	0.51	0.60	0.70	0.93	1.17	1.15	1.09	1.61	2.26	2.40	20.9%
DPS	0.21	0.29	0.28	0.36	0.40	0.46	0.43	0.40	0.65	0.69	0.83	14.9%

KEY RATIOS

	1986	1987	1988	1989	1990	1991	1992	1993	1994	1995	1996	AVG
Pretax Margin	0.9%	1.4%	2.3%	2.7%	2.9%	3.5%	3.2%	1.8%	1.5%	1.7%	4.0%	2.4%
ROE	10.3%	10.1%	16.3%	16.6%	11.7%	11.5%	13.0%	10.4%	11.2%	11.8%	12.8%	12.3%
LT Debt/Total Cap	45.0%	44.0%	43.0%	34.0%	22.7%	41.0%	31.0%	41.0%	40.0%	36.4%	7.8%	35.1%
P/E (Projected)	10.0	7.7	11.4	16.2	15.3	18.5	18.3	19.1	16.0	19.5	23.0	15.9

STOCK PRICE CHART
(fiscal year-end closing price, in U.S. dollars, adjusted for capital changes)

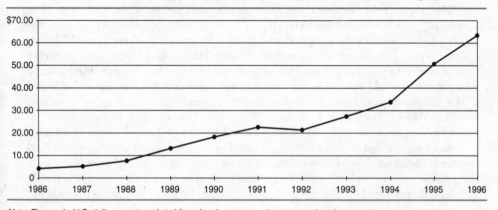

Note: Figures in U.S. dollars are translated from local currency using year-end exchange rates.

GRUMA (GRMBF—OTC)

Address: Paseo de la Reforma 300, 9th Piso / Colonia Juárez / Mexico D.F.
Tel.: (011) 52 8 335 99 00   **Fax:** (011) 52 8 399 33 59   **E-mail:** administracion@gruma.com

BASIC INFORMATION

Country: Mexico
Industry: Food and beverages
Investment thesis: Largest producer of corn in the Western Hemisphere

Market capitalization: $1.30 billion
Share status: Foreign shares trade OTC

COMPANY GRADING BOX

Growth Categories		Quality of Management	
Revenue Growth	20	Return on Equity	5
Operating Income Growth	20	**Risk**	
Earnings per Share Growth	0	Long-Term Debt/Total Capital	0
Share Price Growth	15	**Total QM&R (maximum 20)**	5
Total Growth (maximum 80)	55	**FINAL GRADE**	60

BACKGROUND

Mexico-based Gruma is the largest corn flour producer in the Western Hemisphere, dominating the industry in North America. It receives 50% of its revenues from Mexico, 40% from the United States, and 10% from Central America. Gruma is particularly strong in Mexico, where corn-based tortillas are a staple of life. Gruma has corn flour production plants in five Mexican cities, eleven distribution plants, and 16,000 employees, and generated just under $1.5 billion in revenues in 1996. The company is 22% owned by Archer Daniels Midland, the giant U.S. agricultural conglomerate.

Although tortillas have traditionally been made by using corn paste from boiled corn, the idea of starting with corn flour is catching on: it's less expensive and more efficient (producing more tortilla for the same amount of raw corn product). Corn flour–based tortillas still represent a relatively small percentage of the total tortilla production in Mexico, but that is changing rapidly. For the ten years leading up to 1994, the corn flour industry grew about 10% per annum; that number jumped to 20% in 1995 and 1996, as pressure grew on tortilla producers to bring down costs (supermarkets have been taking market share from corner stores). Gruma also produces prepackaged tortillas, a relatively small business in Mexico but one with plenty of potential.

One caveat: the government subsidizes tortilla consumption in Mexico by providing low-cost corn to the industry, which in turn sells low-priced tortillas to the consumer. Recently these subsidies were capped, and there is no guarantee these caps will be removed, as the government intends to gradually switch to a welfare-based system providing relief directly to poor people. Such a change would be better for Gruma's business in the long run, as it would encourage the more efficient use of corn flour, as opposed to boiled corn, for tortilla production. But in the short run, it could cause earnings to be volatile.

Then there is Gruma's U.S. business. Thirty-nine percent of Gruma's revenues are generated in the United States, where corn and wheat tortillas make up a $1.8 billion market. Over the last few years, Mexican food has been the fastest-growing ethnic food in the United States, and Gruma's Mission Foods (corn chips, tortillas, tacos, salsa, etc.) is considered a market leader. No competitors come close to its 18% share of the tortilla market. Prepackaged tortillas are particularly popular in the United States. In addition, an estimated 70% of all commercial corn tortillas made in the United States are made from flour, and 46% of that flour is supplied by Gruma.

Finally, Gruma also has operations in Central America, where the corn flour industry as a whole represents about 9% of the tortilla market, leaving plenty of room for growth. Today, Central America accounts for about 6% of Gruma's revenues.

COMPANY STATEMENT (from the 1995 annual report)

"In our efforts to be the lowest-cost producer, we continued our strategy of constantly improving our technologies, which are the most advanced in the corn-flour and tortilla industries. Since 1993, we have focused our investment programs and management resources on our core product lines of corn flour and tortillas while divesting non-core businesses. . . . We also continued establishing a base for future growth by building the infrastructure for increased capacity, adding production at our existing facilities. This strategy will reduce future investments needed to expand our corn-flour and tortilla operations, while allowing the Group to increase operating income faster than revenues.

"We are proud to be the world leaders in the corn-flour and tortilla industries. These product categories are expected to grow at rates higher than those of other sectors of the food industry in all areas in which we operate. We will continue to build on the basic principles that have enabled us to achieve this leadership: long-term vision; developing our own state-of-the-art technology, strengthening of our brand names; a strong emphasis on distribution; a commitment to product quality; and the integration of executives from diverse cultures and nationalities into our operations, all of which contribute to the fulfillment of our company's mission."

PERFORMANCE
(Gruma went public in 1994; however, we are using operating numbers going back to 1991)

Gruma received an overall grade of 60 in our grading system, based on its share price performance since the company went public in 1994, and on its operating numbers going back to 1991. Gruma got top scores for growth, with revenues in dollars having compound annual growth of 16% and increasing in four of the last five years (year-over-year revenues in dollars declined in 1994, the year the peso was devalued). EBDIT had compound annual growth of 23%. EPS in dollars, cut in half in 1994, still showed compound annual growth of 11%. In dollars, share price performance has been excellent (though brief), showing compound annual growth of 26%. The share price increased from a low of $2.21 in 1995 to a high of $6.45 in 1996. ROE averaged 16% and was 14% in 1996. The risk profile has improved over the years: the long-term debt to total capital ratio averaged 40% between 1991 and 1996 but was 25% in 1996.

If you had invested $10,000 in Gruma at the end of 1994, you would have purchased around 2,410 shares at about $4.12 each (excluding commissions). During the next two years, there were a one-for-fifty bonus issue in April 1995 and a one-for-twenty bonus issue in May 1996. By the end of 1996, you would have had around 2,600 shares worth an estimated $15,800. You would also have received dividend payments of around $200.

GRUMA

Ticker Symbol and Exchange: GRMBF—OTC   **SEDOL Code: 2392545**

OPERATING AND PER SHARE DATA
(in millions of nominal Mexican pesos and pesos per share)

	1986	1987	1988	1989	1990	1991	1992	1993	1994	1995	1996	CAGR
Sales	N/A	N/A	N/A	N/A	N/A	2,179	2,875	3,238	4,045	7,656	11,738	40.0%
EBDIT	N/A	N/A	N/A	N/A	N/A	210	232	443	329	1,393	1,500	48.2%
Net Profit	N/A	N/A	N/A	N/A	N/A	140	137	317	202	1,064	1,002	48.2%
EPS	N/A	N/A	N/A	N/A	N/A	0.82	0.65	1.38	0.82	4.25	3.58	34.3%
DPS	N/A	N/A	N/A	N/A	N/A	N/A	N/A	N/A	0.12	0.14	0.24	42.3%

OPERATING AND PER SHARE DATA
(in millions of U.S. dollars and dollars per share)

	1986	1987	1988	1989	1990	1991	1992	1993	1994	1995	1996	CAGR
Sales	N/A	N/A	N/A	N/A	N/A	710	921	1,041	826	997	1,493	16.0%
EBDIT	N/A	N/A	N/A	N/A	N/A	68.4	74.4	142.4	67.1	181.4	190.8	22.8%
Net Profit	N/A	N/A	N/A	N/A	N/A	45.6	43.9	101.9	41.2	138.5	127.5	22.8%
EPS	N/A	N/A	N/A	N/A	N/A	0.27	0.21	0.44	0.17	0.55	0.46	11.3%
DPS	N/A	N/A	N/A	N/A	N/A	N/A	N/A	N/A	0.02	0.02	0.03	12.4%

KEY RATIOS

	1986	1987	1988	1989	1990	1991	1992	1993	1994	1995	1996	AVG
EBDIT Margin	N/A	N/A	N/A	N/A	N/A	9.6%	8.1%	13.7%	8.1%	18.2%	12.8%	11.7%
ROE	N/A	N/A	N/A	N/A	N/A	14.3%	10.4%	18.0%	7.4%	29.7%	13.6%	15.6%
LT Debt/Total Cap	N/A	N/A	N/A	N/A	N/A	35.2%	45.4%	39.8%	43.0%	49.0%	24.7%	39.5%
P/E (Projected)	N/A	N/A	N/A	N/A	N/A	N/A	N/A	N/A	7.0	6.0	20.4	11.1

STOCK PRICE CHART
(fiscal year-end closing price, in U.S. dollars, adjusted for capital changes)

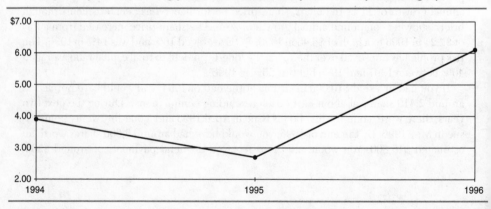

Notes: Gruma shares were listed on the Mexican stock exchange in 1994. Only a few years of data are available. Figures in U.S. dollars are translated from local currency using year-end exchange rates.

HAGEMEYER (HMYEF—OTC)

Address: Rijksweg 69 / P.O. Box 5111 / 1410 AC Naarden / Netherlands
Tel.: (011) 31 35 695 76 11   **Fax:** (011) 31 35 694 43 96

BASIC INFORMATION

Country: Netherlands
Industry: Multi-industry
Investment thesis: A classic Dutch trading firm—everything from auto parts to gourmet foods

Market capitalization: $3.39 billion
Share status: Foreign shares trade OTC

COMPANY GRADING BOX

Growth Categories		Quality of Management	
Revenue Growth	20	Return on Equity	10
Operating Income Growth	20	**Risk**	
Earnings per Share Growth	20	Long-Term Debt/Total Capital	10
Share Price Growth	20	**Total QM&R (maximum 20)**	**20**
Total Growth (maximum 80)	**80**	**FINAL GRADE**	**100**

BACKGROUND

Hagemeyer, based in the Netherlands, is a worldwide trading company with operations in businesses from automotive parts to commercial vehicles to gourmet foods. Founded in 1900 and public since 1937, it is a company built on a national mercantile tradition, home to a number of old Dutch trading houses. It has a market capitalization of $3.4 billion, does business in forty countries, and has 22,000 employees. Growth has been organic and by acquisition and is likely to continue.

Forty-five percent of Hagemeyer's revenues come from the distribution of "electrotechnical" materials, including specialist cable and lighting products. Thirty-six percent of revenues come from its consumer division, including its HCL subsidiary, which represents—acting as an exclusive agent or licensee—such well-known brand names as Bally, Rolex, and General Electric in the Far East. Originally part of a joint venture, Hagemeyer bought out its Swiss partner in 1996. Hagemeyer's Consumer Group also includes a leading retailer (and trading company) in Latin America and a division that develops and distributes small gifts and promotional items (many of which are manufactured in the People's Republic of China) throughout Europe and the United States.

Then there is the specialty foods group, accounting for an estimated 11% of revenues, which distributes gourmet and ethnic foods to retailers all over North America. Finally, there are the electrical distribution group and the automotive and technical products groups. The former distributes electrical equipment in Europe and the United Kingdom (brand names Hagemeyer works with include Panasonic, Samsung, Olympus, and Fuji); the latter handles the marketing, sales, and distribution of cars and automotive products in Europe.

Now, that's diversification.

COMPANY STATEMENT (from the 1996 annual report)

"Hagemeyer is committed to optimizing value for its stakeholders by establishing, maintaining and further building prominent positions in selected markets as a specialist international marketing, sales and distribution group.

"The sustainability and predictability of financial results is enhanced by diversified product categories in combination with geographic spread. The Group's activities are predominantly multi-principal whilst diversification through geographic and product mix counterbalances product and economic cycles, currency fluctuations and seasonal influences which are typical of trading activities.

"The company's growth policy is directed toward achieving and maintaining the critical mass required to occupy prominent positions in each of its markets and to support a quality of infrastructure throughout the Group. The pursuit of a high level organic growth is complemented by focused acquisitions. Criteria evaluated when considering potential acquisitions include strategic fit, quality of management and contributions to earnings per share. The principal financial objective of Hagemeyer is to continue to realize a steady improvement in return to shareholders while maintaining a well balanced capital structure."

PERFORMANCE

Hagemeyer is one of our star companies, receiving a maximum score of 100 points in our grading system. The company has been a model of consistency, with revenues, EBITDA, and EPS increasing every year over the last ten years while the share price finished higher in eight out of the ten years. At the same time, growth has been strong, with revenues, EBITDA, EPS, and share prices increasing at compound annual rates of 24%, 29%, 18%, and 25%, respectively. Moreover, quality of earnings was not sacrificed for growth, as management achieved an average ROE of 21% over the ten-year period. Neither did it take undue risk to achieve this growth, as evidenced by an average long-term debt to total capital ratio of 22%. There is not much to say other than hats off to an outstanding performance.

Investors have clearly been appreciative of Hagemeyer's performance. The share price increased from a low of $5.50 in 1986 to a high of $81.61 in 1996. Dividends increased from $0.32 in 1986 to $1.31 in 1996, with compound growth of 15%, while the company maintained a payout ratio of 38% during the decade.

If you had invested $10,000 in Hagemeyer at the end of 1986, you would have purchased around 280 shares at about $35 each (excluding commissions). During the following ten years, Hagemeyer had a two-for-one stock split in 1993 and a two-for-one stock split in 1995. By the end of 1996, you would have had around 1,140 shares worth an estimated $90,600. You would also have received around $9,000 in dividend payments.

HAGEMEYER

Ticker Symbol and Exchange: HMYEF—OTC   **SEDOL Code: 4414168**

OPERATING AND PER SHARE DATA
(in millions of Dutch guilders and guilders per share)

	1986	1987	1988	1989	1990	1991	1992	1993	1994	1995	1996	CAGR
Sales	1,216	1,277	1,693	2,269	2,483	2,930	3,369	3,871	4,726	5,722	8,216	21.1%
EBITDA	58	62	102	149	165	196	245	263	317	403	573	25.7%
Net Profit	25	31	46	61	74	85	102	123	147	193	285	27.7%
EPS	1.60	1.92	2.55	2.74	2.99	3.33	3.73	4.38	5.10	5.78	6.59	15.2%
DPS	0.70	0.78	0.90	1.00	1.13	1.42	1.50	1.62	1.80	2.00	2.28	12.5%

OPERATING AND PER SHARE DATA
(in millions of U.S. dollars and dollars per share)

	1986	1987	1988	1989	1990	1991	1992	1993	1994	1995	1996	CAGR
Sales	558	721	848	1,188	1,478	1,713	1,851	1,985	2,732	3,554	4,722	23.8%
EBITDA	27	35	51	78	98	115	135	135	183	250	329	28.5%
Net Profit	11	18	23	32	44	50	56	63	85	120	164	30.6%
EPS	0.73	1.08	1.28	1.43	1.78	1.95	2.05	2.25	2.95	3.59	3.79	17.8%
DPS	0.32	0.44	0.45	0.52	0.67	0.83	0.82	0.83	1.04	1.24	1.31	15.1%

KEY RATIOS

	1986	1987	1988	1989	1990	1991	1992	1993	1994	1995	1996	AVG
EBITDA Margin	4.8%	4.9%	6.0%	6.6%	6.6%	6.7%	7.3%	6.8%	6.7%	7.0%	7.0%	6.4%
ROE	14.3%	18.7%	14.5%	16.7%	19.7%	20.1%	22.7%	30.0%	30.9%	21.9%	23.4%	21.2%
LT Debt/Total Cap	13.0%	32.6%	12.0%	11.1%	8.8%	16.4%	18.5%	31.1%	38.9%	28.5%	29.6%	21.9%
P/E (Projected)	9.9	4.4	6.9	9.4	7.7	8.3	6.9	12.2	12.2	12.7	17.9	9.9

STOCK PRICE CHART
(fiscal year-end closing price, in U.S. dollars, adjusted for capital changes)

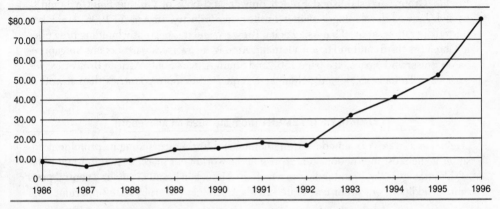

Note: Figures in U.S. dollars are translated from local currency using year-end exchange rates.

HEINEKEN (HINKY—OTC)

Address: Tweede Weteringplantsoen 21/ 1017 ZD Amsterdam / Netherlands
or
Address: P.O. Box 28, 1000 AA Amsterdam / Netherlands
Tel.: (011) 31 20 523 9239   **Fax:** (011) 31 20 626 3503   **Web site:** http://www.heineken.nl

BASIC INFORMATION

Country: Netherlands
Industry: Brewing
Investment thesis: A world powerhouse in the brewing industry

Market capitalization: $8.68 billion
Share status: ADRs trade OTC

COMPANY GRADING BOX

Growth Categories		Quality of Management	
Revenue Growth	10	Return on Equity	5
Operating Income Growth	5	**Risk**	
Earnings per Share Growth	10	Long-Term Debt/Total Capital	10
Share Price Growth	15	**Total QM&R (maximum 20)**	15
Total Growth (maximum 80)	40	**FINAL GRADE**	55

BACKGROUND

Talk about an international company. With brand names such as Heineken, Amstel Light, and Murphy's Irish Stout to call its own, Netherlands-based Heineken is a world powerhouse in the brewery business. It was in 1864 that Gerard Adriaan Heineken bought the brewery De Hooiberg (founded in 1592), put his own name on it, and started expanding. Today, Heineken employs 31,682 people and is active in more than 170 countries. The Heineken brand is the leading beer in Europe and the leading import in the United States.

Heineken may be a company with a long history, but it's not one that is standing still. Facing increasing competition in its core European markets, Heineken has been aggressively expanding overseas as well as closer to home. By the end of 1995 Heineken had bought a 66% stake in the largest Slovakian brewery and malt works, had increased its interest in a Polish brewery, and had completed the integration of an Italian brewery. In 1996 Heineken became the market leader in Italy after buying Italian brewer Birra Moretti, while in France—where it was already number two—Heineken bought the Fischer Group, an established French brewer, and 66% of Groupe Saint-Arnould, a French brewer developing activities in the wine industry. In Asia in 1996, Heineken started operations at the Thai Asia Pacific Brewery, and it is currently building breweries in China (its third) and in Hanoi, Vietnam. Among its overseas partners are Singapore-based Fraser and Neave (see page 156), and South Africa's South African Breweries (see page 321). Heineken's slogan? "Heineken: requested in more countries than any other beer."

COMPANY STATEMENT (from the 1996 annual report)

"Heineken's strategy is aimed at strengthening and further expanding its prominent position as the most international enterprise in the world beer market. An important pillar of this strategy is the brand policy, in which the Heineken brand occupies a central position. In addition, our other corporate brands Amstel and Murphy's are important. The range is completed by a variety of national and regional brands. By offering a broad package of high-quality beers we can respond to the wishes of consumers.

"In canvassing the market, we concentrate primarily on strengthening our position in the premium segment, in which the Company has traditionally been well positioned. This policy offers good possibilities because the interest in premium beer is increasing worldwide—also in the more saturated markets—and furthermore better margins can be achieved in that segment. . . .

"The Company's good position and strong brands make it possible to maintain or reinforce its position in the existing markets and to further expand its presence in growth markets. It is Heineken's policy to enhance the Company's long-term profit potential by means of organic growth and acquisitions."

PERFORMANCE

Heineken's overall score in our grading system was 55 points, reflecting the increased competitiveness of its traditional markets and the company's efforts to expand geographically through acquisitions and investment. Even so, Heineken has been a very consistent performer, the kind of company whose growth rate might not knock your socks off but— if you're prone to worry a lot—might let you sleep better at night. Revenues and EPS in guilders both increased in nine of the last ten years (though the company lost some points when those numbers were translated into dollars), and Heineken's ROE, just over 14% in 1996, has improved every year since 1988. EBDIT increased in eight of the last ten years, with compound annual growth of 9%. The company also has a low risk profile: the long-term debt to total capital ratio averaged a very reasonable 11% during the decade. Heineken's ADR price performance has also been very consistent; the end-of-year ADR price rose every year since 1987, showing a compound annual growth rate of 17% for the same period.

If you had invested $10,000 in Heineken at the end of 1986, you would have purchased around 120 ADRs (or ADR equivalents) at about $82 each (excluding commissions). During the following ten years, there were a one-for-four bonus issue in January 1989 and two four-for-one bonus issues, one in April 1992 and one in April 1995. By the end of the ten-year period, you would have had around 240 ADRs worth an estimated $41,900. You would also have received around $3,500 in dividend payments.

HEINEKEN

Ticker Symbol and Exchange: HINKY—OTC   **CUSIP No.: 423012202**

OPERATING AND PER SHARE DATA
(in millions of Dutch guilders and guilders per share)

	1986	1987	1988	1989	1990	1991	1992	1993	1994	1995	1996	CAGR
Sales	5,626	6,552	7,175	7,677	8,082	8,534	8,748	8,838	9,744	10,144	12,189	8.0%
EBDIT	887	908	975	1,043	1,169	1,287	1,391	1,318	1,520	1,562	1,638	6.3%
Net Profit	285	287	291	325	366	410	463	519	603	664	655	8.7%
EPS	5.69	5.71	5.80	6.49	7.29	8.17	9.22	10.34	12.03	13.24	13.06	8.7%
DPS	1.79	1.79	1.79	2.24	2.24	2.24	2.80	2.80	2.80	3.50	3.50	6.9%

OPERATING AND PER SHARE DATA
(in millions of U.S. dollars and dollars per ADR)

	1986	1987	1988	1989	1990	1991	1992	1993	1994	1995	1996	CAGR
Sales	2,581	3,702	3,593	4,019	4,811	4,991	4,807	4,532	5,632	6,301	7,005	10.5%
EBDIT	407	513	488	546	696	752	764	676	878	970	941	8.7%
Net Profit	131	162	146	170	218	240	254	266	349	413	376	11.1%
EP/ADR	2.61	3.23	2.90	3.40	4.34	4.78	5.07	5.30	6.95	8.22	7.51	11.1%
DP/ADR	0.82	1.01	0.90	1.17	1.33	1.31	1.54	1.44	1.62	2.17	2.01	9.4%

KEY RATIOS

	1986	1987	1988	1989	1990	1991	1992	1993	1994	1995	1996	AVG
EBDIT Margin	15.8%	13.9%	13.6%	13.6%	14.5%	15.1%	15.9%	14.9%	15.6%	15.4%	13.4%	14.7%
ROE	12.7%	11.6%	10.5%	11.0%	11.6%	12.2%	12.7%	13.1%	13.9%	14.0%	14.5%	12.5%
LT Debt/Total Cap	14.6%	13.7%	13.5%	14.7%	12.3%	11.2%	9.9%	7.6%	7.5%	6.0%	10.7%	11.1%
P/E (Projected)	15.9	11.0	11.2	11.1	10.7	10.9	13.3	14.3	15.8	21.8	21.4	14.3

STOCK PRICE CHART
(fiscal year-end closing price, in U.S. dollars, adjusted for capital changes)

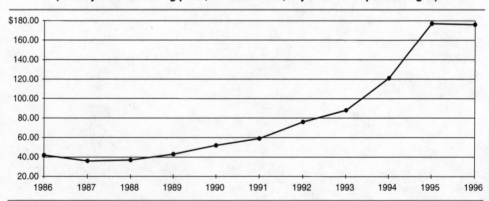

Note: Figures in U.S. dollars are translated from local currency using year-end exchange rates.

HELLENIC BOTTLING (HEBOF—OTC)

Address: Frangoklissias 9 / Marousi / 151 25 Athens / Greece
Tel.: (011) 30 1 61 83 100   **Fax:** (011) 30 1 68 95 515

BASIC INFORMATION

Country: Greece   **Market capitalization:** $1.8 billion
Industry: Food and beverages   **Share status:** Foreign shares trade OTC
Investment thesis: Dominant Coke bottler in Greece, Bulgaria and Armenia, expanding rapidly

COMPANY GRADING BOX

Growth Categories		Quality of Management	
Revenue Growth	20	Return on Equity	10
Operating Income Growth	20	**Risk**	
Earnings per Share Growth	0	Long-Term Debt/Total Capital	10
Share Price Growth	20	**Total QM&R (maximum 20)**	**20**
Total Growth (maximum 80)	**60**	**FINAL GRADE**	**80**

BACKGROUND

Hellenic Bottling serves up Coca-Cola in Greece, Bulgaria, Armenia and the Federal Republic of Yugoslavia and, through its recent merger with Molino Beverage Holding S.A., in the Republic of Ireland, Northern Ireland, part of Romania, Moldova, part of Russia and Nigeria. This $1.2-billion-dollar market capitalization (pre-merger) company got its start as a Coke bottler in 1969. Today Coke has just under 50% of the carbonated soft drink market in Hellenic Bottling's home market, Greece. And the bottler is still aggressively marketing Coca-Cola products (for example, Coca-Cola sponsors the Spartathlon, a running competition between Athens and Sparta.) Hellenic Bottling also bottles and distributes Sprite, Fanta and Nestea (the latest addition to its roster of Coke products). And it produces a few of its own offerings, including Greece's leading line of fruit juices (a market growing at about 10% annually) and bottled water. With the Molino merger, Hellenic Bottling's market for soft drinks increases from 33 million to 200 million people. Not bad.

In the early 1990s the company took some of that cash it's generating at home and began expanding. The company made its first big move into Bulgaria, where today it has 60% of the carbonated soft drink market.

In 1994, Hellenic Bottling also bought 50% of Brewinvest, the company which owns 87% of Bulgaria's largest brewer—the other 50% of Brewinvest is owned by Heineken's Greek affiliate, and the other 13% of the brewer is owned by the Bulgarian government. Then, in 1995, the company started operations in Armenia and through a joint venture, Coca-Cola Bottlers Armenia, the company took a long-term lease with the option to buy a previously state-run bottling plant. In late 1996, it was granted the franchise for the Federal Republic of Yugoslavia, where it acquired 68% of a privatized bottling company. It started operating there in early 1997. Finally, in 1997, Hellenic Bottling merged with Molino Beverage Holdings (in which it previously had a thirty percent stake), a company registered in Luxembourg with the Coca-Cola franchises in the Republic of Ireland, Northern Ireland, part of Romania, Moldova, part of Russia, and—most recently—Nigeria. It also bought 30% of Frigoglass S.A., a new company specializing in commercial coolers and packaging.

Not that Hellenic Bottling's business has always moved along smoothly. Like most of our "emerging markets" picks, this company operates in more volatile markets than its counterparts in developed countries (Bulgaria was particularly difficult in 1996). And it has a relatively short history as a public company. Even so, management has done an excellent job and the company has developed successfully into a multinational firm. After all, it has one of the world's great brand names.

COMPANY STATEMENT (from the 1996 annual report)

"Two elements mark our Group's performance in 1996. The positive aspect reflects our ambitious expansion into new geographical areas as well as related industrial activities. The negative dimension originates from the serious crisis of the Bulgarian economy, tangibly influencing our financial results in 1996.

"In terms of our geographic expansion, we completed negotiations for a bottling investment in the Federal Republic of Yugoslavia, whereby we acquired control and are incorporating into our Group operations the country's main soft drink industry located in Belgrade.

"Likewise, our affiliated company, Molino Beverage Holding, expanded its Russian bottling activities to include a total area of 42 million people. It is worth noting that The Coca-Cola Company will hold a minority equity interest in Molino's operations in Russia. Molino also acquired the majority shareholding of Nigerian Bottling Company, which bottles and distributes The Coca-Cola Company products in Africa's most populous nation."

PERFORMANCE

Hellenic Bottling received an overall score of 80 points in our grading system, with particularly high marks for revenue growth, share price growth and ROE. Revenues in dollars increased in eight of the last nine years, recording compound annual growth of 14%; the share price in dollars increased at a compound annual rate of 28% in the five years since the company went public. And ROE averaged a high 35%. The ratio of long-term debt to total capital was reasonable, averaging 20%—and was just 7% in 1996. Operating income plus depreciation (EBDIT) in dollars increased in seven of the last nine years, recording compound annual growth of 17%. Hellenic Bottling lost points only for its EPS growth rate—a compound rate of only 2% over the last nine years, due in part to the company's aggressive acquisition policy.

If you had invested $10,000 in Hellenic Bottling at the end of 1991, you would have purchased around 470 shares at about $21.25 each (excluding commissions). During the following five years, there were a one-for-two bonus issue in November 1992 and a one-for-two bonus issue in March 1995. By the end of 1996, you would have had around 1,060 shares worth an estimated $34,100. You would also have received dividend payments of around $6,500.

HELLENIC BOTTLING

Ticker Symbol and Exchange: HEBOF—OTC   **SEDOL Code: 4420723**

OPERATING AND PER SHARE DATA
(in billions of Greek drachmas and drachmas per share)

	1986	1987	1988	1989	1990	1991	1992	1993	1994	1995	1996	CAGR
Sales	N/A	22.2	31.7	40.7	48.5	61.3	94.0	120.6	143.8	143.7	143.1	23.0%
EBDIT	N/A	3.7	5.2	6.3	8.3	8.0	16.9	24.7	31.1	39.3	29.9	26.2%
Net Income	N/A	2.1	3.0	3.7	5.6	10.3	10.0	12.7	16.8	21.9	23.2	30.9%
EPS	N/A	192	285	192	293	401	389	494	435	566	451	9.9%
DPS	N/A	112	140	119	218	280	173	103	78	132	142	2.7%

OPERATING AND PER SHARE DATA
(in millions of U.S. dollars and dollars per share)

	1986	1987	1988	1989	1990	1991	1992	1993	1994	1995	1996	CAGR
Sales	N/A	177	215	259	310	350	437	483	599	606	580	14.1%
EBDIT	N/A	29.3	35.5	40.2	53.0	45.6	78.7	99.2	129.6	165.8	121.1	17.1%
Net Income	N/A	16.4	20.7	23.6	36.0	59.0	46.6	51.0	70.1	92.2	94.0	21.4%
EPS	N/A	1.53	1.93	1.23	1.87	2.29	1.81	1.98	1.81	2.39	1.83	2.0%
DPS	N/A	0.89	0.95	0.76	1.40	1.60	0.80	0.41	0.32	0.56	0.58	−4.7%

KEY RATIOS

	1986	1987	1988	1989	1990	1991	1992	1993	1994	1995	1996	AVG
EBDIT Margin	N/A	16.6%	16.5%	15.5%	17.1%	13.0%	18.0%	20.5%	21.6%	27.4%	20.9%	18.7%
ROE	N/A	N/M	N/M	N/M	N/M	43.6%	34.9%	33.7%	33.9%	38.0%	27.3%	35.2%
LT Debt/Total Cap	N/A	43.4%	27.8%	38.2%	30.4%	12.2%	14.8%	10.5%	7.7%	10.3%	6.8%	20.2%
P/E (Projected)	N/A	N/M	N/M	N/M	N/M	4.2	4.9	13.3	10.0	16.9	18.4	11.3

STOCK PRICE CHART
(fiscal year-end closing price, in U.S. dollars, adjusted for capital changes)

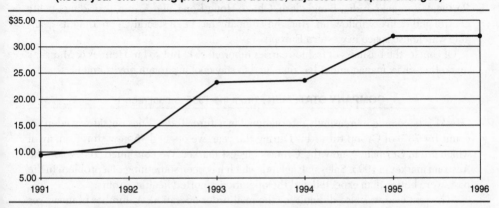

Note: Figures in U.S. dollars are translated from local currency using year-end exchange rates.

HENNES & MAURITZ (HMZBF—OTC)

Address: Jakobsbergsgatan 17 / Box 1421 / 111 84 Stockholm / Sweden
Tel.: (011) 46 8 796 55 00   **Fax:** (011) 46 8 248 078

BASIC INFORMATION

Country: Sweden   **Market capitalization:** $5.33 billion
Industry: Retailing, clothing   **Share status:** Foreign shares trade OTC
Investment thesis: A leading European fashion retailer

COMPANY GRADING BOX

Growth Categories		Quality of Management	
Revenue Growth	20	Return on Equity	10
Operating Income Growth	20	**Risk**	
Earnings per Share Growth	15	Long-Term Debt/Total Capital	10
Share Price Growth	20	**Total QM&R (maximum 20)**	**20**
Total Growth (maximum 80)	**75**	**FINAL GRADE**	**95**

BACKGROUND

Sweden as a fashion capital? Hennes & Mauritz, a Swedish chain, has taken European fashion retailing by storm. Just imagine fashion stores with the price points you would see at the Limited, or even Limited Express, in stores with a more hip "downtown" flavor— a chain a bit like Urban Outfitters or a slightly hipper Gap. The 450-plus stores are a magnet for the European teenage and twenty-something crowds. Stop by a Hennes & Mauritz store on almost any one of western Europe's busiest shopping streets on a Saturday afternoon, and the store will probably be packed.

Although Germany—with 100 stores—is by far Hennes & Mauritz's largest market outside Sweden, the fifty-year-old chain also has stores in Austria, Belgium, the Netherlands, Norway, Denmark, France, Switzerland, and the United Kingdom. In 1996 management opened sixty new stores throughout western Europe. This year, it plans to open another fifty—that despite the recent recessionary climate that has prevailed in much of Europe. As other retailers have been cutting back, Hennes & Mauritz has not only been expanding, it's been taking over prime retail real estate vacated by the competition. The chain does much of its buying through more than 200 representatives based in Turkey, Portugal, Romania, India, Bangladesh, China, Hong Kong, and Korea, providing quality control and delivery follow-up. And the company has been steadily increasing its available warehouse space in western Europe.

Of course, the business of fashion carries inherent risk. But so far, Hennes & Mauritz's marketing-savvy management has managed to stay cool in a tough environment.

COMPANY STATEMENT (from the 1995 annual report)

"H&M is becoming increasingly international in nature. Today, sales outside Sweden account for 73% of Group turnover. During the year, we opened 45 new stores, many of which are in Germany—now the Group's biggest market. We continued to develop the Austrian market in 1995. Sales in England, which has been something of a problem in the past, were better than expected and the operation reported healthy profits.

"The past year was also difficult for the mail-order operation. A number of measures are being planned to improve our competitive advantage, including coordinating purchasing activities with those of the rest of the Group to a greater extent than before.

"We did not enter any new countries during the year, nor do we plan to in 1996. We will, however, keep a close eye on what is happening in Europe. We must remember that our goal is not to open stores in as many countries as possible. Each new market has a new set of problems—and challenges, a fact we have learned in the 30 years that we have been operating internationally. Moreover, there is still a great deal to accomplish in our existing markets.

"From the factory, to the port, to the warehouse and distribution to the store, logistics is playing an increasingly important role. The more the different links in the chain understand one another, the smoother the process and the greater the profit for the Group and the customer alike. . . .

"H&M continues to grow. We currently have some 400 stores in nine countries. Still, we must strive to remain small, as well. Our competitors are often small companies with a strong local presence. We must act locally without giving up our economies of scale and the Group profile that customers associate with H&M."

PERFORMANCE

Hennes & Mauritz is one of our top scorers, having received 95 points in our grading system. In an industry defined by trends, it has been remarkably consistent. Revenues in dollars increased in nine of the last ten years, with compound annual growth of 14%. EBDIT rose in eight of the last ten years (and in every one of the last seven years), with compound annual growth of 22%. EPS in dollars were less consistent but still increased at a compound annual rate of 20%. And the share price, up in each of the last seven years, increased at a compound annual rate of 28%. ROE, 25.8% in 1996, averaged a very impressive 24.3% for the decade. As for risk, the long-term debt to total capital ratio steadily declined from 18% in 1990 to 0.8% in 1996.

If you had invested $10,000 in Hennes & Mauritz in November 1986, you would have purchased around 170 shares at about $58 each (excluding commissions). During the following ten years, there were several small capital changes and a five-for-one stock split in June 1992. By November 1996, you would have had around 860 shares worth an estimated $121,900. You would also have received around $5,600 in dividend payments.

HENNES & MAURITZ

Ticker Symbol and Exchange: HMZBF—OTC   SEDOL Code: 4408224

OPERATING AND PER SHARE DATA
(in millions of Swedish kronor and kronor per share)

	Nov 86	Nov 87	Nov 88	Nov 89	Nov 90	Nov 91	Nov 92	Nov 93	Nov 94	Nov 95	Nov 96	CAGR
Sales	3,763	4,275	4,502	4,703	5,593	6,370	8,080	9,790	11,548	12,350	14,553	14.5%
EBDIT	289	333	304	193	349	623	951	1,258	1,636	1,424	2,071	21.8%
Net Profit	183	210	203	110	200	393	652	823	1,067	973	1,331	21.9%
EPS	5.03	5.61	5.43	2.93	5.34	10.50	17.43	19.90	25.80	23.52	32.16	20.4%
DPS	0.76	0.90	1.00	1.00	1.40	2.80	3.82	6.00	7.75	7.75	11.00	30.6%

OPERATING AND PER SHARE DATA
(in millions of U.S. dollars and dollars per share)

	Nov 86	Nov 87	Nov 88	Nov 89	Nov 90	Nov 91	Nov 92	Nov 93	Nov 94	Nov 95	Nov 96	CAGR
Sales	552	740	737	759	993	1,148	1,141	1,174	1,554	1,860	2,121	14.4%
EBDIT	42	58	50	31	62	112	134	151	220	214	302	21.7%
Net Profit	27	36	33	18	35	71	92	99	144	147	194	21.8%
EPS	0.74	0.97	0.89	0.47	0.95	1.89	2.46	2.39	3.47	3.54	4.69	20.3%
DPS	0.11	0.16	0.16	0.16	0.25	0.50	0.54	0.72	1.04	1.17	1.60	30.6%

KEY RATIOS

	Nov 86	Nov 87	Nov 88	Nov 89	Nov 90	Nov 91	Nov 92	Nov 93	Nov 94	Nov 95	Nov 96	AVG
EBDIT Margin	7.7%	7.8%	6.8%	4.1%	6.2%	9.8%	11.8%	12.8%	14.2%	11.5%	14.2%	9.7%
ROE	26.2%	23.7%	19.9%	10.4%	16.8%	26.4%	32.6%	30.1%	31.0%	24.7%	25.8%	24.3%
LT Debt/Total Cap	14.4%	13.8%	16.4%	17.4%	18.1%	13.1%	11.4%	1.1%	0.9%	1.1%	0.8%	9.8%
P/E (Projected)	14.1	9.9	21.8	8.6	4.9	5.7	6.6	9.4	16.7	12.7	28.1	12.6

STOCK PRICE CHART
(fiscal year-end closing price, in U.S. dollars, adjusted for capital changes)

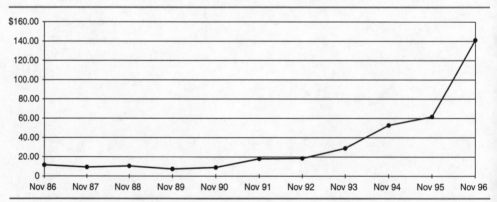

Note: Figures in U.S. dollars are translated from local currency using year-end exchange rates.

HSBC HOLDINGS (HSBHY—OTC)

Address: 10 Lower Thames Street / London EC3R 6AE / United Kingdom
Tel.: (011) 44 171 260 0500 **Fax:** (011) 44 171 260 0501 **Web site:** http://www.hsbcgroup.com

BASIC INFORMATION

Country: United Kingdom
Industry: Financial services
Investment thesis: Global force in the financial industry; 30% of revenues from Asia

Market capitalization: $61.3 billion
Share status: ADRs trade on NASDAQ

COMPANY GRADING BOX

Growth Categories		Quality of Management	
Revenue Growth	20	Return on Equity	5
Gross Profit	20	Return on Assets	0
Earnings per Share Growth	20	**Total QM (maximum 20)**	**5**
Share Price Growth	15		
Total Growth (maximum 80)	**75**	**FINAL GRADE**	**80**

BACKGROUND

HSBC Holdings—parent of the Hongkong and Shanghai Banking Corporation—has actually been based in London since 1993; however, with well over a third of its profits derived from its Hong Kong businesses and a history that is intrinsically linked to the former British colony, it remains an Asian powerhouse. Even so, it has an international reach rivaling U.S.-based Citicorp, with long-established businesses in Europe, the Middle East, and the Americas, as well as the Asia-Pacific region. By March 1997 HSBC's network extended to more than 5,000 offices, with over 120,000 employees in seventy-eight countries. Assets amounted to $402 billion at year-end 1996, making it one of the world's largest banking and financial services organizations. The 1997 "Asian Contagion" took its toll, but this is one company that has weathered many crises, survived and then prospered again.

This is no newcomer to the world of finance. The original Hongkong and Shanghai Banking Corporation (Hongkong Bank) was founded in Hong Kong in 1865 (the company's relatively new, billion-dollar Hong Kong headquarters was built at the same address as that first Hong Kong office). One month later, the bank opened its first Shanghai office. In the ensuing years Hongkong Bank pioneered modern banking practices throughout Asia, opening branches all over the region. The bank weathered years of political turmoil throughout Asia (the chairman has been quoted saying that Hongkong Bank has been kicked out of more countries than Citicorp has ever been in) to retain its status as a preeminent Asian bank.

In the second half of this century, management has worked hard to diversify the company's revenue base. Toward that end, HSBC bought the British Bank of the Middle East in 1959, set up a subsidiary in Canada in 1986, bought U.K.-based James Capel and Midland Bank in 1992, and bought U.S.-based Marine Midland Bank (a stake in 1980; the rest in 1987). In 1997, HSBC bought a financial services holding company in Argentina and a bank in Brazil. The company also diversified within Asia. Among those purchases, HSBC bought a majority stake in a Hong Kong retail bank in 1965. Today, the HSBC Group offers personal and corporate banking, trade services, private banking, investment banking, treasury and capital markets services, consumer and business finance, pension and investment fund management, trustee services, securities and custody services, and insurance.

There is no question that this company has thrived in Hong Kong's favorable regulatory and interest rate climate (among other things, savings deposit rates in Hong Kong are well below bank mortgage rates) and that future political developments in Hong Kong under Chinese rule will have an effect on the bank's future. But this is one company that has had to adapt before and has come through with flying colors.

COMPANY STATEMENT (from the 1996 annual report)

"As the Group Chairman noted in his commentary, 1 July is an historic date for Hong Kong as it becomes a Special Administrative Region of the People's Republic of China. Hong Kong's economic fundamentals remain sound. The banking market will continue to be intensely competitive with pressure on margins, particularly in residential mortgage lending. The HSBC Group remains focused on retaining its position as the leading financial services organization in Hong Kong.

"Elsewhere in Asia-Pacific, the Group will further develop its personal banking capabilities. We believe the demographic growth and deregulation taking place there give us good opportunity to achieve profitable growth by further expanding throughout the region.

"In the UK and continental Europe, Midland will continue to focus on customer service, further using technology to improve the quality of services as well as to improve productivity. Controlling costs remains an essential discipline as competition increases in the financial services sector.

"In North America, the focus for 1997 will be integrating First Federal and the J P Morgan clearing business into our Group, while continuing to improve the productivity and sales penetration of our existing businesses."

PERFORMANCE

HSBC gets high marks for growth and an overall score of 80 points in our grading system. In dollars, revenues and gross profits increased in six of the last seven years (numbers for the previous three were not available), with compound annual growth of 19% and 23%, respectively. EP/ADR increased in nine of the last ten years, with compound annual growth of 21%. ADR price performance was inconsistent but strong, increasing at a compound annual rate of around 22%, while dividends increased at a compound annual rate of 18% (with an average payout ratio of 40%). Average ROE was only 14%; however, it has been going up since 1990 and was 21% in 1996. ROA averaged 0.7% for the decade, a little low, but it has been 1% or higher for the last four years.

If you had invested $10,000 in HSBC in 1986, you would have purchased around 620 ADRs (or ADR equivalents) at about $16 each (excluding commissions). During the following ten years, there were a one-for-eight rights issue in March 1987, a one-for-eight bonus issue in March 1987, a one-for-ten bonus issue in April 1988, a one-for-ten bonus issue in April 1989, a one-for-ten bonus issue in April 1990, and a one-for-four stock consolidation in April 1991. By the end of 1996, you would have had around 320 ADRs (or ADR equivalents) worth an estimated $69,000. You would also have received dividend payments of around $12,500.

HSBC HOLDINGS

Ticker Symbol and Exchange: HSBHY—OTC   **CUSIP No.: 404280307**

OPERATING AND PER SHARE DATA
(in millions of Hong Kong dollars and dollars per share)

	1986	1987	1988	1989	1990	1991	1992	1993	1994	1995	1996	CAGR
Net Revenues	N/A	N/A	N/A	35,657	40,155	44,355	70,000	93,000	92,000	107,000	115,804	18.3%
Gross Profit	N/A	N/A	N/A	14,296	15,218	18,436	30,400	46,100	39,900	49,400	59,943	22.7%
Net Profit	3,056	3,593	4,300	4,774	3,046	6,874	14,321	20,624	24,334	30,044	37,587	28.5%
EPS	2.15	2.39	2.72	3.00	1.93	4.23	7.28	8.20	9.43	11.47	14.20	20.8%
DPS	1.08	1.14	1.32	1.53	1.56	1.85	2.23	2.68	3.26	3.84	5.40	17.5%

OPERATING AND PER SHARE DATA
(in millions of U.S. dollars and dollars per ADR)

	1986	1987	1988	1989	1990	1991	1992	1993	1994	1995	1996	CAGR
Net Revenues	N/A	N/A	N/A	4,571	5,148	5,701	9,044	12,031	11,886	13,842	14,981	18.5%
Gross Profit	N/A	N/A	N/A	1,833	1,951	2,370	3,928	5,964	5,155	6,391	7,755	22.9%
Net Profit	392	463	551	612	391	884	1,850	2,668	3,144	3,887	4,862	28.6%
EP/ADR	2.76	3.08	3.48	3.85	2.47	5.44	9.41	10.61	12.18	14.84	18.37	20.9%
DP/ADR	1.39	1.47	1.69	1.96	2.00	2.38	2.88	3.47	4.21	4.97	6.99	17.6%

KEY RATIOS

	1986	1987	1988	1989	1990	1991	1992	1993	1994	1995	1996	AVG
Profit/Revenues	N/A	N/A	N/A	40.1%	37.9%	41.6%	43.4%	49.6%	43.4%	46.2%	51.8%	44.2%
ROE	11.7%	10.8%	12.0%	9.1%	5.8%	10.1%	15.2%	20.8%	20.4%	20.7%	21.3%	14.4%
ROA	0.4%	0.4%	0.5%	0.5%	0.3%	0.5%	0.7%	1.1%	1.1%	1.3%	1.5%	0.7%
P/E (Projected)	10.0	8.0	7.0	13.9	4.5	4.9	6.8	12.2	7.3	8.2	10.6	8.5

STOCK PRICE CHART
(fiscal year-end closing price, in U.S. dollars, adjusted for capital changes)

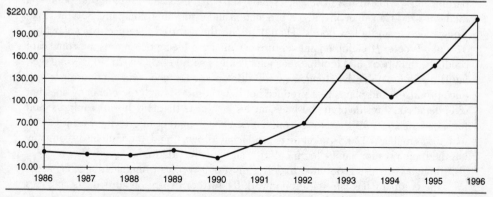

Notes: Results prior to 1992 have been restated and are not strictly comparable to following years'. Figures in U.S. dollars have been translated from local currency using year-end exchange rates.

HUTCHISON WHAMPOA (HUWHY—OTC)

Address: 22/F Hutchison House, Central / Hong Kong
Tel.: (011) 852 2521 6264   **Fax:** (011) 852 2521 6264

BASIC INFORMATION

Country: Hong Kong
Industry: Conglomerate
Market capitalization: $27.05 billion
Share status: ADRs trade OTC
Investment thesis: Hong Kong conglomerate in ports, retail, telecoms, power, hotels, and manufacturing

COMPANY GRADING BOX

Growth Categories		Quality of Management	
Revenue Growth	20	Return on Equity	5
Operating Income Growth	20	**Risk**	
Earnings per Share Growth	20	Long-Term Debt/Total Capital	5
Share Price Growth	20	**Total QM&R (maximum 20)**	10
Total Growth (maximum 80)	**80**	**FINAL GRADE**	**90**

BACKGROUND

Li Ka-shing is the man behind both Hutchison Whampoa and Cheung Kong (Holdings) (see page 99), together valued at an estimated $50 billion. He is a self-made billionaire involved in almost every aspect of Hong Kong's economic life. Technically, Cheung Kong owns just 44.2% of Hutchison Whampoa, but sixty-eight-year-old Mr. Li is chairman of both boards, and is—for the time being—the man in charge (his two American-educated sons are expected to take over when he retires). Although these companies have a range of activities outside Hong Kong, an investment in Hutchison is an investment in the future of this former British colony. Hard hit during the 1997 Asian market turmoil, it's an interesting investment play for when the region turns around.

Among Hutchison's businesses: ports—it's the largest private container port operator in the world; property investment and developing—it has an estimated HK$41 billion of rent-producing investment property; retailing—it controls three Hong Kong retailers that are expanding into other parts of Asia; telecommunications—Hong Kong fixed-line, cellular, and paging services as well as a major U.K. cellular phone company launched in partnership with British Aerospace; a sizable stake in the AsiaSat satellite transponder; a medium-sized Canadian oil and gas production and exploration company; 35% of Hong Kong Electric; and a few hotels. Then there are the assorted manufacturing activities: 31% of a Procter & Gamble joint venture in China producing detergents, personal care products, shampoos, and toothpaste; a joint venture with Pepsi-Cola in Hong Kong (giving Hutchison 20% of the Hong Kong soft drink market); an ice-cream importer; a fruit juice producer; and plants that produce bottled water. Although the company does not offer details on this side of the business, analysts estimate that Hutchison's could account for more than 75% of the Hong Kong bottled water market (a growing business with margins as high as 75%). In addition to producing its own brand, the Hutchison company has the franchises for San Pellegrino, Vittel, and San Benedetto.

Although Hutchison continues to derive most of its profits from its Hong Kong activities, the company has laid the groundwork for further expansion abroad. Its activities throughout Asia, as well as its British cellular phone company, Orange, are expected to contribute significantly to profits by the end of the decade (even though an earlier

Hutchison venture into U.K. telecommunications was an expensive flop). This is a company geared toward the long term and a core holding for investors interested in Hong Kong.

COMPANY STATEMENT (from the 1996 earnings announcement)

"The Group's overall strategy is to continue to expand its core businesses in Hong Kong, China and elsewhere, particularly in Asia. As part of its overall strategy, the Group also seeks to enlarge its recurrent income base and to maximize the coordination of its businesses. The recent reorganization saw the consolidation of the Hongkong Electric group shareholding into its subsidiary, Cheung Kong Infrastructure. This will further enable the Group to focus on its core businesses in China and the region. The Group is most active in China in the areas of port operations, property development, infrastructure, power generation, manufacturing and retailing.

"During 1996 we witnessed a gradual recovery in Hong Kong's economy with rallies in both the stock market and property sectors. This recovery is likely to be further enhanced in the months ahead with expected increases in China's exports and imports. Hong Kong will maintain its pre-eminent regional role given the on-going strengthening of economic ties between itself and China. The Group has complete confidence in the future of Hong Kong. Against that background, the group is committed to continue developing its core businesses in markets with good potential and in those areas in which it has the resources and expertise. With its solid base of recurrent quality income, strong cash flow and financial position the Group is well positioned to move forward to the next century with confidence."

PERFORMANCE

Hutchison Whampoa's received 90 points in our grading system, with top scores in every growth category. Revenues, which increased in eight of the last nine years, had compound annual growth of 15%; EBDIT, which increased in all nine of the last nine years, had compound annual growth of 21%; EP/ADR (or ADR equivalent) in dollars increased in seven of the last nine years at a compound annual rate of 20%; and the ADR price, which increased in eight of the last nine years (remarkable considering the volatility of the Hong Kong equity market), saw compound annual growth of 27%. ROE averaged 14% for the ten-year period, hitting a high 19% in 1996, while the long-term debt to total capital ratio remained moderate, averaging just under 26% for the ten years. Hutchison also rewarded shareholders with a lot of income, maintaining an average dividend payout ratio of 51% of earnings.

If you had invested $10,000 in Hutchison Whampoa at the end of 1987, you would have purchased around 2,220 ADRs (or ADR equivalents) at about $4.50 each (excluding commissions). During the next nine years, there were no capital changes. By the end of 1996, you would still have had around 2,220 ADRs, but their value would have increased to an estimated $87,000. You would also have received dividends worth around $11,600.

HUTCHISON WHAMPOA

Ticker Symbol and Exchange: HUWHY—OTC   **CUSIP No.: 448415208**

OPERATING AND PER SHARE DATA
(in millions of Hong Kong dollars and dollars per share)

	1986	1987	1988	1989	1990	1991	1992	1993	1994	1995	1996	CAGR
Sales	N/A	10,524	12,875	17,685	15,975	19,212	21,030	24,748	30,168	35,026	36,663	14.9%
EBDIT	N/A	3,040	3,974	5,832	6,442	7,111	7,359	9,980	12,806	15,434	16,244	20.5%
Net Profit	N/A	1,846	2,320	3,031	3,519	3,328	3,169	6,304	8,021	8,811	12,020	23.1%
EPS	N/A	0.66	0.77	1.00	1.16	1.09	1.00	1.79	2.22	2.44	3.32	19.7%
DPS	N/A	0.35	0.43	0.54	0.65	0.68	0.55	0.68	0.93	1.18	1.50	17.5%

OPERATING AND PER SHARE DATA
(in millions of U.S. dollars and dollars per ADR)

	1986	1987	1988	1989	1990	1991	1992	1993	1994	1995	1996	CAGR
Sales	N/A	1,356	1,649	2,267	2,048	2,469	2,717	3,202	3,898	4,531	4,743	14.9%
EBDIT	N/A	392	509	748	826	914	951	1,291	1,655	1,997	2,101	20.5%
Net Profit	N/A	238	297	389	451	428	409	816	1,036	1,140	1,555	23.2%
EP/ADR	N/A	0.43	0.49	0.64	0.74	0.70	0.65	1.16	1.43	1.58	2.15	19.7%
DP/ADR	N/A	0.23	0.28	0.35	0.42	0.44	0.36	0.44	0.60	0.76	0.97	17.6%

KEY RATIOS

	1986	1987	1988	1989	1990	1991	1992	1993	1994	1995	1996	AVG
EBDIT Margin	N/A	28.9%	30.9%	33.0%	40.3%	37.0%	35.0%	40.3%	42.4%	44.1%	44.3%	37.6%
ROE	N/A	12.9%	14.7%	13.5%	14.3%	12.0%	8.8%	12.8%	14.0%	15.0%	19.0%	13.7%
LT Debt/Total Cap	N/A	17.5%	30.7%	31.1%	28.6%	26.3%	22.6%	22.0%	34.7%	33.6%	25.3%	27.2%
P/E (Projected)	N/A	9.1	8.6	7.6	11.0	14.6	8.4	17.3	12.8	14.2	18.1	12.2

STOCK PRICE CHART
(fiscal year-end closing price, in U.S. dollars, adjusted for capital changes)

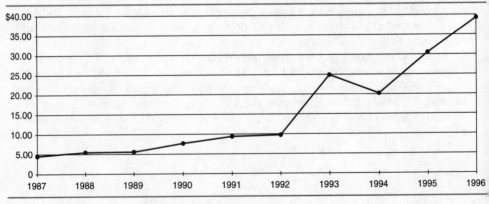

Note: Figures in U.S. dollars are translated from local currency using year-end exchange rates.

IHC CALAND (ICHHF—OTC)

Address: Postbus 31 / 3100 AA Schledam / Netherlands
Tel.: (011) 31 10 2466980   **Fax:** (011) 31 10 2466990

BASIC INFORMATION

Country: Netherlands
Industry: Oil services
Investment thesis: Leading oil services company; 60% of sales outside Europe

Market capitalization: $1.23 billion
Share status: Foreign shares trade OTC

COMPANY GRADING BOX

Growth Categories		Quality of Management	
Revenue Growth	20	Return on Equity	5
Operating Income Growth	20	Risk	
Earnings per Share Growth	20	Long-Term Debt/Total Capital	10
Share Price Growth	20	Total QM&R (maximum 20)	15
Total Growth (maximum 80)	**80**	**FINAL GRADE**	**95**

BACKGROUND

Equipping the offshore oilfield service industry and the dredging, shipping, and mining industries does not sound glamorous, but for IHC Caland it has been very profitable. This Netherlands-based "marine technology oriented" company (its own description), which mostly custom builds floating equipment and provides industrial engineering services, has been building Dutch ships for hundreds of years and has been listed on the Dutch stock exchange since 1965. Over the years it has supplied Dutch industry with the equipment to "reclaim" or add land to make the tiny country bigger.

Today, however, IHC Caland is a truly international company, a holding group for complementary businesses. In 1995 (the most recent year for which data were available) just 13.5% of the group's nearly $900 million in annual revenue was generated in Holland. More than 27% was from Europe as a whole, 4.6% from North and South America, 16.8% from Africa, and 37.6% from Australia and Asia. Management sees the rapid development of Asian markets as holding its greatest potential for growth.

Today international oil companies are budgeting more for offshore exploration and development in an effort to keep pace with the world's appetite for oil. Demand is growing for floating production and floating storage systems (contracted to oil companies by IHC Caland and its competitors). Dredging activities are strong in Asia, along with increased land development, and all over the world companies are replacing equipment to keep up with changing technology (a movement toward "green," or more environmentally correct, dredging equipment is helping to fuel those sales).

COMPANY STATEMENT (from the 1995 annual report)

"IHC Caland's mission is to excel in its chosen fields of business and thereby realize on a long-term basis a return on its invested capital substantially higher than its cost of capital. In this way it aims to provide the shareholders with a return on their investment, commensurate with the risk involved, and so also to secure the continuity and independence of the corporation.

" . . . The Group's present activities comprise the design and supply of floating loading and unloading systems, tanker-based storage and production systems based on the single point mooring concept, custom built and standard dredgers, custom built ships and hydraulic pile hammers. The Group is also in the business of owning and operating Floating Production and Floating Storage systems. These units are contracted on long-term charters, including their operation, to oil companies in various parts of the world. . . .

"In all these different activities the Group companies are among the market leaders, both in terms of market share and technical expertise. The above mentioned products are developed by the individual Group companies and are marketed under their own identity. Much of the Group companies' fundamental technology is protected by patents. Within an agreed financial and strategic framework, Group companies have considerable operational and entrepreneurial freedom. Cohesion is created in that they all have potential to support each other using one or more of their individual core competencies."

PERFORMANCE

IHC Caland, which received 95 points overall in our grading system, got top marks in most of our categories and turned in a spectacular share price performance. The share price in dollars increased at a compound annual rate of 48%, increasing in every one of the last nine years. EPS in dollars also increased in every one of the last nine years, recording incredible compound annual growth of around 47%. And EBDIT in dollars increased in eight of the last nine years and recorded compound annual growth of 24%. Revenues in dollars were down a bit in the late 1980s but increased in every one of the last seven years and recorded compound annual growth of 28%. Although ROE averaged 17% for the ten-year period, it reached 21% in 1996. And the ratio of long-term debt to total capital, which averaged an acceptable 11%, fell to an even more impressive 3% in 1996.

If you had invested $10,000 in IHC Caland at the end of 1987, you would have purchased around 1,480 shares at about $6.75 each (excluding commissions). During the following nine years, there was a four-for-one stock split in June 1993, as well as a few other minor changes in the capital structure. By the end of 1996, you would have had around 5,900 shares worth an estimated $335,600. You would also have received dividend payments of around $32,000.

IHC CALAND

Ticker Symbol and Exchange: ICHHF—OTC

SEDOL Code: 4441155

OPERATING AND PER SHARE DATA
(in millions of Dutch guilders and guilders per share)

	1986	1987	1988	1989	1990	1991	1992	1993	1994	1995	1996	CAGR
Sales	N/A	165	156	134	441	453	557	775	886	928	1,512	27.9%
EBDIT	N/A	22.6	28.3	33.0	42.4	47.2	70.6	122.1	124.4	137.7	148.7	23.3%
Net Profit	N/A	2.8	4.0	17.0	27.0	32.7	45.5	53.5	64.2	75.3	93.0	47.6%
EPS	N/A	0.12	0.18	0.74	1.17	1.41	1.96	2.28	2.72	3.19	3.70	46.4%
DPS	N/A	N/M	N/M	0.73	0.75	1.00	1.05	1.20	1.40	1.60	1.84	14.1%

OPERATING AND PER SHARE DATA
(in millions of U.S. dollars and dollars per share)

	1986	1987	1988	1989	1990	1991	1992	1993	1994	1995	1996	CAGR
Sales	N/A	93	78	70	263	265	306	397	512	576	869	28.2%
EBDIT	N/A	12.8	14.2	17.3	25.2	27.6	38.8	62.6	71.9	85.5	85.5	23.5%
Net Profit	N/A	1.6	2.0	8.9	16.1	19.1	25.0	27.4	37.1	46.8	53.4	23.5%
EPS	N/A	0.07	0.09	0.39	0.70	0.82	1.08	1.17	1.57	1.98	2.13	47.9%
DPS	N/A	N/M	N/M	0.38	0.45	0.58	0.58	0.62	0.81	0.99	1.06	46.6%
												15.6%

KEY RATIOS

	1986	1987	1988	1989	1990	1991	1992	1993	1994	1995	1996	AVG
EBDIT Margin	N/A	13.7%	18.1%	24.6%	9.6%	10.4%	12.7%	15.8%	14.0%	14.8%	9.8%	14.4%
ROE	N/A	1.5%	3.0%	12.1%	17.5%	17.5%	22.0%	23.9%	25.6%	25.9%	21.4%	17.0%
LT Debt/Total Cap	N/A	23.0%	20.9%	6.3%	8.2%	5.0%	17.8%	15.5%	2.8%	2.2%	16.9%	10.5%
P/E (Projected)	N/A	16.7	6.6	7.7	8.2	6.9	9.5	14.3	13.8	14.6	22.8	12.1

STOCK PRICE CHART
(fiscal year-end closing price, in U.S. dollars, adjusted for capital changes)

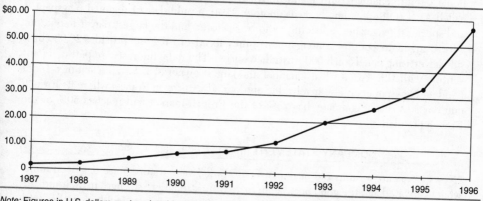

Note: Figures in U.S. dollars are translated from local currency using year-end exchange rates.

INDEPENDENT NEWSPAPERS (INWS.L—LONDON)

Address: 1–2 Upper Hatch Street / Dublin 2 / Ireland
Tel.: (011) 353 1 475 8432   **Fax:** (011) 353 1 475 2126   **Web site:** http://www.indnews.com

BASIC INFORMATION

Country: Ireland   **Market capitalization:** $1.1 billion
Industry: Printing and publishing   **Share status:** Foreign shares trade on London Exchange
Investment thesis: Media and communications; holdings in Ireland, South Africa, and Australia, among others

COMPANY GRADING BOX

Growth Categories		Quality of Management	
Revenue Growth	20	Return on Equity	5
Operating Income Growth	20	**Risk**	
Earnings per Share Growth	20	Long-Term Debt/Total Capital	5
Share Price Growth	20	**Total QM&R (maximum 20)**	10
Total Growth (maximum 80)	80	**FINAL GRADE**	90

BACKGROUND

The *Irish Independent,* Ireland's largest newspaper, was launched in Dublin in 1905. Today the paper is the flagship of Independent Newspapers, a media and communications group with holdings in Ireland, South Africa, Britain, Australia, New Zealand, France, Portugal, and Mexico. Its newspaper division dominates in high-growth markets such as Ireland—with five national and ten regional titles; New Zealand—where it owns 85% of the country's leading newspaper and magazine publishing company (it also has interests in educational publishing); and South Africa—where it owns more than 59% of the leading newspaper company (publisher of the leading English-language newspaper in the country). In total, the Group publishes 160 newspaper and magazine titles, employs more than 13,500 people, had revenues of $694 million in 1995, and had a market capitalization of $1.1 billion at the end of 1996. The group's chairman and largest shareholder is A. J. F. "Tony" O'Reilly, also chairman of H. J. Heinz, the giant U.S. food company.

Apart from newspapers, the company owns the second largest multichannel television signal distributor (allowing for the reception of U.K.-based TV channels and international satellite channels) in Ireland. In Australia it indirectly holds 23% of a company called APN (O'Reilly's family owns another 21%), a publisher of regional newspapers and specialist magazines, a leading radio broadcaster, and the largest player in outdoor advertising in the country (among other venues, its advertising unit provides 20,000 busside advertising panels on 5,000 Australian buses). The radio interests are part of a joint venture with U.S.-based Clear Channel, the largest owner of U.S. radio stations. Independent Newspapers is also involved in outdoor advertising in France, where its French outdoor advertising company has 25% of the French market and reaches 50% of the French population.

COMPANY STATEMENT (from the 1996 annual report)

"Newspapers are a funny old business. Like Mark Twain, their demise has been somewhat overstated and the good ones seem to go from strength to strength in their individual marketplaces. Try to give the *New York Times* away in Dublin or the *Irish*

Independent in Capetown, and you can't. The populace are wedded to their local brand. The collection of editors, writers, columnists, commentators, journalists, photographers and layout artists respond to local needs and local tastes, and the consumer tends to enjoy (or dislike at times) his or her local news and comment and an accurate, digestible international snapshot. Independent Newspapers is now the number one newspaper in seven major cities and in six countries throughout the world. In each country and in each city, there is an overarching awareness that they are all part of the one Group—and they all try to achieve the one common standard of fairness and objectivity, that in good days and bad, is the overwhelming ambition of most newspapers throughout the world.

"The Group is commercial, and strives to be the low cost operator wherever it can. But unlike manufactured goods, you can't build an inventory of yesterday's papers, and so ambitions for efficiency must be matched against the need to publish every day and often twice a day throughout the world. . . .

"But the Independent is happily about more than newspapers and as the spectacular results achieved by Liam Healy (Chief Executive) and his team throughout the world are examined, you can see success and effort in radio, pay TV, cable, outdoor advertising in various countries—all reminding us that the customers and advertisers are our life blood and we ignore them at our own peril."

PERFORMANCE

Independent Newspapers gets high marks for growth and a total of 90 points in our grading system. In dollars, revenues and EPS increased in eight of the last ten years, recording compound annual growth of 21% and 18%, respectively. EBDIT in dollars increased in nine of the last ten years, recording compound annual growth of 28%. Shareholders did well: the share price in dollars recorded compound annual growth of 21%, and the dividend payout ratio averaged 45%.

Independent Newspapers lost points only for ROE, which averaged 12%—fine but not as high as that of some of the other companies on our list—and the long-term debt to total capital ratio, which averaged 26%—also fine but a little higher than that of some of the other companies on our list.

If you had invested $10,000 in Independent Newspapers at the end of 1986, you would have purchased around 2,000 shares at about $5 each (excluding commissions). During the next ten years, there were a one-for-two bonus issue in April 1989, a two-for-three bonus issue in June 1993, a one-for-two bonus issue in April 1994, a two-for-three bonus issue in June 1996, and a one-for-three rights issue in July 1996. By the end of 1996, you would have had around 12,500 shares worth an estimated $64,500. You would also have received dividend payments of around $8,300.

INDEPENDENT NEWSPAPERS

Ticker Symbol and Exchange: INWS.L—London   **SEDOL Code: 4699103**

OPERATING AND PER SHARE DATA
(in millions of Irish punts and punts per share)

	1986	1987	1988	1989	1990	1991	1992	1993	1994	1995	1996	CAGR
Sales	76.0	89.0	134.0	148.0	155.0	156.0	170.0	174.0	271.4	368.0	419.0	18.6%
EBDIT	8.1	11.5	15.8	22.1	19.8	21.4	28.8	32.9	49.1	59.7	78.8	25.5%
Net Profit	5.2	7.4	8.8	10.7	8.5	7.0	13.0	22.4	30.8	40.0	56.8	27.0%
EPS	0.04	0.05	0.06	0.06	0.07	0.04	0.08	0.10	0.12	0.14	0.16	16.2%
DPS	0.02	0.02	0.02	0.03	0.03	0.03	0.03	0.04	0.05	0.06	0.07	13.6%

OPERATING AND PER SHARE DATA
(in millions of U.S. dollars and dollars per share)

	1986	1987	1988	1989	1990	1991	1992	1993	1994	1995	1996	CAGR
Sales	106	149	202	230	275	272	276	245	420	589	709	20.9%
EBDIT	11.3	19.3	23.8	34.4	35.1	37.4	46.8	46.3	76.0	95.6	133.3	28.0%
Net Profit	7.3	12.4	13.3	16.7	15.1	12.1	21.1	31.5	47.7	64.0	96.1	29.4%
EPS	0.05	0.08	0.09	0.09	0.12	0.08	0.13	0.14	0.19	0.22	0.27	18.4%
DPS	0.03	0.04	0.04	0.04	0.05	0.06	0.05	0.06	0.08	0.09	0.11	15.7%

KEY RATIOS

	1986	1987	1988	1989	1990	1991	1992	1993	1994	1995	1996	AVG
EBDIT Margin	10.7%	12.9%	11.8%	14.9%	12.8%	13.7%	16.9%	18.9%	18.1%	16.2%	18.8%	15.1%
ROE	20.5%	10.7%	11.8%	12.5%	1C.4%	5.0%	9.0%	12.0%	12.5%	13.9%	14.4%	12.1%
LT Debt/Total Cap	19.3%	18.7%	35.9%	44.3%	39.5%	9.7%	19.7%	11.8%	21.3%	31.7%	32.8%	25.9%
P/E (Projected)	11.4	9.6	15.0	16.4	13.2	9.1	9.3	14.8	11.9	14.5	16.6	12.9

STOCK PRICE CHART
(fiscal year-end closing price, in U.S. dollars, adjusted for capital changes)

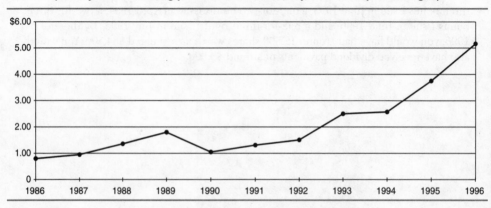

Note: Figures in U.S. dollars are translated from local currency using year-end exchange rates.

INVESTEC BANK (IVBOY—OTC)

Address: 55 Fox Street, Johannesburg 2001 / South Africa
or
Address: P.O. Box 11177, Johannesburg 2000 / South Africa
Tel.: (011) 27 11 498 2000   **Fax:** (011) 27 11 498 2100

BASIC INFORMATION

Country: South Africa   **Market capitalization:** $1.75 billion
Industry: Banking   **Share status:** ADRs trade OTC
Investment thesis: Fifth largest South African bank; now expanding overseas

COMPANY GRADING BOX

Growth Categories		Quality of Management	
Revenue Growth	20	Return on Equity	10
Operating Income Growth	20	Return on Assets	10
Earnings per Share Growth	20	**Total QM (maximum 20)**	**20**
Share Price Growth	20		
Total Growth (maximum 80)	**80**	**FINAL GRADE**	**100**

BACKGROUND

Investec Bank has been making waves in conservative South African banking circles for years. Formed as a leasing company in 1974, Investec became a full-fledged bank in 1980 and, through aggressive expansion into new business areas and acquisitions, has grown to become South Africa's fifth largest bank. Along the way, Investec has compiled a track record that would be the envy of any bank in the world, increasing its revenues in dollars by 35% per annum over the last decade and recording compound annual share price growth (also in dollars) of 29% during the period.

Today, Investec focuses on corporate and investment banking, private banking, securities trading, asset management, and property (trading and management) and trade finance. Its greatest strength has been its reputation as a specialist in each of its niche markets.

Since the end of apartheid, Investec has made itself a part of the movement to address some of South Africa's social ills, with its "economic uplift program." And, with South Africa again an accepted member of the international community, South African banks have been able to rejoin the international banking community. That has meant new technology, greater liquidity, renewed lines of credit and a jump in business activity (as well as competition).

Investec has made several acquisitions overseas, including a small bank and discount house in the United Kingdom; it also has operations in the United States and in Israel and a stake in a private bank in the Netherlands. Management has said that eventually it would like to generate 50% of its revenues in foreign currencies, up from 30% now. In early 1997 Investec formed an alliance with Crédit Suisse First Boston to offer general corporate finance advice to companies incorporated in South Africa, as well as advice on raising capital in international markets.

COMPANY STATEMENT (from the 1996 annual report)

"Investec's mission is to be a significant and highly respected independent, international investment and investment banking group which focuses on providing its selected clients with specialized financial services.

"In pursuit of this mission we seek to be the foremost investment banking group in Southern Africa, maintaining a high level of recognition and respect for the professional manner in which we conduct our business, for our ability to respond creatively to our changing markets' needs, for attracting and retaining quality people who are motivated to perform in an extraordinary way, and for our consistent and substantial growth in earnings per share and assets under management.

"Prospects: Investec is well poised to take advantage of the opportunities arising out of the globalization of South Africa's economy and financial markets and intends to maintain a very visible presence in local, regional and international markets. The group's independence, substantial capital base, breadth of skills and products and emphasis on quality growth have combined to render Investec one of the leading financial institutions in the country today. These qualities will ensure that it maintains and builds upon this position in the future. We are confident that in the coming year Investec will show strong growth in earnings and dividends consistent with its historic performance."

PERFORMANCE

Investec is another of our star performers, with a perfect score of 100 in our grading system. Revenues in dollars increased in each of the last six years—all the years for which data were available—with compound annual growth of 35%. EBDIT increased in each of the last five years—all the years for which that data were available—with compound annual growth of an astounding 54%. And EP/ADR (or ADR equivalent) in dollars increased in each of the last ten years, with compound annual growth of 20%.

ROE averaged an excellent 19%, and return on assets averaged 2%, very high for a bank. ADR price growth in dollars was also impressive, though it is important to remember that the sanctions against South Africa were in force through 1994, making foreign investment in those shares impossible. Even so, the ADR equivalent price hit a new high in each of the last seven years and increased at a compound annual rate of 29%. The dividend payout ratio averaged 47%, and the dividend increased in each of the last ten years.

If you had invested $10,000 in Investec Bank in March 1987, you would have purchased around 4,000 ADRs (or ADR equivalents) at about $2.50 each (excluding commissions). There were no significant capital changes during the next ten years. By March 1997, your 4,000 ADRs would have been worth an estimated $123,700. You would also have received dividend payments of around $12,000.

INVESTEC BANK

Ticker Symbol and Exchange: IVBOY—OTC   **CUSIP No.: 46128U103**

OPERATING AND PER SHARE DATA
(in millions of South African rand and rand per share)

	Mar 87	Mar 88	Mar 89	Mar 90	Mar 91	Mar 92	Mar 93	Mar 94	Mar 95	Mar 96	Mar 97	CAGR
Net Revenues	N/A	N/A	N/A	N/A	127.0	185.0	269.8	296.8	500.5	751.3	1,249.0	46.4%
Pretax Income	N/A	N/A	N/A	N/A	N/A	N/A	64.5	99.2	207.7	317.2	515.2	68.1%
Net Profit	6.9	11.0	14.0	17.5	24.0	33.2	54.0	80.0	147.5	235.0	365.0	48.6%
EPS	0.42	0.55	0.70	0.88	1.18	1.45	1.72	2.24	3.11	4.20	5.58	29.6%
DPS	0.18	0.24	0.32	0.40	0.56	0.70	0.90	1.15	1.50	2.00	2.60	30.6%

OPERATING AND PER SHARE DATA
(in millions of U.S. dollars and dollars per ADR)

	Mar 87	Mar 88	Mar 89	Mar 90	Mar 91	Mar 92	Mar 93	Mar 94	Mar 95	Mar 96	Mar 97	CAGR
Net Revenues	N/A	N/A	N/A	N/A	47	65	85	86	140	189	278	34.6%
Pretax Income	N/A	N/A	N/A	N/A	N/A	N/A	20.3	28.6	58.2	79.7	114.5	54.0%
Net Profit	3.4	5.2	5.5	6.6	8.8	11.6	17.0	23.1	41.3	59.0	81.1	37.2%
EP/ADR	0.21	0.26	0.27	0.33	0.43	0.51	0.54	0.65	0.87	1.06	1.24	19.7%
DP/ADR	0.09	0.11	0.13	0.15	0.21	0.24	0.28	0.33	0.42	0.50	0.58	20.6%

KEY RATIOS

	Mar 87	Mar 88	Mar 89	Mar 90	Mar 91	Mar 92	Mar 93	Mar 94	Mar 95	Mar 96	Mar 97	AVG
Pretax/Revenue	N/A	N/A	N/A	N/A	N/A	N/A	23.9%	33.4%	41.5%	42.2%	41.2%	36.5%
ROE	18.3%	19.6%	22.4%	23.5%	22.4%	19.9%	15.5%	20.4%	17.1%	15.5%	15.0%	19.1%
ROA	2.2%	2.0%	1.7%	1.6%	1.5%	1.4%	1.8%	2.0%	2.3%	2.5%	2.5%	2.0%
P/E (Projected)	9.1	5.4	4.7	5.7	9.6	11.9	12.5	14.5	15.5	16.1	21.7	11.5

STOCK PRICE CHART
(fiscal year-end closing price, in U.S. dollars, adjusted for capital changes)

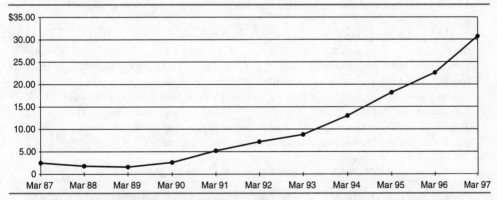

Notes: Due to minimal reporting requirements for banks in South Africa prior to 1993, a lot of historical data for Investec is unavailable, including 1987–90 net revenue, 1987–92 pretax income, and 1987–89 high and low share prices. Figures in U.S. dollars are translated from local currency using year-end exchange rates.

LEIGHTON HOLDINGS (LEI.AX—SYDNEY)

Address: 472 Pacific Highway / Saint Leonards, NSW 2065 / Australia
Tel.: (011) 61 2 9925 6666   **Fax:** (011) 61 2 9925 6005

BASIC INFORMATION

Country: Australia   **Market capitalization:** $1.0 billion
Industry: Construction   **Share status:** Foreign shares trade on Sydney Exchange
Investment thesis: Civil engineering, construction, and mining; operations in Australia and Asia

COMPANY GRADING BOX

Growth Categories		Quality of Management	
Revenue Growth	10	Return on Equity	5
Operating Income Growth	20	**Risk**	
Earnings per Share Growth	5	Long-Term Debt/Total Capital	0
Share Price Growth	20	**Total QM&R (maximum 20)**	5
Total Growth (maximum 80)	55	**FINAL GRADE**	60

BACKGROUND

Leighton Holdings' principal activities include civil engineering and infrastructure, non-residential building, and contract mining (of gold, coal, nickel, and iron ore). Structurally, the company is made up of five revenue-producing units: Leighton Contractors, based in Australia and accounting for 44% of overall revenue; Leighton Asia, the Asian arm of Leighton Contractors, which accounts for about 15% of revenue; Australia-based Theiss Contractor, bought by Leighton in 1983 and accounting for about 34% of revenue; Leighton Properties, the company's property development unit, accounting for a mere 2% of revenue; and Welded Mesh, an Australian manufacturing company that represents about 5% of revenue. Hong Kong, Thailand, Indonesia, Malaysia, and Vietnam are all major markets for this company, which now is also aggressively seeking business in the Philippines and beginning to push into China.

Begun in 1949 in Victoria, Australia, as a small civil engineering company, today Leighton, with 10,500 employees and 1996 sales of $1.9 billion, is Australia's largest construction and contract mining company. It has been publicly traded in Australia since 1962 and has had an Asian regional headquarters in Hong Kong since 1975, shortly after it set up operations in Hong Kong.

Already Leighton has been a beneficiary of skyrocketing infrastructure spending throughout those developing markets. Among its recent projects, the group has been involved with the construction of parts of the new Hong Kong airport (including earth-moving and land reclamation), countless highway and bridge projects in Australia, utilities, and the giant Sydney Casino project (a publicly traded company of which Leighton owns 5%). Leighton is now gearing up to help create the infrastructure for the Sydney Olympics in the year 2000 and is beginning to export its expertise in contract mining to its already established business bases outside Australia.

COMPANY STATEMENT (from the 1996 annual report)

"Leighton remains the largest construction and mining group in Australia, with more extensive Asian operations than any of its Australian competitors. We have reached this position by building a strong balance sheet, sticking to a disciplined strategy of adding value through innovation and performance and only pursuing projects where we can have an acceptable return.

"The Group is not driven by the need to maintain revenue, to bid the lowest price, or to build monuments. Our goal is to increase shareholder wealth. We are very careful that the projects we take on are suited to the Group in terms of our financial, technical and operational skills. As a matter of policy we match risk with return, and avoid speculative developments in favor of long term high quality projects. . . .

"The prospects for the Group are excellent as economic confidence in Australia returns. The Olympics will trigger a number of civil, building and infrastructure projects in and around Sydney, and we have already been successful in securing some of this work. The Games will also give rise to a new and positive atmosphere, especially in the tourism and hospitality industries, which we believe will stimulate the nation as a whole. The outlook for the resources sector is also positive."

PERFORMANCE

Leighton scored reasonably well in terms of growth, garnering 60 points, and showed particular strength in operating income and share price performance. EBDIT increased in nine of the last 10 years, with impressive compound annual growth of 20%, while share price also increased nine out of ten years and grew at a compound rate of 24% in dollar terms. Revenue growth was respectable at 10% per annum and reasonably consistent, but not strong enough to gain top marks. EPS grew strongly in dollars, rising from $0.02 in 1987 to $0.27 in 1997. Although Leighton received just 5 points for ROE and no points for the long-term debt to capital ratio, in both areas the company has shown significant improvement over the last few years. ROE reached 16% in 1997, up from about 5% in 1987 (and −10% in 1986), and the long-term debt to total capital ratio fell to 15% in 1997, down from 44.5% in 1987.

Since the company began issuing a dividend in 1988, dividends per share have increased an average of 20% per annum, and the payout averaged 52% of earnings during the period. The dividend per share in dollars reached $0.17 in 1997, up from $0.03 in 1988.

If you had invested $10,000 in Leighton in June of 1987, you would have purchased around 8,800 shares at about $1.12 each (excluding commissions). During the following ten years, Leighton had a one-for-one bonus issue in April 1988. By the end of June 1997, you would have had around 17,600 shares worth an estimated $88,000. You would also have received around $15,000 in dividend payments.

LEIGHTON HOLDINGS

Ticker Symbol and Exchange: LEI.AX—Sydney   **SEDOL Code: 6511227**

OPERATING AND PER SHARE DATA
(in millions of Australian dollars and dollars per share)

	Jun 87	Jun 88	Jun 89	Jun 90	Jun 91	Jun 92	Jun 93	Jun 94	Jun 95	Jun 96	Jun 97	CAGR
Sales	1,328	1,489	1,431	1,587	1,710	1,590	1,581	1,808	2,031	2,520	3,161	9.1%
EBDIT	57	75	76	104	109	122	133	138	185	238	319	18.9%
Net Profit	7	17	17	21	21	23	48	37	51	65	93	20.4%
EPS	0.03	0.15	0.14	0.16	0.11	0.12	0.24	0.17	0.22	0.27	0.35	9.9%
DPS	N/A	0.04	0.07	0.08	0.08	0.08	0.08	0.08	0.12	0.15	0.22	20.9%

OPERATING AND PER SHARE DATA
(in millions of U.S. dollars and dollars per share)

	Jun 87	Jun 88	Jun 89	Jun 90	Jun 91	Jun 92	Jun 93	Jun 94	Jun 95	Jun 96	Jun 97	CAGR
Sales	956	1,191	1,084	1,260	1,315	1,195	1,054	1,320	1,440	1,984	2,470	10.0%
EBDIT	40.8	60.0	57.4	82.4	83.8	91.9	88.5	100.5	130.9	187.7	249.0	19.8%
Net Profit	4.8	13.9	12.5	16.3	16.2	16.9	31.9	27.0	36.3	51.4	72.4	20.1%
EPS	0.02	0.12	0.11	0.13	0.08	0.09	0.16	0.12	0.16	0.21	0.27	9.6%
DPS	N/A	0.03	0.05	0.06	0.06	0.06	0.05	0.06	0.09	0.12	0.17	20.5%

KEY RATIOS

	Jun 87	Jun 88	Jun 89	Jun 90	Jun 91	Jun 92	Jun 93	Jun 94	Jun 95	Jun 96	Jun 97	AVG
EBDIT Margin	4.3%	5.0%	5.3%	6.5%	6.4%	7.7%	8.4%	7.6%	9.1%	9.5%	10.1%	7.3%
ROE	5.2%	12.9%	11.0%	12.6%	9.2%	9.2%	16.8%	12.2%	14.9%	13.8%	16.4%	12.2%
LT Debt/Total Cap	44.5%	40.7%	43.9%	44.5%	30.8%	36.9%	43.5%	40.2%	37.6%	24.2%	15.2%	36.5%
P/E (Projected)	5.3	5.3	3.9	7.2	9.0	6.1	11.1	9.5	9.2	14.5	16.8	8.9

STOCK PRICE CHART
(fiscal year-end closing price, in U.S. dollars, adjusted for capital changes)

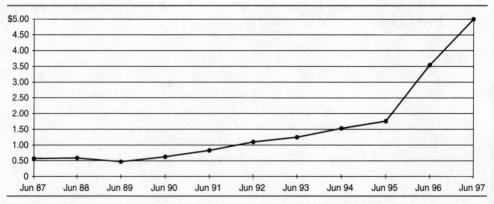

Note: Figures in U.S. dollars are translated from local currency using year-end exchange rates.

L'ORÉAL (LORLY—OTC)

Address: 41 Rue Martre / 92117 Clichy / France
Tel.: (011) 33 1 47 56 70 00 **Fax:** (011) 33 1 47 56 86 42 **Web site:** http://www.bourse-de-paris.fr

BASIC INFORMATION

Country: France
Industry: Health and personal care
Investment thesis: World's largest cosmetics company, with high-profile brand names

Market capitalization: $25 billion
Share status: ADRs trade OTC

COMPANY GRADING BOX

Growth Categories		Quality of Management	
Revenue Growth	20	Return on Equity	5
Operating Income Growth	20	**Risk**	
Earnings per Share Growth	20	Long-Term Debt/Total Capital	10
Share Price Growth	20	**Total QM&R (maximum 20)**	**15**
Total Growth (maximum 80)	**80**	**FINAL GRADE**	**95**

BACKGROUND

How about a stable of cosmetics brand names that includes Maybelline, Lancôme, Helena Rubenstein, L'Oréal, Garnier, Biotherm, and Vichy? And perfume brand names that include Cacherel, Guy Laroche, Paloma Picasso, and Ralph Lauren? Then there is the Lanvin fashion label, including a new line of Lanvin handbags; 49% of the Marie-Claire international stable of magazines; and a well-known contemporary Parisian art gallery, Artcurial. It's not a bad assortment that France-based L'Oréal has pulled together. Active in 150 countries, this $25 billion market capitalization company is the largest on the French stock exchange. Founded by a French chemist nearly a hundred years ago, L'Oréal quickly established a reputation for quality and innovation in the world of beauty. Today it is the largest cosmetics company in the world.

In the last few years, L'Oréal has bought Maybelline, inaugurated its first factory in China, announced plans to build an industrial unit in Poland, consolidated its businesses in Japan, and bought the Chilean company Unisa, a specialist in mass-market cosmetics, from the Gillette Company. Closer to home, L'Oréal has signed a licensing agreement with U.K.-based Laura Ashley. In 1996, 79% of L'Oréal's sales were generated overseas.

Of course, L'Oréal's best-known products are its hair dyes. And that's a business that's going strong. Remember the old Clairol ad: "Does she or doesn't she?" Today, who watches television and has not seen ads for Préférence by L'Oréal? Women are dyeing their hair in record numbers, and they generally do not care who knows. While Clairol has been losing market share here in the United States, L'Oréal has been gaining—dramatically (between the two, they have about 90% of the U.S. market). And L'Oréal is not letting up. Today about half of all American women between the ages of thirteen and seventy reportedly dye their hair—up 50% in the last ten years—and one in eight men. More than 60% of women in France, Germany, and Spain, and 40% of women in Japan, have also jumped on the bandwagon. And hair coloring is big in South America and eastern Europe too. In the international market, Clairol is not even a key player.

Finally, L'Oréal owns 56% of Synthelabo, currently the third largest pharmaceutical company in France, whose revenues are increasing about 15% annually. As it happens, Synthelabo—which accounts for about 17% of L'Oréal's total sales—is also one of our Top 100 (see page 327).

COMPANY STATEMENT (from the 1996 annual report)

"World leader in cosmetics, L'Oréal offers a unique portfolio of famous, quality brands to consumers across five continents. Founded nearly a century ago by French chemist Eugène Schueller, today the group comprises four main cosmetics divisions: Salon, Consumer, Perfumes & Beauty, and Active Cosmetics. It also operates in pharmaceuticals, dermatology and other related fields. Its capacity for research and innovation, and the high caliber of its personnel have earned L'Oréal an outstanding international reputation. As a result of its worldwide presence and the extent and variety of its cosmetics ranges, L'Oréal's activities are harmoniously divided across all types of distribution channels. At the service of health and beauty, L'Oréal is now developing products and markets for the third millennium."

PERFORMANCE

L'Oréal's numbers are a model of consistency, garnering the company 95 points in our grading system. EP/ADR (or ADR equivalent) in dollars increased in every one of the last ten years, recording compound annual growth of 17%. In dollars, revenues and EBDIT increased in nine of the last ten years, recording compound annual growth of 15% and 18%, respectively. The ADR price in dollars set a new high in each of the last ten years, increasing at a compound annual rate of 27%. The dividend payout ratio averaged 23%, with dividends also increasing in each of the last ten years. ROE averaged a very respectable 16%. The long-term debt to total capital ratio averaged a low 11% and was 6% in 1996.

If you had invested $10,000 in L'Oréal at the end of 1986, you would have purchased about 100 ADRs (or ADR equivalents) at around $95 each (excluding commissions). During the following ten years, there were a one-for-five bonus issue in June 1987, a ten-for-one stock split in July 1990, and a one-for-ten bonus issue in July 1996. By the end of 1996, you would have had about 1,400 ADRs worth an estimated $106,700. You would also have received dividend payments of around $3,800.

L'ORÉAL

Ticker Symbol and Exchange: LORLY—OTC   **CUSIP No.: 502117203**

OPERATING AND PER SHARE DATA
(in millions of French francs and francs per share)

	1986	1987	1988	1989	1990	1991	1992	1993	1994	1995	1996	CAGR
Sales	18,130	20,095	24,445	27,170	30,360	33,445	37,568	40,163	47,624	53,371	60,347	12.8%
EBDIT	2,279	2,644	3,126	3,740	4,425	4,356	5,651	5,902	7,444	8,007	9,141	14.9%
Net Profit	872	1,060	1,262	1,806	1,965	2,342	2,413	2,579	3,086	3,310	3,728	15.6%
EPS	13.99	16.59	19.30	22.90	26.40	31.50	35.90	40.40	46.20	50.00	55.15	14.7%
DPS	2.51	3.36	4.55	5.45	6.34	7.64	8.73	9.82	11.09	12.09	14.00	18.8%

OPERATING AND PER SHARE DATA
(in millions of U.S. dollars and dollars per ADR)

	1986	1987	1988	1989	1990	1991	1992	1993	1994	1995	1996	CAGR
Sales	2,815	3,349	4,104	4,265	5,581	5,930	7,102	7,096	8,596	10,702	11,810	15.4%
EBDIT	354	441	525	587	813	772	1,068	1,043	1,344	1,606	1,789	17.6%
Net Profit	135	177	212	283	361	415	456	456	557	664	730	18.3%
EP/ADR	0.43	0.55	0.65	0.72	0.97	1.12	1.36	1.43	1.67	2.01	2.16	17.4%
DP/ADR	0.08	0.11	0.15	0.17	0.23	0.27	0.33	0.35	0.40	0.48	0.55	21.5%

KEY RATIOS

	1986	1987	1988	1989	1990	1991	1992	1993	1994	1995	1996	AVG
EBDIT Margin	12.6%	13.2%	12.8%	13.8%	14.6%	13.0%	15.0%	14.7%	15.6%	15.0%	15.1%	14.1%
ROE	12.7%	15.0%	15.3%	19.4%	18.6%	19.0%	17.4%	16.6%	14.5%	14.6%	14.1%	16.1%
LT Debt/Total Cap	28.7%	14.8%	13.0%	6.8%	8.5%	9.9%	11.2%	10.2%	5.9%	4.8%	5.8%	10.9%
P/E (Projected)	13.9	12.0	17.5	17.1	13.6	19.0	24.0	25.7	19.8	21.6	30.6	19.5

STOCK PRICE CHART
(fiscal year-end closing price, in U.S. dollars, adjusted for capital changes)

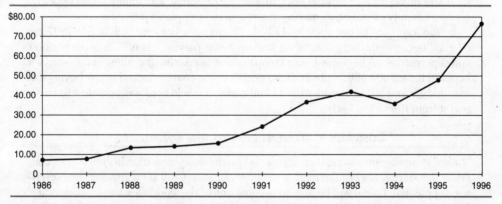

Note: Figures in U.S. dollars are translated from local currency using average exchange rates.

LUKOIL (LUKOY—OTC)

Address: 11 Stretensky Boulevard / Moscow / 101000 Russia
Tel.: (011) 7 095 927 4884   **Fax:** (011) 7 095 281 9072   **Web site:** http://www.lukoil.com

BASIC INFORMATION

Country: Russia
Industry: Oil and gas
Market capitalization: $17.92 billion
Share status: ADRs trade OTC
Investment thesis: Russia's largest vertically integrated oil company; owns vast crude oil reserves

COMPANY GRADING BOX

Growth Categories		Quality of Management	
Revenue Growth	20	Return on Equity	0
Operating Income Growth	20	**Risk**	
Earnings per Share Growth	20	Long-Term Debt/Total Capital	10
Share Price Growth	15	**Total QM&R (maximum 20)**	10
Total Growth (maximum 80)	**75**	**FINAL GRADE**	**85**

BACKGROUND

Russian oil and gas giant Lukoil is the closest we could find to a Russian blue chip. One of the first Russian companies to be privatized, it accounts for 22% of Russia's oil and gas output and has among the largest proven crude oil reserves in the world. As fund managers begin allocating more money to the Russian market, it will likely be a beneficiary. Stock performance at this early stage has been impressive (see score above and performance below), and many of its investors have been well rewarded. Analysts expect Lukoil to participate when the Russian government sells off its remaining major oil and gas holdings.

All that said, however, even a blue chip in Russia is not for the faint of heart. As a whole the Russian stock market has been extremely volatile since it was opened to foreign investors. Moreover, Russian accounting standards are different from U.S. standards, so disclosure is not as clear as it could be, and the rights of shareholders also are not well defined. Lukoil has to deal with an extremely difficult economy (and nonpaying large industrial customers), high corporate taxes, and high production and transportation costs, as most of its reserves are in western Siberia. On the other hand, the company does have strong ties to the Russian government; its president and founder was once the country's deputy oil minister and played a role in the company's privatization.

By the way, keep an eye open for Lukoil at a grocery store near you: in July 1997 the oil giant began supplying gas to filling stations in the parking lots of U.S. grocery stores and supermarkets. The Texas-based company that is opening the filling stations says it hopes to have 2,000 of them built in the next five years (so far, Lukoil is just buying unbranded gas and selling it under the Lukoil name; it would not be economical to transport it from Russia just yet).

COMPANY STATEMENT (from the 1996 annual report)

"Lukoil is steadily increasing its reserves and production potential, which makes us confident that our profits and the market prices of our shares will keep growing. By exercising its potential, Lukoil will be able to become one of the world's leading oil companies. Increasing reserves, and high-yielding reserves in particular, is a strategic goal that

Lukoil will carry out through more exploration and participation in oil field tenders both in Russia and abroad.

"Another strategic goal is to further develop crude oil production, currently our most profitable sector. We plan to sustain our crude output volumes in regions where we have been around for a while and increase it in new regions, primarily in the Caspian. We plan to build a refinery in Novorossiisk and acquire new refineries in Russia and other former Soviet Republics. To raise the quality and increase the range of our oil products, we will continue to renovate our refineries. Laying pipelines will enable us to reduce our transport expenses. We are working to increase our range of high-quality products and sell them in new markets both in Russia and abroad."

PERFORMANCE

Lukoil, though we have just four years of numbers to go on, received a total of 85 points in our grading system with unbelievable growth numbers (keep in mind this company was starting, with tremendous potential, from a low base). In dollars, revenues, pretax profit and earnings per ADR grew 301%, 156%, and 51% respectively over the last four years. The company only offered a dividend beginning in 1995, so a dividend growth rate would be meaningless. ROE averaged a respectable 10% while the long-term debt to total capital ratio averaged a tiny 2% (more than respectable). Of course, we want to reiterate here that this company is not for the investor who is faint of heart; as we discuss in our company description, the possibility of outsized gain in a company like this is accompanied by the risk of outsized loss. In this case, the ADRs have increased at a compound annual rate of 48% over the last four years.

If you had invested $10,000 in Lukoil in 1993, you would have bought around 24 ADRs for $425 each (excluding commissions). In 1995 there were three stock splits: five-for-one; 411:1000; and eight-for-one. At the end of 1996, you would have had around 3,000 ADRs worth an estimated $32,700. You would also have received around $300 in dividends.

LUKOIL

Ticker Symbol and Exchange: LUKOY—OTC   **CUSIP No.: 677862104**

OPERATING AND PER SHARE DATA
(in millions of U.S. dollars and dollars per ADR)

	1986	1987	1988	1989	1990	1991	1992	1993	1994	1995	1996	CAGR
Sales	N/A	N/A	N/A	N/A	N/A	N/A	N/A	134	2,628	5,128	8,631	300.9%
Pretax Profit	N/A	N/A	N/A	N/A	N/A	N/A	N/A	55	442	750	928	156.5%
Net Profit	N/A	N/A	N/A	N/A	N/A	N/A	N/A	36	309	526	753	175.6%
EP/ADR	N/A	N/A	N/A	N/A	N/A	N/A	N/A	N/M	0.46	0.73	1.05	51.1%
DP/ADR	N/A	N/A	N/A	N/A	N/A	N/A	N/A	N/M	N/M	0.04	0.06	N/M

KEY RATIOS

	1986	1987	1988	1989	1990	1991	1992	1993	1994	1995	1996	AVG
Pretax Margin	N/A	N/A	N/A	N/A	N/A	N/A	N/A	41.0%	16.8%	14.6%	10.8%	20.8%
ROE	N/A	N/A	N/A	N/A	N/A	N/A	N/A	N/M	13.9%	7.9%	8.1%	10.0%
LT Debt/Total Cap	N/A	N/A	N/A	N/A	N/A	N/A	N/A	3.9%	0.5%	1.5%	2.2%	2.0%
P/E (Projected)	N/A	N/A	N/A	N/A	N/A	N/A	N/A	7.2	8.4	4.3	11.3	7.8

STOCK PRICE CHART
(fiscal year-end closing price, in U.S. dollars, adjusted for capital changes)

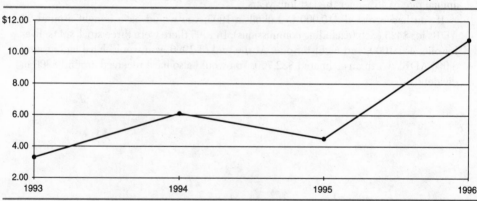

Note: Data for Lukoil are available only from 1993 and only in U.S. dollars.

LUXOTTICA (LUX—NYSE)

Address: 32021 Agordo (BL) / Italy
Tel.: (011) 39 437 62641   **Fax:** (011) 39 437 63223   **Web site:** http://www.luxottica.it

BASIC INFORMATION

Country: Italy

Industry: Health and personal care

Investment thesis: Leading manufacturer of mid- to high-priced eyeglasses; also owns Lenscrafters

Market capitalization: $2.46 billion

Share status: Shares trade on NYSE

COMPANY GRADING BOX

Growth Categories		Quality of Management	
Revenue Growth	20	Return on Equity	10
Operating Income Growth	20	**Risk**	
Earnings per Share Growth	20	Long-Term Debt/Total Capital	10
Share Price Growth	20	**Total QM&R (maximum 20)**	**20**
Total Growth (maximum 80)	**80**	**FINAL GRADE**	**100**

BACKGROUND

In a world where brand names are international currency, the founder of Italy's Luxottica, Leonardo Del Vecchio, knows how to capitalize on his assets. It was founded in 1961 as a manufacturer of parts for eyeglass framers. But Del Vecchio quickly realized he would make more money making the eyeglasses himself and went into that business. Then he saw how much money the eyeglass distributors were making and added that business to his growing company. Today, Del Vecchio credits his success to the way he integrated his business vertically. His company takes its products right through the process, now even to the end user.

Of course, no industry remains stagnant. Beginning in the early 1990s, HMOs in the United States sent consumers in search of cheaper glasses, and Luxottica—which made most of its money in medium- and high-priced frames—had to rethink its U.S. business strategy. In response, Del Vecchio spent about $700 million for the largest U.S. retail chain, LensCrafters (he quickly sold off the parent company, U.S. Shoe, which was part of the deal).

Now, though Luxottica remains a leader at the upper end with brand names such as Giorgio Armani, Byblos, and Yves Saint-Laurent, it also has a huge presence at the other end of the retail spectrum. And Del Vecchio is working hard to turn the Luxottica name itself into a recognized symbol of quality. It is hard to doubt him. Today Luxottica is one of the largest eyeglass manufacturers in the world. In 1996 it sold more than 16 million metal and plastic prescription and sunglass frames in around 2,000 styles, manufactured in the company's Italian production facilities. It's also hard to argue with success: Luxottica's products are available in seventy countries; the company has more than 17,000 employees; and in 1996 revenues hit $1.5 billion.

COMPANY STATEMENT (from the 1996 annual report)

"Luxottica is the world leader in the design, manufacture and marketing of quality eyewear, both eyeglass frames and sunglasses in the mid- and premium-priced market segments. The company has also become, thanks to LensCrafters, the largest optical retailer in the world with 645 super optical stores at the end of 1996.

"The company's products are designed and produced in five facilities based in Northern Italy and include over 2,000 styles available in a wide array of colors and sizes.

"The vertical integration has allowed the Company to create, thanks to in-house designers, unique styles and shapes and utilize proprietary flexible manufacturing processes in order to be the lowest cost producer of quality frames. . . . Unlike most competitors, Luxottica's success to date has been based on total vertical integration, whereby the Company directly controls the design, production and distribution of its frames and sunglasses.

"Luxottica's strategy for the nineties: Implement diversification strategies

- From the mid- and premium-price to the designer segment
- Into the sunglass market
- Into the sports accessories market
- Further geographic expansion
- Focus on image, marketing and advertising
- Entry into retail in North America."

PERFORMANCE

Luxottica is among our star companies, having received 100 points in our grading system. By every one of our measures, its performance has been excellent. Revenues increased in each of the last six years, with compound annual growth of 30.5%. EBDIT and EPS increased in five of the last six years, with compound annual growth of 25% and 22%, respectively. ROE averaged an impressive 28%. And the ratio of long-term debt to total capital averaged a reasonable 16%, despite the fact that it shot up briefly in 1995 in the wake of the U.S. Shoe acquisition (by 1996 it was back down to 15%). Investors have done well by this company: the share price saw compound annual growth of 31%.

If you had invested $10,000 in Luxottica at the end of 1990, you would have purchased around 490 shares at $20.25 each (excluding commissions). There was a two-for-one stock split in July 1992. By the end of 1996, you would have had 980 shares worth an estimated $51,100. You would also have received dividend payments of around $3,300.

LUXOTTICA

Ticker Symbol and Exchange: LUX—NYSE   **CUSIP No.: 55068R202**

OPERATING AND PER SHARE DATA
(in millions of U.S. dollars and dollars per ADR)

	1986	1987	1988	1989	1990	1991	1992	1993	1994	1995	1996	CAGR
Sales	N/A	N/A	N/A	N/A	312	372	425	419	504	1,135	1,538	30.5%
EBIT	N/A	N/A	N/A	N/A	60	90	105	115	142	182	225	24.6%
Net Profit	N/A	N/A	N/A	N/A	41	48	55	59	78	99	133	21.7%
EPS	N/A	N/A	N/A	N/A	0.92	1.07	1.22	1.31	1.74	2.22	2.97	21.6%
DPS	N/A	N/A	N/A	N/A	0.35	0.48	0.38	0.47	0.50	0.57	0.65	10.8%

KEY RATIOS

	1986	1987	1988	1989	1990	1991	1992	1993	1994	1995	1996	AVG
EBIT Margin	N/A	N/A	N/A	N/A	19.2%	24.2%	24.7%	27.4%	28.2%	16.0%	14.6%	22.1%
ROE	N/A	N/A	N/A	N/A	27.8%	27.7%	25.8%	26.7%	29.0%	30.2%	27.9%	27.9%
LT Debt/Total Cap	N/A	N/A	N/A	N/A	8.4%	7.2%	6.4%	3.5%	2.8%	70.4%	15.2%	16.3%
P/E (Projected)	N/A	N/A	N/A	N/A	9.5	22.5	19.2	16.8	15.4	19.7	14.9	16.9

STOCK PRICE CHART
(fiscal year-end closing price, in U.S. dollars, adjusted for capital changes)

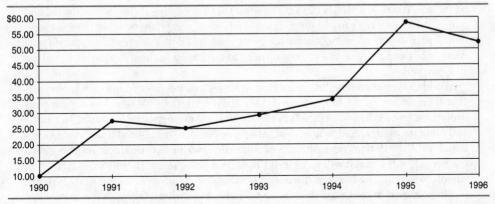

Notes: Luxottica shares became publicly traded in 1990 and are listed on the NYSE. Data are available only in U.S. dollars.

MAGNA INTERNATIONAL (MGA—NYSE)

Address: 36 Apple Creek Boulevard / Markham, Ontario L3R 4Y4 / Canada
Tel.: (905) 477-7766 **Fax:** (905) 475-0776 **Web site:** http://www.magnaint.com

BASIC INFORMATION

Country: Canada
Industry: Industrial equipment
Investment thesis: A world leader in automotive parts; independent supplier to auto companies

Market capitalization: $3.51 billion
Share status: ADRs trade on NYSE

COMPANY GRADING BOX

Growth Categories		Quality of Management	
Revenue Growth	20	Return on Equity	5
Operating Income Growth	20	**Risk**	
Earnings per Share Growth	15	Long-Term Debt/Total Capital	10
Share Price Growth	5	**Total QM&R (maximum 20)**	15
Total Growth (maximum 80)	60	**FINAL GRADE**	75

BACKGROUND

This company is a world leader in automotive parts, an independent supplier to some of the world's largest auto companies. It was founded in 1957 as a tool and die shop called Multimac by the man who is still chairman (first-year sales: $13,000). In 1960 the company signed its first auto parts contract with General Motors, and in 1969 it merged with Magna Electronics, a manufacturer of industrial components. Now called Magna, it was on its way. Today Magna has 32,000 employees, 118 operating divisions worldwide, and annual sales of more than $4 billion. It sells systems of components rather than just individual parts—part of an ongoing strategy to raise its "dollar content" per car. Magna wants more and more of the auto companies to outsource to them. So far, it's a strategy that has worked.

Worldwide auto companies are looking to larger independent suppliers who can service them more fully, often wherever they have operations. Magna already supplies everything from instrument panels to electronics and door systems to seating to chassis and body stampings. And in late 1996, Magna entered a "strategic alliance" with Ohio-based TRW to design, develop, and manufacture automotive products for the global market. TRW has said it will focus on air bags, seat belts, inflators, sensors, and steering wheels, while Magna has said it will focus on vehicle interiors and total body systems.

Magna's most recent expansion has been in Europe, where the push for automotive companies toward using fewer independent suppliers (for more parts) is a few years behind that in the United States, leaving plenty of room for this kind of industry behemoth.

COMPANY STATEMENT (from the 1996 annual report)

"Fiscal year 1996 proved to be another milestone for the Company, which achieved record sales and saw a significant increase in the dollar content per vehicle of Magna supplied components and systems to the global automotive industry. Of particular long term significance, the past fiscal year saw the Company substantially broaden its customer and shareholder base. In addition, we strengthened our balance sheet, and cash balances of approximately $1 billion will enable us to capitalize on opportunities as the automotive industry continues to restructure, consolidate and become solid.

"We have completed three significant acquisitions in the past year. . . . Much of our focus in the year ahead will be to integrate the new companies into Magna's unique entrepreneurial corporate culture, and to consolidate the new technologies and processes with Magna's existing systems capabilities. Through these actions, Magna has strategically enhanced its core systems capabilities, expanded its product line and added new processes for future growth.

"We continue to build upon our record of customer service and close, cooperative relationships with all of our customers. Magna was proud to be named the General Motors Worldwide Corporation of the Year for the second consecutive year—a testimonial to our strong customer focus and our stated commitment of supplying quality systems and components at globally competitive prices."

PERFORMANCE

Magna scored just 75 points overall in our grading system, but the company still turned out to be a great investment. The company received top marks for both revenue growth and EBDIT, although it did not do as well in terms of EP/ADR (or ADR equivalent) growth or share price performance. Revenues in dollars increased every year over the last ten years, recording compound annual growth of 20%. EBDIT increased in nine of the past ten years, showing compound annual growth of just under 27%. EP/ADR increased in just seven of the last ten years and grew by 17%, brought down a little by a 1990–91 company restructuring and a series of rights offerings to raise cash for acquisitions. The ADR price also suffered from this lack of consistency, as investors reacted nervously to the company's up-and-down earnings record, with compound annual growth of about 10%, increasing from a low of $1.96 in 1991 to a high of $67.15 in 1997.

Magna received 5 out of 10 points both for its ROE, which averaged just under 13% for the decade, and 10 points for its long-term debt to total capital ratio, which averaged just under 26% for the decade.

If you had invested $10,000 in Magna in July 1987, you would have purchased around 400 ADRs (or ADR equivalents) at about $25 each (excluding commissions). During the following decade, there were rights offerings and debt conversions to raise cash for the restructuring and acquisitions; however, the company made no changes in its capital structure (shares were simply diluted). By July 1997, your 400 ADRs would have been worth an estimated $27,000. You would also have received around $2,600 in dividend payments.

MAGNA INTERNATIONAL

Ticker Symbol and Exchange: MGA—NYSE   **CUSIP No.: 559222401**

OPERATING AND PER SHARE DATA
(in millions of Canadian dollars and dollars per share)

	Jul 87	Jul 88	Jul 89	Jul 90	Jul 91	Jul 92	Jul 93	Jul 94	Jul 95	Jul 96	Jul 97	CAGR
Sales	1,182	1,536	2,093	2,107	2,212	2,576	2,878	3,884	4,795	5,856	7,692	20.6%
EBDIT	96	98	142	(109)	132	217	264	372	480	499	1,065	27.2%
Net Profit	40	20	34	(224)	17	98	140	234	317	309	617	31.4%
EPS	1.52	0.70	1.19	(8.06)	0.58	2.08	2.55	3.87	5.16	4.71	7.60	17.5%
DPS	0.48	0.48	0.48	0.12	—	0.30	0.60	0.93	1.08	1.08	1.14	9.0%

OPERATING AND PER SHARE DATA
(in millions of U.S. dollars and dollars per ADR)

	Jul 87	Jul 88	Jul 89	Jul 90	Jul 91	Jul 92	Jul 93	Jul 94	Jul 95	Jul 96	Jul 97	CAGR
Sales	891	1,269	1,774	1,832	1,923	2,183	2,248	2,814	3,526	4,274	5,615	20.2%
EBDIT	72	81	120	(95)	115	184	206	270	353	364	777	26.8%
Net Profit	30	16	28	(195)	14	83	110	170	233	226	450	31.0%
EP/ADR	1.15	0.58	1.01	(7.01)	0.50	1.76	1.99	2.80	3.79	3.44	5.55	17.1%
DP/ADR	0.36	0.40	0.41	0.10	—	0.25	0.47	0.67	0.79	0.79	0.83	8.7%

KEY RATIOS

	Jul 87	Jul 88	Jul 89	Jul 90	Jul 91	Jul 92	Jul 93	Jul 94	Jul 95	Jul 96	Jul 97	AVG
EBDIT Margin	8.1%	6.4%	6.8%	−5.2%	6.0%	8.4%	9.2%	9.6%	10.0%	8.5%	13.8%	7.4%
ROE	9.0%	4.4%	7.2%	N/A	6.2%	16.6%	16.6%	17.8%	19.9%	13.3%	18.5%	12.9%
LT Debt/Total Cap	38.0%	38.6%	38.7%	34.7%	41.5%	20.9%	10.0%	4.3%	7.9%	16.2%	6.6%	23.4%
P/E (Projected)	47.16	11.34	N/A	6.21	6.15	11.88	13.05	11.14	13.33	10.95	14.46	14.6

STOCK PRICE CHART
(fiscal year-end closing price, in U.S. dollars, adjusted for capital changes)

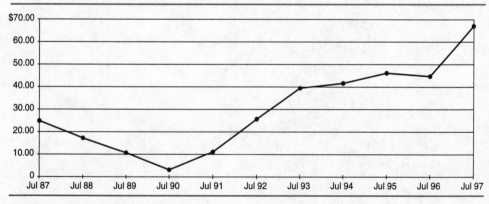

Note: Figures in U.S. dollars are translated from local currency using year-end exchange rates.

MAGNUM (MGMS.KL—KUALA LUMPUR)

Address: 33rd Floor, Menara Multi-Purpose/ Capital Square No. 8 / Jalan Munshi Abdullah /
50100 Kuala Lumpur / Malaysia
Tel.: (011) 60 3 298 8033   **Fax:** (011) 60 3 298 9885

BASIC INFORMATION

Country: Malaysia   **Market capitalization:** $2.45 billion
Industry: Gaming   **Share status:** Foreign shares trade on Kuala Lumpur Exchange
Investment thesis: Market leader in Malaysian gaming industry

COMPANY GRADING BOX

Growth Categories		Quality of Management	
Revenue Growth	20	Return on Equity	10
Operating Income Growth	20	**Risk**	
Earnings per Share Growth	20	Long-Term Debt/Total Capital	10
Share Price Growth	15	**Total QM&R (maximum 20)**	20
Total Growth (maximum 80)	75	**FINAL GRADE**	95

BACKGROUND

Three companies control 95% of Malaysia's gaming industry—and Magnum, with 44% of the market, is the largest of the three. Gaming is tightly regulated in Malaysia but tolerated, mostly for Malaysia's largest ethnic minority. Twenty-six percent of the Malaysian population is Chinese, and the Chinese are known as avid gamblers. Competition? With the Muslim-dominated government so far unwilling to issue gaming licenses to new operators, the dominant players are likely to remain so. Altogether, Magnum has more than 490 outlets and 1,800 gambling terminals. In 1996 revenues totaled $1.1 billion, having increased at a compound annual rate of 23% over the last nine years (see performance below for more details). Founded in 1968, Magnum has been listed on the Kuala Lumpur Stock Exchange since 1970.

Although during the last few years Magnum has been under pressure from its competitors, who have been targeting a younger generation with new forms of gaming entertainment, Magnum still has a lot in its favor. As the pioneer of the most popular form of gaming in Malaysia, the relatively simple 4D game (customers bet on four-digit numbers to win selected prizes), it is operating from a strong base and has a long and consistently profitable track record, conservative management, and a sensible expansion plan. Recently, Magnum has used its prodigious cash flow to expand into property development and hotels in Malaysia and abroad, particularly in the Philippines and China (through joint ventures).

Domestically, Magnum also should be able to profit from an increase in disposable income, new outlets (and relocated outlets) in areas with more people, and the continued shift by bettors from illegal to legal games. Although the possibility of increased government regulation presents risks, Magnum has thrived facing such risks in the past, and it's a good bet it will continue to do so in the future. Of course, the Asian market turmoil of 1997 and 1998 has clouded the picture for all companies in the region; however, Magnum could offer an interesting opportunity when this market does turn around.

COMPANY STATEMENT (from the 1996 annual report)

"With Malaysia's economic fundamentals remaining strong, the Group's principal business activities will continue to benefit from the steady economic growth which is expected to average 8% this year. As for the other ASEAN countries, especially the Philippines, the economic growth for 1997 is projected to remain on target with growth emanating from, amongst others, high rates of investment and domestic demand. Against this background, the outlook for the Group's business ventures in the region remains encouraging for the year ahead.

"Magnum is committed to realizing the full potential of its core operations through numerous development and expansion programs in Malaysia as well as abroad, and managing its resources to maximize returns to its shareholders."

PERFORMANCE

With stellar past performance, Magnum received 95 points in our grading system. Revenues in dollars increased in every one of the last eight years, with compound annual growth of 23%. EBDIT and EPS increased in seven of the last eight years, recording compound annual growth of 42% and 52%, respectively. ROE averaged 24%. As for risk, the ratio of long-term debt to total capital averaged 9%—and was a minimal 1% in 1996. Share price performance has also been impressive: the share price in dollars saw compound annual growth of 42%. Keep in mind, however, that nine years ago it would have been difficult to invest in this company and that—going forward—it would be tough for any company to sustain Magnum's incredible historic growth rate. Even so, the numbers indicate that management knows what it is doing. And, with those caveats, (plus the above mentioned Asian economic turmoil) Magnum remains an interesting candidate for investment.

If you had invested $10,000 in Magnum at the end of 1988, you would have purchased around 7,200 shares at about $1.25 each (excluding commissions). During the next eight years, there were a one-for-eight bonus issue in August 1980, a two-for-one stock split in December 1991, a one-for-ten bonus issue in July 1992, a three-for-two bonus issue in September 1993, and a one-for-two bonus issue in February 1996. By the end of 1996, you would have had around 67,000 shares worth an estimated $130,000. You would also have received dividend payments of around $10,300.

MAGNUM

Ticker Symbol and Exchange: MGMS.KL—KUALA LUMPUR   SEDOL Code: 6554006

OPERATING AND PER SHARE DATA
(in millions of Malaysian ringgit and ringgit per share)

	1986	1987	1988	1989	1990	1991	1992	1993	1994	1995	1996	CAGR
Sales	N/A	N/A	544	746	1,051	1,217	1,556	2,249	2,230	2,332	2,794	22.7%
EBDIT	N/A	N/A	30	64	110	221	325	431	400	402	462	40.9%
Net Profit	N/A	N/A	7	30	53	121	181	256	250	241	284	57.8%
EPS	N/A	N/A	0.01	0.03	0.05	0.08	0.12	0.17	0.17	0.16	0.19	51.1%
DPS	N/A	N/A	0.04	0.05	0.20	0.25	0.10	0.05	0.05	0.03	0.05	2.8%

OPERATING AND PER SHARE DATA
(in millions of U.S. dollars and dollars per share)

	1986	1987	1988	1989	1990	1991	1992	1993	1994	1995	1996	CAGR
Sales	N/A	N/A	201	276	389	447	596	836	875	918	1,104	23.7%
EBDIT	N/A	N/A	11.0	23.7	40.6	81.2	124.6	160.2	156.7	158.1	182.8	42.1%
Net Profit	N/A	N/A	2.7	11.2	19.6	44.6	69.2	95.3	98.0	94.7	112.2	59.1%
EPS	N/A	N/A	0.00	0.01	0.02	0.03	0.05	0.06	0.07	0.06	0.08	52.4%
DPS	N/A	N/A	0.01	0.02	0.07	0.09	0.04	0.02	0.02	0.01	0.02	3.7%

KEY RATIOS

	1986	1987	1988	1989	1990	1991	1992	1993	1994	1995	1996	AVG
EBDIT Margin	N/A	N/A	5.5%	8.6%	10.4%	18.1%	20.9%	19.2%	17.9%	17.2%	16.5%	14.9%
ROE	N/A	N/A	7.8%	21.4%	21.2%	32.8%	34.9%	32.4%	24.4%	19.9%	19.5%	23.8%
LT Debt/Total Cap	N/A	N/A	43.8%	26.2%	4.2%	2.6%	1.9%	1.1%	0.8%	1.1%	1.0%	9.2%
P/E (Projected)	N/A	N/A	10.7	7.8	9.8	9.0	13.3	31.5	18.8	16.8	21.3	15.4

STOCK PRICE CHART
(fiscal year-end closing price, in U.S. dollars, adjusted for capital changes)

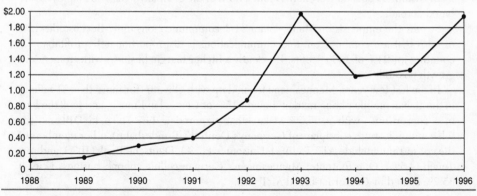

Note: U.S. dollar figures translated from local currency using year-end exchange rate.

MANNESMANN (MNNSY—OTC)

Address: Mannesmannufer 2 / 40027 Düsseldorf / Germany
Tel.: (011) 49 211 8 200   **Fax:** (011) 49 211 8 202554

BASIC INFORMATION

Country: Germany   **Market capitalization:** $13.97 billion
Industry: Multi-industry   **Share status:** ADRs trade OTC
Investment thesis: Industrial conglomerate, aggressively expanding in telecommunications

COMPANY GRADING BOX

Growth Categories		Quality of Management	
Revenue Growth	10	Return on Equity	0
Operating Income Growth	10	**Risk**	
Earnings per Share Growth	5	Long-Term Debt/Total Capital	10
Share Price Growth	15	**Total QM&R (maximum 20)**	10
Total Growth (maximum 80)	40	**FINAL GRADE**	50

BACKGROUND

Mannesmann, based in Düsseldorf, Germany, is a company that made some right moves at the right time; it's an industrial conglomerate that saw trouble ahead and diversified, beginning back in the 1960s. Mannesmann's biggest growth business today? Telecommunications. Not where you expect to find them, but Mannesmann is doing just fine. Five years after starting operations, Mannesmann's mobile phone network business, Mannesmann Mobilfunk, is running neck and neck with recently privatized Deutsche Telekom, until recently the sole player in the German telecommunications market. In August 1996 Mannesmann became the first German mobile telecommunications operator to have more than 2 million subscribers in its network.

Mannesmann was founded in 1890 by two Mannesmann brothers, the first to produce seamless steel tubes by rolling a solid ingot. Through the 1960s, the company grew into a giant vertically integrated coal and steel company. Today 43% of sales are in machinery and engineering, 22% are in automotive engineering, 19% are in tubulars and trading, 12% are in telecommunications (that's up from 8% for 1995), and 4% are in other smaller businesses. Total annual sales: more than $22 billion, more than half of which comes from customers outside Germany. About a third of the company's 120,000 employees are based abroad.

So why the emphasis on Mannesmann's telecommunications unit? Because the 12% of sales that are coming from telecommunications is disproportionately profitable, accounting for 94% of 1996 profits. It's clearly a higher-margin business with tremendous growth possibilities.

In the last few years, Mannesmann teamed up with Olivetti (for more than $1 billion) in the Italian mobile phone market, bought 15% of Cegetel in France, and took the lead in a consortium—with a 55.5% stake—that acquired a 49% stake in DBkom (the telecommunications subsidiary of Germany's Deutsche Bundesbahn); other members of the consortium include AT&T (15%), Unisource (15%), Deutsche Bank (10%), and AirTouch (4.5%). One footnote: Mannesmann's German cellular phone business is itself 35.2% owned by California-based AirTouch.

COMPANY STATEMENT (from the 1996 annual report)

"In managing Mannesmann on your behalf, we are guided by the principles of increasing value and return on investment. In the past year we have put a concrete figure on our ambitions: in the medium term we intend to provide you with a return of 15 percent based on our gross operating assets. In 1996, we attained a return of 8 percent.

"In 1996 we had substantial weakness and therefore heavy losses in Demag's Metallurgical Engineering subdivision, Building Materials Trading and at our tubes company in Brazil. In all three subdivisions we initiated measures in 1996 that will eliminate these weaknesses. . . . In the Engineering and Automotive sectors, we must make portfolio improvements in order to achieve the 15 percent return. . . . In 1996, we made even greater strides than in recent years with our growth strategy in the Telecommunications sector. . . . More than half of Mannesmann's investments were channeled into Telecommunications in 1996. We project this also to be the case in 1997. We believe that the opportunities for high value increases in this sector remain promising. In 1996, we reached a general agreement concerning an investment in telecommunications in our neighboring market in France which will be made in 1997. . . . For years now, Mannesmann has been prevented from carrying out a strategy based solely on growth and expansion in steel tubes by world economic conditions and product criteria. We plan to found a joint venture for seamless steel tubes in 1997 together with our major French competitor. . . . Mannesmann's commitment of assets to its Tubes & Trading sector will tend to decline in relative terms due to growth in the other sectors."

PERFORMANCE

Mannesmann's best numbers are its stock price performance: its ADR (or ADR equivalent—the sponsored ADR was listed in 1994) recorded 24% compound annual growth over the last nine years. It has also done reasonably well in terms of consistency, recording increases in revenues in dollars in eight of the last ten years and in EBDIT—also in dollars—in seven of the last ten years. Mannesmann's overall score of 50 in our grading system reflects both its sizable investment in the rapidly growing telecommunications business and the less impressive growth in the more mature segments of the company. Revenues in dollars had compound annual growth of just under 10%. EBDIT had compounded annual growth of 13%. EP/ADR showed compound annual growth of 14% despite a downturn in the early 1990s, right before Mannesmann diversified into telecommunications. ROE averaged a moderate 9% for the decade but moved up to 13% in 1996. As for risk, this company has very little long-term debt; the ratio of long-term debt to total capital averaged just 6%.

If you had invested $10,000 in Mannesmann at the end of 1987, you would have purchased around 150 ADRs (or ADR equivalents) at about $66.25. During the next nine years there were two major capital changes, a one-for-nine rights issue in November 1989, a one-for-ten rights issue in September 1990, and a one-for-eight rights issue in September 1993. By the end of 1996, you would have had around 160 ADRs worth an estimated $66,900. You would also have received dividend payments of around $6,700.

MANNESMANN

Ticker Symbol and Exchange: MNNSY—OTC   **CUSIP No.: 563775303**

OPERATING AND PER SHARE DATA
(in millions of German marks and marks per share)

	1986	1987	1988	1989	1990	1991	1992	1993	1994	1995	1996	CAGR
Sales	17,234	16,655	20,422	22,330	23,943	24,315	28,018	27,963	30,397	32,094	34,683	7.2%
EBDIT	1,129	1,091	1,669	1,963	1,879	1,637	1,589	1,322	2,538	2,755	3,182	10.9%
Net Profit	197	157	463	658	667	450	258	(146)	549	630	610	12.0%
EPS	7.52	6.00	17.37	23.78	21.93	14.00	8.00	(3.99)	15.00	21.00	22.00	11.3%
DPS	N/M	4.83	6.27	8.92	9.00	9.00	6.00	5.00	6.00	8.00	9.00	7.2%

OPERATING AND PER SHARE DATA
(in millions of U.S. dollars and dollars per ADR)

	1986	1987	1988	1989	1990	1991	1992	1993	1994	1995	1996	CAGR
Sales	8,976	10,608	11,538	13,213	16,069	15,997	17,295	16,071	19,611	22,288	22,233	9.5%
EBDIT	588	695	943	1,162	1,261	1,077	981	760	1,638	1,913	2,040	13.2%
Net Profit	103	100	261	389	448	296	160	(84)	354	438	391	14.3%
EP/ADR	3.92	3.82	9.81	14.07	14.72	9.21	4.94	(2.29)	9.68	14.58	14.10	13.7%
DP/ADR	N/M	3.08	3.54	5.28	6.04	5.92	3.70	2.87	3.87	5.56	5.77	7.2%

KEY RATIOS

	1986	1987	1988	1989	1990	1991	1992	1993	1994	1995	1996	AVG
EBDIT Margin	6.5%	6.6%	8.2%	8.8%	7.8%	6.7%	5.7%	4.7%	8.4%	8.6%	9.2%	7.4%
ROE	6.4%	4.5%	12.9%	15.1%	12.5%	8.2%	4.7%	-2.4%	9.1%	11.8%	13.5%	8.8%
LT Debt/Total Cap	3.7%	6.2%	8.2%	3.7%	3.2%	3.7%	5.6%	8.3%	9.4%	5.8%	6.0%	5.8%
P/E (Projected)	N/M	5.8	8.6	16.8	18.8	30.4	(57.4)	28.2	20.1	20.8	25.0	11.7

STOCK PRICE CHART
(fiscal year-end closing price, in U.S. dollars, adjusted for capital changes)

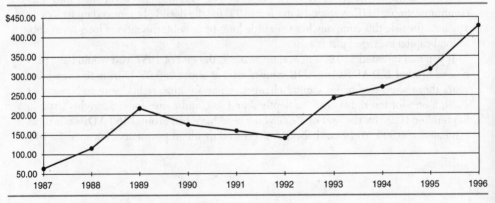

Note: Figures in U.S. dollars are translated from local currency using year-end exchange rates.

MANUTAN (MATP.PA—PARIS)

Address: 32 bis Boulevard de Picpus / 75583 Paris Cedex 12 / France
Tel.: (011) 33 1 53 33 40 00   **Fax:** (011) 33 1 53 33 40 28

BASIC INFORMATION

Country: France
Industry: Retailing, specialty
Investment thesis: A leading mail-order company specializing in industrial equipment

Market capitalization: $573 million
Share status: Foreign shares trade on Paris Exchange

COMPANY GRADING BOX

Growth Categories		Quality of Management	
Revenue Growth	20	Return on Equity	10
Operating Income Growth	20	**Risk**	
Earnings per Share Growth	20	Long-Term Debt/Total Capital	10
Share Price Growth	20	**Total QM&R (maximum 20)**	**20**
Total Growth (maximum 80)	**80**	**FINAL GRADE**	**100**

BACKGROUND

When most of us think of the mail-order business, we think of J. Crew or Land's End. France-based Manutan is a mail-order business of a different ilk. Thirty years ago this company began selling industrial equipment to industrial users by mail order. And it has been growing pretty much ever since. The company has compiled a track record that got it a top grade in this book. Among the (mostly European) products Manutan offers are handling, lifting, and storage equipment; office and workshop furniture as well as general office supplies; and equipment for maintenance and security. A range of catalogs is mailed free to customers and prospects, including 800-page general catalogs and specialty catalogs tailored to different businesses.

Today Manutan is the leader in most of its markets (a key exception being Germany), with 60% of revenues now generated outside France. It has more than 500,000 customers—predominantly in western Europe—and thirteen operating companies located throughout the Continent and the United Kingdom, and it generates about $342 million in sales annually. Just two years ago Manutan bought Netherlands-based Overtoom, the market leader in Holland and a company just about half its size, consolidating its position in the Benelux countries. Going forward, that acquisition should also give the company greater negotiating power with manufacturers, as well as efficiencies of scale.

This is a company with tremendous growth potential in all of its markets. Overall, the mail-order industry is making inroads in industrial orders, and Manutan is an industry veteran. By continuing to broaden its product range, it should be able to draw new customers interested in working with a single supplier and bring in new business from its existing customer base. Manutan is now focusing on Portugal and the Middle East for further overseas expansion.

COMPANY STATEMENT (from the 1994–95 annual report)

"Manutan's Thirtieth Birthday

"... The unifying idea is, of course, selling industrial equipment by mail order. We wanted to have the best catalog. A catalog of industrial equipment for industrial users.

Inspired by moral principles, we have created the right conditions to foster responsibility and loyalty which are essential to the company. . . .

"Highlights of the Year

"1/ Overtoom joins the Manutan Group: the quality of the company and its team, its position as market leader in the Netherlands and Belgium, and its size, which is half of ours, give the Manutan group a new dimension. Manutan will from now on be one of the (very restricted) companies leading the European market for business-to-business mail order.
"2/ General Growth: All companies in the group, without exception, increased their turnover.
"3/ Development of our logistical methods:

- notable acquisitions, at very competitive prices, together with recent building developments (warehouses and offices) in Sweden and Germany give these two companies the means to ensure their future development.
- centralization of our warehouse and offices in Italy in one location; this geographic concentration of our locations has already given a significant improvement in productivity and customer service.
- construction of a large office complex in the United Kingdom."

PERFORMANCE

Manutan's track record is impressive, garnering the full 100 points in our grading system. Investors who got in when Manutan was a small-capitalization company (it still has a market capitalization of only $573 million) have made a lot of money. Over the last ten years, the share price in dollars increased at a compound annual rate of 31%. Manutan's revenues in dollar terms grew in every one of the last ten years, with compound annual growth of 18%. EBDIT increased in nine of the last ten years, showing compound annual growth of 21%. EPS in dollars increased from $0.35 in 1986 to $3.19 in 1996, with compound annual growth of 25%. And dividends in dollars increased from $0.04 to $0.73, with compound annual growth of 35%. ROE was 16% in 1996 and averaged 21.5% for the ten-year period. Manutan has also kept down the ratio of its long-term debt to total capital, which averaged 8.1%. Although Manutan's debt jumped to 27% after the Overtoom acquisition in 1995, by the end of 1996 management had brought it back down to 17%.

If you had invested $10,000 in Manutan in September 1986, you would have purchased around 150 shares at about $66.50 each (excluding commissions). During the following ten years, there were six capital changes, including a bonus issue in June of 1991 and two one-for-one stock splits, in September 1994 and in June 1996. By September 1996, you would have had 1,800 shares worth an estimated $146,400. You would also have received around $5,000 in dividend payments.

MANUTAN

Ticker Symbol and Exchange: MATP.PA—PARIS   **SEDOL Code: 4564869**

OPERATING AND PER SHARE DATA
(in millions of French francs and francs per share)

	Sep 86	Sep 87	Sep 88	Sep 89	Sep 90	Sep 91	Sep 92	Sep 93	Sep 94	Sep 95	Sep 96	CAGR
Sales	449	481	616	743	889	991	1,013	955	994	1,391	1,763	14.7%
EBDIT	44	50	96	98	113	132	127	106	122	180	226	17.7%
Net Profit	17	19	41	49	58	65	74	68	74	111	119	21.7%
EPS	2.31	2.69	5.68	6.75	8.09	8.94	10.21	9.42	10.22	15.35	16.45	21.7%
DPS	0.25	0.33	0.50	0.84	1.25	1.45	1.63	1.63	2.10	4.50	3.77	31.2%

OPERATING AND PER SHARE DATA
(in millions of U.S. dollars and dollars per share)

	Sep 86	Sep 87	Sep 88	Sep 89	Sep 90	Sep 91	Sep 92	Sep 93	Sep 94	Sep 95	Sep 96	CAGR
Sales	68	78	97	117	170	174	212	168	188	283	342	17.6%
EBDIT	6.7	8.2	15.1	15.5	21.6	23.2	26.6	18.6	23.0	36.5	43.8	20.7%
Net Profit	2.5	3.2	6.4	7.7	11.1	11.4	15.5	12.0	14.0	22.6	23.0	24.8%
EPS	0.35	0.44	0.89	1.06	1.54	1.57	2.14	1.66	1.93	3.12	3.19	24.8%
DPS	0.04	0.05	0.08	0.13	0.24	0.26	0.34	0.29	0.40	0.91	0.73	34.5%

KEY RATIOS

	Sep 86	Sep 87	Sep 88	Sep 89	Sep 90	Sep 91	Sep 92	Sep 93	Sep 94	Sep 95	Sep 96	AVG
EBDIT Margin	9.8%	10.5%	15.6%	13.2%	12.8%	13.3%	12.5%	11.1%	12.2%	12.9%	12.8%	12.4%
ROE	20.6%	20.0%	30.1%	27.5%	25.9%	22.9%	22.0%	17.4%	16.5%	17.2%	16.0%	21.5%
LT Debt/Total Cap	7.0%	5.1%	3.1%	1.9%	1.1%	9.2%	7.7%	5.8%	4.4%	26.6%	17.4%	8.1%
P/E (Projected)	13.6	7.6	8.6	15.0	11.0	13.5	15.2	15.9	15.2	18.1	21.9	14.1

STOCK PRICE CHART
(fiscal year-end closing price, in U.S. dollars, adjusted for capital changes)

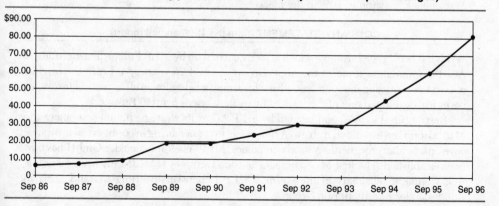

Note: Figures in U.S. dollars are translated from local currency using average exchange rates.

MARSCHOLLEK (MCPG.F—FRANKFURT)

Address: Forum 7 / 69126 Heidelberg / Germany
Tel.: (011) 49 62 21 3 08-0   **Fax:** (011) 49 62 21 3 08-158

BASIC INFORMATION

Country: Germany   **Market capitalization:** $1.37 billion
Industry: Financial services   **Share status:** Foreign shares trade on Frankfurt Exchange
Investment thesis: Insurance and financial management services for professionals in Germany

COMPANY GRADING BOX

Growth Categories		Quality of Management	
Revenue Growth	20	Return on Equity	10
Operating Income Growth	20	**Risk**	
Earnings per Share Growth	20	Long-Term Debt/Total Capital	10
Share Price Growth	20	**Total QM&R (maximum 20)**	**20**
Total Growth (maximum 80)	**80**	**FINAL GRADE**	**100**

BACKGROUND

We all know what has happened to the mutual fund industry in the United States: Fidelity, T. Rowe Price, Vanguard . . . they're household names today. And they're financial giants. Germany's Marschollek may be heading in the same direction. The German economy is in a state of transition; state benefits are being rolled back, and individuals are taking greater responsibility for their financial well-being. Employees are beginning to think about their own retirement funds. And a stock culture is beginning to take hold. Marschollek is ready. This financial services firm, with a market capitalization today of $1.37 billion, was started twenty-five years ago to provide independent advice for young academics on their insurance coverage. It has been building on that concept ever since.

Today in Germany, Marschollek is a major player in life, health, and property insurance, and its mutual funds are booming. In 1994 Marschollek managers began offering to manage clients' fund money directly, choosing the funds for clients. And in 1995 more than 95 percent of the firm's clients chose to use the service. Marschollek continues to draw medical school graduates as clients and has a 40% market share among Germany's doctors. Among its other target groups—economists, engineers and natural scientists—Marschollek has around 10% of the market.

COMPANY STATEMENT (from the 1995 annual report)

"With the brokerage business, which is today carried on by MLP Finanzdienstleistungen AG, the foundation stone of the MLP Group was laid 25 years ago. From the original concept of providing independent advice for young academics on all aspects of insurance cover has developed one of the leading financial services firms in Europe.

"Restructured in 1993 and headed by MLP AG as its strategic holding company, the MLP Group has expanded its base. A new company specializing in commercial insurance cover, particularly for medium sized companies, MLP Assekuranzmakler GmbH has now been established. The first MLP company outside Germany is MLP-Lebensversicherung AG, Vienna, a subsidiary of the German MLP Lebensversicherung AG and Austrian Bundesländer und Raiffeisen Group.

"All companies have contributed by their growth to the positive overall performance of the MLP Group. From a business point of view this has resulted in an increasingly broader base, which contains considerable future potential."

PERFORMANCE

Marschollek's growth has been strong and consistent, garnering a perfect score of 100 in our grading system. This company has increased its revenues in dollars in each of the last ten years, recording compound annual growth of 25% per annum. EBDIT increased in nine of the last ten years, with compound annual growth of 36%. And EPS increased in eight of the last ten years, with compound annual growth of 26%. ROE averaged a very high 29% (although in 1996 it was down to 13%) and the ratio of debt to long-term capital averaged just 8%.

Shareholders have done well in this company. If you had invested $10,000 in Marschollek at the end of 1990, you would have purchased around ten shares for about $807.25 each (excluding commissions). Over the next six years, there were a one-for-eight rights issue in June 1991, a one-for-two bonus issue in July 1992, a one-for-one bonus issue in July 1993, a ten-for-one stock split in September 1996, and a one-for-ten rights issue in October 1996. At the end of 1996, you would have had around 375 shares worth an estimated $58,000. You would also have received dividend payments of around $2,500.

MARSCHOLLEK

Ticker Symbol and Exchange: MCPG.F—Frankfurt   **SEDOL Code: 4569392**

OPERATING AND PER SHARE DATA
(in millions of German marks and marks per share)

	1986	1987	1988	1989	1990	1991	1992	1993	1994	1995	1996	CAGR
Sales	33.0	41.0	53.0	64.0	72.0	91.0	119.0	142.0	167.0	193.0	249.0	22.4%
EBDIT	3.2	6.5	6.6	11.4	16.8	19.8	30.2	33.1	39.4	46.9	56.4	33.2%
Net Income	1.2	2.1	1.8	2.6	7.6	9.6	11.2	13.1	17.6	20.1	26.7	36.4%
EPS	0.48	0.84	0.36	0.52	1.57	1.58	1.83	2.14	2.87	3.28	4.04	23.7%
DPS	N/M	0.66	0.33	0.41	0.84	0.84	1.00	1.52	1.76	2.25	2.21	14.4%

OPERATING AND PER SHARE DATA
(in millions of U.S. dollars and dollars per share)

	1986	1987	1988	1989	1990	1991	1992	1993	1994	1995	1996	CAGR
Revenues	17.2	26.1	29.9	37.9	48.3	59.9	73.5	81.6	107.7	134.0	159.6	25.0%
EBDIT	1.7	4.1	3.7	6.7	11.3	13.0	18.6	19.0	25.4	32.6	36.2	36.0%
Net Income	0.6	1.3	1.0	1.5	5.1	6.3	6.9	7.5	11.4	14.0	17.1	39.2%
EPS	0.25	0.54	0.20	0.31	1.05	1.04	1.13	1.23	1.85	2.28	2.59	26.3%
DPS	N/M	0.42	0.19	0.24	0.56	0.55	0.62	0.87	1.14	1.56	1.42	14.5%

KEY RATIOS

	1986	1987	1988	1989	1990	1991	1992	1993	1994	1995	1996	AVG
Operating Margin	9.7%	15.9%	12.5%	17.8%	23.3%	21.8%	25.4%	23.3%	23.6%	24.3%	22.7%	20.0%
ROE	32.4%	48.8%	31.6%	29.2%	60.8%	16.2%	18.9%	20.6%	24.3%	26.1%	12.9%	29.3%
LTD/TC	19.4%	8.8%	7.5%	20.7%	5.8%	1.4%	2.2%	4.7%	4.3%	4.7%	5.0%	7.7%
P/E (Projected)	N/M	N/M	N/M	N/M	25.1	21.7	20.3	29.3	26.4	25.2	49.7	28.2

STOCK PRICE CHART
(fiscal year-end closing price, in U.S. dollars, adjusted for capital changes)

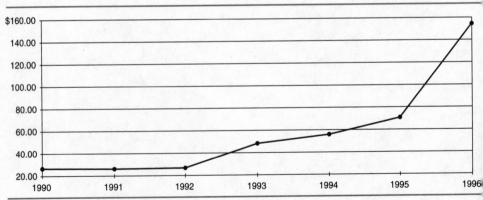

Note: Figures in U.S. dollars are translated from local currency using year-end exchange rates.

MISYS (MSY.L—LONDON)

Address: Burleigh House Chapel Oak / Salford Priors / Worcestershire WR11 5SH / United Kingdom
Tel.: (011) 44 1386 871 373   **Fax:** (011) 44 1386 871 045   **Web site:** http://www.misysplc.com

BASIC INFORMATION

Country: United Kingdom
Industry: Business services
Market capitalization: $1.7 billion
Share status: Foreign shares trade on London Exchange
Investment thesis: Supplies software, management systems and service to corporate information technology departments

COMPANY GRADING BOX

Growth Categories		Quality of Management	
Revenue Growth	20	Return on Equity	0
Operating Income Growth	20	**Risk**	
Earnings per Share Growth	20	Cash Flow / Interest Expenses	10
Share Price Growth	15	**Total QM&R (maximum 20)**	10
Total Growth (maximum 80)	**75**	**FINAL GRADE**	**85**

BACKGROUND

Misys is a software outsourcing company—a British leader in a relatively young, high-growth industry, pursuing growth by acquisition. It specializes in supplying software, management systems, and services to corporate information technology departments. Through 1997 about 45% of its revenues came from recurring license fees (renewals); 30% came from initial sales (to new and existing customers); and the rest came from related services. Misys takes on all or part of a company's information technology needs and provides low-cost, efficient solutions.

Misys's main focus is the financial sector (stockbrokerage, transaction processing, etc.), although the group services a range of clients, from the construction, contracting, and utilities sector to health care providers. In 1996 banks accounted for about 50% of revenues and 60% of profits; the insurance industry accounted for 14% of sales and 23% of profits; and information systems accounted for 36% of sales and 17% of profits.

Misys was incorporated in 1979 as a supplier of systems to the U.K. insurance industry. It started branching out in the mid-1980s, went public in 1987, and has since grown organically and by acquisition. Today, Misys is the largest application software company in the United Kingdom and one of the top ten in the world, with customers in more than ninety countries. Almost half the company's 1996 sales were generated overseas before Misys agreed to buy North Carolina–based Medic Computer Systems for $922.8 million. Misys spends around 13% of annual revenue on its research and development efforts, and about 25% of the company's 4,140 employees are involved with product development.

COMPANY STATEMENT (from a 1996 corporate overview)

"Our philosophy is based on enhancing shareholder value, measured by the growth and stability of long term cash flows. Misys has an outstanding track record, achieved through

- committed and experienced management
- proven financial controls
- substantial ongoing investment in product development
- selective investment in well positioned businesses.

"The success of this philosophy has made Misys one of the world's largest and most financially successful providers of commercial software applications and associated services.

"Misys is also well positioned for the future. Consolidation in the software industry is being driven by a need to recover product development costs from larger user bases and by the scale required to support the pullthrough of escalating levels of professional services. Scale is also critical if software and services companies are to have credibility in the eyes of large customers seeking outsourcing partners. As the consolidation process accelerates, larger companies such as Misys should enjoy significant competitive advantage."

PERFORMANCE

Misys received top scores for growth, and its long-term debt to total capital ratio, compiling an overall score of 85 in our grading system. In dollars, EPS and EBDIT increased in nine of the last ten years, with compound annual growth of 21% and 55%, respectively. Revenues in dollars, though up in just eight of the ten years, increased at an incredible compound annual rate of 60%. (ROE numbers are distorted by U.K. GAAP, which requires the company to immediately write off from shareholders' equity any goodwill incurred from acquisitions so we deemed them N/M.) To try to determine risk, we used a different measure, cash flow divided by interest expense, to assess the company's ability to cover interest payments on outstanding debt. In this regard, Misys appears to be well covered and receives maximum points. Share price performance was less impressive over the longer term, increasing at a compound annual rate of 16%—though the stock price more than doubled from 1995 to 1996.

If you had invested $10,000 in Misys in May 1988, you would have purchased around 1,700 shares at about $5.75 each (excluding commissions). During the next eight years, there were an 11-for-57 rights issue in May 1989, a 1-for-10.231 rights issue in March 1991, and a 2-for-13 rights issue in April 1994. By May 1997, you would have had around 1,780 shares worth an estimated $39,000. You would also have received dividend payments of around $2,100.

MISYS

Ticker Symbol and Exchange: MSY.L—LONDON **SEDOL Code: 596606**

OPERATING AND PER SHARE DATA
(in millions of British pounds and pounds per share)

	May 87	May 88	May 89	May 90	May 91	May 92	May 93	May 94	May 95	May 96	May 97	CAGR
Sales	3.0	8.0	26.0	77.0	67.0	68.0	74.0	93.0	153.0	280.0	325.0	59.8%
EBDIT	0.9	2.2	6.3	12.9	7.8	10.7	16.9	20.4	29.1	58.4	71.5	54.9%
Net Profit	0.6	1.5	3.7	7.2	3.7	6.2	10.5	12.9	18.6	36.8	45.9	54.3%
EPS	0.08	0.15	0.23	0.23	0.11	0.17	0.27	0.32	0.35	0.44	0.53	21.1%
DPS	0.02	0.03	0.05	0.05	0.06	0.06	0.07	0.08	0.09	0.11	0.12	21.0%

OPERATING AND PER SHARE DATA
(in millions of U.S. dollars and dollars per share)

	May 87	May 88	May 89	May 90	May 91	May 92	May 93	May 94	May 95	May 96	May 97	CAGR
Sales	5	15	41	128	114	124	116	141	243	438	533	59.8%
EBDIT	1.5	4.0	9.8	21.5	13.2	19.5	26.4	30.9	46.2	91.3	117.2	54.9%
Net Profit	1.0	2.7	5.8	12.0	6.3	11.3	16.4	19.5	29.5	57.5	75.2	54.3%
EPS	0.13	0.27	0.36	0.38	0.19	0.32	0.42	0.48	0.56	0.69	0.86	21.1%
DPS	0.03	0.06	0.07	0.09	0.09	0.11	0.11	0.12	0.15	0.17	0.20	21.0%

KEY RATIOS

	May 87	May 88	May 89	May 90	May 91	May 92	May 93	May 94	May 95	May 96	May 97	AVG
EBDIT Margin	30.0%	27.5%	24.2%	16.8%	11.6%	15.7%	22.8%	21.9%	19.0%	20.9%	22.0%	21.1%
ROE	N/M	N/M	N/M	N/M	N/M	N/M	N/M	N/M	N/M	N/M	N/M	N/M
CF/Int Exp	N/A	N/A	43.0	21.8	14.0	26.7	32.3	30.8	55.5	14.4	20.5	30.6
P/E (Projected)	N/A	13.5	18.9	13.1	9.0	10.7	15.7	13.8	8.5	15.9	21.9	11.9

STOCK PRICE CHART
(fiscal year-end closing price, in U.S. dollars, adjusted for capital changes)

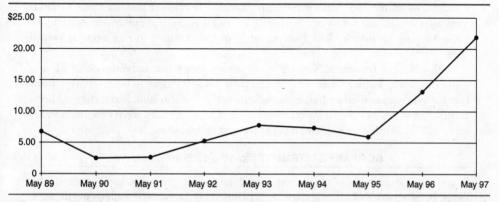

Notes: Misys consistently reports low or negative shareholders' equity because according to U.K. GAAP it must write off the goodwill on any acquisitions from shareholders' equity immediately. Under U.S. GAAP, a U.S. company could write off goodwill over a forty-year period. To measure risk for Misys, we therefore analyzed interest payment coverage, or cash flow divided by interest expense. Figures in U.S. dollars are translated from local currency using year-end exchange rates.

NATUZZI (NTZ—NYSE)

Address: Via iazzitiello 47 / 70029 Santeramo in Colle (Bari) / Italy
Tel.: (011) 39 80 882 0111   **Fax:** (011) 39 80 837 637
or
Address: P.O. Box 2438 / High Point, NC 27261
Tel.: (910) 887-8300   **Fax:** (910) 887-8500

BASIC INFORMATION

Country: Italy
Industry: Household goods
Investment thesis: World leader in leather-upholstered furniture

Market capitalization: $1.3 billion
Share status: ADRs trade on NYSE

COMPANY GRADING BOX

Growth Categories		Quality of Management	
Revenue Growth	20	Return on Equity	10
Operating Income Growth	20	**Risk**	
Earnings per Share Growth	20	Long-Term Debt/Total Capital	10
Share Price Growth	15	**Total QM&R (maximum 20)**	**20**
Total Growth (maximum 80)	**75**	**FINAL GRADE**	**95**

BACKGROUND

Industrie Natuzzi is Italy's largest furniture manufacturer—and the world leader in leather upholstered furniture. A family business, Natuzzi was founded in 1959 by Pasquale Natuzzi—who still heads the company—when he was nineteen years old. Today, Natuzzi is a New York Stock Exchange–listed company (it is not listed in Italy) with 1996 revenues of $554 million, a market capitalization of $1.3 billion, and 2,631 employees. The company's furniture is available in more than 15,000 locations in 118 markets, as well as through an Italian franchise furniture chain, made up of sixty-four stores throughout Italy.

The company, credited with popularizing leather furniture, is well known for appealing to a broad range of customers; it offers a tremendous variety of colors and styles at various price points and introduces an average of 100 new models every year. (It has around 25% of the U.S. leather furniture market.) Because it manufactures furniture only after orders are received ("just-in-time" delivery), it can customize its products while keeping inventories low. Everything from hide tanning to marketing is kept in house.

Within the last few years, Natuzzi has expanded into fabric upholstery and a line of more traditional leather furniture (the company made its name in contemporary furniture). Along with two other Italian manufacturers, it has also launched a chain of home furnishings stores in Italy. In 1996 around 50% of Natuzzi's sales were generated in Europe, 41% in North America, and most of the rest in Asia.

COMPANY STATEMENT (from the 1995 annual report)

"Growth is, and always has been, the first item on Natuzzi's agenda. Our growth has never been a matter of mere chance. It is planned on the basis of analysis of the world markets and the Group's potential to increase its market share.

"Our analysis shows the world upholstery market is made up of 55% contemporary and 45% traditional and transitional styles. Leather represents 20% of the coverings and fabric 80%. We have grown to become one of the world's largest furniture companies by concentrating on contemporary leather upholstery, a niche of only 11% of all upholstered furniture. We believe our share of all upholstery sold in the world is approximately 2%.

"Our objective for the future is to continue to stimulate expansion of the contemporary leather segment, which shows excellent opportunities for growth. At the same time, we aim to increase sales in traditional leather with our new 'Classics by Pasquale Natuzzi' collection. This will enable us to occupy more space on the floors of the existing 15,000 retail outlets currently selling our products, while attracting new dealers."

PERFORMANCE

Natuzzi is one of our top-performing companies, garnering 95 out of a possible 100 points in our grading system. Natuzzi's six-year operating financial history and four-year history as a public company are shorter than those of many of the companies in this book and make it difficult to extrapolate much about the company's performance over time. Nonetheless, in those six years Natuzzi management turned in a strong, consistent performance. Revenues and EP/ADR increased in every one of the last five years, with compound annual growth of 16% and 27%, respectively. EBDIT increased in four of the last five years, with compound annual growth of 22%. ROE averaged an incredible 29%. And long-term debt stayed minimal: the ratio of long-term debt to total capital averaged 2%. The ADR price increased at a compound annual rate of 18%—but, of course, over a relatively short time horizon.

If you had invested $10,000 in Natuzzi at the end of 1993, you would have purchased around 350 ADRs at $14 each (excluding commissions). In December 1996, there was a two-for-one stock split. At the end of 1996, your 700 ADRs would have been worth an estimated $16,400. You would also have received dividend payments of around $350.

NATUZZI

Ticker Symbol and Exchange: NTZ—NYSE   **CUSIP No.: 456478106**

OPERATING AND PER SHARE DATA
(in millions of U.S. dollars and dollars per ADR)

	1986	1987	1988	1989	1990	1991	1992	1993	1994	1995	1996	CAGR
Sales	N/A	N/A	N/A	N/A	N/A	259.7	227.0	271.1	426.1	529.7	554.0	16.4%
EBDIT	N/A	N/A	N/A	N/A	N/A	28.3	30.4	54.5	55.4	78.4	77.1	22.2%
Net Profit	N/A	N/A	N/A	N/A	N/A	23.5	21.4	36.9	47.2	60.5	76.1	26.5%
EP/ADR	N/A	N/A	N/A	N/A	N/A	0.41	0.38	0.66	0.84	1.07	1.34	26.5%
DP/ADR	N/A	N/A	N/A	N/A	N/A	0.14	0.11	0.09	0.10	0.10	0.17	3.9%

KEY RATIOS

	1986	1987	1988	1989	1990	1991	1992	1993	1994	1995	1996	AVG
EBDIT Margin	N/A	N/A	N/A	N/A	N/A	10.9%	13.4%	20.1%	13.0%	14.8%	13.9%	14.4%
ROE	N/A	N/A	N/A	N/A	N/A	N/A	26.1%	34.9%	29.7%	27.2%	25.2%	28.6%
LT Debt/Total Cap	N/A	N/A	N/A	N/A	N/A	N/A	4.0%	2.4%	2.2%	1.5%	1.1%	2.2%
P/E (Projected)	N/A	N/A	N/A	N/A	N/A	N/A.	N/A	16.7	15.8	17.0	18.4	17.0

STOCK PRICE CHART
(fiscal year-end closing price, in U.S. dollars, adjusted for capital changes)

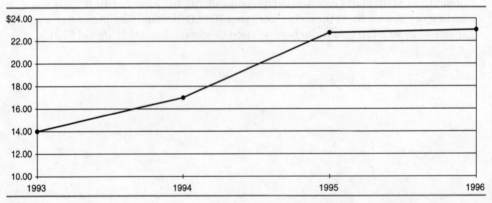

Notes: Natuzzi shares became publicly traded in 1993 and are listed on the NYSE. Data are available only in U.S. dollars.

NOKIA (NOKA—NYSE)

Address: Etelaesplanadi 12 / P.O. Box 226 / 00101 Helsinki / Finland
Tel.: (011) 358 0 180 71   **Fax:** (011) 358 0 656 388   **Web site:** http://www.nokia.com
or
Address: 2300 Valley View Lane, Suite 100 / Irving, TX 75062
Tel.: (214) 257-9880   **Fax:** (214) 257-9831

BASIC INFORMATION

Country: Finland   **Market capitalization:** $17.89 billion
Industry: Telecommunications equipment   **Share status:** ADRs trade on NYSE
Investment thesis: Second largest manufacturer of mobile phones in the world

COMPANY GRADING BOX

Growth Categories		Quality of Management	
Revenue Growth	20	Return on Equity	5
Operating Income Growth	15	**Risk**	
Earnings per Share Growth	10	Long-Term Debt/Total Capital	5
Share Price Growth	15	**Total QM&R (maximum 20)**	**10**
Total Growth (maximum 80)	**60**	**FINAL GRADE**	**70**

BACKGROUND

Finland's telecommunications giant Nokia traces its roots back to 1865 to a forest industry company founded by a Finnish mining engineer. He named the company after a mill on Finland's Nokia River. But it was not until a hundred years later that Nokia, Finnish Cable Works, and Finnish Rubber Works merged under the Nokia name and the company began to take on its current guise. By 1990 Nokia management had decided to focus on what it considered high-growth core operations, that is, consumer electronics and telecommunications equipment; by the end of the 1980s it had sold off its "soft-tissue" businesses. The company then divested its remaining noncore businesses, the basic industry operations, and restructured. Today Nokia is one of the largest telecommunications equipment manufacturers in the world, with more than 31,000 employees in forty-five countries, sales in 120 countries, revenues topping $8 billion, and a market capitalization of $18 billion.

The company is made up of three business units: Nokia Telecommunications, which develops and manufactures cellular phone networks and systems for fixed networks and represents 27% of revenues; Nokia Mobile Phones, which is the second largest manufacturer of mobile phones in the world and represents 43% of revenues; and Nokia General Communications Products, which focuses on consumer and industrial electronics—everything from the development of interactive products for televisions to satellite receivers to car audio systems—and represents 29% of revenues.

Going forward, Nokia should continue to benefit from the worldwide shift to digital telecommunications systems, gradual liberalization of the global telephone industry, steady demand for more sophisticated (higher-margin) equipment, the development of multimedia systems, and the booming markets for cellular communications—keeping in mind the still low penetration rates around the world (particularly in countries such as China and India). Although it is operating in an increasingly competitive environment, this is the era of telecommunications, and Nokia is one of the companies leading the charge.

COMPANY STATEMENT (from the 1996 annual report)

"The future need for telecommunications has no limits. More and more users will want a thousand times more bits than are being transmitted in today's networks. But the increased number of bits does not only mean that a single person will require and receive larger amounts of information. It means that the data quality will be vastly enhanced, resulting in clearer images and sounds at the chosen location. Telecommunications will eliminate distances. . . .

"One explanation of Nokia's success is the early investments in digital and wireless technologies. We introduced our first digital transmission systems in 1969. The decision to develop digital periodic switches was made already in the 1970s. At that time there was no general consensus to start digitizing. As a result of this decision, Nokia could deliver Europe's first full digital switch which started operating in 1982. The world's first digital GSM (Global System for Mobile Communications) network, including exchange, was delivered in 1991 by Nokia.

"Nokia, having developed and expanded in a challenging market environment, has created solutions on the cutting edge of international technology. The strength of our know-how and pioneering vision has been demonstrated many times. Examples are our introductions of new mobile phone generations and base stations, our state-of-the-art solution facilitating wireless data traffic and the almost futuristic world-class Nokia Communicator 9000."

PERFORMANCE

Nokia is a company that did not score particularly high in our grading system (receiving a total score of 70) because of massive restructuring over the last decade. But it made a fortune for investors who stuck with the company through thick and thin. Over the last ten years, revenues grew at a compound rate of 13% while EBDIT grew by almost 18%. EP/ADR grew by a respectable 15%. Plenty of firms would be happy with such results, but it is worth noting that Nokia achieved them while completely recasting itself in the late 1980s and early 1990s. From 1991, when most of the restructuring was completed, Nokia had compound annual growth in revenues, EBDIT, and EP/ADR of 18%, 50%, and 62%, respectively. The ADR price followed this pattern, growing at a strong compound annual rate of 32% over the decade but with most of the good performance coming subsequent to the restructuring. Since 1991, Nokia's ADR price has increased at a compound annual rate of 62%. Our measurements for quality of management and risk also reflect this trend. ROE averaged a respectable 12% for the decade but has averaged 18% since 1991. The long-term debt to total capital ratio averaged a reasonable 31% for the decade, but this ratio has fallen to the teens over the last few years.

Dividends increased from $0.13 in 1986 to $0.75 in 1996, growing by a healthy 20% per annum, and were paid even during years of declining earnings. The dividend payout ratio has been good, averaging 33% of earnings.

If you had invested $10,000 in Nokia at the end of 1986, you would have purchased around 600 ADRs (or ADR equivalents) at about $16.25 each (excluding commissions). During the following ten years, Nokia had a one-for-six rights issue in 1988, a one-for-ten bonus issue in 1988, and a four-for-one stock split in 1995. By the end of 1996, you would have had around 2,800 ADRs worth an estimated $160,700. You would also have received around $11,100 in dividend payments.

NOKIA

Ticker Symbol and Exchange: NOKA—NYSE   **CUSIP No.: 654902204**

OPERATING AND PER SHARE DATA
(in millions of Finnish marks and marks per share)

	1986	1987	1988	1989	1990	1991	1992	1993	1994	1995	1996	CAGR
Sales (bn marks)	12.0	14.0	21.8	22.8	22.1	15.5	18.2	23.7	30.2	36.8	39.3	12.6%
EBDIT	1,310	1,762	2,076	1,673	1,945	757	1,040	2,365	5,035	6,321	6,502	17.4%
Net Profit	502	769	641	101	301	(373)	(314)	768	2,971	4,063	3,044	19.7%
EPS	2.65	3.83	3.43	1.10	1.38	(1.48)	(1.29)	3.07	10.97	14.36	10.73	15.0%
DPS	0.60	0.83	0.80	0.70	0.70	0.50	0.50	0.70	2.50	3.00	3.50	19.3%

OPERATING AND PER SHARE DATA
(in millions of U.S. dollars and dollars per ADR)

	1986	1987	1988	1989	1990	1991	1992	1993	1994	1995	1996	CAGR
Sales (bn $)	2.5	3.6	5.3	5.3	5.8	3.8	4.1	4.2	5.8	8.4	8.5	12.9%
EBDIT	275	447	500	389	509	188	232	415	963	1,446	1,398	17.7%
Net Profit	105	195	154	23	79	(93)	(70)	135	568	930	655	20.0%
EP/ADR	0.56	0.97	0.83	0.26	0.36	(0.37)	(0.29)	0.54	2.10	3.29	2.31	15.3%
DP/ADR	0.13	0.21	0.19	0.16	0.18	0.12	0.11	0.12	0.48	0.69	0.75	19.6%

KEY RATIOS

	1986	1987	1988	1989	1990	1991	1992	1993	1994	1995	1996	AVG
EBDIT Margin	10.9%	12.6%	9.5%	7.3%	8.8%	4.9%	5.7%	10.0%	16.7%	17.2%	16.5%	10.9%
ROE	12.2%	17.1%	11.6%	1.9%	5.4%	−6.3%	−5.2%	12.5%	26.7%	33.0%	19.1%	11.6%
LT Debt/Total Cap	37.9%	40.9%	42.2%	43.4%	38.0%	32.6%	24.8%	31.0%	18.3%	19.3%	13.2%	31.1%
P/E (Projected)	4.4	7.3	17.3	11.6	N/M	N/M	6.5	6.6	12.1	15.9	16.8	10.9

STOCK PRICE CHART
(fiscal year-end closing price, in U.S. dollars, adjusted for capital changes)

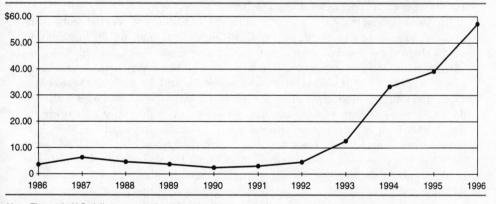

Note: Figures in U.S. dollars are translated from local currency using year-end exchange rates.

NOVARTIS (NVTSY—OTC)

Address: Lischstrasse 35 / 4002 Basel / Switzerland
Tel.: (011) 41 61 324 1111   **Fax:** (011) 41 61 321 0985   **Web site:** http://www.Novartis.com

BASIC INFORMATION

Country: Switzerland
Industry: Health and personal care
Investment thesis: Leading drug company created by the 1996 merger of Ciba-Geigy and Sandoz

Market capitalization: $83.06 billion
Share status: ADRs trade OTC

COMPANY GRADING BOX

Growth Categories		Quality of Management	
Revenue Growth	20	Return on Equity	5
Operating Income Growth	20	**Risk**	
Earnings per Share Growth	5	Long-Term Debt/Total Capital	10
Share Price Growth	10	**Total QM&R (maximum 20)**	15
Total Growth (maximum 80)	55	**FINAL GRADE**	70

BACKGROUND

This is one of the few companies we write about in this book that technically has no operating history. Novartis officially came into being on December 20, 1996, created by the $83 billion (market capitalization) combination of Sandoz, which traces its history back to 1886, and Ciba-Geigy, which traces its roots back to 1758, two giant old-time pharmaceutical rivals based in Basel, Switzerland. For our purposes, we looked at financial data on both companies and decided to include three years of combined numbers provided by the company (going back to 1993), then Sandoz numbers going back to 1986. The new corporate name is derived from Latin: *novo,* meaning "new," and *artis,* meaning "skills" (it apparently does not offend any group of people and is easy to pronounce in various languages).

Novartis is now the second largest drug group in the world, with $27 billion in 1996 revenues, tremendous cash flow, and clout in the marketplace that neither Sandoz nor Ciba-Geigy had on its own. By combining research efforts, management hopes to bring new products to market faster and distribute them more efficiently. Initial cost cutting is expected to save the company 8% of total overhead. Today, Novartis employs more than 100,000 people and operates in more than 100 countries.

Investor response to the merger was enthusiastic. In trading just after the deal was announced, Sandoz shares jumped 20% and Ciba-Geigy shares jumped 30%. In addition to a 4.4% share of the world pharmaceutical market (only Glaxo Wellcome, with 4.7%, has a larger share), the new company will be a leader in biotechnology, agricultural chemicals (Novartis paid $910 million for Merck's insecticide and fungicide business in May 1996), and nutrition products (Gerber is a Novartis brand name). Asked what it plans to do with its cash, Novartis management has said it may buy products that are already under development or push further into the over-the-counter drug market (although its popular Ex-Lax brand laxative was temporarily pulled off the market in mid-1997 after the FDA proposed banning one ingredient; Novartis has said it will reformulate the product without the questionable ingredient). Either way, the outlook for continued growth is good.

COMPANY STATEMENT (1997 "Welcome to the New World of Novartis")

"On 7 March 1996 we set out to build a new company, by combining two strong enterprises to create an even stronger one—Novartis. Having gained the approval of shareholders and regulatory authorities our vision is rapidly becoming reality. Much has already been accomplished. Our management team and the new organization are in place, and we look to the future with great confidence.

"Through our unique focus on healthcare, agribusiness and nutrition, we immediately take our place as the world leader in life sciences. We all live in a world that faces many challenges—disease, crop failure and malnutrition. We believe that our know-how and our comprehensive portfolio of products and services will provide lasting solutions to these challenges.

"With an annual investment in research and development of three billion Swiss francs we demonstrate our commitment to develop life science solutions for tomorrow.

"The combined and focused efforts of the 100,000 Novartis associates will allow Novartis to grow successfully and to create value for all its stakeholders."

PERFORMANCE

Keeping in mind that financial data prior to 1993 and ADR prices prior to 1995 are for Sandoz only, and that this company was born only in 1996, Novartis's score of 70 points in our grading system is pretty remarkable. Revenues increased in eight of the last ten years (with a jump in 1993 due to the aforementioned accounting adjustments), with compound annual growth of 18%. EBDIT increased in nine of the last ten years, with compound annual growth of 32%. ROE averaged a good 16% and the long-term debt to total capital ratio averaged a relatively low 12%. Again, using Sandoz numbers alone prior to 1995, ADR price performance looks a little less spectacular, with compound annual growth of just under 16%. Dividends (just Sandoz prior to 1995) increased in nine of the last ten years, with compound annual growth of 19%.

If you had invested $10,000 in Novartis at the end of 1986, you would have purchased 30 ADRs (or ADR equivalents) of Novartis at $336 each. During the following ten years, there were two five-for-one stock splits, one in May 1991 and the other in May 1994. By the end of the ten-year period, you would have had around 750 ADRs worth an estimated $42,400. You would also have received around $3,000 in dividend payments.

NOVARTIS

Ticker Symbol and Exchange: NVTSY—OTC　　　　**CUSIP No.: 66987V109**

OPERATING AND PER SHARE DATA
(in millions of Swiss francs and francs per share)

	1986	1987	1988	1989	1990	1991	1992	1993	1994	1995	1996	CAGR
Sales	8,361	8,979	10,151	12,497	12,367	13,444	14,416	37,747	37,919	35,943	36,233	15.8%
EBDIT	541	627	761	958	967	1,114	1,495	6,290	6,922	7,514	7,437	30.0%
Net Profit	680	747	815	1,080	1,081	1,132	1,413	3,485	3,647	4,216	2,304	13.0%
EPS	20.17	21.56	23.53	31.18	31.20	28.94	34.61	37.16	55.00	62.00	33.00	5.0%
DPS	4.20	4.40	4.80	6.00	6.00	7.00	9.40	12.00	15.00	16.80	20.00	16.9%

OPERATING AND PER SHARE DATA
(in millions of U.S. dollars and dollars per ADR)

	1986	1987	1988	1989	1990	1991	1992	1993	1994	1995	1996	CAGR
Sales	5,193	7,070	6,767	8,115	9,738	9,885	9,807	25,334	28,946	31,255	27,040	17.9%
EBDIT	336	494	507	622	761	819	1,017	4,221	5,284	6,534	5,550	32.4%
Net Profit	422	588	543	701	851	833	961	2,339	2,784	3,666	1,719	15.1%
EP/ADR	0.63	0.85	0.78	1.01	1.23	1.06	1.18	1.25	2.10	2.70	1.23	7.0%
DP/ADR	0.13	0.17	0.16	0.19	0.24	0.26	0.32	0.40	0.57	0.73	0.75	19.1%

KEY RATIOS

	1986	1987	1988	1989	1990	1991	1992	1993	1994	1995	1996	AVG
EBDIT Margin	6.5%	7.0%	7.5%	7.7%	7.8%	8.3%	10.4%	16.7%	18.3%	20.9%	20.5%	11.9%
ROE	14.5%	13.7%	13.9%	17.0%	15.1%	13.6%	15.7%	15.0%	29.2%	17.6%	8.7%	15.8%
LT Debt/Total Cap	7.5%	7.9%	8.3%	7.5%	6.9%	12.0%	11.1%	13.1%	16.6%	26.4%	19.3%	12.4%
P/E (Projected)	20.2	21.9	12.8	15.4	12.4	14.2	16.9	15.9	11.2	32.2	20.1	17.6

STOCK PRICE CHART
(fiscal year-end closing price, in U.S. dollars, adjusted for capital changes)

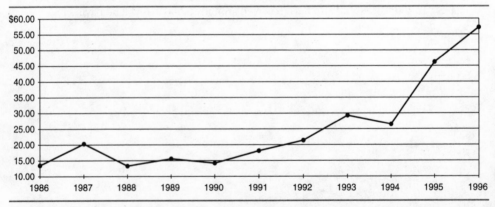

Notes: 1986–87 year-end share prices are estimated from midpoint of high and low, using year-end exchange rates. Financial data prior to 1993 and share prices prior to 1995 are for Sandoz only. Novartis was formed from the merger of Ciba-Geigy and Sandoz in March 1996. The first day of trading for the new shares was December 23, 1996.

NOVO NORDISK (NVO—NYSE)

Address: Novo Alle / 2880 Bagsvaerd / Denmark
Tel.: (011) 45 4444 8888   **Fax:** (011) 45 4449 0555   **Web site:** http://www.novo.dk
or
Address: 405 Lexington Avenue, Suite 6400 / New York, NY 10017
Tel.: (212) 867-0123   **Fax:** (212) 867-0298

BASIC INFORMATION

Country: Denmark   **Market capitalization:** $7.78 billion
Industry: Health, personal care   **Share status:** ADRs trade on NYSE
Investment thesis: Leader in products for diabetics; world's largest producer of industrial enzymes

COMPANY GRADING BOX

Growth Categories		Quality of Management	
Revenue Growth	20	Return on Equity	0
Operating Income Growth	20	**Risk**	
Earnings per Share Growth	10	Long-Term Debt/Total Capital	10
Share Price Growth	15	**Total QM&R (maximum 20)**	10
Total Growth (maximum 80)	65	**FINAL GRADE**	75

BACKGROUND

Novo Nordisk is a leading supplier of products for diabetics and the world's largest producer of industrial enzymes, used in everything from alcohol to baked goods to contact lens solutions to detergents. By the end of 1996 the company had 13,395 employees in sixty-one countries, manufacturing facilities in six countries, and a $7.78 billion market capitalization.

Half the company, Nordisk, was founded in Denmark in 1923 by a Nobel prize–winning physiologist and his diabetic wife to produce insulin. The other half, Novo, was founded in Denmark a year later by a fired Nordisk employee, also to produce insulin. Over the next sixty years the two companies raced against each other to bring new and better insulin products to market, even as they both developed other small businesses. Novo developed its industrial enzyme business and launched some new health care products, including contraceptive pills and an antidepressant. Nordisk became a major producer and exporter of the human growth hormone. Finally, in 1989, they merged and created the largest producer of insulin in the world.

In the last few years, Novo Nordisk has concentrated on streamlining itself, focusing attention on its core businesses. In the health care division, that has meant products for diabetic care; women's health care, including products for the treatment of osteoporosis and the treatment of menopausal symptoms; and human growth hormones—products for the treatment of "hormone insufficiency-related disorders." In the enzyme division, that has meant increasing volume without increasing costs. In the mid-1990s Novo Nordisk closed a plant on the Japanese island of Hokkaido and started building one in China. In 1996 the company divested its Plasma Product Unit.

Novo Nordisk continues to spend heavily on research and development, about 14% of revenue annually; it has built a reputation over the years for consistently developing and manufacturing new and innovative products.

COMPANY STATEMENT (from the 1996 annual report)

"At the beginning of 1994, we initiated a process of radical change. The purpose of this process is to place Novo Nordisk among the top performers in our industries before the turn of the century. An ambitious goal, both in terms of scope and the time that we have allowed ourselves to achieve it.

"Anticipating and responding to more radical changes in the sciences we use, in our markets and in the demands of all our stakeholders, we changed our basic business strategy. We focused on our core businesses and divested businesses, products and projects in areas where we did not believe we could achieve global leadership positions. On the surface, an uncomplicated and straightforward task, yet one which demanded significant organizational change and new thinking. A challenge which has been handled with great skill by the management teams involved and with a remarkable level of buy-in from the Novo Nordisk people."

PERFORMANCE

Novo Nordisk received top scores for revenue and operating income growth during the last decade, with each growing at a compound rate of about 16% per annum. Novo Nordisk lost a few points on both earnings growth (11% compound rate) and share price growth (19% compound rate), both just one point below our thresholds for higher scores. Where Novo Nordisk really stands out is in its consistency; this is a company you can depend on. During the past decade, operating income increased every year, revenues and net earnings increased in nine out of ten years, and the ADR (or ADR equivalent) price finished higher in eight out of ten years. Novo Nordisk lost ground on ROE, where an 11% average return was low compared with other firms. However, the company did score maximum points on risk, with a long-term debt to total capital ratio of just 15%.

Novo Nordisk's ADR price increased from a low of $6.47 in 1986 to a high of $47.40 in 1996. Dividends increased from $0.14 to $0.31 during the period, and the dividend payout ratio averaged 15%.

If you had invested $10,000 in Novo Nordisk at the end of 1986, you would have purchased around 1,170 ADRs (or ADR equivalents) at about $8.50 each (excluding commissions). During the following ten-year period, Novo Nordisk had a one-for-six rights issue in 1991. By the end of 1996, you would have owned around 1,220 ADRs worth an estimated $57,000. You would also have received around $2,900 in dividend payments.

NOVO NORDISK

Ticker Symbol and Exchange: NVO—NYSE　　　**CUSIP No.: 670100205**

OPERATING AND PER SHARE DATA
(in millions of Danish krone and krone per share)

	1986	1987	1988	1989	1990	1991	1992	1993	1994	1995	1996	CAGR
Sales	4,210	4,912	5,263	7,334	8,066	9,361	10,699	12,163	13,524	13,723	14,873	13.5%
EBDIT	915	891	1,153	1,494	1,657	1,908	2,202	2,501	2,962	3,218	3,451	14.2%
Net Profit	521	477	637	746	778	928	1,276	1,426	1,432	1,563	1,799	13.2%
EPS	10.22	9.37	12.49	11.79	12.31	13.51	17.06	19.01	19.09	20.83	23.98	8.9%
DPS	2.00	2.00	2.00	2.00	2.00	2.00	2.00	2.00	2.50	2.50	3.75	6.5%

OPERATING AND PER SHARE DATA
(in millions of U.S. dollars and dollars per ADR)

	1986	1987	1988	1989	1990	1991	1992	1993	1994	1995	1996	CAGR
Sales	578	807	774	1,113	1,388	1,584	1,706	1,791	2,224	2,468	2,495	15.8%
EBDIT	125	146	170	227	285	323	351	368	487	579	579	16.5%
Net Profit	72	78	94	113	134	157	203	210	236	281	302	15.5%
EP/ADR	0.70	0.77	0.92	0.89	1.06	1.14	1.36	1.40	1.57	1.87	2.01	11.1%
DP/ADR	0.14	0.16	0.15	0.15	0.17	0.17	0.16	0.15	0.21	0.22	0.31	8.7%

KEY RATIOS

	1986	1987	1988	1989	1990	1991	1992	1993	1994	1995	1996	AVG
EBDIT Margin	21.7%	18.1%	21.9%	20.4%	20.5%	20.4%	20.6%	20.6%	21.9%	23.4%	23.2%	21.2%
ROE	10.6%	9.3%	11.5%	11.9%	10.8%	9.8%	12.1%	12.0%	10.9%	10.8%	11.3%	11.0%
LT Debt/Total Cap	15.8%	14.3%	12.9%	19.5%	13.7%	15.0%	19.4%	21.5%	18.8%	8.2%	5.6%	15.0%
P/E (Projected)	13.0	5.5	11.3	13.5	13.3	15.5	14.4	17.4	13.9	15.8	20.0	14.0

STOCK PRICE CHART
(fiscal year-end closing price, in U.S. dollars, adjusted for capital changes)

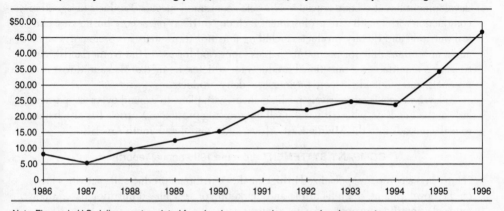

Note: Figures in U.S. dollars are translated from local currency using year-end exchange rates.

NUTRICIA (NUTVc.AS—AMSTERDAM)

Address: Rokkeveenseveg 49 / 2712 PJ Zoetermeer / Netherlands
Tel.: (011) 31 79 353 9000   **Fax:** (011) 31 79 353 9620   **Web site:** http://www.nutricia.com

BASIC INFORMATION

Country: Netherlands   **Market capitalization:** $3.56 billion
Industry: Food and beverages   **Share status:** Foreign shares trade on Amsterdam Exchange
Investment thesis: Dominant producer of infant formula in Europe

COMPANY GRADING BOX

Growth Categories		Quality of Management	
Revenue Growth	20	Return on Equity	10
Operating Income Growth	15	**Risk**	
Earnings per Share Growth	20	Long-Term Debt/Total Capital	10
Share Price Growth	20	**Total QM&R (maximum 20)**	20
Total Growth (maximum 80)	75	**FINAL GRADE**	95

BACKGROUND

Nutricia is the largest manufacturer of infant formula in Europe with carefully protected brand names that connote quality in many of the world's major markets and lines of products for healthy babies as well as babies with special needs (low birth weight, premature, allergies, etc.). It had revenues of $1.7 billion in 1996, has a market capitalization of $3.56 billion, and has operations throughout Europe, the Far East, the Caribbean, South America, the Commonwealth of Independent States, Australia, and New Zealand (it also exports to countries in Africa and the Middle East). In addition to infant formula, Nutricia's most important product group includes cereals, milks, drinks, and juices for babies and toddlers. Altogether, the group accounts for 54% of the company's total revenues. Key to the company's success: relationships with pediatricians, clinics, and hospitals throughout its markets. Nutricia focuses on baby foods made from natural raw materials, without preservatives, artificial coloring, odors, or flavorings—a concept that has also caught on in the United States.

Founded in 1901 by a physician and his industrialist brother, this Dutch company has shown consistent organic growth, and—particularly within the last few years—made a series of targeted acquisitions expanding its market share and product reach. New product development has also been crucial to Nutricia's continued success. Products designed in conjunction with health care professionals include Nutricia's other core businesses: clinical nutrition and dietary products, including nutritional products for pregnant women and a new infant milk for premature babies (approved for use in the Netherlands). Nutricia also manufactures nutritional products for athletes, a range of skin and throat care products, and—outside its core businesses—dairy products.

Today, Nutricia is aggressively pushing ahead with plans to expand overseas, particularly in the Far East, where it has a small but growing presence. Nutricia has also begun to make inroads into the Middle East, Africa, and Central and South America.

COMPANY STATEMENT (from the 1996 annual report)

"Nutricia is a company specialized in high quality nutritional products. Its activities focus on the development, manufacturing and marketing of specialized nutrition based upon medical scientific concepts and with a high added value.

"Nutricia's strategy is based upon specialization, continuing internationalization and profitable growth, partly by acquisitions as well as by strategic alliances, and safeguarding of the highest quality in all stages of production and services. An important factor related hereto is maintaining good relationships with the medical and paramedical professions, based on mutual trust as well as constant improvement of products. Research & Development play an essential role in this.

"Nutricia distinguishes core and other activities. The core activities comprise the following product groups:

- infant milk formula
- enteral clinical nutrition (highly specialized nutritional products and related administration systems, developed for hospital and community use on medical recommendation)
- dietary food and health food (products for people with metabolic disorders, deficiencies or specific nutritional requirements such as elderly and sportsmen)
- meals, drinks, juices and cereals for babies and toddlers
- skin and throat-care products.

"The other activities consist mainly of consumer products on a dairy basis, such as chocolate milk and yogurt drinks, etc."

PERFORMANCE

Nutricia received an almost perfect score of 95, losing only a few points due to some inconsistency in its operating income growth. On all other fronts, Nutricia is a standout. Revenues in dollars increased nine of the last ten years, recording compound annual growth of 17%; EBDIT, although it increased in only seven of the ten years, had compound annual growth of 22%; and EPS in dollars increased in eight of the last ten years, with compound growth of 19%. Equally impressive, ROE averaged 24% during the period and was 38% in 1996. This is a signal that Nutricia did not sacrifice quality of earnings for growth but made high average returns on money invested in the business. The risk profile is moderate: the long-term debt to total capital ratio jumped to 52% in 1995, after a major acquisition; however, it averaged 18% during the ten-year period.

Share price performance in dollars has also been impressive, with compound annual growth of about 25%. Dividends increased at a compound annual rate of 20.3%. If you had invested $10,000 in Nutricia at the end of 1986, you would have bought around 75 shares at $132 each (excluding commissions). During the following ten years, there were two capital changes, including a two-for-one stock split in 1994. By the end of 1996, you would have had around 600 shares worth an estimated $91,500. You would also have received around $5,700 in dividend payments.

NUTRICIA

Ticker Symbol and Exchange: NUTVc.AS—Amsterdam　　　**SEDOL Code: 4588126**

OPERATING AND PER SHARE DATA
(in millions of Dutch guilders and guilders per share)

	1986	1987	1988	1989	1990	1991	1992	1993	1994	1995	1996	CAGR
Sales	744	732	838	905	1,143	1,244	1,253	1,404	1,490	1,928	2,911	14.6%
EBDIT	75.3	56.2	91.2	115.7	154.1	177.4	163.0	172.7	228.3	270.0	428.2	19.0%
Net Profit	38.7	52.9	47.9	60.3	87.3	99.2	87.2	100.5	136.2	151.8	231.7	19.6%
EPS	2.05	2.74	2.46	3.05	4.15	4.72	4.12	4.72	6.35	6.85	9.58	16.7%
DPS	0.63	0.65	0.73	0.88	1.25	1.43	1.45	1.50	1.90	2.10	3.20	17.6%

OPERATING AND PER SHARE DATA
(in millions of U.S. dollars and dollars per share)

	1986	1987	1988	1989	1990	1991	1992	1993	1994	1995	1996	CAGR
Sales	341	414	420	474	680	727	688	720	861	1,198	1,673	17.2%
EBDIT	34.5	31.8	45.7	60.6	91.7	103.7	89.6	88.6	132.0	167.7	246.1	21.7%
Net Profit	17.8	29.9	24.0	31.6	52.0	58.0	47.9	51.5	78.7	94.3	133.2	22.3%
EPS	0.94	1.55	1.23	1.60	2.47	2.76	2.26	2.42	3.67	4.25	5.51	19.3%
DPS	0.29	0.37	0.37	0.46	0.74	0.84	0.80	0.77	1.10	1.30	1.84	20.3%

KEY RATIOS

	1986	1987	1988	1989	1990	1991	1992	1993	1994	1995	1996	AVG
EBDIT Margin	10.1%	7.7%	10.9%	12.8%	13.5%	14.3%	13.0%	12.3%	15.3%	14.0%	14.7%	12.6%
ROE	17.0%	20.9%	18.0%	21.3%	24.5%	25.5%	19.5%	20.4%	24.9%	30.8%	37.9%	23.7%
LT Debt/Total Cap	6.6%	5.8%	12.4%	19.3%	20.1%	13.1%	8.5%	8.7%	8.0%	51.6%	47.5%	18.3%
P/E (Projected)	13.1	14.6	10.2	10.9	11.3	18.8	12.2	10.3	12.4	13.5	23.4	13.7

STOCK PRICE CHART
(fiscal year-end closing price, in U.S. dollars, adjusted for capital changes)

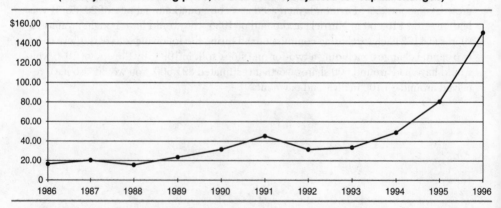

Note: Figures in U.S. dollars are translated from local currency using year-end exchange rates.

PANAMCO (PB—NYSE)

Address: Panamerican Beverages, Inc. / Tiburcio Montiel No. 15 / Colonia San Miguel Chapultepec / C.P. 11850 Mexico D.F.

Tel.: 52 5 272 2322   **Fax:** 52 5 272 2802   **Web site:** http://www.panamco.com

BASIC INFORMATION

Country: Mexico

Industry: Food and beverages

Investment thesis: Coca-Cola anchor bottler; the largest bottler in Latin America

Market capitalization: $3.07 billion

Share status: ADRs trade on NYSE

COMPANY GRADING BOX

Growth Categories		Quality of Management	
Revenue Growth	20	Return on Equity	5
Operating Income Growth	20	**Risk**	
Earnings per Share Growth	20	Long-Term Debt/Total Capital	10
Share Price Growth	5	**Total QM&R (maximum 20)**	15
Total Growth (maximum 80)	65	**FINAL GRADE**	80

BACKGROUND

Yes, it's another Coca-Cola anchor bottler—the largest soft drink bottler in Latin America and one of the largest Coca-Cola bottlers in the world. In 1996 Panama-based Panamco's sales represented about 17% of Latin America's Coke sales and 4% of worldwide Coke sales. The company was founded in Mexico in 1941 and has franchises in Mexico, Brazil, Costa Rica, and Colombia. In its most recent major acquisition, in May 1996, Panamco added Venezuela to the list when it bought Venezuela's powerful Cisneros business out for $1.01 billion in stock and cash—not long after the family switched its bottlers from Pepsi-Cola to Coca-Cola. That translates into a market of 100 million existing and potential customers, with great demographics, and potential revenues 50% higher in 1997 than they were in 1996. Per capita soda consumption is still low relative to that of many of the world's more developed economies, translating into ample growth opportunities.

By the end of 1996, Panamco held strong market positions in each of its major markets: 72% in Mexico, 59% in Colombia, and 89% in Costa Rica—all higher than a year earlier. In the summer of 1997, Panamco bought the sole bottler of Coca-Cola products in Nicaragua for $19.1 million, giving it a 78% share of Nicaragua's soft drink market. In the giant Brazilian market, Panamco's local subsidiary (of which it owns 96%) in the São Paulo, Campinas, and Santos regions, Spal, has a 90.3% market share in the cola segment. Spal is also the exclusive distributor of Kaiser and Heineken beers (see page 174) in those regions. Finally, the Cisneros deal gives Panamco 86% of the market in Venezuela.

Having weathered the recession in Mexico and managed rapid growth in Brazil (while bringing more capacity on line, Spal had to import cans from the United States), Panamco is now positioning itself for the future. In its push for greater market share, Panamco has put a big emphasis on nonreturnable packages (lower margins but higher volume), on new product introductions (such as Fresca and a new apple-flavored Coca-Cola in Mexico and Cherry Coke in Brazil), and on the placement of company-owned coolers. Panamco now has more than 176,000 company-owned coolers placed throughout its territories.

Panamco also expects further growth through acquisition, specifically citing the more than 110 Coca-Cola bottlers throughout Latin America as possibly ripe for the picking. Targeted areas: Brazil, Mexico, the northern part of South America, and Central America.

COMPANY STATEMENT (from the 1996 annual report)

"Panamco is focused on optimizing our use of products, people and capital to create shareholder value. We benefited in 1996 from having the best in all three of these foundations of a business enterprise: Panamco's products are among the best consumer products in the world; our people are talented, dedicated and hard working; and Panamco has excellent access to capital, having favorable credit ratings and a receptive public market for our securities, a strong balance sheet, and the long-term support of the Coca-Cola company. . . .

"To further build on our foundation of long-term shareowner value, in 1996 we began adopting the concept of Economic Value Added (EVA®), long used by the Coca-Cola Company as a measure of performance and as a tool in evaluating our investment decisions. Naturally, using EVA will not guarantee our future success. Economic and industry growth are essential elements in the equation. In this respect Panamco has a huge advantage over soft drink bottlers in developed markets: the tremendous growth potential in the Latin American region. Per capita consumption of soft drinks in the region is significantly below that of the U.S. and other developed nations. This, coupled with a rapidly growing population, an increasingly affluent consumer base and our proven operating ability, leaves enormous growth opportunities for Panamco in the coming years."

PERFORMANCE

Panamco gets high marks for consistency and growth and an overall score of 80 in our grading system, despite operating in some of the most volatile economies in the world. Revenues and EBDIT increased in each of the last eight years, recording compound annual growth of 19% and 21% respectively. EP/ADR, which recorded compound annual growth of 23%, increased in seven of the last eight years, showing a year-over-year decline only from 1994 to 1995, at the height of Mexico's recent economic problems. Mexico's economic woes are more strongly reflected in the company's ADR price performance: in the three years since Panamco went public, the ADR price has seen compound annual growth of only 7%. ROE averaged an acceptable 15%. And debt stayed low, with the long-term debt to total capital ratio averaging 8% over six years.

If you had invested $10,000 in Panamco at the end of 1993, you would have purchased around 260 ADRs at $38.25 each, adjusted for changes in the capital structure. Three years later, your 260 ADRs would have been worth an estimated $12,300. You would also have received about $300 in dividend payments during the period.

PANAMCO

Ticker Symbol and Exchange: PB—NYSE   **CUSIP No.: P74823108001**

OPERATING AND PER SHARE DATA
(in millions of U.S. dollars and dollars per ADR)

	1986	1987	1988	1989	1990	1991	1992	1993	1994	1995	1996	CAGR
Revenues	N/A	N/A	493	606	752	861	957	1,111	1,339	1,609	1,993	19.1%
EBDIT	N/A	N/A	64	79	126	135	163	188	219	235	283	20.5%
Net Income	N/A	N/A	14	16	22	31	37	43.5	68.5	70.6	118	30.0%
EP/ADR	N/A	N/A	0.48	0.52	0.75	1.04	1.25	1.47	1.81	1.75	2.44	22.5%
DP/ADR	N/A	N/A	N/M	N/M	N/M	N/M	N/M	0.26	0.28	0.32	0.36	11.5%

KEY RATIOS

	1986	1987	1988	1989	1990	1991	1992	1993	1994	1995	1996	AVG
EBDIT Margin	N/A	N/A	12.9%	13.0%	16.7%	15.7%	17.0%	16.9%	16.4%	14.6%	14.2%	15.3%
ROE	N/A	N/A	13.7%	13.0%	16.9%	19.7%	19.7%	11.2%	12.8%	11.6%	12.0%	14.5%
LT Debt/Total Cap	N/A	N/A	N/A	N/A	N/A	1.8%	3.6%	3.9%	5.0%	14.9%	16.6%	7.6%
P/E (Projected)	N/A	N/A	N/A	N/A	N/A	N/M	N/M	21.1	18.1	13.1	16.5	17.2

STOCK PRICE CHART
(fiscal year-end closing price, in U.S. dollars, adjusted for capital changes)

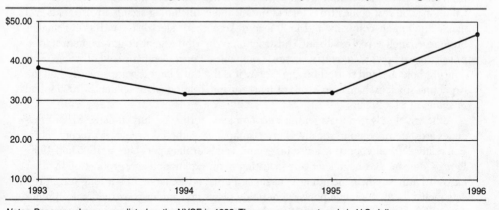

Notes: Panamco shares were listed on the NYSE in 1993. The company reports only in U.S. dollars.

PEREZ COMPANC (CNPZY—OTC)

Address: Maipu 1 (1599) / Buenos Aires / Argentina
Tel.: (011) 54 1 331 8393   **Fax:** (011) 54 1 345 1243

BASIC INFORMATION

Country: Argentina   **Market capitalization:** $6.04 billion
Industry: Oil and gas   **Share status:** Foreign shares trade OTC
Investment thesis: Dynamic oil and gas company, expanding into telecoms and electricity

COMPANY GRADING BOX

Growth Categories		Quality of Management	
Revenue Growth	15	Return on Equity	5
Operating Income Growth	5	**Risk**	
Earnings per Share Growth	20	Long-Term Debt/Total Capital	10
Share Price Growth	0	**Total QM&R (maximum 20)**	15
Total Growth (maximum 80)	40	**FINAL GRADE**	55

BACKGROUND

Perez Companc, an oil and gas company that is involved with much more than oil and gas, is a great way to invest in the energy sector in Latin America. This fifty-year-old Argentine company, started by the Perez family as a shipping company in 1946, today receives 31% of its net income from oil production, 6% from gas production, 6% percent from oil services (directional drilling), 13% from petrochemicals, and 14% from gas distribution. The rest comes from telecommunications (including sizable investments in a major equipment company and in Telecom Argentina), electricity, and a few smaller businesses, such as real estate and construction. When the Argentine government started privatizing some of the country's largest companies, Perez Companc sold off some of its noncore holdings and started buying. Today it is the third largest company listed on the Argentine stock exchange, in terms of market capitalization, at $6 billion; in 1996 it had revenues of $1.4 billion.

Although closely tied to Argentina's economic performance (an estimated 87% of revenues are generated domestically), Perez Companc weathered Argentina's recent recession relatively well, reporting a rise in revenues and earnings per share in 1995 and 1996. Perez Companc has begun actively investing in oil exploration and production in other parts of Latin America, including Venezuela, Peru, and Ecuador. Other long-term projects include a $230 million power generation plant, now under construction in Buenos Aires; 50% of a mining company in southern Argentina where gold has been found; and 50% of a styrene plant in Brazil. The company has also teamed up with YPF, Argentina's largest oil company, to build a $450 million urea plant to supply both the domestic and international fertilizer markets.

COMPANY STATEMENT (from the 1996 annual report)

"We believe that our company is well prepared to sustain growth in all of the sectors that make up its activity, particularly in the power generating area, in which we continue exploring new business opportunities, both in Argentina and in the rest of Latin America. In this respect, our goals focus on expansion based on the use of the latest technologies, the comprehensive development of our human resource and commitment with an environmental protection policy.

"As regards oil and gas, by the end of the century we hope to reach reserves equivalent to twelve years of production. In the petrochemical and refining activities, our projects focus on maintaining our share in the local market and establishing a solid position in the Mercosur area. We also hope to improve even more our production efficiency and to widen our range of products.

"The optimism underlying these plans originates, as we see it, in the strength, flexibility and endeavor to change showed by the Company in its first 50 years and in the short-term recovery of the Argentine economy we foresee."

PERFORMANCE

Perez Companc received a score of 55 in our grading system, receiving top points for consistency and EPS growth during its five-year history as a public company. Revenues and EPS have increased every year since the company went public, with compound annual growth of 11% and 20%, respectively. Dividends grew faster than EPS, with compound annual growth of 28%. EBDIT increased in three of the last four years, showing compound annual growth of 9%. ROE, 15% in 1996, averaged an impressive 24%. And the long-term debt to total capital ratio, our measurement of risk, was a moderate 26.5% in 1996 and averaged 24%.

If you had invested $10,000 in Perez Companc in August 1992, you would have bought around 1,460 shares at about $6.75 each (excluding commissions). During the following four years, there were a 28-for-100 bonus issue in April 1993, a 0.25-for-1 bonus issue in April 1994, an 18-for-100 bonus issue in March 1995, and a 13-for-100 bonus issue in February 1996. By December 1996, you would have had around 3,000 shares worth an estimated $17,000. You would also have received around $1,600 in dividend payments.

PEREZ COMPANC

Ticker Symbol and Exchange: CNPZY—OTC   **CUSIP No.: 713665107**

OPERATING AND PER SHARE DATA
(in millions of U.S. dollars and dollars per share)

	Aug 86	Aug 87	Aug 88	Aug 89	Aug 90	Aug 91	Aug 92	Aug 93	Dec 94	Dec 95	Dec 96	CAGR
Sales	N/A	N/A	N/A	N/A	N/A	N/A	916	918	1,027	1,320	1,413	11.4%
EBIT	N/A	N/A	N/A	N/A	N/A	N/A	257	205	308	323	367	9.3%
Net Profit	N/A	N/A	N/A	N/A	N/A	N/A	111	146	215	242	266	24.5%
EPS	N/A	N/A	N/A	N/A	N/A	N/A	0.17	0.27	0.28	0.32	0.35	19.8%
DPS	N/A	N/A	N/A	N/A	N/A	N/A	0.06	0.09	0.11	0.11	0.16	27.8%

KEY RATIOS

	Aug 86	Aug 87	Aug 88	Aug 89	Aug 90	Aug 91	Aug 92	Aug 93	Dec 94	Dec 95	Dec 96	AVG
EBIT Margin	N/A	N/A	N/A	N/A	N/A	N/A	28.1%	22.3%	30.0%	24.5%	25.9%	26.2%
ROE	N/A	N/A	N/A	N/A	N/A	N/A	11.5%	13.3%	19.1%	16.5%	15.4%	15.2%
LT Debt/Total Cap	N/A	N/A	N/A	N/A	N/A	N/A	12.9%	29.3%	27.0%	26.4%	26.5%	24.4%
P/E (Projected)	N/A	N/A	N/A	N/A	N/A	N/A	12.4	11.0	8.6	11.8	15.0	11.8

STOCK PRICE CHART
(fiscal year-end closing price, in U.S. dollars, adjusted for capital changes)

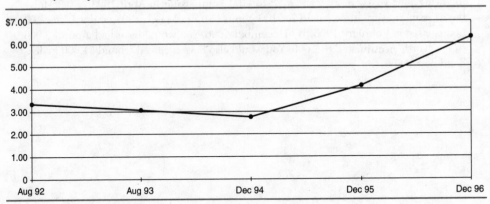

Notes: Company changed fiscal year from August to December in 1994. The Argentine peso trades at parity with the U.S. dollar, so results are shown in U.S. dollars only.

PERPETUAL (PER.L—LONDON)

Address: 47–89 Station Road / Henley-on-Thames, Oxon RG9 1AF / United Kingdom
Tel.: (011) 44 1491 417000   **Fax:** (011) 44 1491 416000

BASIC INFORMATION

Country: United Kingdom   **Market capitalization:** $1.15 billion
Industry: Financial services   **Share status:** Foreign shares trade on London Exchange
Investment thesis: One of the top-performing mutual fund companies in the United Kingdom

COMPANY GRADING BOX

Growth Categories		Quality of Management	
Revenue Growth	20	Return on Equity	10
Operating Income Growth	20	**Risk**	
Earnings per Share Growth	20	Long-Term Debt/Total Capital	10
Share Price Growth	15	**Total QM&R (maximum 20)**	**20**
Total Growth (maximum 80)	**75**	**FINAL GRADE**	**95**

BACKGROUND

You probably know all about Fidelity and Franklin Resources. And you also probably know how rapidly mutual funds have grown over the last five years. Perpetual is a U.K.-based fund company, small by comparison with the U.S. giants but with the kind of track record that any fund company would envy. Perpetual was started in 1974. In 1990 the firm had £420 million under management. By the end of its 1996 fiscal year, Perpetual had £6.6 billion under management, up from £4.7 billion at the end of its 1995 fiscal year. Profits have also risen steadily, up 46% compared to a year earlier. Of course, the bull market helped. But the outstanding performance of Perpetual's funds, relative to those of comparable funds, hasn't hurt.

Of Perpetual's twenty U.K.-based funds, ranging from its International Growth Fund to a U.K. Tax Exempt Fund, sixteen have been ranked in the top quartile of peer group funds since they were launched. Nearly 93% of Perpetual's funds that are five years or older, including Perpetual's number one–ranked Income Fund, were in the top quartile over that period. Perpetual's overall share of the U.K. mutual fund business (known as authorized unit trusts in the United Kingdom) moved up to 4.2% in 1996 from 3.7% in 1995.

In the financial industry, the mutual fund business is very highly valued because it is relatively stable and generates strong cash flows. Most other financial businesses rely on commissions or transactions to generate income and thus are more vulnerable to economic slowdowns or market corrections. The mutual fund business, on the other hand, generates income through fees collected on assets. While the business can't completely escape the effects of a bad market, earnings growth in the mutual fund business nevertheless is much less volatile than in other segments of the financial industry.

These favorable characteristics apply to Perpetual, which operates in the second largest financial center in the world, London, and has an outstanding track record to build on and attract new assets.

COMPANY STATEMENT (from the 1996 annual report)

"Some world stock markets are currently trading at new highs, but we believe that shares are generally not overpriced in the current low inflationary environment. While our actual and relative investment performance necessarily influences both sales and funds under management, if markets were to come under selling pressure, the effect would inevitably affect our revenue flows.

"While we recognize the challenges that are implicit within these issues, we believe that the Group is well placed to meet them, and the long term outlook remains encouraging. In the shorter term a significant improvement on results that already reflect material advance on previous years may be difficult to achieve in the event of adverse reaction to any of these issues."

PERFORMANCE

Perpetual received top scores for growth, ROE, and the ratio of long-term debt to total capital, lagging other companies in this book only in the consistency of its share price performance. Overall, Perpetual received 95 points in our grading system, making it one of our top scorers. In dollars, revenues and EBDIT increased in eight of the last ten years, with compound annual growth of 24% and 30%, respectively. EPS in dollar terms also increased in eight of the last ten years, with compound annual growth of an even more impressive 29%. ROE averaged a stellar 39%. And the long-term debt to total capital ratio was minimal, averaging 1.4%. The share price in dollars, though inconsistent, increased at a compound annual rate of 28% in the nine years after the company went public. And dividends increased at a compound annual rate of 41%, with an average payout ratio of 40%.

If you had invested $10,000 in Perpetual in September 1987, you would have bought around 2,620 shares at about $3.75 each (excluding commissions). There were no capital changes over the next nine years. By September 1996, your 2,620 shares would have been worth an estimated $93,000. You would also have received dividend payments of around $7,700.

PERPETUAL

Ticker Symbol and Exchange: PER.L—London   **SEDOL Code: 682389**

OPERATING AND PER SHARE DATA
(in millions of British pounds and pounds per share)

	Sep 86	Sep 87	Sep 88	Sep 89	Sep 90	Sep 91	Sep 92	Sep 93	Sep 94	Sep 95	Sep 96	CAGR
Sales	189	184	77	59	116	182	247	842	1,523	1,169	1,458	22.7%
EBDIT	4.3	5.2	2.0	1.4	1.3	2.8	4.5	14.4	34.7	36.2	52.7	28.5%
Net Profit	2.9	3.7	1.7	1.1	1.3	2.0	3.3	10.3	24.6	25.7	37.7	29.2%
EPS	0.12	0.15	0.07	0.04	0.05	0.08	0.13	0.39	0.92	0.95	1.35	27.8%
DPS	0.01	0.03	0.03	0.03	0.03	0.03	0.05	0.15	0.35	0.40	0.57	47.1%

OPERATING AND PER SHARE DATA
(in millions of U.S. dollars and dollars per share)

	Sep 86	Sep 87	Sep 88	Sep 89	Sep 90	Sep 91	Sep 92	Sep 93	Sep 94	Sep 95	Sep 96	CAGR
Sales	274	299	130	96	218	318	441	1,259	2,403	1,851	2,282	23.6%
EBDIT	6.2	8.4	3.4	2.3	2.4	4.9	8.0	21.5	54.7	57.3	82.5	29.5%
Net Profit	4.2	6.0	2.9	1.8	2.4	3.5	5.9	15.4	38.8	40.7	59.0	30.2%
EPS	0.17	0.24	0.12	0.07	0.10	0.14	0.23	0.58	1.46	1.50	2.11	28.8%
DPS	0.02	0.04	0.04	0.04	0.05	0.06	0.09	0.22	0.55	0.63	0.89	48.3%

KEY RATIOS

	Sep 86	Sep 87	Sep 88	Sep 89	Sep 90	Sep 91	Sep 92	Sep 93	Sep 94	Sep 95	Sep 96	AVG
EBDIT Margin	2.3%	2.8%	2.6%	2.4%	1.1%	1.5%	1.8%	1.7%	2.3%	3.1%	3.6%	2.3%
ROE	65.9%	51.4%	20.0%	12.0%	13.3%	18.0%	25.2%	52.8%	70.5%	51.6%	52.4%	39.4%
LT Debt/Total Cap	2.2%	1.4%	0.0%	0.0%	0.0%	0.0%	0.0%	2.0%	4.1%	2.7%	2.5%	1.4%
P/E (Projected)	N/A	34.6	21.3	18.9	5.5	8.1	3.7	8.3	12.3	12.5	16.1	14.1

STOCK PRICE CHART
(fiscal year-end closing price, in U.S. dollars, adjusted for capital changes)

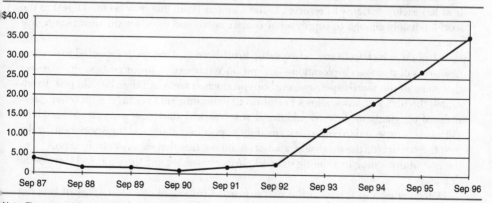

Note: Figures in U.S. dollars are translated from local currency using year-end exchange rates.

PETROBRAS (PTBRY—OTC)

Address: Avenida Republica do Chile, 65 / 20035-900 Rio de Janeiro / Brazil
Tel.: (011) 55 21 534 4477   **Fax:** (011) 55 21 220 5052

BASIC INFORMATION

Country: Brazil
Industry: Oil and gas
Investment thesis: Monopoly integrated oil company in Brazil; vast untapped resources

Market capitalization: $29.11 billion
Share status: ADRs trade OTC

COMPANY GRADING BOX

Growth Categories		Quality of Management	
Revenue Growth	5	Return on Equity	0
Operating Income Growth	20	**Risk**	
Earnings per Share Growth	5	Long-Term Debt/Total Capital	10
Share Price Growth	15	**Total QM&R (maximum 20)**	**10**
Total Growth (maximum 80)	**45**	**FINAL GRADE**	**55**

BACKGROUND

Petrobras supplies about 60% of Brazil's oil; its reserve base is one of the largest among international oil companies, and it owns about 98% of Brazil's refining capacity—not a bad position for a company in one of the largest and fastest-developing nations in the world. Petrobras's poor track record does little to illuminate the company's tremendous potential. Having been run by the government during times of acute economic turmoil in Brazil, the company was not necessarily managed with efficiency or profitability in mind. In fact, Petrobras was used to subsidize domestic oil prices, while little money was invested to develop resources. All this is set to change.

In November 1995 the Brazilian government took steps to begin deregulating Brazil's oil industry. Although Petrobras will soon have to contend with some measure of competition, deregulation also means opportunity for the still state-run company. Today, despite its vast proven reserves, Petrobras can supply about only 60% of Brazil's oil needs; most of the remainder is imported (at market rates, though Petrobras has been selling it domestically at below-market rates—a shortfall the government has said it will pay back). The new legislation should allow Petrobras to tap into its own resources by allowing it to raise capital and invest aggressively to develop its enormous reserve base. In fact, Petrobras has exclusive rights to reserves in the Campos Basin that may be the largest in the world, possibly enough to supply all of Brazil's needs and more for the next twenty-five years.

Petrobras, which has a special expertise in offshore exploration, is expected to develop new areas of deep-sea exploration—and produce more oil at lower cost (analysts expect that some of the more expensive, onshore production areas will then be sold off). In addition, the new legislation allows Petrobras to enter into joint ventures with other international oil giants to develop additional reserves and start new projects. Meanwhile, Petrobras is expected to continue its near monopoly in refining and transportation for the next three years (on the downside, analysts point out that that means Petrobras now faces the cost of upgrading its refining network on its own, assuming the expected increase in demand).

Deregulation also is paving the way to market pricing of oil. After years of keeping prices artificially low as part of the fight against inflation, the Brazilian government recently began to allow larger price increases. Finally, Petrobras has improved its operating efficiency, reducing staff by about 27% since 1989 amid intense political pressure. Today the government owns 51.1% of the total shares outstanding (81.7% of the voting shares), and about 36% is publicly traded. The government has announced its intention to continue to reduce its stake—good news for continued efficiency gains at the company.

COMPANY STATEMENT (from the 1996 annual report)

"Description: Petrobras is a mixed capital corporation that operates in the exploration, production, refining, commercialization, transportation, import and export of oil and oil products. It also operates in the natural gas segment, in oil product distribution, in petrochemicals and in fertilizers. Founded in 1953, the company is currently the sixteenth largest oil concern in the world, according to *Petroleum Intelligence Weekly*.

"Message from the Chairman: In abidance with Constitutional Amendment no. 9, enacted on November 9, 1995, Brazil's oil sector is now part of a new institutional and legal reality that has opened all segments of this vital activity to competition among companies incorporated under Brazilian law.

"Petrobras is confident that this decision opens the door to many chances for new conquests by expanding business opportunities and affording greater corporate autonomy. The company is ready to operate in a competitive market while continuing to fulfill its commitment to supply Brazilian consumers as efficiently as possible."

PERFORMANCE

Petrobras received top marks in two categories in our grading system—for growth in EBDIT and a low ratio of long-term debt to total capital. However, its overall grade of 55 points reflects its less-than-stellar track record. Unlike most of the companies we chose to include in this book, Petrobras came to our attention because of its potential rather than its past success. Public since just 1993 and only now in the process of being deregulated, it is an interesting vehicle for investors who do not mind the greater risk—and volatility—inherent in a company like this one, with vast resources but little experience as a truly profit-oriented enterprise. EP/ADR are still well below their peak in 1994, though they showed year-over-year improvement from 1995 to 1996. Revenues in dollars have seen compound annual growth of just 6% over the last four years, while the ROE averaged a paltry 5%.

Even so, shareholders have done well. If you had invested $10,000 in Petrobras at the end of 1993, you would have purchased around 5,500 ADRs at around $1.75 each (excluding commissions). In March 1994, Petrobras offered a 0.33-for-1 bonus issue. By the end of 1996, you would have owned 7,353 ADRs worth $121,324. Petrobras does not pay a dividend.

PETROBRAS

Ticker Symbol and Exchange: PTBRY—OTC   **CUSIP No.: 71654V101**

OPERATING AND PER SHARE DATA
(in millions of U.S. dollars and dollars per ADR)

	1986	1987	1988	1989	1990	1991	1992	1993	1994	1995	1996	CAGR
Net Revenues	N/A	N/A	N/A	N/A	N/A	N/A	N/A	15,029	17,353	16,387	18,074	6.3%
Operating Income	N/A	N/A	N/A	N/A	N/A	N/A	N/A	789	1,791	2,702	2,902	54.4%
Net Income	N/A	N/A	N/A	N/A	N/A	N/A	N/A	687	1,432	639	643	-2.2%
EP/ADR	N/A	N/A	N/A	N/A	N/A	N/A	N/A	0.63	1.32	0.59	0.62	-0.5%
DP/ADR	N/A	N/A	N/A	N/A	N/A	N/A	N/A	N/M	N/M	N/M	N/M	N/M

KEY RATIOS

	1986	1987	1988	1989	1990	1991	1992	1993	1994	1995	1996	AVG
Operating Margin	N/A	N/A	N/A	N/A	N/A	N/A	N/A	5.2%	10.3%	16.5%	16.1%	12.0%
ROE	N/A	N/A	N/A	N/A	N/A	N/A	N/A	5.4%	8.5%	3.3%	3.3%	5.1%
LT Debt/Total Cap	N/A	N/A	N/A	N/A	N/A	N/A	N/A	18.7%	8.4%	7.8%	12.4%	11.8%
P/E (Projected)	N/A	N/A	N/A	N/A	N/A	N/A	N/A	1.0	18.1	13.4	17.3	12.5

STOCK PRICE CHART
(fiscal year-end closing price, in U.S. dollars, adjusted for capital changes)

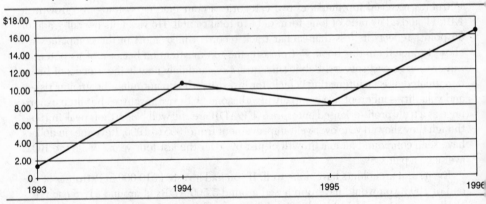

Note: Data for Brazilian companies are available only in U.S. dollars.

PHOENIX MECANO (PHOZ.S—ZURICH)

Address: Seestrasse 35 / 8700 Kusnacht / Switzerland
Tel.: (011) 41 1 910 36 66 **Fax:** (011) 41 1 910 75 70 **Web site:** http://www.phoenix-mecano.ch

BASIC INFORMATION

Country: Switzerland
Industry: Electrical and electronic
Market capitalization: $518 million
Share status: Foreign shares trade on Zurich Exchange
Investment thesis: A leading, cost-efficient components supplier to equipment manufacturers

COMPANY GRADING BOX

Growth Categories		Quality of Management	
Revenue Growth	15	Return on Equity	10
Operating Income Growth	15	**Risk**	
Earnings per Share Growth	15	Long-Term Debt/Total Capital	0
Share Price Growth	20	**Total QM&R (maximum 20)**	10
Total Growth (maximum 80)	65	**FINAL GRADE**	75

BACKGROUND

Phoenix Mecano describes itself as a company that makes the "little things every equipment maker, every designer, every development engineer uses of necessity, day after day." This Swiss company, with revenues of $255 million in 1996, has achieved success by making those little things better and more efficiently than many of its competitors. And it keeps bringing its costs down, most recently by moving production to lower-cost locations. It got into the market early and developed relationships with its customers, as well as tremendous economies of scale. The business has taken off with the recent European boom in outsourcing. Phoenix Mecano supplies the parts, while the equipment manufacturers focus on their core businesses.

Founded in 1975 as a manufacturer of industrial gases for the welding industry, Phoenix Mecano (then called Phoenix Maschinentechnik) quickly moved into the production of welding torches, then evolved into a component manufacturer for the electrical equipment industry. By the mid-1990s, almost half the company's revenues were generated by enclosures for electrical equipment, an area that continues to grow (think about all those infrastructure projects, particularly in telecommunications, in eastern Europe). Phoenix Mecano is the market leader for aluminum, plastic, and fiber glass enclosures in Europe. The company's other businesses: electromechanical components, including code switches, connectors, and keyboards, and mechanical components, including linear drives for beds and slatted bed frames (used in the booming health care industry), linear drives for medical treatment couches and chairs (also used by health care professionals), and profile assembly components for easy-to-assemble working platforms, automatic assembly machines, and workstations.

Over the years, the company has moved into businesses that looked profitable and moved out of ones where it did not have a competitive advantage. Determined to remain a relatively low-cost provider, it has also shifted much of its production from older facilities in Germany, by far its largest market, to lower-cost plants in Hungary.

COMPANY STATEMENT (from the 1996 *Investor Handbook*)

"The strategic foundation of a component manufacturer is its cost situation, not so much its product portfolio. Components do not differ much in design or quality. Price is the determining factor for the buyer. Corresponding to the shape of the learning curve the price is declining longer-term. The one who is the first to lower his costs will be victorious in competition. Because this is the rule of the game Phoenix Mecano has taken three strategic decisions:

- switch of operations to lower-cost locations
- globalization of procurement
- emphasis on volume sold

"For the time being the move of the enclosure and drive production to Kecskemét and of the production of electrical components to Budapest, both in Hungary, are the most important instances of switching of operations. For the electrical components an additional low-cost location was found in China. In electro-mechanical components we currently explore switching 50 percent of the production of Kundisch to Hungary (one 7th of German costs) and India (one tenth of German costs) and where Phoenix Mecano already has its own qualified people at hand.

"In globalization of procurement the focus is on the sourcing of electronic components of which Phoenix Mecano buys several million pieces each year. . . . Suppliers are located mostly in Taiwan or Korea. In electromechanical components Phoenix Mecano is currently examining the sourcing of foil keyboards in China, problem being that the manufacturing process is labor-intensive but not low-tech.

"The emphasis on volume is a more subtle strategic decision: Without a high volume business it makes no sense to talk of switching locations or outsourcing. . . . Therefore volume has to be generated by conquering markets. In order to avoid that the cat chases its own tail one cannot wait to lower prices until the corresponding volume has been generated. To the contrary: by lowering price in advance of the corresponding cost situation one can create volume business which then warrants the preceding price decrease."

PERFORMANCE

Phoenix Mecano got high marks for share price performance and ROE, garnering a total of 75 points in our grading system. The share price in dollars increased at a compound annual rate of 30%. And ROE averaged an impressive 26% over the last decade. EBDIT in dollars increased in eight of the last ten years, with compound annual growth of 14%. Revenues and EPS increased in just six of the last ten years, recording compound annual growth of 14% and 22%, respectively. The ratio of long-term debt to total capital was a little high, compared with some of our other companies, averaging 38% (although it was down to 27% in 1996.)

If you had invested $10,000 in Phoenix Mecano at the end of 1988, you would have purchased 16 shares at $630 each. In July 1992 there was a ten-for-one stock split. At the end of 1996, you would have had around 160 shares worth an estimated $82,900. You would also have received dividend payments of around $2,500.

PHOENIX MECANO

Ticker Symbol and Exchange: PHOZ.S—Zurich   **SEDOL Code: 4687595**

OPERATING AND PER SHARE DATA
(in millions of Swiss francs and francs per share)

	1986	1987	1988	1989	1990	1991	1992	1993	1994	1995	1996	CAGR
Net Sales	109	120	138	168	201	210	271	247	270	311	336	11.9%
EBDIT	21.7	27.0	32.7	38.6	43.6	47.4	60.0	52.4	61.5	65.8	68.9	12.2%
Net Income	5.5	6.3	7.4	11.3	14.3	16.5	19.6	21.0	23.8	28.7	32.6	19.4%
EPS	5.00	5.70	6.70	10.20	13.00	14.90	17.80	19.10	21.60	26.10	29.60	19.5%
DPS	N/M	N/M	1.30	1.70	2.10	2.30	2.60	2.80	3.10	3.60	4.00	15.1%

OPERATING AND PER SHARE DATA
(in millions of U.S. dollars and dollars per share)

	1986	1987	1988	1989	1990	1991	1992	1993	1994	1995	1996	CAGR
Net Sales	67.7	94.5	92.0	109.1	158.3	154.4	184.4	165.5	205.7	270.7	250.7	14.0%
EBDIT	13.5	21.3	21.8	25.1	34.3	34.9	40.8	35.2	46.9	57.2	51.4	14.3%
Net Income	3.4	5.0	4.9	7.3	11.3	12.1	13.4	14.1	18.2	25.0	24.3	21.6%
EPS	3.11	4.49	4.47	6.62	10.24	10.96	12.11	12.82	16.49	22.70	22.09	21.7%
DPS	N/M	N/M	0.87	1.10	1.65	1.69	1.77	1.88	2.37	3.13	2.99	16.7%

KEY RATIOS

	1986	1987	1988	1989	1990	1991	1992	1993	1994	1995	1996	AVG
EBIT Margin	19.9%	22.5%	23.7%	23.0%	21.7%	22.6%	22.1%	21.2%	22.8%	21.1%	20.5%	21.9%
ROE	22.8%	25.5%	23.5%	26.1%	26.4%	23.7%	36.1%	25.4%	25.4%	25.9%	23.7%	25.9%
LT Debt/Total Cap	38.4%	38.9%	27.7%	39.5%	34.6%	40.4%	51.6%	47.1%	38.8%	33.0%	26.6%	37.9%
P/E (Projected)	N/A	N/A	9.3	14.0	13.4	13.1	13.4	18.8	16.3	19.5	20.1	15.3

STOCK PRICE CHART
(fiscal year-end closing price, in U.S. dollars, adjusted for capital changes)

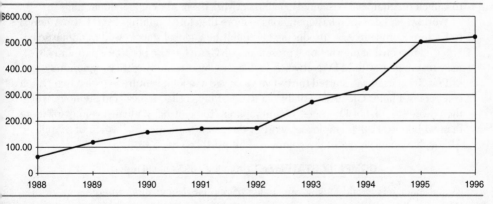

Note: Figures in U.S. dollars are translated from local currency using year-end exchange rates.

POLYGRAM (PLG—NYSE)

Address: 8 St. James's Square / London SW1Y 4JU / England
Tel.: (011) 44 171 747 4000   **Web site:** http://www.polygramnv.com
or
Address: Worldwide Plaza / 825 Eighth Avenue / New York, NY 10019
Tel.: (212) 333-8000   **Fax:** (212) 333-8281

BASIC INFORMATION

Country: Netherlands   **Market capitalization:** $9.2 billion
Industry: Leisure and entertainment   **Share status:** ADRs trade on NYSE
Investment thesis: Entertainment powerhouse in music and movies

COMPANY GRADING BOX

Growth Categories		Quality of Management	
Revenue Growth	20	Return on Equity	10
Operating Income Growth	20	**Risk**	
Earnings per Share Growth	15	Long-Term Debt/Total Capital	10
Share Price Growth	15	**Total QM&R (maximum 20)**	20
Total Growth (maximum 80)	70	**FINAL GRADE**	90

BACKGROUND

Netherlands-based PolyGram is probably our coolest company. It is the only pure enter-tainment company that made our international Top 100 list. Its record labels include Mercury, Deutsche Grammophon, Motown, Island, and Verve. Its current talent roster includes Sheryl Crow, Boyz II Men, Bon Jovi, Jessye Norman, Dee Dee Bridgewater, and Luciano Pavarotti—not to mention the Vienna Philharmonic. Together, PolyGram's thousands of artists account for an estimated 17% of global music sales.

Then there are the movies. Among PolyGram's releases in the mid-1990s were Jane Campion's *Portrait of a Lady, Mr. Holland's Opus* with Richard Dreyfuss, Tim Robbins's *Dead Man Walking,* and the Coen brothers' *Fargo.* They represent a small but growing percentage of PolyGram's overall business, accounting for about 14% of revenues in 1995 (and an operating loss). For PolyGram, they are an investment in its future as a con-tent provider as the number of outlets for content increases dramatically worldwide. PolyGram has also bought the rights to many old movies and television shows, building a backlog of programming, and partnered with Robert Redford and Showtime Networks to launch the Sundance Channel, a cable network devoted to independent films.

Worldwide, PolyGram has operations in more than forty countries from Latin America to Eastern Europe to Asia, producing and publishing global stars as well as domestic tal-ent. Building on that international presence, PolyGram has also become a partner in MTV Asia, teaming up with MTV Networks to deliver Chinese and English programming.

PolyGram itself was started thirty-five years ago as a joint venture between two Dutch companies, Philips Gloeilampenfabrieken (now Philips Electronics) and Siemens, which then owned the label Deutsche Grammophon. Today it has annual revenues of more than $5 billion, 12,000 employees worldwide, and a market capitalization of $9 billion. Although Siemens is out of the company, Philips still owns 75%.

COMPANY STATEMENT (from the 1995 annual report)

"Some managers would look at our melee of pop labels and shout 'merge, cut, prune.' What possible use can we have for so many different labels, all competing with each other? Between them, PolyGram's labels share roughly 17% of the world's music market. By keeping each of the label's identities intact, they can access the world and respond more quickly to changes in taste, and artists are not submerged by that 'big company' feeling.

"How do you market classical music so that it retains its appeal to serious music lovers, whilst reaching out to a wider, younger audience? By building the profile of our new artists, maximizing the value of our superstars, and focusing on each label's identity, we are expanding the definition of classical music to provide something for everyone.

"How do you maximize the value of a few choice words scribbled on the back of an envelope? 'Hold me, thrill me, kiss me, kill me' by U2 earned a synchronization fee for its use in the *Batman Forever* film . . . and earned mechanical income from sales of the single and soundtrack album plus any subsequent income if it's covered in the future . . . and earned performance income every time it was played on the road, on TV, in cinemas and in live performances. . . .

"Everyone can see there are great profits to be made in film and video, but how do you try and avoid the pitfalls? We spread film production over several companies; we produce local language films and acquire catalogues; we've got strong cash flow from music to help cover our start-up costs; we're building up our own distribution channels; and we've got strong financial controls."

PERFORMANCE

PolyGram gets high marks for consistency, revenue growth, and an excellent ROE, compiling a total score of 90 points in our grading system. EBDIT in dollars increased in each of the last nine years (PolyGram went public seven years ago), with compound annual growth of 22%. Revenues in dollars and EP/ADR increased in eight of the last nine years, both with compound annual growth of around 14%. ROE averaged an impressive 30%. And the long-term debt to capital ratio stayed at reasonable levels, averaging 7%. ADR price performance reflected PolyGram's solid growth, increasing at a compound annual rate of 19% over the last seven years.

If you had invested $10,000 in PolyGram at the end of 1989, you would have purchased around 680 ADRs at around $14.50 each (excluding commissions). There were no capital changes during the next seven years. At the end of 1996, your 680 ADRs would have been worth an estimated $34,500. You would also have received dividend payments of around $2,300.

POLYGRAM

Ticker Symbol and Exchange: PLG—NYSE   **CUSIP No.: 731733101**

OPERATING AND PER SHARE DATA
(in millions of Dutch guilders and guilders per share)

	1986	1987	1988	1989	1990	1991	1992	1993	1994	1995	1996	CAGR
Sales	N/A	2,924	3,426	4,105	5,252	6,326	6,617	7,416	8,600	8,798	9,488	14.0%
EBDIT	N/A	297	374	503	654	806	903	1,205	1,500	1,604	1,781	22.0%
Net Profit	N/A	191	262	333	357	446	506	614	738	741	722	15.9%
EPS	N/A	1.24	1.64	2.08	2.10	2.62	2.98	3.56	4.10	4.12	4.01	13.9%
DPS	N/A	N/M	N/M	0.62	0.50	0.60	0.65	0.75	0.85	0.95	0.95	6.3%

OPERATING AND PER SHARE DATA
(in millions of U.S. dollars and dollars per ADR)

	1986	1987	1988	1989	1990	1991	1992	1993	1994	1995	1996	CAGR
Sales	N/A	1,652	1,716	2,149	3,126	3,699	3,636	3,803	4,971	5,465	5,453	14.2%
EBDIT	N/A	168	187	263	389	471	496	618	867	996	1,024	22.3%
Net Profit	N/A	108	131	174	213	261	278	315	427	460	415	16.1%
EP/ADR	N/A	0.70	0.82	1.09	1.25	1.53	1.64	1.83	2.37	2.56	2.30	14.1%
DP/ADR	N/A	N/M	N/M	0.32	0.30	0.35	0.36	0.38	0.49	0.59	0.55	7.7%

KEY RATIOS

	1986	1987	1988	1989	1990	1991	1992	1993	1994	1995	1996	AVG
EBDIT Margin	N/A	10.2%	10.9%	12.3%	12.5%	12.7%	13.6%	16.2%	17.4%	18.2%	18.8%	14.3%
ROE	N/A	32.9%	30.5%	33.9%	32.2%	39.4%	39.5%	25.3%	26.8%	24.5%	18.9%	30.4%
LT Debt/Total Cap	N/A	3.3%	2.8%	7.6%	6.9%	11.5%	6.3%	10.5%	7.8%	6.9%	5.3%	6.9%
P/E (Projected)	N/A	N/A	N/A	13.3	11.5	13.6	12.6	18.8	19.6	21.2	19.6	16.3

STOCK PRICE CHART
(fiscal year-end closing price, in U.S. dollars, adjusted for capital changes)

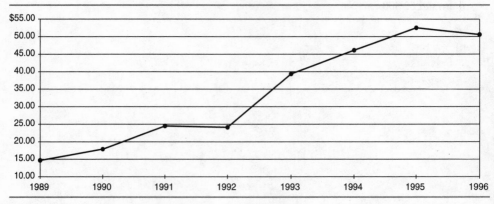

Note: Figures in U.S. dollars are translated from local currency using year-end exchange rates.

POTASH CORPORATION OF SASKATCHEWAN (POT—NYSE)

Address: Suite 500, 122—1st Avenue South / Saskatoon, Saskatchewan S7K 7G3 / Canada
Tel.: (306) 933-8520 **Fax:** (306) 933-8844 **Web site:** http://www.potashcorp.com

BASIC INFORMATION

Country: Canada
Industry: Mining
Investment thesis: World's largest producer of potash, second largest of nitrogen, and third largest of phosphate

Market capitalization: $3.44 billion
Share status: ADRs trade on NYSE

COMPANY GRADING BOX

Growth Categories		Quality of Management	
Revenue Growth	15	Return on Equity	0
Operating Income Growth	20	**Risk**	
Earnings per Share Growth	10	Long-Term Debt/Total Capital	10
Share Price Growth	20	**Total QM&R (maximum 20)**	10
Total Growth (maximum 80)	65	**FINAL GRADE**	75

BACKGROUND

Potash mining may not be on your list of growth industries, but if the company in question is the Potash Corporation of Saskatchewan (PCS), you might want to add it. A combination of strong management, a string of strategic acquisitions, and booming demand have made this company an industry leader in an industry that is going strong. Why potash? Potash and this company's other major products, phosphate and nitrogen, are three of the major ingredients in fertilizer. And worldwide demand for fertilizer is surging, along with the world's population. Currently, PCS, with 1996 revenues of $1.4 billion and a year-end market capitalization of $3.8 billion, provides more than 15% of the world's potash, and most of its revenue is from outside Canada.

When CEO Charles Childers took over PCS back in 1987, it was a giant government-owned mining operation, one of the largest potash producers in the world—and a steady money loser. Childers took the company in hand. He shepherded PCS through a dramatic restructuring, cut back on production to give prices a boost (PCS today has 50% of the world's excess potash capacity), slashed debt, and took the company public. Finally, he went on a buying spree, spending U.S. $1.1 billion to buy two giant phosphate producers and making PCS the largest fertilizer company in the world. Then he spent another U.S. $1.2 billion on the world's second largest nitrogen producer.

Childers wants to be in fertilizer everywhere. And he is probably right. The world's population may be growing, but the amount of arable land is not, and Childers's fertilizers will help feed future generations. The most recent annual report stresses PCS's strong balance sheet, the synergies between its businesses, and its tremendous excess capacity—ready when necessary.

COMPANY STATEMENT (from the 1996 annual report)

"When it became a public company seven years ago, PCS analyzed its business and identified the strengths that would achieve its objective of increasing value for its shareholders. Its major strength was its operating strategy of matching production to demand to maximize profitability, coupled with its excess capacity. Well-established in the mature US market, the Company identified the growing export market as offering the best potential for increased use of its excess potash capacity, and for higher earnings. Adopting an acquisition strategy to capitalize on its financial and industry strengths, it built its future on its past and present, making PCS first a potash export leader and then an integrated international fertilizer supplier. . . .

"PCS has played a major role in the consolidation of the fertilizer industry, first in potash and then in phosphate. Through its acquisitions, it has transformed itself from the world's largest potash company to the world's largest company producing all three primary nutrients. A strong, integrated, market-oriented fertilizer corporation, it is a low-cost producer and market leader.

"Its customer-oriented sales force handles all three nutrients, offering customers the convenience of a single salesperson, a single billing system and computer linkups with one major company that is able to serve them better. With three nutrients, PCS is an efficient one-stop shop for its fertilizer customers."

PERFORMANCE

Potash Corporation of Saskatchewan scored an overall grade of 75 points in our grading system, a reasonably high score but one that does not do this firm justice. The truth is that since 1990, when restructuring (noted above) was completed, performance has been explosive and investors have made a great deal of money. Over the last nine years, revenues grew at a compound rate of 25% while EBDIT grew by 29%. EP/ADR grew by around 6% per annum. However, using 1990, the fulcrum year, as a base, revenue, EBDIT, and EP/ADR grew at compound annual rates of 35%, 32%, and 42%, respectively, through 1996. Although Potash received no points for ROE, again the company has shown significant improvement since its restructuring. In 1990 Potash had ROE of 2%; in 1996 ROE was 15%. As for risk, Potash scores well, averaging 12% for the nine-year period, although this ratio rose to 36% in 1996.

Potash's ADR price increased from a low of $12.50 in 1989 to a high of $87 in 1996. Since the company began issuing a dividend in 1989, dividends per share have increased at a compound annual rate of 31% per annum. The dividend per ADR reached $1.06 in 1996, up from $0.16 in 1989, with an average payout ratio of 45% of earnings during the period.

If you had invested $10,000 in Potash at the end of 1989, you would have purchased around 740 ADRs (or ADR equivalents) at $13.50 each. There were no significant changes in the capital structure during the following nine years. By the end of 1996, your 740 ADRs would have been worth an estimated $63,000. You would also have received around $2,900 in dividend payments.

POTASH CORPORATION OF SASKATCHEWAN

Ticker Symbol and Exchange: POT—NYSE   **CUSIP No.: 73755L107**

OPERATING AND PER SHARE DATA
(in millions of Canadian dollars and dollars per share)

	1986	1987	1988	1989	1990	1991	1992	1993	1994	1995	1996	CAGR
Sales	N/A	252	353	311	266	290	300	298	509	1,164	1,923	25.3%
EBDIT	N/A	53.0	161.0	134.8	85.4	94.0	112.2	124.3	193.2	401.6	533.6	29.2%
Net Profit	N/A	(20.8)	104.9	80.9	24.3	43.9	55.8	62.7	127.9	216.9	286.3	13.4%
EPS	N/A	N/M	3.56	2.31	0.66	1.14	1.44	1.59	2.97	5.00	6.29	7.4%
DPS	N/A	N/M	N/M	0.18	0.72	0.72	0.72	0.74	1.08	1.44	1.45	34.5%

OPERATING AND PER SHARE DATA
(in millions of U.S. dollars and dollars per ADR)

	1986	1987	1988	1989	1990	1991	1992	1993	1994	1995	1996	CAGR
Sales	N/A	194	296	268	230	251	236	225	364	856	1,404	24.6%
EBDIT	N/A	41	135	116	74	81	88	94	138	295	390	28.5%
Net Profit	N/A	(16)	88	70	21	38	44	48	91	160	209	11.4%
EP/ADR	N/A	N/M	2.99	2.00	0.57	0.98	1.14	1.20	2.12	3.68	4.59	5.5%
DP/ADR	N/A	N/M	N/M	0.16	0.62	0.62	0.56	0.56	0.77	1.06	1.06	31.3%

KEY RATIOS

	1986	1987	1988	1989	1990	1991	1992	1993	1994	1995	1996	AVG
EBDIT Margin	N/A	N/M	45.7%	43.4%	32.1%	32.4%	37.4%	41.8%	37.9%	34.5%	27.7%	37.0%
ROE	N/A	N/M	8.8%	7.9%	2.3%	4.1%	5.1%	4.9%	9.5%	12.9%	14.9%	7.8%
LT Debt/Total Cap	N/A	N/M	7.8%	8.3%	7.4%	6.4%	5.6%	2.2%	0.2%	37.8%	36.1%	12.4%
P/E (Projected)	N/A	N/M	N/M	23.7	14.2	14.4	16.2	11.4	9.5	15.3	16.6	15.2

STOCK PRICE CHART
(fiscal year-end closing price, in U.S. dollars, adjusted for capital changes)

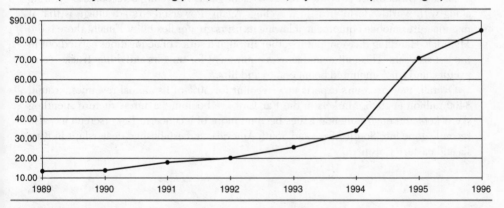

Note: Figures in U.S. dollars are translated from local currency using year-end exchange rates.

POWERSCREEN (POITF—OTC)

Address: Coalisland Road / Dungannon / County Tyrone / Northern Ireland BT71 4DR
Tel.: (011) 44 1 868 740701 **Fax:** (011) 44 1 868 748816 **Web site:** http://www.powerscreen.co.uk

BASIC INFORMATION

Country: Northern Ireland
Industry: Industrial equipment
Investment thesis: Manufacturer of machinery for screening, crushing, recycling building materials

Market capitalization: $876 million
Share status: Foreign shares trade OTC

COMPANY GRADING BOX

Growth Categories		Quality of Management	
Revenue Growth	20	Return on Equity	10
Operating Income Growth	20	**Risk**	
Earnings per Share Growth	20	Long-Term Debt/Total Capital	10
Share Price Growth	15	**Total QM&R (maximum 20)**	20
Total Growth (maximum 80)	75	**FINAL GRADE**	95

BACKGROUND

This engineering company, based in Northern Ireland, is a leading manufacturer of machinery used in the building and construction industries—primarily for screening, crushing and recycling—leaving it well positioned as governments around the world become increasingly concerned with environmental issues. The screening division, which accounts for well over half the company's operating profits, provides machinery that is used to separate different sizes of materials: different rocks from a quarry, or waste products left after a building demolition.

Powerscreen has an estimated 45% of the world market for mobile screening, which allows companies to screen materials with equipment that is less expensive to put into operation than larger static screening machinery and easier to move from site to site (rather than moving the material, contractors move the machinery). To date, mobile screening machinery accounts for only 10% of the market worldwide. Recycling accounts for 50% of Powerscreen's U.S. screening sales and forty percent of U.K. screening sales. A landfill tax established in the United Kingdom in 1996 gave Powerscreen a big boost, giving dumpers greater incentive to screen materials for usable products.

Next in profitability is Powerscreen's Crushing and Recycling division, also growing along with worldwide interest in recycling. Again, Powerscreen's advantage is that it manufactures mobile equipment, allowing its users greater flexibility. Finally, there is the Materials Handling division, put together through a series of acquisitions carried out in the last six years. This unit manufactures equipment for tractors and dump trucks, compactors, and truck-mounted boom cranes and lifts.

Overall, Powerscreen's exports now account for 50% of its annual revenues, around $400 million in 1996. Markets in the Far East are booming as infrastructure spending skyrockets and environmental issues become more of a concern. Powerscreen has also recently gone into South Africa and South America, and established dealerships in Russia and eastern Europe.

COMPANY STATEMENT (from the 1996 annual report)

"Screening Division:

- ... The use of mobile screening in a number of the Far Eastern countries is under-developed and this fact presents tremendous opportunities for growth of business in the area.
- Ongoing product development and enhancement is essential to our screening business. Best prices are achieved in the newer markets and with newer updated product lines. ...
- The UK landfill levy has provided further incentive and additional economic rationale for the reduction in both volume and weight of material going to landfill.

"Crushing and Recycling Division:

- As the availability of suitable tipping sites particularly in urban areas becomes scarce so the pressure for recycling increases. In the UK, the government target is to double the use of secondary and recycled material in Britain to around 55 million tons by the year 2006. Tightening the licensing system for waste dumps later this year will more than double the average tipping costs.
- The shortage of natural materials in certain geographical areas due to planning limitations, for example, in South East England, or an actual supply shortage such as in the Netherlands and Germany, are both factors which influence the recycling demand. Mobile crushing equipment sales benefit from these factors. The ability to move crushing equipment to operate at demolition sites and recycling stations highlights the advantage of mobile as opposed to static equipment in certain circumstances.

"Materials Handling Divisions:

Overall the Materials Handling Divisions has seen vibrant growth in the last three years and management are confident that 1996/97 should show further progress in both sales and profits."

PERFORMANCE

Powerscreen received a total of 95 points in our grading system, making it one of our top scoring companies. Revenues in dollars increased in nine of the last ten years, recording compound annual growth of 19%. EBDIT increased in every one of the last ten years, recording compound annual growth of 17%. And EPS in dollars increased in eight of the last ten years, recording compound annual growth of 15%. ROE averaged an excellent 32%. And the long-term debt to total capital ratio remained low, averaging 7% over the ten year period. Share price performance was less consistent, but the shares in dollars still increased at a compound annual rate of about 20%.

If you had invested $10,000 in Powerscreen in March 1987, you would have bought around 6,250 shares at about $1.60 each (excluding commissions). There were no capital changes over the next ten years. By March 1997, your 6,250 shares would have been worth around $60,000. You also would have received dividend payments of around $5,500.

POWERSCREEN

Ticker Symbol and Exchange: POITF—OTC   **SEDOL Code: 128689**

OPERATING AND PER SHARE DATA
(in millions of British pounds and pounds per share)

	Mar 87	Mar 88	Mar 89	Mar 90	Mar 91	Mar 92	Mar 93	Mar 94	Mar 95	Mar 96	Mar 97	CAGR
Sales	51.0	49.0	45.0	66.0	72.0	88.0	108.0	122.0	197.0	261.0	305.0	19.6%
EBDIT	9.3	10.0	12.8	16.2	18.3	20.5	24.8	25.7	31.1	39.6	46.9	17.6%
Net Profit	6.5	7.5	9.3	11.2	13.1	13.8	14.9	19.3	21.8	26.9	32.1	17.3%
EPS	0.09	0.10	0.12	0.14	0.16	0.16	0.17	0.22	0.25	0.30	0.36	15.1%
DPS	0.02	0.04	0.04	0.05	0.06	0.06	0.07	0.07	0.08	0.09	0.10	17.7%

OPERATING AND PER SHARE DATA
(in millions of U.S. dollars and dollars per share)

	Mar 87	Mar 88	Mar 89	Mar 90	Mar 91	Mar 92	Mar 93	Mar 94	Mar 95	Mar 96	Mar 97	CAGR
Sales	82	92	76	109	126	153	164	181	319	398	477	19.3%
EBDIT	14.9	18.8	21.6	26.6	32.0	35.6	37.6	38.1	50.4	60.4	73.3	17.2%
Net Profit	10.4	14.1	15.7	18.4	22.9	24.0	22.6	28.6	35.3	41.0	50.2	17.0%
EPS	0.14	0.19	0.20	0.23	0.28	0.28	0.26	0.33	0.41	0.46	0.56	14.8%
DPS	0.03	0.07	0.07	0.08	0.10	0.10	0.10	0.11	0.13	0.14	0.16	17.4%

KEY RATIOS

	Mar 87	Mar 88	Mar 89	Mar 90	Mar 91	Mar 92	Mar 93	Mar 94	Mar 95	Mar 96	Mar 97	AVG
EBDIT Margin	18.2%	20.4%	28.4%	24.5%	25.4%	23.3%	23.0%	21.1%	15.8%	15.2%	15.4%	21.0%
ROE	40.4%	39.5%	44.3%	36.7%	30.8%	28.8%	23.1%	25.8%	25.1%	27.2%	29.3%	31.9%
LT Debt/Total Cap	9.6%	11.1%	12.7%	6.0%	5.4%	12.4%	6.2%	3.8%	5.3%	5.8%	2.2%	7.3%
P/E (Projected)	10.0	10.5	7.3	9.1	11.2	14.6	16.3	11.1	8.2	12.1	14.9	11.4

STOCK PRICE CHART
(fiscal year-end closing price, in U.S. dollars, adjusted for capital changes)

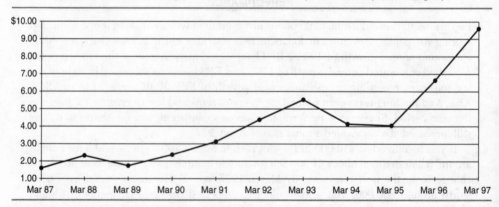

Note: Figures in U.S. dollars are translated from local currency using year-end exchange rates.

PROVIDENT FINANCIAL (PFG.L—LONDON)

Address: Colonnade / Sunbridge Road / Bradford BD1 2LQ / United Kingdom
Tel.: (011) 44 1274 731111   **Fax:** (011) 44 1274 727300

BASIC INFORMATION

Country: United Kingdom   **Market capitalization:** $2.48 billion
Industry: Financial services   **Share status:** Foreign shares trade on London Exchange
Investment thesis: Financial services company specializing in home credit, door to door

COMPANY GRADING BOX

Growth Categories		Quality of Management	
Revenue Growth	10	Return on Equity	10
Operating Income Growth	20	**Risk**	
Earnings per Share Growth	20	Long-Term Debt/Total Capital	10
Share Price Growth	20	**Total QM&R (maximum 20)**	**20**
Total Growth (maximum 80)	**70**	**FINAL GRADE**	**90**

BACKGROUND

Provident Financial, a U.K. financial services firm, prides itself on knowing its markets better than anyone else and on being part of every community in which it operates. The fastest-growing part of the company, Home Collected Credit, brings in an estimated 74% of this company's $430 million in annual revenues—and the division has consistently increased its earnings. Profits for the division were up 21% in 1996. Home Collected Credit's target market is lower-income homes, often those that have been rejected by other credit companies. And it generally advances credit immediately, in the customer's home; credit is advanced in the form of cash, checks, or shopping vouchers, and agents call on customers weekly to work out repayment schedules. Rather than relying on traditional techniques for determining creditworthiness, Provident relies on its agents in the communities, 85% of them women, who come from the communities where they work to determine good and bad risks. Though risky, it is a unique strategy that thus far has proven to be very successful.

The other 26% of Provident's revenues come from the insurance side of the business, mostly noncomprehensive car insurance covering women and second cars. By concentrating in this specialist insurance market and bringing an innovative approach to its niche, Provident hopes to maintain its profitability in an increasingly competitive marketplace. Over the past few years, the company has raised its premiums (at the expense of volume and market share) to maintain its margins. But it remains a low-cost provider of low-premium coverage.

COMPANY STATEMENT (from the 1996 annual report)

"Provident Financial is a personal financial services group, focused on credit, cash collections and insurance. We aim to achieve consistent, above average growth by developing, both organically and by acquisition, a balanced portfolio of businesses within our areas of special expertise. Our objectives are to increase the value of the Company to our shareholders and maintain our excellent dividend record by developing strong market positions and maximizing returns on capital in all our businesses, whilst adhering to conservative financial principles.

"... Much of our success is due to concentrating on the growth strategy in Home Credit together with our group-wide focus on improving performance and containing costs. . . .

"The market for home credit continues to grow: first, because many people in the communities we serve prefer to borrow in the comfort and privacy of their own home from an agent who understands their circumstances and, secondly, because we are able to serve those people efficiently. Our success is due to our agents' knowledge of their customers which enables us to lend responsibly and profitably."

PERFORMANCE

Provident Financial received 90 points in our grading system, with particularly good EPS growth in dollars and an excellent ROE. EPS in dollars increased in eight of the last ten years, with compound annual growth of 19%. EBDIT increased in nine of the last ten years, with compound annual growth of 20%. Revenues in dollars also increased in nine of the last ten years but at a slower rate, with compound annual growth of around 9%. Share price performance, on the other hand, kept pace with EPS growth, increasing at a compound annual rate of 26%. And dividends per share showed compound annual growth of 22%, with an average payout ratio of 49%. ROE averaged a high 23%. And the long-term debt to total capital ratio averaged 15% (it went up to 45% in 1993 but was back down to 33% by 1996).

If you had invested $10,000 in Provident Financial at the end of 1986, you would have bought around 2,400 shares at about $4 each (excluding commissions). During the next ten years, there were a one-for-two stock consolidation in May 1993, a five-for-one stock split in May 1993, and a one-for-one bonus issue in May 1996. By the end of 1996, you would have had around 12,000 shares worth an estimated $103,600. You would also have received dividend payments of around $16,800.

PROVIDENT FINANCIAL
Ticker Symbol and Exchange: PFG.L—London   **SEDOL Code: 701433**

OPERATING AND PER SHARE DATA
(in millions of British pounds and pounds per share)

	1986	1987	1988	1989	1990	1991	1992	1993	1994	1995	1996	CAGR
Sales	208.2	216.3	251.2	286.2	317.6	359.9	371.3	399.9	445.3	448.4	429.7	7.5%
EBDIT	22.3	26.7	28.2	31.7	36.2	34.1	40.7	62.5	81.2	101.1	118.5	18.2%
Net Profit	14.4	17.8	18.6	21.6	24.4	24.1	28.1	41.9	54.4	67.8	79.4	18.6%
EPS	0.06	0.07	0.07	0.09	0.10	0.09	0.14	0.16	0.20	0.25	0.29	17.5%
DPS	0.03	0.03	0.04	0.04	0.05	0.05	0.06	0.08	0.10	0.14	0.17	20.3%

OPERATING AND PER SHARE DATA
(in millions of U.S. dollars and dollars per share)

	1986	1987	1988	1989	1990	1991	1992	1993	1994	1995	1996	CAGR
Sales	309	408	454	461	614	671	561	590	697	695	736	9.1%
EBDIT	33.0	50.4	51.0	51.1	69.9	63.6	61.5	92.3	127.2	156.7	202.9	19.9%
Net Profit	21.3	33.6	33.6	34.8	47.1	44.9	42.4	61.9	85.2	105.1	135.9	20.3%
EPS	0.09	0.14	0.13	0.14	0.19	0.17	0.21	0.23	0.32	0.39	0.50	19.2%
DPS	0.04	0.06	0.07	0.07	0.09	0.09	0.09	0.12	0.16	0.22	0.28	22.0%

KEY RATIOS

	1986	1987	1988	1989	1990	1991	1992	1993	1994	1995	1996	AVG
EBDIT Margin	10.7%	12.3%	11.2%	11.1%	11.4%	9.5%	11.0%	15.6%	18.2%	22.5%	27.6%	14.7%
ROE	21.9%	23.9%	21.7%	18.3%	19.3%	17.6%	18.2%	23.7%	27.2%	29.2%	29.5%	22.8%
LT Debt/Total Cap	1.4%	1.2%	2.7%	1.3%	0.9%	0.4%	0.1%	45.2%	43.3%	37.3%	33.1%	15.2%
P/E (Projected)	7.8	8.9	7.5	8.0	8.7	6.0	8.8	11.2	10.9	14.0	15.0	9.7

STOCK PRICE CHART
(fiscal year-end closing price, in U.S. dollars, adjusted for capital changes)

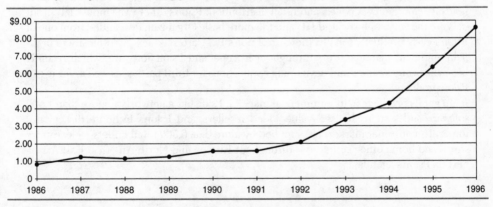

Note: Figures in U.S. dollars are translated from local currency using year-end exchange rates.

PSION (PSIOF—OTC)

Address: Alexander House / 85 Frampton Street / London NW8 8NQ / United Kingdom
Tel.: (011) 44 171 262 5580   **Fax:** (011) 44 171 258 7340   **Web site:** http://www.psion.com

BASIC INFORMATION

Country: United Kingdom
Industry: Electrical and electronic
Investment thesis: High-tech firm with 33% of the world market for handheld computers

Market capitalization: $474 million
Share status: Foreign shares trade OTC

COMPANY GRADING BOX

Growth Categories		Quality of Management	
Revenue Growth	20	Return on Equity	10
Operating Income Growth	20	**Risk**	
Earnings per Share Growth	15	Long-Term Debt/Total Capital	10
Share Price Growth	20	**Total QM&R (maximum 20)**	**20**
Total Growth (maximum 80)	**75**	**FINAL GRADE**	**95**

BACKGROUND

Like many U.S. high-tech companies, U.K.-based Psion has experienced explosive growth. This sixteen-year-old manufacturer of handheld computers has grown at a compound rate of more than 35 percent per annum since inception. Today it is an industry leader, with an estimated 33% of the handheld market worldwide (according to a 1995 study by Forrester Research). The company, which manufactures all its products at two U.K. plants, sells five product groups to four different market segments.

Best known are its handheld computers sold for the consumer markets, accounting for 55 percent of Psion's total sales. Its Series 3 handhelds were launched in 1991, and the company has been improving on them ever since. The current model, the Series 3c, includes a word processor, database and spreadsheet applications, Internet access, e-mail, and up to 16 megabytes of memory . . . along with daily, monthly, and weekly planners, alarms, an address database, and a telephone autodialer. You get the idea. The software titles available even include Scrabble and Monopoly.

For the industrial market, Psion offers three product lines with different specialized applications. The most recently introduced, the Workabout, is built for outdoor use. The Workabout's target markets are field service, the utilities, trucking, inventory and warehousing, emergency services, and retail distribution. Psion's other two "industrial" products are the very sophisticated HC and the more basic Organizer, descended from one of Psion's early products. Finally, there are Psion's PC Card modems, sold mostly to original equipment manufacturers throughout Europe, and Psion Software, which recently began licensing systems and developing applications for third parties, as well as for use in Psion products.

To get its products to its commercial markets, Psion has a network of more than 1,500 software and systems houses, value-added resellers, and Psion's in-house direct sales forces. Its consumer markets are supplied by more than 6,500 retail outlets—electronics stores and home office suppliers—throughout Europe and North America. East Asia is next on Psion's agenda.

COMPANY STATEMENT (from the 1996 annual report)

"The growth of Psion has been based around skills in microprocessor software and electronics. We use these skills to create new products which we manufacture in volume and market through our distribution network.

"Psion has been very successful in the palmtop computer market. Such success makes it inevitable that others will enter the market, competition will increase and much larger volumes will in due course be established. Psion's strategy is based on continuous technological and market innovation, an essential approach in an industry which is driven by flux and change. Psion leverages its in-house, core technologies as a means to exploit emerging market opportunities at the front wave of technology. By cultivating the Group's ability to innovate, we are able to operate in high-margin markets and avoid lower-margin commodity markets. . . .

"The market sectors that the Group addresses are exciting, dynamic and growing. Although competition is increasing, there are many opportunities for us in our key markets. We will be launching new products in Psion Computers, Psion Industrial and Psion Dacom, while Psion Software is expected to obtain new licensees for its 'EPOC' operating systems."

PERFORMANCE

Psion is another of our top performing companies, garnering 95 of a possible 100 points in our grading system, even though it is the smallest of our companies in terms of market capitalization. Not surprising for a growth company of this size, share price performance stands out, with the share price in dollars increasing at a compound annual rate of 30%. As is the case with other fast-growing small companies we chose to include, it is only fair to note that it would have been difficult to get into this stock when it first began trading, making the eight-year stock performance a bit misleading.

Nonetheless, management's performance in other areas also stands out. Despite a downturn in the late 1980s, revenues, EBDIT, and EPS soared in the 1990s. In its nine-year operating history, these three key growth measures increased at compound annual rates of 28%, 26%, and 19%, respectively. ROE averaged a healthy 18% and was 23% in 1996, while the ratio of long-term debt to total capital declined from 20% in 1987 to 6% in 1996.

If you had invested $10,000 in Psion at the end of 1988, you would have purchased around 3,550 shares at around $2.75 each. During the next eight years, there were a one-for-ten rights issue in October 1989 and a two-for-one bonus issue in May 1996. By the end of 1996, you would have had around 10,700 shares worth an estimated $80,860. You would also have received dividend payments of around $1,900.

PSION

Ticker Symbol and Exchange: PSIOF—OTC   **SEDOL Code: 709545**

OPERATING AND PER SHARE DATA
(in millions of British pounds and pounds per share)

	1986	1987	1988	1989	1990	1991	1992	1993	1994	1995	1996	CAGR
Sales	N/A	12.0	19.0	31.0	31.0	21.0	35.1	41.2	61.3	91.0	124.2	29.6%
EBDIT	N/A	2.2	3.1	4.2	1.9	(0.7)	3.1	4.9	8.7	14.8	19.8	27.7%
Net Profit	N/A	1.4	1.8	2.0	0.3	(1.8)	1.0	2.0	4.2	7.5	10.4	25.0%
EPS	N/A	0.03	0.04	0.03	0.00	(0.03)	0.01	0.03	0.05	0.11	0.16	20.7%
DPS	N/A	0.00	0.00	0.01	0.01	0.01	0.01	0.01	0.01	0.02	0.02	24.4%

OPERATING AND PER SHARE DATA
(in millions of U.S. dollars and dollars per share)

	1986	1987	1988	1989	1990	1991	1992	1993	1994	1995	1996	CAGR
Sales	N/A	23	34	50	60	39	53	61	96	141	213	28.3%
EBDIT	N/A	4.2	5.6	6.8	3.7	(1.3)	4.7	7.2	13.6	22.9	33.9	26.3%
Net Profit	N/A	2.6	3.3	3.2	0.6	(3.4)	1.5	3.0	6.6	11.6	17.8	23.6%
EPS	N/A	0.06	0.06	0.05	0.01	(0.05)	0.02	0.04	0.09	0.17	0.27	19.4%
DPS	N/A	—	0.01	0.01	0.02	0.01	0.01	0.01	0.02	0.03	0.04	23.6%

KEY RATIOS

	1986	1987	1988	1989	1990	1991	1992	1993	1994	1995	1996	AVG
EBDIT Margin	N/A	18.3%	16.3%	13.5%	6.1%	−3.3%	8.8%	11.9%	14.2%	16.3%	15.9%	11.8%
ROE	N/A	45.2%	31.6%	15.4%	2.3%	−17.1%	8.9%	15.7%	25.6%	32.5%	22.6%	18.3%
LT Debt/Total Cap	N/A	20.0%	10.8%	9.1%	8.5%	5.3%	5.0%	4.4%	6.2%	6.5%	6.2%	8.2%
P/E (Projected)	N/A	N/A	15.5	N/M	N/M	28.2	11.6	11.1	7.7	16.2	21.0	13.9

STOCK PRICE CHART
(fiscal year-end closing price, in U.S. dollars, adjusted for capital changes)

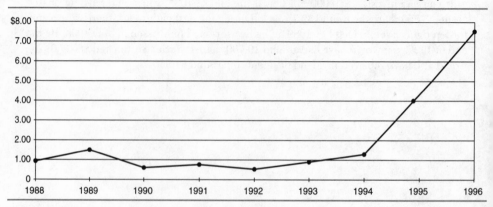

Note: Figures in U.S. dollars are translated from local currency using year-end exchange rates.

RANDSTAD (RANHF—OTC)

Address: Diemermere 25 / 1112 TC Dieman / Netherlands
Tel.: (011) 31 20 569 5911   **Fax:** (011) 31 20 569 55 20   **Web site:** http://www.randstad.com

BASIC INFORMATION

Country: Netherlands
Industry: Temporary employment
Investment thesis: Fourth largest employment agency in the world; 960 offices in nine countries

Market capitalization: $3.65 billion
Share status: Foreign shares trade OTC

COMPANY GRADING BOX

Growth Categories		Quality of Management	
Revenue Growth	20	Return on Equity	10
Operating Income Growth	15	**Risk**	
Earnings per Share Growth	20	Long-Term Debt/Total Capital	10
Share Price Growth	20	**Total QM&R (maximum 20)**	**20**
Total Growth (maximum 80)	**75**	**FINAL GRADE**	**95**

BACKGROUND

Take a look at Randstad, the fourth largest temporary employment agency in the world. Based in the Netherlands, this thirty-six-year-old outsourcing company has seen its revenues and profits grow by an average of more than 20% annually over the past twenty-five years. It has more than 960 offices in nine countries, is responsible for staffing around 130,000 employees daily, and is the market leader in the Benelux countries (nearly 40% market share in the Netherlands; 26% in Belgium).

Perfectly positioned to take advantage of corporate restructuring throughout Europe, Randstad is now projecting 15% annual profit growth based on a conservative estimate of 10% annual market growth. In the first half of 1996, the temporary staffing market grew in every one of Randstad's markets except France, and there Randstad increased its market share. After years of fighting for recognition and room in European industry (for example, temporary agencies are still illegal in Italy), some European governments are now looking at temp agencies as a way to help bring down European unemployment rates. Despite a spate of regulations still in place to limit the industry's growth, a recent headline in *The Wall Street Journal* announced: "Off the Dole—Europe Sees Market in Temporary Workers Profit from Job Crisis."

Randstad is aggressively pushing ahead. Today it is active in cleaning, security, technical staffing, automation, and training, as well as traditional temp staffing. It also consults with corporations about staffing needs; offers staff management services, interim management on-site reassignment and outplacement for employees; runs call centers; and is working with the Dutch government to retrain hard-to-place workers.

In the United States, Randstad, with seventy-eight offices in the Southeast, has become the leading temporary employment agency in Georgia and Tennessee, even supplying the temporary staff for the Atlanta Olympics.

COMPANY STATEMENT (from the 1996 annual report)

"Randstad was established as a temporary staffing agency in 1960. The core activity was and still is 'linking the demand for labor with the supply.' Over the years, a whole range of activities has been developed around this concept. The company has grown into an international business services supplier.

"Emphasis on autonomous growth: All-important for the development of the company is autonomous growth. The preference for autonomous growth ties in with the wish to maintain the culture that is rooted within the Group. The keywords for this culture are 'to know, to serve and to trust.' . . . The choice not to operate with the franchise formula but only to use its own branches also fits into Randstad's strategy. Thanks to its excellent financial position, Randstad is in a position to acquire suitable staffing firms should appropriate opportunities arise.

"Strong positions in local markets: Randstad focuses primarily on attaining a leading position in local markets in order to serve its clients well within the local situation.

"Randstad's growth strategy: Randstad's growth scenario takes various paths. It involves the further penetration of existing markets, entering new markets with existing products, and developing new products in both existing and new markets."

PERFORMANCE

Randstad does not have as long a track record as a publicly traded company as some of our other picks, but the reported historical figures compiled from the years before it went public and its share price performance over the last six years show a formidable track record. Randstad's overall grade of 95 puts it among our highest scorers. This is a company that got top scores in five out of our six categories, the only exception being consistency of growth in EBDIT (operating income rose in just seven of the last ten years; however, it showed compound annual growth of just under 21%). Revenues in dollars grew in nine of the last ten years, recording compound annual growth of 18%. EPS in dollars showed compound annual growth of 23%. ROE was an impressive 39% in 1996 and averaged 31% for the decade. And the long-term debt to total capital ratio was just under 9% in 1996 and averaged around 14% for the decade. It is rare indeed to find a company with such consistently high growth, above-average returns, and low risk.

Then there is Randstad's share price performance. The share price in dollars increased from a low of $10.49 in 1992 to a high of $85.00 in 1996; from 1990 to 1996, the share price saw compound annual growth of 32%. Since 1990, dividends increased at a compound annual rate of 14%.

If you had invested $10,000 in Randstad in 1990, you would have bought around 370 shares at around $27 each (excluding commissions). In September 1995 the company had a two-for-one stock split. By the end of 1996, you would have had around 740 shares worth an estimated $52,600. And you would have received dividend payments of around $8,500.

RANDSTAD

Ticker Symbol and Exchange: RANHF—OTC   **SEDOL Code: 4717362**

OPERATING AND PER SHARE DATA
(in millions of Dutch guilders and guilders per share)

	1986	1987	1988	1989	1990	1991	1992	1993	1994	1995	1996	CAGR
Sales	1,477	1,611	1,887	2,197	2,542	2,607	3,012	3,006	3,759	4,702	5,953	15.0%
EBDIT	70.2	72.6	93.9	121.5	171.0	173.0	172.2	151.6	214.5	288.7	361.9	17.8%
Net Profit	33.6	35.6	44.6	64.8	92.9	98.5	91.5	72.3	112.4	163.3	207.4	20.0%
EPS	0.78	0.83	1.03	1.50	2.15	2.28	2.12	1.67	2.60	3.78	4.80	19.9%
DPS	N/M	N/M	N/M	0.60	0.86	0.92	0.92	0.92	1.04	1.52	1.92	18.1%

OPERATING AND PER SHARE DATA
(in millions of U.S. dollars and dollars per share)

	1986	1987	1988	1989	1990	1991	1992	1993	1994	1995	1996	CAGR
Sales	678	910	945	1,150	1,513	1,525	1,655	1,542	2,173	2,920	3,421	17.6%
EBDIT	32	41	47	64	102	101	95	78	124	179	208	20.5%
Net Profit	15	20	22	34	55	58	50	37	65	101	119	22.7%
EPS	0.36	0.47	0.52	0.79	1.28	1.33	1.16	0.86	1.50	2.35	2.76	22.7%
DPS	N/M	N/M	N/M	N/M	0.51	0.54	0.51	0.47	0.60	0.94	1.10	13.7%

KEY RATIOS

	1986	1987	1988	1989	1990	1991	1992	1993	1994	1995	1996	AVG
EBDIT Margin	4.8%	4.5%	5.0%	5.5%	6.7%	6.6%	5.7%	5.0%	5.7%	6.1%	6.1%	5.6%
ROE	25.9%	23.9%	19.5%	29.7%	33.9%	29.6%	34.2%	26.9%	35.9%	40.2%	38.8%	30.8%
LT Debt/Total Cap	15.0%	16.7%	15.2%	14.7%	12.5%	11.0%	14.1%	17.2%	13.8%	10.4%	8.5%	13.6%
P/E (Projected)	N/A	N/A	N/A	N/A	10.0	9.3	13.8	11.2	12.4	15.2	22.4	13.5

STOCK PRICE CHART
(fiscal year-end closing price, in U.S. dollars, adjusted for capital changes)

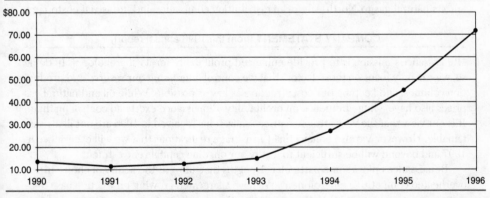

Notes: Randstad shares did not begin trading publicly until 1990. Figures in U.S. dollars are translated from local currency using year-end exchange rates.

RENAISSANCE (RES.TO—TORONTO)

Address: Suite 3000, 425 First Street S.W. / Calgary, Alberta T2P 3L8 / Canada
Tel.: (403) 750-1400   **Fax:** (403) 750-1468

BASIC INFORMATION

Country: Canada   **Market capitalization:** $3.23 billion
Industry: Oil and gas   **Share status:** Foreign shares trade on Toronto Exchange
Investment thesis: Oil and gas company with abundant proven reserves and unexplored land

COMPANY GRADING BOX

Growth Categories		Quality of Management	
Revenue Growth	20	Return on Equity	0
Operating Income Growth	20	**Risk**	
Earnings per Share Growth	15	Long-Term Debt/ Total Capital	10
Share Price Growth	20	**Total QM&R (maximum 20)**	10
Total Growth (maximum 80)	75	**FINAL GRADE**	85

BACKGROUND

This Canadian oil and gas company sticks to what it knows. One hundred percent of revenues come from its core businesses, oil and gas exploration and production. Its activities are centered in the Western Canadian Sedimentary Basin: 500,000 square miles including Alberta, Saskatchewan, and Manitoba with known oil and gas resources, and plenty of room for growth. Renaissance (and its competitors) generally acquire mineral rights from local governments, the largest landowners. In 1996 Renaissance bought an additional 2.5 million acres, increasing its inventory of unexplored land to 10.6 million acres. Today Renaissance has the largest land position in its corner of the industry, and on a relatively low-cost basis. The company is also using new technology to explore land considered "mature" where management believes there is more oil and gas to be found.

This is a company that has increased its earnings from $5 million in 1986 to $131 million in 1996. On average, it drills 4.5 wells a day, and it has recently added or expanded ten oil and ten natural gas facilities, as well as 500 additional miles of pipeline gathering systems. Oil production volumes rose by 26% in 1996; natural gas production was up 6%. Renaissance directly markets all its crude oil to refiners in Canada and the United States and its natural gas to North American distribution companies and industrial customers.

COMPANY STATEMENT (from the 1996 annual report)

"Renaissance's mission is to provide enhanced profitability for its shareholders. In doing so, we can only focus on those factors that we control: increasing our reserve and production volumes, and keeping our cost structure as low as possible. While oil and natural gas prices also have a huge influence on profitability, Renaissance exerts no control on them. It is our view that the very attractive price realizations received in 1996 are not likely sustainable. However, we also believe that the average realizations that we will experience in 1997 and beyond will be sufficient to justify our ongoing capital reinvestment.

"Renaissance enjoys some particular strengths that allow us the luxury of choice in this overheated competitive environment. We have a large and growing production base to finance our capital program. We are an exploration driven company—it is our belief that only exploration creates true lasting value in our business. The momentum of our program is very important to sustaining our activity levels. Our inventory of undeveloped lands is the largest in North America and is concentrated in geologically familiar settings. We have built solid relationships with many members of the service sector and continue to enjoy a price and service advantage. Most importantly, our balanced team of share-holder employees has the necessary skills and vision to direct our efforts. While we are not immune to the competitive pressures that exist in our industry today, we can rely on these strengths to grow our reserves and production volumes at a relatively low cost."

PERFORMANCE

Renaissance gets high marks for consistency and growth and received an overall grade of 85. Revenues in dollars have grown every year for the last ten years, with compound annual growth of just over 40%. EBDIT also increased in each of the last ten years, showing compound annual growth of about 37%. Although Renaissance's EPS numbers have been somewhat inconsistent, the company still had compound annual EPS growth of 30%. Share price performance has also been impressive, showing compound annual growth of 32%. Finally, Renaissance got its full 10 points for a low long-term debt to total capital ratio, which averaged 23% during the decade. Renaissance received no points for ROE, which averaged 6.8%. But at least it is going in the right direction: in 1996, ROE was 9%, up from 4.4% one year earlier. Renaissance's share price in dollars increased from a low of $1.20 in 1986 to a high of $37.23 in 1996.

If you had invested $10,000 in Renaissance at the end of 1986, you would have purchased around 1,150 shares at $8.50 each (excluding commissions). During the following ten years, Renaissance had two two-for-one stock splits, one in October 1987 and another in May 1990. By the end of 1996, you would have had 4,600 shares worth an estimated $157,100. Renaissance did not issue any dividends.

RENAISSANCE

Ticker Symbol and Exchange: RES.TO—Toronto   **SEDOL Code: 2731513**

OPERATING AND PER SHARE DATA
(in millions of Canadian dollars and dollars per share)

	1986	1987	1988	1989	1990	1991	1992	1993	1994	1995	1996	CAGR
Sales	32	57	86	131	180	206	266	382	522	603	953	40.4%
EBDIT	27	49	70	78	101	112	143	216	293	355	608	36.6%
Net Profit	7	10	7	18	23	21	25	49	63	63	180	38.4%
EPS	0.12	0.22	0.14	0.31	0.38	0.32	0.35	0.60	0.70	0.66	1.61	30.2%
DPS	N/M	N/M	N/M	N/M	N/M	N/M	N/M	N/M	N/M	N/M	N/M	N/M

OPERATING AND PER SHARE DATA
(in millions of U.S. dollars and dollars per share)

	1986	1987	1988	1989	1990	1991	1992	1993	1994	1995	1996	CAGR
Sales	23	44	72	113	155	178	209	289	373	443	696	40.5%
EBDIT	19.5	38.0	59.0	67.2	87.4	97.1	112.3	163.3	209.6	260.8	443.8	36.7%
Net Profit	5.1	7.7	5.9	15.5	19.8	18.2	19.4	37.1	45.1	46.4	131.4	38.5%
EPS	0.08	0.17	0.11	0.27	0.33	0.28	0.28	0.45	0.50	0.49	1.18	30.3%
DPS	N/M	N/M	N/M	N/M	N/M	N/M	N/M	N/M	N/M	N/M	N/M	N/M

KEY RATIOS

	1986	1987	1988	1989	1990	1991	1992	1993	1994	1995	1996	AVG
EBDIT Margin	84.2%	87.3%	81.5%	59.4%	56.3%	54.4%	53.6%	56.4%	56.2%	58.8%	63.8%	64.7%
ROE	5.6%	7.8%	4.4%	8.9%	9.8%	6.7%	5.5%	6.9%	6.0%	4.4%	9.1%	6.8%
LT Debt/Total Cap	8.5%	18.4%	31.2%	27.3%	32.2%	32.3%	27.9%	18.0%	24.5%	19.4%	14.6%	23.1%
P/E (Projected)	13.6	45.2	20.5	33.7	49.1	38.0	31.0	40.3	41.1	21.0	30.7	33.1

STOCK PRICE CHART
(fiscal year-end closing price, in U.S. dollars, adjusted for capital changes)

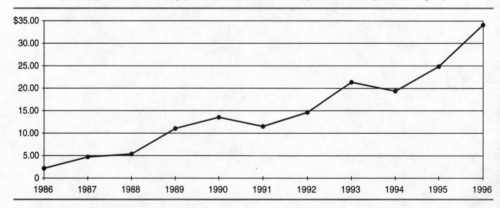

Note: Figures in U.S. dollars are translated from local currency using year-end exchange rates.

RENTOKIL INITIAL (RTOKY—OTC)

Address: Felcourt, East Grinstead, West Sussex RH19 2JY / United Kingdom
Tel.: (011) 44 1342 833 022   **Fax:** (011) 44 1342 326 229

BASIC INFORMATION

Country: United Kingdom   **Market capitalization:** $8.5 billion
Industry: Environmental services   **Share status:** ADRs trade OTC
Investment thesis: The largest business services group in the world; began with pest control

COMPANY GRADING BOX

Growth Categories		Quality of Management	
Revenue Growth	20	Return on Equity	10
Operating Income Growth	20	**Risk**	
Earnings per Share Growth	20	Long-Term Debt/Total Capital	10
Share Price Growth	20	**Total QM&R (maximum 20)**	20
Total Growth (maximum 80)	**80**	**FINAL GRADE**	**100**

BACKGROUND

U.K.-based Rentokil started as a pest control company and has gone way beyond its roots. Today, it is a major player in the booming world of "outsourcing." Hospitals, medical offices, hotels, and corporations all use Rentokil for everything from pest control (including of insects, rodents, and "pest birds") to security services to cleaning services to machine maintenance. Then there are the Tropical Plants division (Rentokil supplies, designs, and maintains indoor tropical plant displays), personnel services (permanent and temporary jobs), contract catering for schools and businesses, management of luxury condominiums and resorts, timber treatment, and the replacement and refurbishment of all types of roofing. And the list goes on. Today Rentokil is a multinational company with $4 billion in 1996 revenues and 140,000 employees in more than forty countries.

Begun in 1927 as a subsidiary of Denmark-based Sophus Berendsen (see page 315), by 1969 Rentokil had grown so large that the parent company decided to float some of the stock on the London Exchange (that was four years before Sophus Berendsen itself floated its own stock on the Copenhagen Exchange). Today, Rentokil is 36% owned by Sophus Berendsen, though the Danish company owned 51.7% as recently as the beginning of 1996 (its stake was reduced as a result of the BET purchase discussed below).

Rentokil has followed a path of growth by acquisition as well as organic growth. Over the last fifteen years, it has bought more than 200 companies and integrated them under the Rentokil umbrella. Last year Rentokil made its largest acquisition to date, actually buying a larger U.K.-based services company, BET, for £2.1 billion. In the process, Rentokil changed its name to Rentokil Initial, adding BET's best known brand name, and doubled its employees. It's an acquisition that offers Rentokil tremendous opportunity for growth: in the rationalization of BET's business, in the integration of the two companies, and finally, in Rentokil's proven ability to grow its existing and new businesses.

COMPANY STATEMENT (from the 1996 annual report)

"Rentokil Initial is an international service company whose consistent objective is to provide for its shareholders growth of at least 20% per annum in profits and earnings per share, whilst not detracting from long term growth prospects. . . .

"Traditionally known for pest control and towel services, Rentokil Initial today is a major provider of electronic security and manned guarding, hygiene and cleaning services, distribution and plant services, personnel services and conference and training facilities. The company also provides a range of property services, and is the world's leading supplier and maintainer of indoor tropical plants. Within Rentokil Initial is the world's largest commercial pest control company.

"Rentokil Initial's 140,000 employees provide services in over 40 countries worldwide, including all the major developed economies of Europe, North America, Asia Pacific and Africa. The two major brands, Rentokil and Initial, are widely recognized internationally. During the next few years all Rentokil Initial services will be rebranded under Rentokil or Initial, to take greater advantage of the established reputations of their brands for delivering consistent high standards of service irrespective of geography or cultures."

PERFORMANCE

Rentokil got great scores across the board and a perfect score of 100 points in our grading system. EBDIT and EP/ADR increased in every one of the last ten years, with compound annual growth of 29% and 26%, respectively. Revenues increased in nine of the last ten years, with compound annual growth of 32%. Shareholders did well, with the ADR price increasing at a compound annual rate of about 34% and dividends increasing at a compound rate of 26%—with a payout ratio of 28%. ROE averaged an incredible 47%, and the long-term debt to total capital ratio averaged a very moderate 6% (note that in 1996 ROE declined and the debt ratio rose in the wake of the BET deal).

If you had invested $10,000 in Rentokil at the end of 1986, you would have purchased around 480 ADRs (or ADR equivalents) at $20.75 each (excluding commissions). During the next ten years, there were a two-for-one stock split in May 1990 and a five-for-two stock split in May 1992. By the end of 1996, you would have had around 2,400 ADRs worth an estimated $179,800. You would also have received dividend payments of around $9,300.

RENTOKIL INITIAL

Ticker Symbol and Exchange: RTOKY—OTC   **CUSIP No.: 760125104**

OPERATING AND PER SHARE DATA
(in millions of British pounds and pounds per share)

	1986	1987	1988	1989	1990	1991	1992	1993	1994	1995	1996	CAGR
Sales	167	174	213	279	309	389	474	600	735	875	2340	30.2%
EBDIT	41	47	61	78	95	119	147	177	212	250	450	27.0%
Net Income	19	23	32	39	47	60	78	94	115	139	219	28.0%
EPS	0.02	0.02	0.03	0.04	0.05	0.06	0.08	0.10	0.12	0.14	0.17	24.4%
DPS	0.01	0.01	0.01	0.01	0.01	0.02	0.02	0.03	0.03	0.04	0.05	24.6%

OPERATING AND PER SHARE DATA
(in millions of U.S. dollars and dollars per ADR)

	1986	1987	1988	1989	1990	1991	1992	1993	1994	1995	1996	CAGR
Revenues	247	328	385	449	597	725	716	886	1,151	1,356	4,006	32.1%
EBDIT	61	89	109	126	184	221	222	261	332	387	770	28.8%
Net Income	27	43	57	63	91	112	118	139	179	216	375	29.9%
EP/ADR	0.29	0.45	0.59	0.65	0.94	1.17	1.21	1.43	1.84	2.20	2.93	26.2%
DP/ADR	0.08	0.12	0.16	0.17	0.26	0.32	0.35	0.43	0.54	0.65	0.87	26.4%

KEY RATIOS

	1986	1987	1988	1989	1990	1991	1992	1993	1994	1995	1996	AVG
Operating Margin	24.7%	27.1%	28.4%	28.0%	30.7%	30.5%	31.0%	29.5%	28.8%	28.5%	19.2%	27.9%
ROE	28.2%	29.2%	46.0%	41.1%	45.0%	53.4%	54.0%	87.1%	65.7%	60.6%	10.5%	47.3%
LTD Debt/Total Cap	8.2%	9.1%	4.6%	2.3%	3.9%	2.6%	2.7%	2.4%	1.5%	3.2%	27.9%	6.2%
P/E (Projected)	11.90	10.61	11.29	15.42	14.06	18.85	21.63	20.51	16.10	19.56	20.90	16.4

STOCK PRICE CHART
(fiscal year-end closing price, in U.S. dollars, adjusted for capital changes)

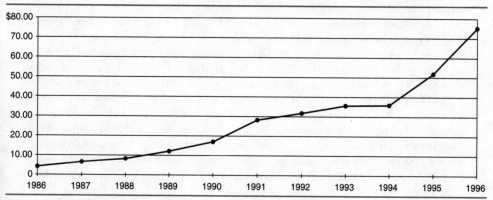

Note: Figures in U.S. dollars are translated from local currency using year-end exchange rates.

REUTERS (RTRSY—NASDAQ)

Address: 85 Fleet Street / London EC4P 4AJ / United Kingdom
Tel.: (011) 44 171 250 1122   **Fax:** (011) 44 171 324 8144   **Web site:** http://www.reuters.com
or
Address: 1700 Broadway, 2nd Floor / New York, NY 10019
Tel.: (212) 603-3300

BASIC INFORMATION

Country: United Kingdom
Industry: Business and public services
Investment thesis: The world's largest financial information company

Market capitalization: $16.36 billion
Share status: ADRs trade on NASDAQ

COMPANY GRADING BOX

Growth Categories		Quality of Management	
Revenue Growth	20	Return on Equity	10
Operating Income Growth	20	**Risk**	
Earnings per Share Growth	20	Long-Term Debt/Total Capital	10
Share Price Growth	20	**Total QM&R (maximum 20)**	**20**
Total Growth (maximum 80)	**80**	**FINAL GRADE**	**100**

BACKGROUND

Reuters has competitors, but it remains the world's biggest financial information company. Reuters information flows to 362,000 computer screens around the world, giving it significantly higher penetration than the acknowledged number two, Dow Jones' Markets (this division of Dow Jones, formerly known as Dow Jones Telerate, does not release specific numbers). Neither Automatic Data Processing nor the most recent major entry into the business, Bloomberg, is thought to be close. Reuters controls 68% of the world market for foreign exchange data, 33% of the world market for equity information, and 24% of the world market for fixed income information. This 145-year-old British news agency has gone way beyond its roots. Today, only 6% of Reuters' revenues comes from sales to the media.

The company made a good bet. Over the last ten years, Reuters' earnings per share in dollars have risen an average of 23.5% annually, and the share price has risen an average of 26.9%. During the same period of time, management has been continuously upgrading, introducing, or acquiring transaction systems that allow clients to do more transactions faster over their Reuters systems. Today's Dealing 2000 is a direct descendent of earlier Reuters products, improvements on the original system created for foreign exchange transactions. And back in 1987 Reuters bought Instinet for equity trading. More recently, Reuters has launched the 3000 series, offering real-time equity and bond information, extensive historical data, Internet access, and a Reuters e-mail system.

Now Reuters, with its prodigious cash flow, is looking into new businesses to complement the old. Among Reuters' recent projects: providing news to forty-five Web sites; designing Web sites for discount brokers that will allow clients to trade on-line; an invoice tracking system for spot TV and radio sales (leading toward a transaction system); and nationwide health information networks in France and England. As for the rest of the cash, at the end of 1997 the company announced a one-time payout to shareholders of $2.53 billion.

COMPANY STATEMENT (from the 1996 annual report)

"It is Reuters' core business to handle the whole process leading up to and including the successful trade, in the right instrument at the right price, taking into account the news that may influence its value. The growth ahead of us lies not only in the older industrialized world, where people fret about the value of their future pensions, but also in the emerging economies, where wealth is now being created in sufficient mass to make individuals concerned about how it should be invested for the future.

"Confidence in this scenario makes it easy for us to decide where to invest our time—in pursuit of doing better and better what we have been doing for a long time already. Competition is fierce. But with the right combination of open technologies and our unique breadth of data and service, we shall have nothing to fear but complacency and loss of concentration."

PERFORMANCE

Reuters is one of our premium companies that received a perfect score of 100. Its growth rates in all categories, ROE, and long-term debt to total capital ratio are remarkable, given the large size of this company. In dollars, revenues and EBDIT increased in nine of the last ten years, with compound annual growth of 18% and 20%, respectively. EP/ADR increased from $0.43 in 1986 to $3.12 in 1996, with compound annual growth of 22%. The ADR price increased at a compound annual rate of 24%, while dividends increased at a compound annual rate of 26%—with an average payout ratio of 33%. ROE averaged a high 46%. And, as for risk, the long-term debt to total capital ratio averaged 8% and was just 3% in 1996.

If you had invested $10,000 in Reuters at the end of 1986, you would have purchased around 280 ADRs (or the equivalent) at $35.50 each (excluding commissions). During the next ten years, there was a four-for-one stock split in April 1994. By the end of 1996, you would have had around 1,100 ADRs worth an estimated $86,600. You would also have received dividend payments of $6,104.

REUTERS

Ticker Symbol and Exchange: RTRSY—NASDAQ   **CUSIP No.: 761324201**

OPERATING AND PER SHARE DATA
(in millions of British pounds and pounds per share)

	1986	1987	1988	1989	1990	1991	1992	1993	1994	1995	1996	CAGR
Sales	621	867	1,003	1,187	1,369	1,467	1,568	1,874	2,309	2,703	2,914	16.7%
EBITDA	176	245	302	374	429	484	502	584	682	801	924	18.1%
Net Profit	80	109	126	181	207	230	236	299	347	414	491	19.9%
EPS	0.05	0.07	0.08	0.11	0.12	0.14	0.16	0.18	0.22	0.26	0.30	20.1%
DPS	0.01	0.02	0.02	0.03	0.04	0.04	0.05	0.07	0.08	0.10	0.12	23.9%

OPERATING AND PER SHARE DATA
(in millions of U.S. dollars and dollars per ADR)

	1986	1987	1988	1989	1990	1991	1992	1993	1994	1995	1996	CAGR
Sales	920	1,636	1,814	1,912	2,645	2,736	2,369	2,767	3,616	4,189	4,989	18.4%
EBITDA	260	462	546	602	829	902	759	862	1,068	1,241	1,582	19.8%
Net Profit	119	206	228	292	400	428	356	441	543	642	841	21.6%
EP/ADR	0.43	0.74	0.87	1.05	1.44	1.53	1.40	1.59	2.04	2.40	3.12	21.9%
DP/ADR	0.12	0.21	0.24	0.31	0.43	0.48	0.48	0.58	0.75	0.91	1.21	25.7%

KEY RATIOS

	1986	1987	1988	1989	1990	1991	1992	1993	1994	1995	1996	AVG
EBITDA Margin	28.3%	28.3%	30.1%	31.5%	31.4%	33.0%	32.0%	31.2%	29.5%	29.6%	31.7%	30.6%
ROE	44.2%	55.2%	51.8%	53.6%	43.2%	36.2%	29.9%	39.5%	50.8%	50.4%	45.6%	45.5%
LT Debt/Total Cap	7.3%	8.0%	21.2%	4.9%	4.4%	3.8%	2.8%	3.9%	11.7%	14.2%	3.3%	7.8%
P/E (Projected)	15.4	15.4	11.9	20.6	12.8	16.6	19.6	20.6	18.1	19.4	23.0	17.6

STOCK PRICE CHART
(fiscal year-end closing price, in U.S. dollars, adjusted for capital changes)

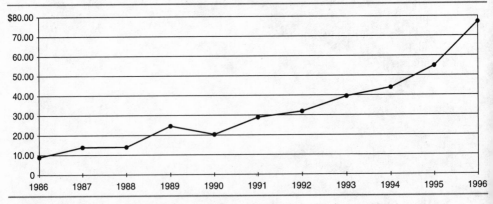

Note: Figures in U.S. dollars are translated from local currency using year-end exchange rates.

REXEL (CDM.PA—PARIS)

Address: 25 Rue de Londres / 75009 Paris / France
Tel.: (011) 33 1 42 85 85 00   **Fax:** (011) 33 1 45 26 25 83

BASIC INFORMATION

Country: France
Industry: Electronics
Investment thesis: World's leading distributor of electrical parts and supplies

Market capitalization: $3.4 billion
Share status: Foreign shares trade on Paris Exchange

COMPANY GRADING BOX

Growth Categories		Quality of Management	
Revenue Growth	20	Return on Equity	5
Operating Income Growth	20	**Risk**	
Earnings per Share Growth	20	Long-Term Debt/Total Capital	5
Share Price Growth	20	**Total QM&R (maximum 20)**	10
Total Growth (maximum 80)	**80**	**FINAL GRADE**	**90**

BACKGROUND

Paris-based Rexel is another one of those companies you are likely not to have heard of—but its products probably help your life run more smoothly. As one of the world's leading distributors of electrical parts and supplies, its parts are probably part of your infrastructure. They help your lights go on, your air conditioner cool your house, and your computer connect to the Internet. We're not talking really high tech, but the company has to stay on top of its market. Rexel supplies electrical fittings, heating and ventilation equipment, wires, cables, and ducts to electrical contractors—with a bent toward smaller, sometimes more specialized, players. Increasingly its business also consists of supplying equipment to set up video monitoring and products used in the connection of computer peripherals.

In France, where Rexel controls around 40% of the market, about 70% of Rexel's business comes from the construction industry—21% of that being new construction and 49% maintenance and renovation. Overall, French sales represent 44% of Rexel's revenue (down from 65% in 1993). While a majority of Rexel's business in Europe is maintenance and repair work, a majority of business in the United States is new construction (and 90% of that is on commercial and industrial sites). In all of its major markets, Rexel is seeing growth in sales to customers outside its traditional audience of electrical contractors—in France it's do-it-yourself stores; in the United States it's companies specializing in products used in the connection of computer peripherals; and in the United Kingdom it's the security business.

All in all, Rexel—just over 70% owned by French group Pinault-Printemps-Redoute—has seventy-three subsidiaries in fourteen countries. And it is expanding rapidly. In 1996 alone Rexel made twelve acquisitions throughout the United States and Europe (only one of the twelve is in France). Its largest foreign market is the United States, representing 24% of revenues, then the rest of Europe, representing about 32% of sales. Worldwide, through 909 sales outlets, its 13,856 employees generated sales of $4.8 billion in 1996.

COMPANY STATEMENT (from the 1995 annual report)

"The Rexel group's 73 subsidiaries are above all service companies. Their vocation is to help each of their customers understand, master and order products that meet their needs, supplying them on time and in the desired quantities. They anticipate the needs of their electrical contractors and industrial customers through attentiveness, advice and training assistance. The approach is the same in each of the fourteen countries where Rexel operates.

"Rexel's objectives are expressed in the four strategic axes of its three-year business plan:

- continue striving for improved productivity;
- expand the group's customer base and extend its product range;
- practice new modes of distribution;
- pursue growth by acquisition. . . .

"Since its origins and throughout its development, through growth by acquisition or via its own internally generated expansion, Rexel has never wanted to impose a single brand, nor standardized services on its network. The group's vocation has always been to assist its subsidiaries and their branches to strengthen their market positions by offering them high-performance management and training tools and the advantage of economies of scale."

PERFORMANCE

Rexel received top scores for growth and an overall score of 90 in our grading system. Over the last ten years the share price in dollars increased at a compound annual rate of 26.7%. Revenues in dollars and EBDIT increased in nine of the last ten years, with compound annual growth of 16% and 18%, respectively. EPS growth and dividends in dollars were only a little less consistent, increasing in eight of the last ten years, at compound annual rates of 18% and 16%, respectively. So where did Rexel lose points? Rexel's historic ROE is not as impressive as its growth, averaging 15.4% between 1986 and 1996. And the long-term debt to total capital ratio, which moved up to 37% in 1996 as the company made a series of acquisitions, averaged 32%—still comfortable but higher than that of many of the companies on our list.

If you had invested $10,000 in Rexel at the end of 1986, you would have bought around 80 shares at around $125 each (excluding commissions). In May 1990, the board approved a five-for-one stock split. By 1996, you would have had around 400 shares worth an estimated $120,400. You would also have received around $7,800 in dividend payments.

REXEL

Ticker Symbol and Exchange: CDM.PA—PARIS   **SEDOL Code: 4169338**

OPERATING AND PER SHARE DATA
(in millions of French francs and francs per share)

	1986	1987	1988	1989	1990	1991	1992	1993	1994	1995	1996	CAGR
Sales	7,010	7,010	7,620	10,408	12,313	13,891	15,049	14,326	21,153	22,084	24,395	13.3%
EBDIT	347	347	473	667	794	842	824	764	1,071	1,217	1,428	15.2%
Net Income	95	95	127	235	259	274	289	292	402	520	611	20.5%
EPS	13.68	13.68	18.26	29.56	31.95	31.10	32.20	33.85	41.50	51.50	55.25	15.0%
DPS	5.20	5.00	5.60	6.40	6.80	7.50	8.20	10.00	11.50	14.50	16.99	12.6%

OPERATING AND PER SHARE DATA
(in millions of U.S. dollars and dollars per share)

	1986	1987	1988	1989	1990	1991	1992	1993	1994	1995	1996	CAGR
Revenues	1,089	1,168	1,279	1,634	2,263	2,463	2,845	2,531	3,818	4,428	4,774	15.9%
Operating Income	53.9	57.8	79.4	104.7	146.0	149.3	155.7	134.9	193.3	244.0	279.5	17.9%
Net Income	14.8	15.8	21.3	36.9	47.6	48.6	54.7	51.7	72.6	104.3	119.6	23.3%
EPS	2.12	2.28	3.07	4.64	5.87	5.51	6.09	5.98	7.49	10.33	10.81	17.7%
DPS	0.81	0.83	0.94	1.00	1.25	1.33	1.55	1.77	2.08	2.91	3.32	15.2%

KEY RATIOS

	1986	1987	1988	1989	1990	1991	1992	1993	1994	1995	1996	AVG
Operating Margin	5.0%	5.0%	6.2%	6.4%	6.4%	6.1%	5.5%	5.3%	5.1%	5.5%	5.9%	5.7%
ROE	13.8%	12.8%	15.0%	22.6%	20.5%	17.3%	15.1%	13.1%	13.0%	15.4%	11.2%	15.4%
LT Debt/Total Cap	59.8%	20.3%	19.6%	34.3%	35.8%	39.0%	30.5%	30.0%	22.3%	18.4%	37.4%	31.6%
P/E (Projected)	12.1	8.2	8.4	11.5	9.5	9.8	11.9	15.9	13.6	15.0	24.4	12.8

STOCK PRICE CHART
(fiscal year-end closing price, in U.S. dollars, adjusted for capital changes)

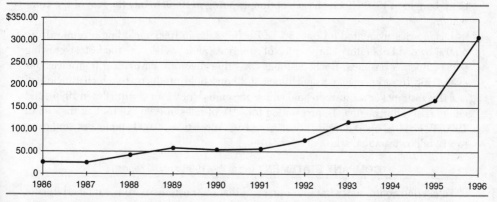

Note: Figures in U.S. dollars are translated from local currency using average exchange rates.

ROCHE (ROHHY—OTC)

Address: 4070 Basel / Switzerland
Tel.: (011) 41 61 688 88 88   **Fax:** (011) 41 61 688 2780   **Web site:** http://www.roche.com

BASIC INFORMATION

Country: Switzerland
Industry: Health and personal care
Market capitalization: $70 billion
Share status: ADRs trade OTC
Investment thesis: 100-year-old leading drug company; bid to become world leader in diagnostics

COMPANY GRADING BOX

Growth Categories		Quality of Management	
Revenue Growth	15	Return on Equity	0
Operating Income Growth	20	**Risk**	
Earnings per Share Growth	20	Long-Term Debt/Total Capital	5
Share Price Growth	20	**Total QM&R (maximum 20)**	**5**
Total Growth (maximum 80)	**75**	**FINAL GRADE**	**80**

BACKGROUND

Switzerland-based Roche has been on a multibillion-dollar buying binge. In May 1997 it announced an $11 billion deal to buy Germany-based Corange, parent of the second largest diagnostics company in the world and the controlling shareholder in a U.S. manufacturer of orthopedic products. With the deal, subject to regulatory approval, Roche became the largest medical diagnostics company in the world, ahead of U.S.-based Abbott Laboratories. Just months before, Roche announced it was buying Connecticut-based Tastemaker for $1.1 billion, to bulk up its flavors and fragrances division.

This 100-year-old Switzerland-based pharmaceuticals giant—which gave the world Aleve, Invirase (one of the leading AIDS drugs), and Accutane (an acne medicine)—has traditionally derived the bulk of its revenues from pharmaceuticals, which accounted for 65% of Roche's revenues in 1996. Like American pharmaceutical giants such as Pfizer and Merck, whose names might seem more familiar, Roche, although smaller, spends heavily on research and development. New drugs include Posicor for the treatment of high blood pressure and angina pectoris, an antiobesity product, and a drug for the treatment of Parkinson's disease. Roche also has a joint venture in the U.S. OTC market with Bayer. Then there is Roche's 66% stake in Genentech, a leading U.S. biotechnology company, bought in 1990 (Roche has an option, expiring in 1999, to buy the rest of the company).

Diagnostics accounted for only 5% of Roche's sales in 1996, including revenues from 49.9%-owned Laboratory Corporation of America, but it has become the fastest-growing part of Roche's business. Roche also has two other divisions: flavors and fragrances, for everything from beverages to perfumes and household products, to which Roche will add the Tastemaker acquisition (and which accounted for 9% of group sales in 1996), and vitamins and fine chemicals, accounting for 21% of sales in 1996. All told, at the end of 1996, Roche had operations in fifty-six countries, more than 50,000 employees, and close to $12 billion in annual sales.

COMPANY STATEMENT (from the 1996 annual report)

"We need to continuously remind ourselves that our customers are the final arbiters of our business success. Our activities are a systematic response to this fact. The objective is to recognize genuine market needs and then satisfy those needs with innovative products and services. Early on we decided to focus on our core businesses, and the wisdom of this course is becoming increasingly apparent. As a result, we now rank among the leading suppliers in most areas in which we compete. Our strong financial base has also contributed greatly to our competitiveness, and it will continue to enable us to seize opportunities to strengthen our position in selected areas. We are well aware of the fact that past and present achievements are no guarantee of future success. What is of decisive importance is that we maintain our ability to respond to changing market conditions with foresight and without hesitation."

PERFORMANCE

Despite some uneven years for the health care industry as a whole, Roche has rewarded investors handsomely. In the last ten years, the ADR price increased at a compound annual rate of 28%, and dividends per ADR increased at a compound annual rate of 20%. For its overall performance, Roche received a score of 80 in our grading system. Although Roche showed mediocre revenue growth (a compound rate of 9%), EP/ADR, which increased in each of the last ten years, had compound annual growth of 27%. EBDIT rose in each of the last nine years, with compound annual growth of 21%. ROE averaged 11% during the ten-year period; however, it hit 19% in both 1995 and 1996. In our risk category, Roche received 5 of the possible 10 points: the long-term debt to total capital ratio averaged 29% during the ten-year period.

If you had invested $10,000 in Roche at the end of 1986, you would have purchased around 15 ADRs (or ADR equivalents) at about $727.75 each (excluding commissions). During the following ten years, there was a capital change in June 1989, a four-for-one rights issue in August 1989, a one-for-three bonus issue in August 1989, a one-for-one rights issue in November 1991, and a one-for-twenty-six bonus issue in 1991. By the end of 1996, you would have had around 1,530 ADRs worth an estimated $118,700. You would also have received dividend payments of around $4,200.

ROCHE

Ticker Symbol and Exchange: ROHHY—OTC   **CUSIP No.: 771195104**

OPERATING AND PER SHARE DATA
(in millions of Swiss francs and francs per share)

	1986	1987	1988	1989	1990	1991	1992	1993	1994	1995	1996	CAGR
Sales	7,822	7,705	8,690	9,814	9,670	11,451	12,953	14,315	14,748	14,722	15,966	7.4%
Cash Earnings	913	974	1,180	1,449	1,469	2,304	2,796	3,408	3,839	4,491	5,108	18.8%
Net Profit	416	482	642	852	948	1,482	1,916	2,478	2,860	3,372	3,899	25.1%
EPS	52.00	60.00	80.00	103.00	115.00	172.00	222.00	287.00	332.00	391.00	456.81	24.3%
DPS	12.00	13.00	14.00	19.00	21.00	28.00	37.00	48.00	55.00	64.00	75.33	20.2%

OPERATING AND PER SHARE DATA
(in millions of U.S. dollars and dollars per ADR)

	1986	1987	1988	1989	1990	1991	1992	1993	1994	1995	1996	CAGR
Revenues	4,858	6,067	5,793	6,373	7,614	8,420	8,812	9,607	11,258	12,802	11,915	9.4%
Cash Earnings	567	767	787	941	1,157	1,694	1,902	2,287	2,931	3,905	3,812	21.0%
Net Profit	258	380	428	553	746	1,090	1,303	1,663	2,183	2,932	2,910	27.4%
EP/ADR	0.32	0.47	0.53	0.67	0.91	1.26	1.51	1.93	2.53	3.40	3.41	26.6%
DP/ADR	0.07	0.10	0.09	0.12	0.17	0.21	0.25	0.32	0.42	0.56	0.56	22.4%

KEY RATIOS

	1986	1987	1988	1989	1990	1991	1992	1993	1994	1995	1996	AVG
Operating Margin	11.7%	12.6%	13.6%	14.8%	15.2%	20.1%	21.6%	23.8%	26.0%	30.5%	32.0%	20.2%
ROE	5.8%	5.5%	6.4%	7.3%	7.2%	10.3%	11.9%	13.8%	17.4%	19.2%	18.8%	11.2%
LT Debt/Total Cap	15.4%	24.3%	21.7%	20.0%	30.5%	32.7%	29.7%	30.6%	37.9%	39.9%	38.0%	29.2%
P/E (Projected)	17.6	11.0	11.7	15.3	10.8	11.7	14.5	19.0	16.2	20.0	19.6	15.2

STOCK PRICE CHART
(fiscal year-end closing price, in U.S. dollars, adjusted for capital changes)

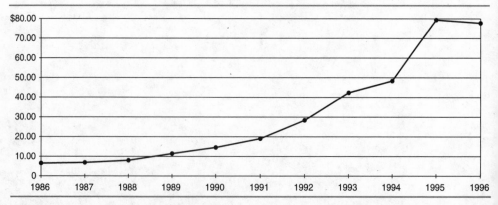

Notes: Cash earnings are net income plus depreciation and amortization. 1986 year-end share price is average of high and low. Figures in U.S. dollars are translated from local currency using year-end exchange rates.

ROHM (ROHCF—OTC)

Address: 21 Saiin Mizosaki-cho / Ukyo-ku / Kyoto 615 / Japan
Tel.: (011) 81 75 311 2121   **Fax:** (011) 81 75 315 0172

BASIC INFORMATION

Country: Japan
Industry: Electrical and electronic
Investment thesis: Manufactures specialized, custom-designed semiconductors

Market capitalization: $23.06 billion
Share status: Foreign shares trade OTC

COMPANY GRADING BOX

Growth Categories		Quality of Management	
Revenue Growth	20	Return on Equity	0
Operating Income Growth	20	**Risk**	
Earnings per Share Growth	15	Long-Term Debt/Total Capital	10
Share Price Growth	15	**Total QM&R (maximum 20)**	10
Total Growth (maximum 80)	70	**FINAL GRADE**	80

BACKGROUND

Rohm is a Japanese semiconductor memory manufacturer that describes itself as a niche player amid global giants—although with a market capitalization of $23 billion and 1996 revenues of $2.1 billion it's hardly a shrimp. Until recently a manufacturer of passive electronic components, today Rohm generates an estimated 80% of its revenues from semiconductors. And an estimated 70% of those semiconductors are customized for clients; they're higher-margin "value-added" products mostly for personal computer, cellular phone, and communications equipment manufacturers. Needless to say, the boom in multimedia and wireless communications has helped this company survive and prosper during a very difficult seven years for the Japanese economy—and the future looks even brighter.

Over the years, Rohm, founded in 1958 in Kyoto, has also developed a reputation for cost competitiveness. In the 1980s it began shifting production to Asia and introduced its own version of "just-in-time" inventory management. Then, in 1990, Rohm initiated a "reengineering" program to focus the company more on profitability than on volume and market share. Since then Rohm has also pushed to be on the cutting edge of technology, to offer more than cost competitiveness.

What's next? Today, semiconductors need to support more and more activities—as we move closer to communications devices that can support mobile computing, as personal digital assistants (PDAs) become more powerful, and as digital video discs (DVDs) catch on. Through two Rohm LSI Research centers, one based in California, the other in Kyoto, Rohm is working with manufacturers to develop multimedia technology. And in September 1996 Rohm announced it would produce products based on its own and U.S.-based Ramtron International's FRAM (ferroelectric random access memory) technology. It's Rohm's kind of business: FRAM technology is difficult to mass-produce and has tremendous potential.

COMPANY STATEMENT (from the 1996 annual report)

"An important facet of our strategy is our focus on the future direction of markets rather than on their size. In other words, we cultivate markets that have potential for Rohm.

Whether in Japan or overseas, we accurately grasp the developments in changing markets and respond quickly.

"One example is the shift of production from Japan to Southeast Asia. Rohm has been expanding its production and marketing capabilities in Southeast Asia to be prepared for increases in demand. Many electronic equipment manufacturers are currently shifting production of personal computer peripherals, such as floppy disk drives and CD-ROM drives. Rohm anticipated that trend and shifted its own production at an early stage. As a result, when demand for audio and video equipment declined, Rohm was able to maintain a high rate of growth in Asia overall.

"In Japan, the United States, and Europe, meanwhile, the trend toward more advanced, higher value-added products continues unabated. Key trends in Japan include the spread of new mobile communications systems, such as the personal handy-phone system and pagers, and the rapid development in advanced multimedia products, such as digital video equipment. Rohm is well positioned for these trends because the Company anticipated the growing importance of such products as personal computers and cellular phones."

PERFORMANCE

Rohm's share price performance—the stock has increased at a compound rate of nearly 26% since 1989—has been remarkable considering the state of the Japanese equity market during the same period. Overall, Rohm received a grade of 80 in our grading system, with particularly high marks for consistency and growth. EBDIT in dollars saw compound annual growth of 20%. EPS in dollars, up every year since 1991, saw compound annual growth of 18%, while dividends per share, up every year since 1990, rose at a compound annual rate of 17%. Revenues in dollars, up in seven of the last eight years, saw compound annual growth of 10%. ROE is low compared to some of our other companies; however, it has been rising. In 1997 ROE was up to 13.6% from a low of 3.4% in 1991. As for risk, the long-term debt to total capital ratio declined in every year since 1990 and was a low 4.5% in 1997.

If you had invested $10,000 in Rohm in March 1989, you would have purchased around 400 shares at about $24.75 each. Over the next eight years, there were a 5-for-100 bonus issue in April 1989, a 35-for-100 bonus issue in November 1990, and a 2-for-10 bonus issue in April 1992. By March 1997, you would have had around 700 shares worth an estimated $51,000. You would also have received dividend payments of around $800.

ROHM

Ticker Symbol and Exchange: ROHCF—OTC   **SEDOL Code: 6747204**

OPERATING AND PER SHARE DATA
(in billions of Japanese yen and yen per share)

	Mar 87	Mar 88	Mar 89	Mar 90	Mar 91	Mar 92	Mar 93	Mar 94	Mar 95	Mar 96	Mar 97	CAGR
Sales	N/A	N/A	146.0	167.0	190.0	205.0	187.0	200.0	241.0	292.0	298.0	9.3%
EBDIT	N/A	N/A	29.8	35.2	36.0	45.9	44.4	50.0	82.4	109.4	118.8	18.9%
NPG	N/A	N/A	6.5	5.9	5.4	7.0	7.6	12.5	22.7	35.9	47.0	28.1%
EPS	N/A	N/A	123	72	58	71	78	125	216	323	395	15.7%
DPS	N/A	N/A	8.2	7.4	10.0	10.0	12.0	14.5	19.0	25.0	19.0	11.0%

OPERATING AND PER SHARE DATA
(in millions of U.S. dollars and dollars per share)

	Mar 87	Mar 88	Mar 89	Mar 90	Mar 91	Mar 92	Mar 93	Mar 94	Mar 95	Mar 96	Mar 97	CAGR
Sales	N/A	N/A	1,106	1,057	1,348	1,553	1,640	1,961	2,786	2,729	2,423	10.3%
EBDIT	N/A	N/A	226	223	255	348	389	490	953	1,022	966	19.9%
Net Profit	N/A	N/A	49	37	38	53	67	123	262	336	382	29.2%
EPS	N/A	N/A	0.93	0.46	0.41	0.54	0.68	1.23	2.50	3.02	3.21	16.8%
DPS	N/A	N/A	0.06	0.05	0.07	0.08	0.11	0.14	0.22	0.23	0.15	12.0%

KEY RATIOS

	1986	1987	1988	1989	1990	1991	1992	1993	1994	1995	1996	AVG
EBDIT Margin	N/A	N/A	20.4%	21.1%	18.9%	22.4%	23.7%	25.0%	34.2%	37.5%	39.9%	27.0%
ROE	N/A	N/A	7.0%	4.5%	3.4%	4.0%	4.1%	6.2%	9.6%	12.3%	13.6%	7.2%
LT Debt/Total Cap	N/A	N/A	39.8%	40.4%	25.9%	21.5%	19.6%	27.0%	18.6%	9.6%	4.5%	23.0%
P/E (Projected)	N/A	N/A	26.7	40.9	28.5	23.1	17.7	18.0	11.7	12.7	19.0	22.0

STOCK PRICE CHART
(fiscal year-end closing price, in U.S. dollars, adjusted for capital changes)

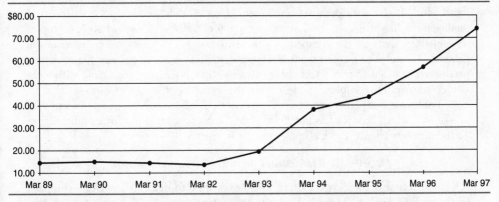

Note: Figures in U.S. dollars are translated from local currency using year-end exchange rates.

SAP (SAPHY—OTC)

Address: P.O. Box 1461 / 69185 Walldorf / Germany
Tel.: (011) 49 6227 34 0   **Fax:** (011) 49 6227 34 1282   **Web site:** http://www.sap.com
or
Address: 701 Lee Road / Wayne, PA 19087
Tel.: (610) 725-4500   **Fax:** (610) 725-4555

BASIC INFORMATION

Country: Germany
Industry: Business services
Market capitalization: $16.97 billion
Share status: ADRs trade OTC
Investment thesis: World's fourth largest software company; clients include Microsoft, IBM, Coca-Cola

COMPANY GRADING BOX

Growth Categories		Quality of Management	
Revenue Growth	20	Return on Equity	10
Operating Income Growth	20	**Risk**	
Earnings per Share Growth	20	Long-Term Debt/Total Capital	10
Share Price Growth	20	**Total QM&R (maximum 20)**	**20**
Total Growth (maximum 80)	**80**	**FINAL GRADE**	**100**

BACKGROUND

On March 14, 1997, there was a very telling article on the front page of *The Wall Street Journal.* The headline: "This German Software Is Complex, Expensive—and Wildly Popular." Pretty good as far as publicity goes (though the company took issue with the somewhat negative tone). The article went on at great length about SAP's most popular product, R/3, an extensive software program that ties together all of a company's business operations, from accounting to sales to plant maintenance and inventories. An open format, it can also link your software to customers, or facilitate commerce over the Internet. And it has taken corporate America by storm. The *Journal* described it as "the new standard equipment of global big business."

By the mid-1990s, SAP had 7,000 employees and included among its clients Microsoft, Burger King, IBM, Coca-Cola, Compaq, Deutsche Telekom . . . the list reads like a Who's Who of international giants. Founded in 1972 by five former IBM employees, today it is the world's fourth largest software company, smaller than only Microsoft (with which it has a cooperative agreement), Oracle, and Computer Associates. And management has projected 1997 revenue growth of between 25% and 30%, on top of 38% in 1996. Even so, the company continues to invest 15% of its annual revenues in product research and development, acknowledging that it needs to keep improving its products to stay ahead of the technological curve. SAP is already coming out with technology it says is less complex (and less expensive to install) than earlier versions.

SAP software is expensive and complicated (tens of millions of dollars often spent over one or two years), but that has not stopped the business community from embracing it. To its corporate clients, R/3 has apparently been worth it.

COMPANY STATEMENT (from the 1996 annual report)

"Over the course of its 25 year history, SAP has evolved from a small software company to the world's market leader in business application software. Through its own subsidiaries, branches or representative offices, it is now present in virtually all of the world's industrialized markets.

"Products have been central to SAP's success story. In 1979, the company launched the R/2 System for mainframe computers. Its client/server R/3 System was launched in 1992 and has proven a spectacular success, accounting for the bulk of the company's current sales. Well over one million end users now work with the R/3 System, which has established itself as the software standard in key industries.

"SAP has continued to strengthen its dominant position as a vendor of client/server applications. According to a study by International Data Corporation, a U.S. market research firm, SAP led the worldwide client/server industry with a more than 29% market share. While this achievement is due in large measure to its technological leadership, SAP and its hardware and software partners have also based their success on a strict customer orientation and a comprehensive program of service and support."

PERFORMANCE

SAP has made a great deal of money for investors over the last eight years. The ADR (or ADR equivalent) price increased at a compound annual rate of 46%. Not surprisingly, it is also one of the star companies in this book, receiving a score of 100 in our grading system. In dollars, revenues and EBDIT increased in every one of the last nine years, with compound annual growth of 46% and 34%, respectively. EP/ADR increased in eight of the last nine years, with compound annual growth of 32%. Even dividend per ADR growth has been impressive, with compound annual growth of 31%. ROE was 28% in 1996 and averaged an excellent 33% over the nine-year period. Finally, the long-term debt to total capital ratio was a tiny 0.1% in 1996 and averaged 0.3% over the nine years. That's pretty good.

If you had invested $10,000 in SAP at the end of 1988, you would have bought around 70 ADRs (or the equivalent) at about $2.25 each (excluding commissions). During the following eight years, there were a capital change in July 1990, a rights issue in May 1992, a four-for-one bonus issue in August 1994, and a ten-for-one stock split in August 1995. By 1996, you would have had around 4,000 ADRs worth an estimated $200,300. You would also have received dividend payments worth around $5,500.

SAP

Ticker Symbol and Exchange: SAPHY—OTC   **CUSIP No.: 803054204**

OPERATING AND PER SHARE DATA
(in millions of German marks and marks per share)

	1986	1987	1988	1989	1990	1991	1992	1993	1994	1995	1996	CAGR
Sales	N/A	125	245	367	500	707	831	1,102	1,831	2,696	3,722	45.8%
EBDIT	N/A	75	99	135	138	213	203	278	525	787	1,070	34.3%
Net Profit	N/A	36	51	70	81	118	126	145	281	405	567	35.7%
EPS	N/A	0.45	0.63	0.87	0.91	1.32	1.26	1.45	2.78	4.00	5.48	32.0%
DPS	N/A	N/M	0.14	0.23	0.29	0.34	0.36	0.44	1.75	1.35	1.75	37.1%

OPERATING AND PER SHARE DATA
(in millions of U.S. dollars and dollars per ADR)

	1986	1987	1988	1989	1990	1991	1992	1993	1994	1995	1996	CAGR
Sales	N/A	80	138	217	336	465	513	633	1,181	1,872	2,386	45.9%
EBDIT	N/A	48.0	55.8	80.0	92.8	139.9	125.0	159.9	338.6	546.7	685.6	34.4%
Net Profit	N/A	23.1	28.5	41.2	54.6	77.8	77.8	83.3	181.4	281.2	363.5	35.8%
EP/ADR	N/A	0.09	0.12	0.17	0.20	0.29	0.26	0.28	0.59	0.92	1.16	32.1%
DP/ADR	N/A	N/M	0.03	0.04	0.06	0.07	0.07	0.08	0.37	0.31	0.37	39.3%

KEY RATIOS

	1986	1987	1988	1989	1990	1991	1992	1993	1994	1995	1996	AVG
EBDIT Margin	N/A	60.3%	40.3%	36.8%	27.7%	30.1%	24.4%	25.3%	28.7%	29.2%	28.7%	33.1%
ROE	N/A	89.4%	38.4%	42.9%	20.1%	24.3%	14.7%	15.1%	24.5%	29.1%	28.2%	32.7%
LT Debt/Total Cap	N/A	0.0%	0.7%	0.6%	0.3%	0.3%	0.0%	0.0%	0.2%	0.2%	0.1%	0.3%
P/E (Projected)	N/A	N/A	14.0	27.6	20.3	21.8	24.6	12.9	22.0	39.6	30.6	11.2

STOCK PRICE CHART
(fiscal year-end closing price, in U.S. dollars, adjusted for capital changes)

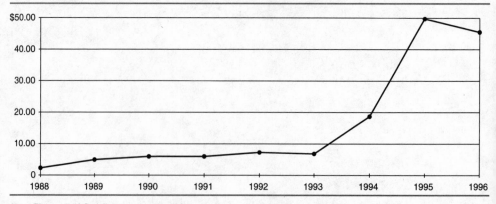

Note: Figures in U.S. dollars are translated from local currency using year-end exchange rates.

SEB (SEBF.PA—PARIS)

Address: Les 4 M, Chemin du Petit-Bois / B.P. 172 / 69132 Ecully Cedex / France
Tel.: (011) 33 72 18 18 18   **Fax:** (011) 33 72 18 16 55

BASIC INFORMATION

Country: France   **Market capitalization:** $2.73 billion
Industry: Household goods   **Share status:** Foreign shares trade on Paris Exchange
Investment thesis: World leader in cookware, bakeware, and small household electric appliances

COMPANY GRADING BOX

Growth Categories		Quality of Management	
Revenue Growth	20	Return on Equity	5
Operating Income Growth	20	**Risk**	
Earnings per Share Growth	15	Long-Term Debt/Total Capital	10
Share Price Growth	20	**Total QM&R (maximum 20)**	**15**
Total Growth (maximum 80)	**75**	**FINAL GRADE**	**90**

BACKGROUND

SEB is a world leader in cookware, bakeware, and small household electrical appliances. Founded in Burgundy, France, in 1857, SEB launched its first pressure cooker in 1953; entered the domestic electrical appliance market and started selling electric fryers in 1967; then, in the late sixties and early seventies, bought two major brand names: Tefal, a leader in nonstick cookware, and Calor, a specialist in irons, hair driers, and portable radiators. Finally, in 1988, SEB bought Rowenta, which has plants in Germany and France making irons, electric coffeemakers, toasters, and vacuum cleaners.

New products include steam cookers, water-filtering devices, products for "food conservation"—so far consisting of a "cheese safe" and a vegetable storage box—and a line of baby care products under the Tefal name (already available in more than 1,000 outlets in France, including do-it-yourself stores and chain stores specializing in baby care products). At the end of 1996, the company had 11,280 employees, revenues of about $1.8 billion—more than two thirds of which came from outside France—and more than forty subsidiaries around the world.

Why did we pick this company as a bright prospect for investment? Management has done an excellent job expanding on its existing brand names, with a healthy emphasis on product innovation. SEB is a market leader in many of its markets with a number of its products, particularly nonstick cookware, fryers, steam irons, pressure cookers, and raclette cookers. Management has also shown its ability to keep production costs down in an increasingly competitive environment. And the company's international exposure diversifies some of its risk, while giving it plenty of room to grow.

In early 1996 SEB bought 60% of a leading Chinese steam iron manufacturer based in Shanghai, as part of a major move into Asia. SEB has also expanded aggressively into central and eastern Europe, the NAFTA markets, Brazil, and Argentina. Sales outside the European Union now account for almost 40% of total annual revenues.

COMPANY STATEMENT (from the 1996 annual report)

Groupe SEB is one of the world's leaders in the small domestic appliances sector. . . . Its strategy is built around three main priorities which are interdependent:

- concentration on several product families that meet basic consumer needs, and in which the Group aims to occupy European or world market leadership;
- a policy of ongoing innovation in products, working methods and technologies, in order to have full command of the core of products that offer real value added;
- steady global expansion of its operations, with a local presence in all the world's major markets.

"Under its two international brands, Tefal and Rowenta, the Group offers consumers on all continents products that make day-to-day life easier and more agreeable."

PERFORMANCE

SEB's aggressive expansion policy took a toll on EPS performance; however, in every other growth category, SEB's performance received a top grade. The company's total score: 90 points. Consistency is a hallmark of SEB. Both revenues in dollars and EBDIT increased in nine of the last ten years; compound annual growth was also strong, with revenues up 14% per year and operating income up 16% per year. Shareholders benefited handsomely from that growth: SEB's share price had compound annual growth of 24%. And dividends increased in each of the last ten years, from $0.59 in 1986 to $2.26 in 1996. SEB achieved this growth without undue risk, as shown by the long-term debt to total capital ratio, which averaged 19% for the decade. The company has also had strong, but not stellar, ROE, averaging 15%.

If you had invested $10,000 in SEB at the end of 1986, you would have purchased around 85 shares at $115 each (excluding commissions). In August 1992 there was a five-for-one stock split. By the end of 1996, you would have had around 430 shares worth an estimated $86,500. You would also have received dividends worth around $6,000.

SEB

Ticker Symbol and Exchange: SEBF.PA—PARIS   SEDOL Code: 4792132

OPERATING AND PER SHARE DATA
(in millions of French francs and francs per share)

	1986	1987	1988	1989	1990	1991	1992	1993	1994	1995	1996	CAGR
Sales	3,465	3,743	5,153	6,663	7,490	8,075	8,279	8,387	8,707	9,104	9,857	11.0%
EBDIT	446	596	711	871	1,133	1,285	1,341	1,334	1,375	1,433	1,570	13.4%
Net Profit	122	164	197	171	233	312	314	331	400	450	480	14.7%
EPS	9.55	12.58	14.11	13.45	17.52	22.71	22.91	23.70	28.02	31.02	31.79	12.8%
DPS	3.80	4.40	5.00	5.50	6.00	6.80	7.50	8.30	9.20	10.30	11.54	11.7%

OPERATING AND PER SHARE DATA
(in millions of U.S. dollars and dollars per share)

	1986	1987	1988	1989	1990	1991	1992	1993	1994	1995	1996	CAGR
Sales	538	624	865	1,046	1,377	1,432	1,565	1,482	1,572	1,826	1,929	13.6%
EBDIT	69.3	99.3	119.4	136.7	208.3	227.8	253.5	235.7	248.2	287.3	307.2	16.1%
Net Profit	18.9	27.3	33.1	26.8	42.8	55.3	59.4	58.5	72.2	90.2	93.9	17.4%
EPS	1.48	2.10	2.37	2.11	3.22	4.03	4.33	4.19	5.06	6.22	6.22	15.4%
DPS	0.59	0.73	0.84	0.86	1.10	1.21	1.42	1.47	1.66	2.07	2.26	14.4%

KEY RATIOS

	1986	1987	1988	1989	1990	1991	1992	1993	1994	1995	1996	AVG
EBDIT Margin	12.9%	15.9%	13.8%	13.1%	15.1%	15.9%	16.2%	15.9%	15.8%	15.7%	15.9%	15.1%
ROE	15.4%	16.4%	16.4%	12.2%	15.5%	17.3%	15.0%	13.8%	14.8%	14.5%	13.3%	15.0%
LT Debt/Total Cap	18.1%	15.3%	16.8%	34.0%	29.6%	27.3%	21.2%	13.0%	10.7%	10.3%	14.0%	19.1%
P/E (Projected)	11.9	8.9	12.0	13.0	10.6	14.7	14.4	18.6	17.6	18.7	25.9	15.1

STOCK PRICE CHART
(fiscal year-end closing price, in U.S. dollars, adjusted for capital changes)

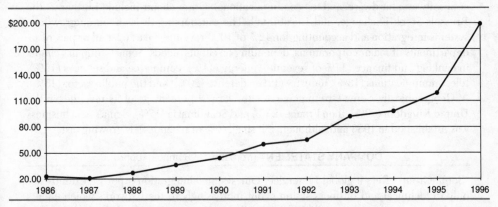

Note: Figures in U.S. dollars are translated from local currency using average exchange rates.

SEMA GROUP (SEM.L—LONDON)

Address: 233 High Holborn / London WC1V 7DJ / United Kingdom
Tel.: (011) 44 171 830 44 44 **Fax:** (011) 44 171 830 1830 **Web site:** http://www.semagroup.com
or
Address: Ashland Green, Suite 460 / 4170 Ashford Dunwoody Road / Atlanta, GA 91457-3031
Tel.: (404) 256-1447   **Fax:** (404) 256-2775

BASIC INFORMATION

Country: United Kingdom   **Market capitalization:** $2.4 billion
Industry: Business services   **Share status:** Foreign shares trade on London Exchange
Investment thesis: A leading European information technology company

COMPANY GRADING BOX

Growth Categories		Quality of Management	
Revenue Growth	20	Return on Equity	10
Operating Income Growth	20	**Risk**	
Earnings per Share Growth	20	Long-Term Debt/Total Capital	5
Share Price Growth	15	**Total QM&R (maximum 20)**	15
Total Growth (maximum 80)	**75**	**FINAL GRADE**	**90**

BACKGROUND

Sema Group is a London-based European information technology (IT) company and another beneficiary of the boom in outsourcing. According to London's *Financial Times*, the British government and Britain-based businesses now spend about £1.7 billion every year on contracting out IT services. That number is expected to grow to £4 billion by the year 2000. Sema Group, one of Britain's leading computer services companies, is well positioned to benefit from this growth.

The company is made up of three core businesses—systems integration (including consulting), outsourcing, and products—all closely related to one another. The systems integration division, which accounts for about 50% of revenues ($1.6 billion in 1996), has developed the command-and-control system for a new-generation nuclear plant on the Franco-Belgian border, an organizational system for Railtrack in the United Kingdom, a smart card system for a number of European banks, and the core system for EURO96, the European Football Championship (coordinating Microsoft, Digital, and British Telecom software, hardware, and telecommunications). Other clients include Lufthansa, the Brussels Stock Exchange, and Eurotunnel. The outsourcing division, an outgrowth of systems integration and accounting for 42% of 1996 revenue, takes over all or part of IT departments of major corporations, depending on clients' needs. Sema Group has clients in banking and finance (17% of revenue), energy (11%), commerce and services (12%), telecommunications (13%), industry (12%), defense (20%), and the public sector (15%).

Geographically, Sema Group generates the largest percentage of its revenues in the United Kingdom (30%), then France (25%) and Scandinavia (17%). Sema's Asia business was established in 1983 and, although still small (6% of revenues), is growing fast.

COMPANY STATEMENT (from the 1996 annual report)

"Sema Group offers a global IT service. Our systems integration expertise extends not only to technical and business systems, but increasingly to the networks which clients need to communicate internally and externally. With the management of IT services under outsourcing agreements, we deliver added value to our clients throughout the life-cycle of their information systems.

"Understanding technology is the core of our expertise. Our research and development activities support all the Group's business areas, with the aim of identifying and evaluating emerging technologies, and judging when they are appropriate and sufficiently mature to be used on client projects. Our R&D team also co-ordinates the development of our own tools and methods as well as developing the application software kernels and packages which constitute our intellectual property and set the scene for the Group's future success.

"Transforming our clients' business challenges into workable high-performance systems depends on other, equally vital factors: a strong foundation of consultancy, the ability to act as a prime contractor, a commitment to deliver against predetermined costs and time-scales, and the project management expertise to ensure that quality and risks are controlled at every stage."

PERFORMANCE

Sema Group received 90 points in our grading system, with strong growth and an excellent ROE. In dollars, revenues, EBDIT, and EPS increased in seven of the last eight years, recording compound annual growth of 24%, 37%, and 49%, respectively. ROE averaged 19%—and was a remarkable 28% in 1996. The long-term debt to total capital ratio was a little higher than for many of our other companies, averaging 27% but still reasonable. The share price in dollars increased at a compound annual rate of 19%—though the price more than doubled in 1996.

If you had invested $10,000 in Sema Group at the end of 1988, you would have purchased around 2,000 shares at about $5.00 each (excluding commissions). In July 1996 there was a two-for-eleven rights issue. By the end of 1996, you would have had around 2,000 shares worth an estimated $40,000. You also would have received dividend payments of around $1,100.

SEMA GROUP

Ticker Symbol and Exchange: SEM.L—London   **SEDOL Code: 172857**

OPERATING AND PER SHARE DATA
(in millions of British pounds and pounds per share)

	1986	1987	1988	1989	1990	1991	1992	1993	1994	1995	1996	CAGR
Sales	N/A	N/A	162.0	293.0	375.0	413.0	417.0	502.0	596.0	678.0	927.0	24.4%
EBDIT	N/A	N/A	7.0	26.2	31.0	30.3	32.9	42.5	56.8	62.5	90.2	37.6%
Net Profit	N/A	N/A	1.0	10.3	9.5	10.0	27.5	23.1	19.7	23.2	31.8	54.1%
EPS	N/A	N/A	0.01	0.11	0.10	0.11	0.13	0.16	0.21	0.24	0.31	50.3%
DPS	N/A	N/A	0.01	0.02	0.02	0.03	0.03	0.03	0.04	0.05	0.06	19.8%

OPERATING AND PER SHARE DATA
(in millions of U.S. dollars and dollars per share)

	1986	1987	1988	1989	1990	1991	1992	1993	1994	1995	1996	CAGR
Sales	N/A	N/A	293	472	724	770	630	741	933	1,051	1,587	23.5%
EBDIT	N/A	N/A	12.7	42.2	59.9	56.5	49.7	62.7	88.9	96.9	154.4	36.7%
Net Profit	N/A	N/A	1.8	16.6	18.4	18.6	41.5	34.1	30.8	36.0	54.4	53.0%
EPS	N/A	N/A	0.02	0.18	0.20	0.21	0.19	0.24	0.32	0.38	0.53	49.3%
DPS	N/A	N/A	0.03	0.04	0.05	0.05	0.04	0.05	0.06	0.08	0.10	19.0%

KEY RATIOS

	1986	1987	1988	1989	1990	1991	1992	1993	1994	1995	1996	AVG
EBDIT Margin	N/A	N/A	4.3%	8.9%	8.3%	7.3%	7.9%	8.5%	9.5%	9.2%	9.7%	8.2%
ROE	N/A	N/A	2.0%	15.7%	18.4%	17.4%	14.3%	14.4%	26.7%	32.7%	27.6%	18.8%
LT Debt/Total Cap	N/A	N/A	16.8%	14.7%	27.0%	30.4%	28.8%	36.8%	26.4%	29.6%	29.5%	26.7%
P/E (Projected)	N/A	N/A	23.3	34.7	44.3	16.4	19.3	14.8	16.5	16.9	27.0	23.7

STOCK PRICE CHART
(fiscal year-end closing price, in U.S. dollars, adjusted for capital changes)

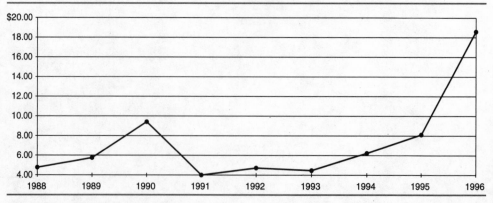

Note: Figures in U.S. dollars are translated from local currency using year-end exchange rates.

SEVEN-ELEVEN JAPAN (SVELY—OTC)

Address: 1-4 Shibakoen 4-chome / Minato-ku / Tokyo 105 / Japan
Tel.: (011) 81 3 3459 3711   **Fax:** (011) 81 3 3438 3724

BASIC INFORMATION

Country: Japan
Industry: Retailing, food
Investment thesis: Dominant convenience store chain in Japan; brought U.S. chain out of bankruptcy

Market capitalization: $23.06 billion
Share status: ADRs trade OTC

COMPANY GRADING BOX

Growth Categories		Quality of Management	
Revenue Growth	20	Return on Equity	10
Operating Income Growth	20	**Risk**	
Earnings per Share Growth	20	Long-Term Debt/Total Capital	10
Share Price Growth	10	**Total QM&R (maximum 20)**	**20**
Total Growth (maximum 80)	**70**	**FINAL GRADE**	**90**

BACKGROUND

No doubt you have heard of Seven-Eleven. But, unless you have been to Japan, you probably have not heard of Seven-Eleven Japan—the largest chain of Japanese convenience stores (and a haven for Americans in Japan looking for relatively inexpensive food) and, since the early 1990s, owner of the U.S. chain. In Japan, where this company built its fortunes, the chain consists of almost 7,000 stores in twenty-four of Japan's forty-seven prefectures. It has a great brand name, a unique strategy, efficiencies of scale, and tremendous room for growth. Despite Japan's ongoing economic problems, Seven-Eleven has managed to grow its customer base, its earnings, and its gross margins. The stores have been described as tiny supermarkets, compact stores that fit into back streets in a country that is still dominated by small retailers. They are open twenty-four hours a day, seven days a week, and carry more than 2,000 different items—with fresh produce restocked (and changed) daily or sometimes hourly. With larger stores constrained by Japan's Large Retail Store Law, the field is wide open for convenience stores.

Since the chain began in 1974, these stores have become an integral part of Japanese communities—more than half the daily sales are of reasonably priced prepared foods such as rice balls, sandwiches, and lunch boxes. Milk, margarine, and magazines are all big sellers. They also have fax machines and color copiers, sell stamps and theater tickets, and allow customers to pay insurance premiums and bills, send parcels, deliver flowers, and draw cash on their credit cards (in 1996 Seven-Eleven stores handled 24.5 million consumer finance transactions). Most recently, they started selling game software (representing $99 million in sales in fiscal 1997). It's a business in which Seven-Eleven Japan sets the pace. The company, which is majority owned by another Japanese retailer, Ito Yokado, says it gets 2.5 billion customer visits a year and has the highest per day sales numbers of all Japanese convenience chains.

Not surprisingly, management is now trying to duplicate its success overseas. Overall, Seven-Eleven Japan has more than 16,400 stores in twenty-two countries. And as of March 1997, it was the third largest retailer in the world, ranked by market value (after Wal-Mart and Home Depot).

As a major part of its overseas ambitions, this Japanese powerhouse is revamping the

American chain of 7-Elevens. Together Ito Yokado and Seven-Eleven Japan bought a chunk of Southland, which controls the U.S. chain, in 1991, after Southland filed for bankruptcy. Over the last six years, the new Japanese management has shut down more than a thousand unprofitable stores, redesigned others, and introduced systems developed in the Japanese stores. The company is now well out of the red and expanding again, though imposing the Japanese systems on U.S. managers has not always gone smoothly. Even so, the chain is generating cash and improving its image. So far, so good.

COMPANY STATEMENT (from the 1997 annual report)

"Seven-Eleven Japan opened its first store in May 1974. Since then, we have constantly refined our systems in order to maintain our ability to meet the constantly changing needs and tastes of consumers. This is reflected in the steady expansion of the product range and services offered by 7-Eleven stores. The Company's ability to continually meet this goal has been due largely to our development of an innovative item-by-item control system—a revolutionary approach to order and inventory management that did not previously exist in the distribution sector—and by building our unique Total System, which integrates this format at all levels, from production through to delivery and sales.

"In the future, product life cycles are expected to continue to shrink as consumers become increasingly discerning in their shopping patterns. However, we are confident that Seven-Eleven Japan will continue to enhance business performance by further developing item-by-item control and by further enhancing and expanding the capabilities of the Total System."

PERFORMANCE

Seven-Eleven Japan got high marks for its impressive ROE (which averaged 18%), its almost nonexistent long-term debt to total capital ratio (which averaged 1.2%), and its ability to manage its growth—adding up to a total score of 90 points in our grading system. Although revenues in dollars grew at a compound annual rate of only 13% over the last ten years, EBDIT and EP/ADR (or ADR equivalent) increased by 16% and 17% per year, respectively. The company's price performance does not compare particularly well with other companies included in this book; however, Seven-Eleven Japan's 15% compound annual growth is impressive relative to the rest of the Japanese equity market. Dividend appreciation outstripped EP/ADR growth, increasing at a compound annual rate of 22%.

If you had invested $10,000 in Seven-Eleven Japan in February of 1987, you would have purchased around 160 ADRs at about $61.25 each (excluding commissions). During the following ten years, there were a one-for-five bonus issue in April 1988, a one-for-five bonus issue in April 1989, a one-for-five bonus issue in April 1990, a one-for-five bonus issue in February 1991, a six-for-five stock split in February 1991, a one-for-ten bonus issue in February 1992, a one-for-ten bonus issue in February 1993, and three eleven-for-ten stock splits, one in February 1994, one in February 1995, and one in February 1996. By February 1997, you would have had around 650 ADRs worth an estimated $40,600. You would also have received dividend payments of around $1,000.

SEVEN-ELEVEN JAPAN

Ticker Symbol and Exchange: SVELY—OTC   **CUSIP No.: 817828205**

OPERATING AND PER SHARE DATA
(in billions of Japanese yen and yen per share)

	Feb 87	Feb 88	Feb 89	Feb 90	Feb 91	Feb 92	Feb 93	Feb 94	Feb 95	Feb 96	Feb 97	CAGR
Sales	95	94	100	114	137	163	182	196	215	231	255	10.4%
EBDIT	39.1	46.1	55.2	62.0	74.3	89.3	101.3	107.0	115.9	122.8	134.4	13.1%
Net Profit	14.4	18.4	22.3	26.2	33.2	40.7	45.0	46.6	49.5	52.6	55.3	14.4%
EPS	35	45	55	63	80	98	108	112	119	126	133	14.1%
DPS	6.90	7.80	9.40	11.20	15.00	19.90	23.20	26.30	28.90	31.80	38.00	18.6%

OPERATING AND PER SHARE DATA
(in millions of U.S. dollars and dollars per ADR)

	Feb 87	Feb 88	Feb 89	Feb 90	Feb 91	Feb 92	Feb 93	Feb 94	Feb 95	Feb 96	Feb 97	CAGR
Sales	620	734	794	765	1,038	1,264	1,542	1,885	2,223	2,200	2,122	13.1%
EBDIT	255	360	438	416	563	692	858	1,029	1,199	1,170	1,120	15.9%
Net Profit	94	144	177	176	252	316	381	448	512	501	461	17.2%
EP/ADR	0.23	0.35	0.43	0.42	0.60	0.76	0.92	1.08	1.23	1.20	1.11	17.0%
DP/ADR	0.05	0.06	0.07	0.08	0.11	0.15	0.20	0.25	0.30	0.30	0.32	21.5%

KEY RATIOS

	Feb 87	Feb 88	Feb 89	Feb 90	Feb 91	Feb 92	Feb 93	Feb 94	Feb 95	Feb 96	Feb 97	AVG
EBDIT Margin	41.2%	49.0%	55.2%	54.4%	54.2%	54.8%	55.7%	54.6%	53.9%	53.2%	52.8%	52.6%
ROE	21.6%	22.2%	18.9%	18.0%	19.1%	19.7%	18.5%	16.7%	15.6%	15.6%	14.7%	18.2%
LT Debt/Total Cap	2.0%	1.8%	1.4%	1.3%	1.2%	1.0%	1.0%	1.1%	0.8%	0.9%	1.0%	1.2%
P/E (Projected)	51.8	52.6	43.7	51.9	41.4	48.0	42.5	58.7	45.4	50.5	51.4	48.9

STOCK PRICE CHART
(fiscal year-end closing price, in U.S. dollars, adjusted for capital changes)

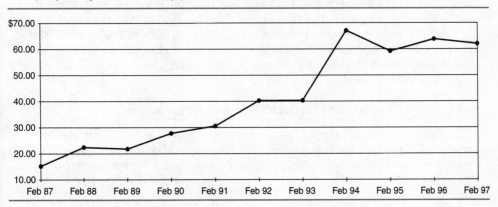

Note: Figures in U.S. dollars are translated from local currency using year-end exchange rates.

SIEBE (SIBEY—OTC)

Address: Saxon House / 2–4 Victoria Street / Windsor, Berkshire SL4 1EN / United Kingdom
Tel.: (011) 44 1753 855 411   **Fax:** (011) 44 1753 830 047

BASIC INFORMATION

Country: United Kingdom
Industry: Industrial equipment
Investment thesis: The United Kingdom's largest diversified engineering group

Market capitalization: $7.08 billion
Share status: ADRs trade OTC

COMPANY GRADING BOX

Growth Categories		Quality of Management	
Revenue Growth	20	Return on Equity	5
Operating Income Growth	20	**Risk**	
Earnings per Share Growth	20	Long-Term Debt/Total Capital	5
Share Price Growth	10	**Total QM&R (maximum 20)**	10
Total Growth (maximum 80)	70	**FINAL GRADE**	80

BACKGROUND

Siebe group (pronounced See-bee) of the United Kingdom is a little tougher to describe than some of our other picks. It is the United Kingdom's largest diversified engineering group, and its products make other products tick: air compressors, safety equipment, fluid controls, and temperature controls for everything from industrial plants to trains to cars to home refrigerators. It is the European market leader in air-conditioning and temperature appliances and has pioneered new ground in industrial plant automation. Along with Microsoft, Siebe recently developed a system that allows plant managers to use their personal computers to manage factory output.

The company says it is "here, there and everywhere." At a U.S. subsidiary, engineers have developed more precise controls for top-of-the-line Jenn-Air "cookers"; Siebe exhaust gas recirculation valves reduce harmful vehicle emissions; and a Siebe environmental control system provides digital control of the ballpark in Arlington, Texas, covering the central plant, offices, locker rooms, and luxury boxes. Together Siebe, made up of 130 companies, had just under $4 billion in revenues in 1996.

Looking forward, Siebe's CEO has said he is shifting the company's emphasis from mechanical and electromechanical products to electrical and electronic components. He hopes that by moving toward "intelligent products" the company will continue to show the kind of margin improvement it has in the past. In 1996 Siebe took a big step in that direction, buying U.K.-based Unitech, a manufacturer of electronic components and power controls with a tremendous presence in the Far East, already one of Siebe's most significant areas of growth.

COMPANY STATEMENT (from the 1996 annual report)

"The stated aims of the Group are that we should be amongst the top three market leaders in each of our core business segments and that we should consistently deliver to our customers superlative design together with excellence of quality. We further commit that we will be within the top ten percent of our peer group over the years ahead on total return to shareholders.

"At this point it is worth noting three distinct and important trends in Siebe's business activity. The first is our growth in emerging markets, wherein our sales in the Far East, Middle East, South America and Eastern Europe grew by 21.3% this year and cumulatively by 86.3% over the past three years.

"Secondly, I would like to highlight the changing technology spread within Siebe. . . . We are effectively managing the transition between mechanical/electro-mechanical technology towards electronic/software-based technology for both ourselves and our customers.

"Finally, the Group's exposure to and dependence upon individual industry and economic sectors has been significantly rebalanced during the past five years. . . . We now serve a very broad set of industries which are well-balanced between early, middle and late economic cycle exposure."

PERFORMANCE

Seibe gets high marks for consistency and growth and an overall score of 80 points in our grading system. In dollars, revenues and EBDIT increased in nine of the last ten years, with compound annual growth of 16% and 20%, respectively. EP/ADR (or ADR equivalent) in dollars increased in eight of the last ten years, with compound annual growth of around 21%. Regarding measurements for quality of management, the operating margin rose from 15% in 1987 to 21% in 1997. ROE also increased, reaching 24%, but averaged 17% for the ten-year period. As for risk, the long-term debt to total capital ratio averaged 35%, a little high. The ADR price increased in each of the last six years, rising at a compound annual rate of around 15%.

If you had invested $10,000 in Siebe in March 1987, you would have purchased around 150 ADRs (or ADR equivalents) at about $67.75 (excluding commissions). During the following ten years, there were a one-for-one bonus issue in September 1987, a two-for-five rights issue in September 1987, a one-for-one bonus issue in September 1992, and a one-for-ten rights issue in November 1993. By March 1997, you would have had around 1,240 ADRs worth an estimated $40,000. You would also have received dividend payments of around $2,800.

SIEBE

Ticker Symbol and Exchange: SIBEY—OTC   **CUSIP No.: 826166209**

OPERATING AND PER SHARE DATA
(in millions of British pounds and pounds per share)

	Mar 87	Mar 88	Mar 89	Mar 90	Mar 91	Mar 92	Mar 93	Mar 94	Mar 95	Mar 96	Mar 97	CAGR
Sales	675	1057	1215	1372	1481	1628	1619	1864	2117	2600	3005	16.1%
EBDIT	102	168	207	242.1	261	300.1	318.5	360	416	494.4	621.7	19.8%
Net Profit	34	69	95.3	106	89	92	106	127	159	189	247	22.0%
EPS	0.08	0.21	0.24	0.27	0.23	0.23	0.27	0.31	0.37	0.44	0.53	21.1%
DPS	0.02	0.04	0.06	0.07	0.08	0.09	0.10	0.11	0.12	0.14	0.15	23.2%

OPERATING AND PER SHARE DATA
(in millions of U.S. dollars and dollars per ADR)

	Mar 87	Mar 88	Mar 89	Mar 90	Mar 91	Mar 92	Mar 93	Mar 94	Mar 95	Mar 96	Mar 97	CAGR
Sales	1,083	1,992	2,047	2,256	2,586	2,826	2,452	2,765	3,433	3,968	4,695	15.8%
EBDIT	164	317	349	398	457	521	482	534	675	754	971	19.5%
Net Profit	54	130	161	175	156	160	160	189	257	288	386	21.6%
EP/ADR	0.25	0.78	0.82	0.89	0.79	0.82	0.81	0.93	1.20	1.34	1.64	20.7%
DP/ADR	0.06	0.16	0.19	0.24	0.28	0.31	0.30	0.33	0.39	0.42	0.46	22.9%

KEY RATIOS

	Mar 87	Mar 88	Mar 89	Mar 90	Mar 91	Mar 92	Mar 93	Mar 94	Mar 95	Mar 96	Mar 97	AVG
EBDIT Margin	15.1%	15.9%	17.0%	17.6%	17.7%	18.4%	19.7%	19.3%	19.7%	19.0%	20.7%	18.2%
ROE	14.3%	17.0%	18.8%	18.2%	14.9%	14.0%	13.0%	13.4%	16.4%	17.8%	24.2%	16.5%
LT Debt/Total Cap	47.4%	32.2%	29.9%	27.5%	46.4%	38.7%	39.0%	30.8%	26.7%	32.1%	34.4%	35.0%
P/E (Projected)	12.2	6.7	8.5	9.9	8.8	11.9	14.1	16.0	12.5	16.6	17.1	12.2

STOCK PRICE CHART
(fiscal year-end closing price, in U.S. dollars, adjusted for capital changes)

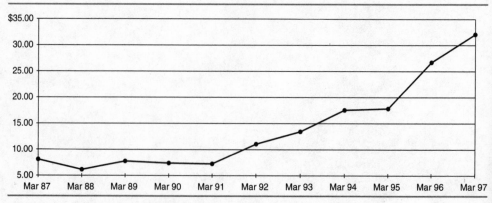

Note: Figures in U.S. dollars are translated from local currency using year-end exchange rates.

SODEXHO ALLIANCE (EXHO.PA—PARIS)

Address: 3 Avenue Newton / 78180 Montigny-le Bretonneux / France
Tel.: (011) 33 1 30 85 75 00   **Fax:** (011) 33 1 30 43 09 58   **Web site:** http://www.sodexho.com

BASIC INFORMATION

Country: France
Industry: Industrial service
Investment thesis: The largest contract food services group in the world

Market capitalization: $3.74 billion
Share status: Foreign shares trade on the Paris Exchange

COMPANY GRADING BOX

Growth Categories		Quality of Management	
Revenue Growth	20	Return on Equity	5
Operating Income Growth	20	**Risk**	
Earnings per Share Growth	5	Long-Term Debt/Total Capital	0
Share Price Growth	20	**Total QM&R (maximum 20)**	5
Total Growth (maximum 80)	65	**FINAL GRADE**	70

BACKGROUND

This is one of the world's largest contract food services groups—a competitor worldwide of Compass Group (see p. 123). In late 1997 Sodexho and Marriott International announced plans to merge their North American contract catering and facilities management businesses in a deal valued at about $2 billion (Sodexho owns 49% of the new merged group which will trade separately on the New York Stock Exchange). Sodexho became an industry giant with its 1995 merger with U.K.-based Gardner Merchant—with 141,000 employees in sixty-two countries, and 77% of its revenue generated outside France, its home country. Sodexho's core business is providing food services to institutions—every kind from schools to prisons to hospitals to sports facilities to industrial plants—that have chosen to contract out non-core functions to help cut costs and to focus more on their core activities. Sodexho provides cooks and serving staff for the Kowloon and Canton Railway Corporation, for VIPs who watch the Tour de France, and for diners at the restaurant of the Sydney Opera House.

Global potential in this business is enormous, with interest in outsourcing gaining momentum. In addition to catering, Sodexho provides clients with such services as grounds and equipment maintenance, cleaning, and even kitchen design and construction. Many of its menus for hospital patients and residents of retirement homes are put together by its own staff of clinical dietitians. And for clients at "remote sites" (such as teams of workers on the new Hong Kong airport, or workers at a Mexican oil company's offshore rigs) a Sodexho subsidiary provides everything from laundry service to catering to entertainment. Sodexho is also developing its more "upscale" business—part of the former Gardner Merchant operations. Among other events catered by the combined group: Wimbledon and Ascot.

COMPANY STATEMENT (from the 1996 annual report)

"Our Strengths:

Flexible: The Group empowers team members to be self-starters. It encourages them to adapt to new, different or changing requirements. Decentralized management ensures national, regional and local knowledge and understanding. Hence, our teams are market-focused, customer-oriented, and ready to personalize service for clients.

Innovative: The Group introduces practices and products in partnership with clients and pioneers in new technology, such as renowned scientific research centers. . . .

Convivial: A vital component of our performance focuses on warm, friendly service. Hence, a convivial atmosphere is central to everything we do. . . .

Expert: The Group's core business is food and management services. For more than thirty years we have built a reputation of outstanding service to customers of all ages. Besides managing our core business units, our expertise also integrates skills such as consulting, architectural design, legal and financial recommendations, equipment and technology advice, training, purchasing, convivial reception, and more.

Multicultural: The Group is multicultural. Its clients and customers cover a broad spectrum of peoples, nationalities and religious beliefs. . . .

Independent: The Group is financially independent of its clients, suppliers and the investment community at large. We have allied geographic spread with diversified businesses to limit the risks of political and economic change. . . ."

PERFORMANCE

Sodexho's overall score of 70 reflects both this company's stellar growth record, and the fact that it has devoted considerable resources to its rapidly expanding businesses. In dollar terms, revenues and EBITDA increased in nine of the last ten years while recording compound annual growth of 21% and 29%, respectively. On the other hand, EPS in dollars grew inconsistently as the company expanded organically and by acquisition, recording compound annual growth of only 11%. Sodexho also lost points because of its relatively high long-term debt to total capital ratio; that number jumped to almost 57% after Sodexho merged with Gardner Merchant in 1995 (by the end of 1996 Sodexho already had brought this ratio down a little, to just under 51%). Even so, Sodexho increased its dividend in nine of the last ten years, from $1.19 in 1986 to $5.14 in 1996. Share price performance also has been impressive; the share price increased at a compound rate of 25% over the ten-year period.

If you had invested $10,000 in Sodexho in August of 1986, you would have purchased around 30 shares at $314 each. During the following ten years, there was a capital change in December 1989 and a one-for-three rights issue in February 1995. By August of 1996, you would have had 200 shares worth $91,600. You also would have received dividend payments worth around $6,000.

SODEXHO ALLIANCE

Ticker Symbol and Exchange: EXHO.PA—PARIS   **SEDOL Code: 4818306**

OPERATING AND PER SHARE DATA
(in millions of French francs and francs per share)

	Aug 86	Aug 87	Aug 88	Aug 89	Aug 90	Aug 91	Aug 92	Aug 93	Aug 94	Aug 95	Aug 96	CAGR
Sales	5,090	5,727	7,104	8,067	7,697	8,918	9,105	10,611	11,239	18,348	24,961	17.2%
EBITDA	155	227	290	297	344	489	508	481	526	1,016	1,457	25.1%
Net Profit	99	105	126	145	166	191	218	231	636	284	684	21.3%
EPS	25.17	23.32	27.86	27.38	34.65	37.97	43.20	45.60	39.80	40.70	54.40	8.0%
DPS	7.95	8.75	10.02	11.42	12.42	14.30	21.00	22.00	22.00	22.00	26.00	12.6%

OPERATING AND PER SHARE DATA
(in millions of U.S. dollars and dollars per share)

	Aug 86	Aug 87	Aug 88	Aug 89	Aug 90	Aug 91	Aug 92	Aug 93	Aug 94	Aug 95	Aug 96	CAGR
Sales	763	942	1,065	1,217	1,458	1,504	1,905	1,814	2,077	3,640	4,933	20.5%
EBITDA	23.3	37.3	43.5	44.8	65.2	82.5	106.2	82.2	97.1	201.6	288.0	28.6%
Net Profit	14.8	17.3	18.9	21.9	31.5	32.2	45.6	39.5	117.5	56.3	135.2	24.7%
EPS	3.77	3.84	4.18	4.13	6.56	6.40	9.04	7.79	7.36	8.08	10.75	11.0%
DPS	1.19	1.44	1.50	1.72	2.35	2.41	4.39	3.76	4.07	4.37	5.14	15.7%

KEY RATIOS

	Aug 86	Aug 87	Aug 88	Aug 89	Aug 90	Aug 91	Aug 92	Aug 93	Aug 94	Aug 95	Aug 96	AVG
EBITDA Margin	3.0%	4.0%	4.1%	3.7%	4.5%	5.5%	5.6%	4.5%	4.7%	5.5%	5.8%	4.6%
ROE	17.2%	17.0%	18.0%	17.8%	19.1%	12.3%	14.0%	13.1%	27.4%	8.0%	15.3%	16.3%
LT Debt/Total Cap	25.8%	50.0%	47.0%	36.8%	30.7%	22.6%	40.7%	37.3%	31.8%	56.5%	50.5%	39.1%
P/E (Projected)	14.3	16.5	15.7	16.8	12.7	16.7	20.6	24.9	22.5	21.9	28.9	19.2

STOCK PRICE CHART
(fiscal year-end closing price, in U.S. dollars, adjusted for capital changes)

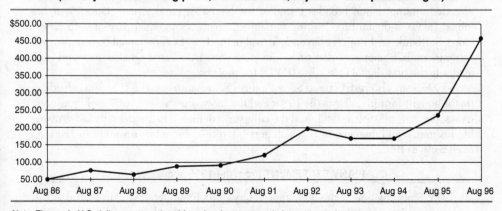

Note: Figures in U.S. dollars are translated from local currency using average exchange rates.

SONY (SNE—NYSE)

Address: 7-35 Kitashinagawa 6-chome / Shinagawa-ku / Tokyo 141 / Japan
Tel.: (011) 81 3 5448 2111   **Fax:** (011) 81 3 5448 2244
Web site: http://www.sony.co.jp/ or http://www.sony.com/
or
Address: 550 Madison Avenue, 33rd Floor / New York, NY 10022-3211
Tel.: (212) 833-6800

BASIC INFORMATION

Country: Japan   **Market capitalization:** $31.3 billion
Industry: Electrical and electronic   **Share status:** ADRs trade on NYSE
Investment thesis: World leader in consumer electronics, film and music; going digital

COMPANY GRADING BOX

Growth Categories		Quality of Management	
Revenue Growth	20	Return on Equity	0
Operating Income Growth	20	**Risk**	
Earnings per Share Growth	10	Long-Term Debt/Total Capital	0
Share Price Growth	5	**Total QM&R (maximum 20)**	**0**
Total Growth (maximum 80)	**55**	**FINAL GRADE**	**55**

BACKGROUND

Sony is one of those ubiquitous brand names—up there with Coca-Cola, Nike, and Heineken in the pantheon of names that almost everybody everywhere has heard of. It also has a market capitalization of $31 billion and 151,000 employees worldwide. This is the company that brought you the Walkman, the movie *Jerry Maguire,* digital camcorders, and PlayStations. Then there are TV shows such as *Mad About You* and *Seinfeld,* which generates strong revenues in syndication, and singer/songwriter Celine Dion's *Falling into You,* a hit overseas. Other Sony Music artists include Mariah Carey, Michael Jackson, and Yo-Yo Ma.

Going forward, Sony's president (installed in 1995) says he wants to build his company, now considered the world leader in audiovisual equipment, into the leading information technology company. Toward that end, he is directing Sony's considerable resources into developing digital technologies, marketing digital consumer products under the powerful Sony brand name, and developing strategic alliances with other key players. Sony is already building digital broadcast studios for NewsCorp and Japan's DirecTV; it has joined JSkyB, a digital broadcasting satellite company, as an equal partner with NewsCorp, Softbank, and Fuji; it is an early arrival in the U.S. PCS (personal communication systems) mobile phone market (in conjunction with U.S.-based Qualcomm); and it's a leader in the new digital video disc (DVD) technology.

In 1996 Sony also restructured Sony Pictures Entertainment, the U.S. film subsidiary that it bought for top dollar in the 1980s and that now generates about 7% of group revenues, down from 9.6% in 1993. And the company continued to build out its fast-growing life insurance and financial unit, which generated 5% percent of revenues in 1996, up from 2.6% in 1993.

COMPANY STATEMENT (from the 1996 annual report)

"In 1996, Sony celebrated the 50th anniversary of its founding, taking its arrival at this milestone as an opportunity to make a fresh start under the theme of Re-Generation.

Sony is endeavoring to re-invent itself to meet the needs of a new era while upholding the spirit of challenge on which it was founded and continuing to emphasize such qualities as freedom, dynamism, originality and creativity.

"In product development, Sony adopted the concept 'Digital Dream Kids,' which expresses Sony's desire to utilize digital technologies to create unique, fun products that fulfill the dreams of customers who have grown up in the digital age. . . .

"In the Electronics Business, Sony is working to strengthen its leading position in audio-visual markets while endeavoring to develop IT business that augments Sony's corporate culture and image. In the Entertainment Business, Sony is seeking to introduce software production technologies that are appropriate for the digital age and striving to fortify its management to further stabilize operations. Sony is endeavoring to bring about a fusion of electronics and entertainment to cultivate new businesses that are expected to expand in line with the rapid development of networking as well as to provide new varieties of hardware and software. Furthermore, to raise its competitiveness and enhance the value of its brand image, Sony is working to maintain its tradition of offering unique products and services, to emphasize further advances in the quality and speed of overall management, and to give high priority to cost control."

PERFORMANCE

Sony received a total of 55 points in our grading system. Although the company got high marks for growth, it lost points for ADR price performance, EP/ADR, and ROE, reflecting tough times in the Japanese equity market and economy. Even so, revenues increased in nine of the last ten years (most recently getting a boost from a strong dollar/weak yen rate), with compound annual growth of 18%. EBDIT in dollars increased in eight of the last ten years, with compound annual growth of 15%.

On the other hand, EP/ADR growth was inconsistent, with compound annual growth of 12%. ROE averaged a paltry 3% but in 1997 climbed to close to 10%. The ratio of long-term debt to total capital, which averaged 36% for the ten-year period, was higher than for many of our other companies. The ADR price increased at a compound annual rate of about 13%—not fantastic compared to other companies in this book but impressive compared with the rest of the Japanese market.

If you had invested $10,000 in Sony in March 1987, you would have purchased around 350 ADRs (or ADR equivalents) at about $28.50 each (excluding commissions). In May 1991 there was a one-for-five bonus issue, and in September 1991 there was an eleven-for-ten stock split. By March 1997, you would have had around 460 ADRs worth an estimated $34,600. You would also have received dividend payments of around $1,600.

SONY

Ticker Symbol and Exchange: SNE—NYSE   **CUSIP No.: 835699307**

OPERATING AND PER SHARE DATA
(in billions of Japanese yen and yen per share)

	Mar 87	Mar 88	Mar 89	Mar 90	Mar 91	Mar 92	Mar 93	Mar 94	Mar 95	Mar 96	Mar 97	CAGR
Sales	1,325	1,431	2,145	2,879	3,617	3,821	3,879	3,610	3,827	4,339	5,663	15.6%
EBDIT	184	188	326	466	521	504	412	372	34	403	637	13.2%
Net Profit	42	37	73	103	117	107	36	15	(293)	54	140	12.8%
EPS	137.4	116.5	194.4	234.7	261.5	286.6	97.3	40.9	(784.5)	145.2	363.0	10.2%
DPS	33.31	33.76	33.76	37.85	37.85	50.00	50.00	50.00	50.00	50.00	50.00	4.1%

OPERATING AND PER SHARE DATA
(in millions of U.S. dollars and dollars per ADR)

	Mar 87	Mar 88	Mar 89	Mar 90	Mar 91	Mar 92	Mar 93	Mar 94	Mar 95	Mar 96	Mar 97	CAGR
Sales	9,089	11,540	16,250	18,222	25,652	28,947	34,026	35,392	44,243	40,551	46,041	17.6%
EBDIT	1,261	1,515	2,470	2,946	3,696	3,820	3,618	3,648	395	3,764	5,177	15.2%
Net Profit	287	296	549	651	829	810	318	150	(3,392)	507	1,134	14.7%
EP/ADR	0.94	0.94	1.47	1.49	1.85	2.17	0.85	0.40	(9.07)	1.36	2.95	12.1%
DP/ADR	0.23	0.27	0.26	0.24	0.27	0.38	0.44	0.49	0.58	0.47	0.41	5.9%

KEY RATIOS

	Mar 87	Mar 88	Mar 89	Mar 90	Mar 91	Mar 92	Mar 93	Mar 94	Mar 95	Mar 96	Mar 97	AVG
EBDIT Margin	13.9%	13.1%	15.2%	16.2%	14.4%	13.2%	10.6%	10.3%	0.9%	9.3%	11.2%	11.7%
ROE	6.9%	5.6%	8.0%	7.2%	7.9%	7.0%	2.5%	1.2%	−29.1%	4.6%	9.5%	2.8%
LT Debt/Total Cap	17.5%	21.2%	17.7%	34.1%	34.7%	38.2%	40.7%	44.5%	48.7%	53.2%	49.1%	36.3%
P/E (Projected)	27.1	20.4	21.6	23.2	17.4	40.4	N/M	N/M	30.0	17.6	20.8	24.3

STOCK PRICE CHART
(fiscal year-end closing price, in U.S. dollars, adjusted for capital changes)

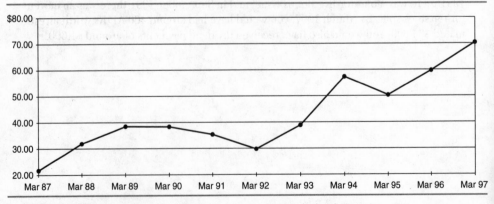

Note: Figures in U.S. dollars are translated from local currency using year-end exchange rates.

SOPHUS BERENDSEN (SBPC.CO—COPENHAGEN)

Address: Klausdalsbrovej 1 / DK-2860 Søborg / Denmark
Tel.: (011) 45 39 69 85 00   **Fax:** (011) 45 39 69 73 00

BASIC INFORMATION

Country: Denmark   **Market capitalization:** $3.34 billion
Industry: Industrial services   **Share status:** Foreign shares trade on Copenhagen Exchange
Investment thesis: Business service group (including outsourcing); owns 36% of Rentokil

COMPANY GRADING BOX

Growth Categories		Quality of Management	
Revenue Growth	20	Return on Equity	10
Operating Income Growth	20	**Risk**	
Earnings per Share Growth	20	Long-Term Debt/Total Capital	10
Share Price Growth	20	**Total QM&R (maximum 20)**	**20**
Total Growth (maximum 80)	**80**	**FINAL GRADE**	**100**

BACKGROUND

No question, one of our favorite themes among international growth stocks is "outsourcing." And Denmark's Sophus Berendsen has been at the forefront of the trend. Over the last ten years, Sophus Berendsen has increased its earnings per share in U.S. dollars by 23.1%. Started in 1854 to trade glass, steel, and iron, in 1904 management saw the future in pest control. The company took over the rights to a pesticide invented to fight rats just as Europe was dealing with a major rat infestation. Then it started pest control subsidiaries around Europe.

Today pest control is included in Rentokil, which is now an associated company rather than a subsidiary—and is another of our Top 100 (see pg. 279). Sophus Berendsen started it as a U.K. pest control subsidiary in 1927, though in the years since it has added a long list of outsourcing services. Although Sophus Berendsen floated stock in Rentokil on the London Exchange in 1969, it was not until 1996 that Sophus Berendsen gave up its majority share (Sophus Berendsen's stake in Rentokil was reduced from 51.7% to 36% after Rentokil issued new shares to complete its acquisition of giant U.K.-based services company BET). Today Rentokil Initial's outsourcing businesses span the gamut from health care and hygiene, catering, security services, distribution, and personnel management to resort and luxury condominium management.

Then there is the rest of Sophus Berendsen, comprising three divisions: Textile Service, Power and Motion Control, and Electronics and Data. Their activities, focused mainly on different types of outsourcing, range from laundry services to the distribution of hydraulics to the marketing of electronic products. In the words of a senior company executive: "We supply services that are inexpensive for the customer but that are incredibly important for his quality image."

COMPANY STATEMENT (from the 1996 annual report)

"The inner cohesion between the Group's activities and business sectors can be best expressed by the term 'Value Added Service.' It means that customers receive extra service in addition to the basic product, adding extra value.

"In its business sectors, Sophus Berendsen will continue to develop its basic products and services—these will ensure its continued progress. This is the context of an overall framework that builds on organic development and on geographic penetration in its markets through acquisitions. Innovation, knowledge, service and efficient logistics are an important part of the Group's development strategy, in which quality always plays a more important role than price. Sophus Berendsen's aim is to secure a leading market position in the places where its three business sectors are represented.

"The Group's size and proliferation allow it to exploit economies of scale and to transfer best practice between its companies and sectors. Synergy and efficiency are created from an increased focus on benchmarking between companies and sectors, greater use of IT and a tighter control of costs. These Group competencies help make Sophus Berendsen an attractive, long-term co-operation partner with a broad and diversely rooted customer base and strong links to its suppliers."

PERFORMANCE

Sophus Berendsen is one of our star companies, receiving a perfect score of 100 points in our grading system. After Sophus Berendsen reduced its stake in Rentokil, it released restated numbers going back to 1987 that show historic figures with a comparable contribution from Rentokil, allowing an apples-to-apples comparison. The result is stunning: Sophus Berendsen's revenues in dollars saw compound annual growth of 20%, rising in eight of the nine years. Pretax profit (restated figures for EBDIT were not available) showed compound annual growth of about 22%, also rising to new highs in eight of the nine years. EPS in dollars had compound annual growth of 20%. As for share price performance, Sophus Berendsen has a great track record: the company's share price has closed at higher levels every year and grown at a compound rate of 29% since 1986. Sophus also received top marks for its ROE and ratio of long-term debt to total capital: ROE averaged 31% over ten years, while the long-term debt to total capital ratio averaged a low 14%.

If you had invested $10,000 in Sophus Berendsen in 1986, you would have purchased around 60 shares at about $164.50 each (excluding commissions). During the following ten-year period, there were a one-for-six rights issue in 1991, a five-for-one stock split in 1992, a one-for-eight bonus issue in 1992, and a one-for-ten bonus issue in 1996. By the end of 1996, you would have owned around 525 shares worth an estimated $66,600. You would also have received around $3,600 in dividend payments during the period.

SOPHUS BERENDSEN

Ticker Symbol and Exchange: SBPC.CO—Copenhagen   **SEDOL Code: 4826451**

OPERATING AND PER SHARE DATA
(in millions of Danish kroner and kroner per share)

	1986	1987	1988	1989	1990	1991	1992	1993	1994	1995	1996	CAGR
Sales	N/A	1,293	1,558	1,731	1,776	2,847	3,129	4,165	5,316	6,314	6,719	20.1%
Pretax Profit	N/A	229	353	453	502	565	699	872	780	1,255	1,294	21.2%
Net Profit	N/A	137	239	310	337	367	462	598	464	875	916	23.5%
EPS	N/A	6.70	12.95	12.59	14.05	15.85	19.10	22.75	17.65	33.21	34.80	20.1%
DPS	N/A	2.03	2.45	2.70	2.70	2.84	3.50	4.00	4.00	5.00	5.50	11.7%

OPERATING AND PER SHARE DATA
(in millions of U.S. dollars and dollars per share)

	1986	1987	1988	1989	1990	1991	1992	1993	1994	1995	1996	CAGR
Sales	N/A	212	229	263	306	482	499	613	874	1,136	1,127	20.4%
Pretax Profit	N/A	38	52	69	86	96	111	128	128	226	217	21.5%
Net Profit	N/A	22	35	47	58	62	74	88	76	157	154	23.8%
EPS	N/A	1.10	1.90	1.91	2.42	2.68	3.05	3.35	2.90	5.97	5.84	20.4%
DPS	N/A	0.33	0.36	0.41	0.46	0.48	0.56	0.59	0.66	0.90	0.92	12.0%

KEY RATIOS

	1986	1987	1988	1989	1990	1991	1992	1993	1994	1995	1996	AVG
Pretax Margin	N/A	18.1%	20.8%	20.3%	21.9%	22.9%	23.6%	21.5%	18.4%	21.1%	19.3%	20.8%
ROE	N/A	16.0%	31.1%	30.5%	31.0%	31.0%	28.1%	30.7%	23.1%	41.3%	50.7%	31.4%
LT Debt/Total Cap	N/A	8.3%	16.1%	12.5%	13.7%	18.5%	11.8%	13.9%	18.6%	12.1%	13.7%	13.9%
P/E (Projected)	N/A	11.0	14.3	18.5	15.9	17.6	17.1	30.7	14.8	17.9	15.7	17.3

STOCK PRICE CHART
(fiscal year-end closing price, in U.S. dollars, adjusted for capital changes)

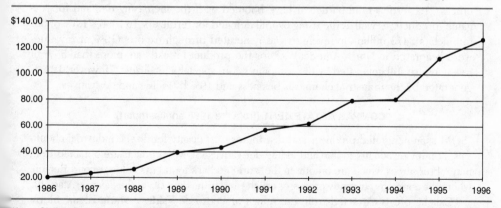

Notes: Sophus Berendsen's stake in Rentokil declined to around 36% in 1996, from over 50% previously, when it did not participate in a share offering by Rentokil to raise money for the acquisition of BET. Accordingly, Rentokil is now reported as an associated company of Sophus Berendsen rather than as a subsidiary. The figures shown above have been restated to reflect the change. Figures in U.S. dollars are translated from local currency using year-end exchange rates.

SOQUIMICHA (SQM—NYSE)

Address: Miraflores 222, 11th Floor / Santiago / Chile
Tel.: (011) 56 2 632 6888   **Fax:** (011) 56 2 633 4223

BASIC INFORMATION

Country: Chile

Industry: Mining

Investment thesis: One of the world's largest producers of specialty fertilizers

Market capitalization: $1.32 billion

Share status: ADRs trade on NYSE

COMPANY GRADING BOX

Growth Categories		Quality of Management	
Revenue Growth	15	Return on Equity	0
Operating Income Growth	15	**Risk**	
Earnings per Share Growth	20	Long-Term Debt/Total Capital	10
Share Price Growth	20	**Total QM&R (maximum 20)**	10
Total Growth (maximum 80)	70	**FINAL GRADE**	80

BACKGROUND

Sociedad Química y Minera de Chile, more commonly known as Soquimicha, was created in 1968 during a reorganization of Chile's sodium nitrate industry, a key part of the Chilean economy since the late 1800s. Initially it was a joint venture between private investors and the state, although in 1971 the state absorbed whatever it did not already own. Finally, in the 1980s, the process of full privatization began, with the company completely out of government hands in 1988.

Over the last ten years, management has been adding products, creating "an integrated producer of specialty fertilizers, industrial chemicals, lithium carbonate, iodine and iodine derivatives" using the abundant natural resources of Chile. Today Soquimicha is one of the world's largest producers of specialty fertilizers based on natural nitrates (the largest producer of nitrates in the world is Potash Corporation of Saskatchewan; see page 261). Soquimicha's products are sold to more than eighty countries through more than fifteen subsidiaries worldwide (including fertilizer-blending plants, warehouses, and offices). Its fertilizers in particular have boomed with the increasing demand for "organic" products, as well as the rising overall demand for fertilizers. In 1996, 71.5% of Soquimicha's $473 million in revenues was generated through exports (19% of revenues were generated in North America). As for the product breakdown, more than 55% of revenues are still generated by the company's core specialty fertilizers. However, 12% is generated by the industrial chemicals business and 19% by iodine and derivatives.

COMPANY STATEMENT (from the 1996 annual report)

"SQM is an integrated producer and distributor of specialty fertilizers, industrial chemicals, lithium carbonate, iodine and iodine derivatives. SQM's products are obtained from natural resources which are unique in the world and are found in Chile's Second Region, where the company currently processes caliche and brine deposits of the Salar de Atacama.

"Caliche ore is extracted from the mines of Pedro de Valdiva, María Elena, Sierra Gorda and Nueva Victoria and, by means of sophisticated processes of crushing, leaching and crystallization, SQM obtains sodium nitrate, potassium nitrate, sodium sulfate and iodine.

"The brine deposits of the Salar de Atacama contain high concentrations of lithium, potassium, sulfate, boron and magnesium. The foregoing, plus the natural conditions of the Atacama Desert, allow SQM to be one of the world's lowest cost producers of potassium chloride and lithium carbonate. Additionally, beginning in 1998 the Company will start production of potassium sulfate and boric acid."

PERFORMANCE

Investors have been well rewarded for their faith in Soquimicha, receiving an average annual return of 42% since the company went public in 1991, although the company did not launch its ADR and become available to U.S. investors until 1991. Overall, Soquimicha received 80 points in our grading system, with earnings per ADR and EBITDA having compound annual growth of 54% and 22%, respectively, over the last six years. Revenues increased at a compound annual rate of just over 11%. Growth was relatively consistent, though 1993 was clearly a tough year across Latin America. ROE was less impressive, averaging not quite 7%; however, by 1996 management had brought it up to 10%. The ratio of long-term debt to total capital averaged an acceptable 19%.

If you had invested $10,000 in Soquimicha at the end of 1991, you would have purchased around 1,100 ADRs at $9 each. In November 1995 there was a capital adjustment amounting to a small bonus increase in shares. By the end of 1996, you would have had 1,120 ADRs worth an estimated $58,600. You would also have received dividend payments of around $3,100. Not a bad investment for a five-year period!

SOQUIMICHA

Ticker Symbol and Exchange: SQM—NYSE   **SEDOL Code: 2819602**

OPERATING AND PER SHARE DATA
(in billions of nominal Chilean pesos and pesos per share)

	1986	1987	1988	1989	1990	1991	1992	1993	1994	1995	1996	CAGR
Sales	N/A	N/A	N/A	N/A	N/A	103.2	112.4	118.4	126.5	166.7	200.4	14.2%
EBITDA	N/A	N/A	N/A	N/A	N/A	14.8	22.4	21.7	19.7	27.8	45.2	25.1%
Net Profit	N/A	N/A	N/A	N/A	N/A	1.5	6.5	9.0	9.4	16.6	29.7	80.8%
EPS	N/A	N/A	N/A	N/A	N/A	12.38	53.10	43.66	45.94	68.78	122.36	58.1%
DPS	N/A	N/A	N/A	N/A	N/A	5.63	6.44	21.70	24.68	21.90	40.80	48.6%

OPERATING AND PER SHARE DATA
(in millions of U.S. dollars and dollars per ADR)

	1986	1987	1988	1989	1990	1991	1992	1993	1994	1995	1996	CAGR
Sales	N/A	N/A	N/A	N/A	N/A	275.2	294.2	276.6	313.9	409.6	473.7	11.5%
EBITDA	N/A	N/A	N/A	N/A	N/A	39.4	58.7	50.8	48.8	68.3	106.9	22.1%
Net Profit	N/A	N/A	N/A	N/A	N/A	4.1	17.1	21.0	23.3	40.7	70.2	76.5%
EP/ADR	N/A	N/A	N/A	N/A	N/A	0.33	1.39	1.02	1.14	1.69	2.89	54.4%
DP/ADR	N/A	N/A	N/A	N/A	N/A	0.15	0.17	0.51	0.61	0.54	0.96	45.1%

KEY RATIOS

	1986	1987	1988	1989	1990	1991	1992	1993	1994	1995	1996	AVG
EBITDA Margin	N/A	N/A	N/A	N/A	N/A	14.3%	20.0%	18.4%	15.5%	16.7%	22.6%	17.9%
ROE	N/A	N/A	N/A	N/A	N/A	2.5%	10.7%	4.7%	5.1%	7.1%	10.0%	6.7%
LT Debt/Total Cap	N/A	N/A	N/A	N/A	N/A	28.4%	23.5%	16.1%	13.5%	7.9%	24.7%	19.0%
P/E (Projected)	N/A	N/A	N/A	N/A	N/A	6.3	13.7	21.0	16.6	15.8	17.0	16.5

STOCK PRICE CHART
(fiscal year-end closing price, in U.S. dollars, adjusted for capital changes)

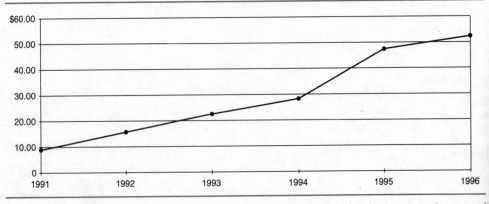

Notes: Soquimicha shares began trading in 1991. Figures in U.S. dollars are translated from local currency using year-end exchange rates.

SOUTH AFRICAN BREWERIES (SBWRY—OTC)

Address: 2 Jan Smuts Avenue / Johannesburg / South Africa
Tel.: (011) 27 11 407 1700   **Fax:** (011) 27 11 339 1830

BASIC INFORMATION

Country: South Africa
Industry: Brewing
Investment thesis: Fourth largest brewer in the world; 98.6% of South African market

Market capitalization: $9.07 billion
Share status: ADRs trade OTC

COMPANY GRADING BOX

Growth Categories		Quality of Management	
Revenue Growth	15	Return on Equity	10
Operating Income Growth	20	**Risk**	
Earnings per Share Growth	10	Long-Term Debt/Total Capital	10
Share Price Growth	10	**Total QM&R (maximum 20)**	20
Total Growth (maximum 80)	55	**FINAL GRADE**	75

BACKGROUND

South African Breweries (SAB) is the fourth largest brewer in the world, with its portfolio of fourteen brands holding 98.6% of the South African market and annual revenues of more than $8 billion—not to mention its Coca-Cola, Schweppes, and Sparletta bottling plants, its hotels, and its retail stores. SAB has 40% of the South African cola market, 50% of the beer market for the whole African continent, 50% of South Africa's three-, four- and five-star hotel rooms (the higher-margin hotels), and 98% of South Africa's glass windshield market (just about 100% of South African auto windshields are made in South Africa). Put it all together, and you'll see why SAB is the third largest conglomerate in South Africa, smaller only than Anglo-American Mining and De Beers.

SAB's best-known beer brands, Castle and Lion, are South Africa's best-sellers. With the end of apartheid and the readmission of South Africa to the international community of nations, SAB has been expanding its beer business overseas at a rapid pace, investing in breweries throughout Africa, as well as in eastern Europe (specifically Hungary, Romania, and Poland) and China, exporting SAB's century of experience in the brewery business. This investment program is in line with SAB's stated goal of capitalizing on its expertise in its core beer business.

At home, the company is also a key player in the retail industry, with fashion chains at different price points and two discount chains. SAB's Southern Sun subsidiary manages and operates sixty South African hotels (everything from five-star resorts to a Holiday Inn Express), and SAB's manufacturing unit is the leading producer of glass in South Africa.

Of course, none of these businesses is immune to the problems roiling South Africa. The political and economic fallout of apartheid is still being felt. Management addresses some of these issues in the annual report, discussing SAB's involvement in developing infrastructure and training programs in South Africa's black communities, as well as SAB's need to train blacks to serve in managerial capacities. But despite the turmoil, SAB has been able to grow earnings per share an average of 21.5% per annum during the last ten years without experiencing a down year, an outstanding record even in the most stable of countries.

COMPANY STATEMENT (from the 1996 annual report)

"The Group continues to concentrate its activities on the mass consumer markets, meeting and responding to consumer needs in a dynamic and creative manner. The core activity, beer, accounts for around 70% of the Group's attributable earnings. Last year's total output of 35 million hectoliters positions SAB as the fifth largest brewer in the world. The most important beneficiary of this steadily growing worldwide competitiveness has been the South African beer drinker, whose real price of refreshment has been halved over the last twenty years—a privilege without equal anywhere in the world!

"Performance of the diversified interests of the Group has been especially gratifying. Their contribution to attributable earnings rose by 39% during the past year, with ongoing recovery recorded in the retail and hotel interests.

"The Group remains committed to pursuing organic growth in its existing interests in South Africa. However, being fully aware of the law of diminishing returns, it becomes increasingly important for SAB to seek out international opportunities, primarily for the development of the core activity, beer. The brewing ventures in emerging and developing environments are complemented by the considerable advances being made in the more mature Western economies through the Group's international Belron arm in the field of automotive glass replacement services."

PERFORMANCE

Over the last ten years, South African Breweries—which compiled an overall score of 75 in our grading system—has been remarkably consistent, despite the dramatic changes in its domestic economy. Revenues in dollars increased every year, with compound annual growth of 9%. EP/ADR and EBDIT increased in nine of the last ten years, showing compound annual growth of 9% and 15%, respectively. Investors fared well. The ADR price had compound annual growth of 13% over the last ten years despite a slight decline in 1996. And the dividend payout ratio averaged 45% of earnings. ROE hit an excellent 28% in 1997 and averaged 23% during the decade. And as for risk, the long-term debt to total capital ratio averaged a comfortable 23% during the decade.

If you had invested $10,000 in South African Breweries in March 1987, you would have purchased around 1,140 ADRs (or ADR equivalents) at about $8.75 each (excluding commissions). There were no capital changes during the following ten years. By March 1997, you would have had around 1,140 ADRs worth an estimated $35,300. You would also have received dividend payments of around $5,200.

SOUTH AFRICAN BREWERIES

Ticker Symbol and Exchange: SBWRY—OTC   **CUSIP No.: 836216309**

OPERATING AND PER SHARE DATA
(in millions of South African rand and rand per share)

	Mar 87	Mar 88	Mar 89	Mar 90	Mar 91	Mar 92	Mar 93	Mar 94	Mar 95	Mar 96	Mar 97	CAGR
Sales	7,083	8,683	10,597	13,250	16,122	17,401	21,779	24,144	27,892	32,597	36,939	18.0%
EBDIT	558	746	1,022	1,316	1,588	1,933	2,335	2,440	2,934	3,474	5,010	24.5%
Net Profit	294	389	502	604	711	779	825	991	1,289	1,663	1,946	20.8%
EPS	1.12	1.47	1.87	2.25	2.65	2.90	3.04	3.63	4.65	5.66	5.95	18.2%
DPS	0.50	0.66	0.84	1.01	1.18	1.30	1.37	1.55	2.00	2.50	2.87	19.1%

OPERATING AND PER SHARE DATA
(in millions of U.S. dollars and dollars per ADR)

	Mar 87	Mar 88	Mar 89	Mar 90	Mar 91	Mar 92	Mar 93	Mar 94	Mar 95	Mar 96	Mar 97	CAGR
Sales	3,506	4,098	4,139	5,019	5,927	6,084	6,870	6,958	7,813	8,190	8,209	8.9%
EBDIT	276	352	399	498	584	676	737	703	822	873	1,113	15.0%
Net Profit	146	184	196	229	261	272	260	286	361	418	432	11.5%
EP/ADR	0.55	0.69	0.73	0.85	0.97	1.01	0.96	1.05	1.30	1.42	1.32	9.1%
DP/ADR	0.25	0.31	0.33	0.38	0.43	0.45	0.43	0.45	0.56	0.63	0.64	9.9%

KEY RATIOS

	Mar 87	Mar 88	Mar 89	Mar 90	Mar 91	Mar 92	Mar 93	Mar 94	Mar 95	Mar 96	Mar 97	AVG
EBDIT Margin	7.9%	8.6%	9.6%	9.9%	9.8%	11.1%	10.7%	10.1%	10.5%	10.7%	13.6%	10.2%
ROE	18.4%	20.0%	22.0%	22.3%	22.7%	21.2%	18.3%	23.3%	28.4%	29.8%	28.3%	23.2%
LT Debt/Total Cap	20.6%	21.3%	27.7%	22.7%	24.6%	23.5%	29.0%	24.7%	23.0%	19.2%	16.0%	22.9%
P/E (Projected)	12.1	9.5	10.2	12.8	16.3	18.6	16.3	17.4	17.7	19.3	20.8	15.5

STOCK PRICE CHART
(fiscal year-end closing price, in U.S. dollars, adjusted for capital changes)

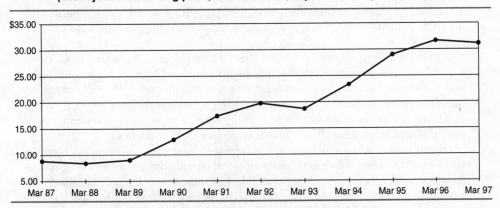

Note: Figures in U.S. dollars are translated from local currency using year-end exchange rates.

SUN HUNG KAI PROPERTIES (SUHJY—OTC)

Address: 45/F Sun Hung Kai Centre / 30 Harbour Road / Hong Kong
Tel.: (011) 852 2827 8111   **Fax:** (011) 852 2827 2862

BASIC INFORMATION

Country: Hong Kong
Industry: Property
Investment thesis: Largest, most successful Hong Kong property company—where property is king

Market capitalization: $26.3 billion
Share status: ADRs trade OTC

COMPANY GRADING BOX

Growth Categories		Quality of Management	
Revenue Growth	20	Return on Equity	5
Operating Income Growth	20	**Risk**	
Earnings per Share Growth	20	Long-Term Debt/Total Capital	10
Share Price Growth	20	**Total QM&R (maximum 20)**	15
Total Growth (maximum 80)	**80**	**FINAL GRADE**	**95**

BACKGROUND

Sun Hung Kai Properties is not typical of the companies that came up in our screens. But its track record is so good and its executives have shown themselves to be such good managers that we decided to include it—despite the fact that this company does not operate in what is traditionally considered a "growth" industry. The chairman of this group has been involved in Hong Kong real estate for more than forty years and appears to have put together a team that understands the vagaries of this very volatile market. Like most companies in the region, it was hard hit during the 1997 "Asian contagion," but it represents another interesting investment play for the future.

In Hong Kong and the New Territories, Sun Hung Kai is involved in every part of the real estate industry, having built and operated some of the area's most visible commercial and residential properties, including shopping centers, luxury and middle-income apartment buildings, hotels, and industrial and office buildings. It also has a tremendous "land bank" of Hong Kong real estate; land bought well below today's prices that it plans to develop over the next five years (of course, it will then have to replenish that "land bank" at current prices). In addition, the group has been involved in recent infrastructure projects, including construction at the new international airport. Although historically Sun Hung Kai has focused on property development, recently management has been building up its property investment and management division in an effort to create more recurrent income.

This is not a company with extensive international holdings. Sun Hung Kai sticks to what it knows. Its overseas operations have been focused on China, and management has said it does not want its China business to represent more than 10% of the company's overall revenues. Its interests outside real estate are minimal, although one stands out: Sun Hung Kai has invested some money in the booming telecommunications industry, buying 40% of Hong Kong–based SmarTone Mobile Communications.

Of course, we cannot talk about this company without mentioning recent events in Hong Kong. No one really knows what China will do with Hong Kong's existing institutions and regulatory framework now that it has assumed leadership in Hong Kong after a century of British domination. And for good or for bad, whatever China decides could have tremendous ramifications for Sun Hung Kai. Nevertheless, we feel there is reason to be optimistic about the prospects for Hong Kong going forward, and Sun Hung Kai is likely to remain a vibrant and successful company should Hong Kong continue to thrive.

COMPANY STATEMENT (from the 1996–97 annual report)

"With the smooth reunification of Hong Kong with China on 1st July 1997, and the establishment of Hong Kong Special Administrative Region, "one-country, two-systems" and "the government of Hong Kong by the people of Hong Kong" have been realized. Confidence in Hong Kong's future has been strengthened. The economy remains prosperous, employment opportunities are increasing and the unemployment rate is falling. The recent financial crisis in Southeast Asia has led to the devaluation of currencies in the region. Hong Kong's economic foundations, however, are strong. Hong Kong's healthy monetary system and substantial foreign exchange reserves, coupled with the backing of China, contribute to the stability of Hong Kong's investment market and currency. Closer economic relations between Hong Kong and mainland China will further reinforce Hong Kong's status as an international center for finance and commerce.

"The Group will continue its ongoing policy of focusing on property business in Hong Kong, reducing risk through diversification in property location and usage. The Group's long-term goal is to achieve an equal balance between profit from property sales and recurrent income. The Group will continue to expand its portfolios of investment properties and infrastructure projects in Hong Kong and rental properties in mainland China in order to strengthen recurrent income."

PERFORMANCE

Sun Hung Kai Properties is one of our highest scorers, with a total of 95 points in our grading system—and excellent ADR (or ADR equivalent) price performance: the ADR price in dollars increased at a compound annual rate of 21% between 1987 and 1997. Revenues in dollars increased in every one of those ten years, recording compound annual growth of 23%. EBDIT in dollars increased in nine of the ten years, with compound annual growth of 26%, as did EP/ADR, which had compound annual growth of 16%. The long-term debt to total capital ratio averaged 17%. ROE averaged a moderate 12% and was 10% in 1997. Sun Hung Kai Properties also provided investors with a great income, maintaining an average payout ratio of 49% of earnings and increasing its dividends in line with EPS at 17% per annum.

If you had invested $10,000 in Sun Hung Kai Properties in June 1987, you would have purchased around 4,900 ADRs (or ADR equivalents) at about $2.00 each (excluding commissions). During the following ten years, there was a one-for-ten bonus issue in November 1993. By the end of June 1997, you would have had around 5,500 ADRs worth an estimated $66,800. You would also have received around $10,800 in dividend payments.

SUN HUNG KAI PROPERTIES

Ticker Symbol and Exchange: SUHJY—OTC   **CUSIP No.: 86676H302**

OPERATING AND PER SHARE DATA
(in millions of Hong Kong dollars and dollars per share)

	Jun 87	Jun 88	Jun 89	Jun 90	Jun 91	Jun 92	Jun 93	Jun 94	Jun 95	Jun 96	Jun 97	CAGR
Sales	3,678	5,781	4,506	6,429	8,755	10,657	13,475	17,780	19,845	22,619	28,960	22.9%
EBDIT	1,725	2,386	2,308	2,855	4,119	5,374	7,849	10,479	12,311	12,717	17,139	25.8%
Net Profit	1,359	1,835	2,020	2,465	3,430	4,681	6,694	8,819	10,363	11,039	14,502	26.7%
EPS	1.29	1.18	1.21	1.40	1.85	2.62	3.48	3.91	4.46	4.69	5.92	16.5%
DPS	0.53	0.59	0.60	0.84	1.01	1.29	1.70	1.92	2.13	2.24	2.73	17.8%

OPERATING AND PER SHARE DATA
(in millions of U.S. dollars and dollars per ADR)

	Jun 87	Jun 88	Jun 89	Jun 90	Jun 91	Jun 92	Jun 93	Jun 94	Jun 95	Jun 96	Jun 97	CAGR
Sales	474	740	578	824	1,125	1,377	1,743	2,297	2,567	2,926	3,737	22.9%
EBDIT	222	305	296	366	529	694	1,015	1,354	1,593	1,645	2,211	25.8%
Net Profit	175	235	259	316	441	605	866	1,139	1,341	1,428	1,871	26.7%
EP/ADR	0.17	0.15	0.16	0.18	0.24	0.34	0.45	0.51	0.58	0.61	0.76	16.5%
DP/ADR	0.07	0.08	0.08	0.11	0.13	0.17	0.22	0.25	0.28	0.29	0.35	17.8%

KEY RATIOS

	Jun 87	Jun 88	Jun 89	Jun 90	Jun 91	Jun 92	Jun 93	Jun 94	Jun 95	Jun 96	Jun 97	AVG
EBDIT Margin	46.9%	41.3%	51.2%	44.4%	47.0%	50.4%	58.2%	58.9%	62.0%	56.2%	59.2%	52.4%
ROE	22.6%	11.2%	11.8%	13.3%	11.7%	11.6%	9.2%	10.8%	10.2%	10.2%	10.5%	12.1%
LT Debt/Total Cap	22.5%	21.6%	23.0%	20.1%	17.7%	13.2%	15.6%	14.1%	11.5%	11.5%	20.5%	17.4%
P/E (Projected)	11.8	8.6	5.1	7.4	6.6	9.5	9.0	10.0	12.2	13.9	13.7	9.8

STOCK PRICE CHART
(fiscal year-end closing price, in U.S. dollars, adjusted for capital changes)

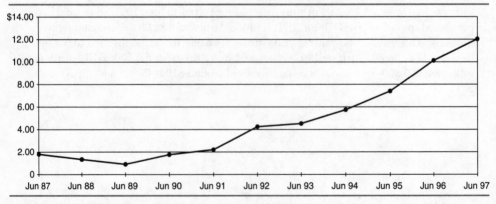

Note: Figures in U.S. dollars are translated from local currency using year-end exchange rates.

SYNTHELABO (SYTBF—OTC)

Address: 22 Avenue Galilée / B.P. 72 / 92352 Le Plessis Robinson Cedex / France
Tel.: (011) 33 1 45 37 57 42   **Fax:** (011) 33 1 45 37 58 46

BASIC INFORMATION

Country: France
Industry: Health and personal care
Investment thesis: Third largest pharmaceutical company in France; 56% owned by L'Oréal

Market capitalization: $4.98 billion
Share status: Foreign shares trade OTC

COMPANY GRADING BOX

Growth Categories		Quality of Management	
Revenue Growth	20	Return on Equity	5
Operating Income Growth	20	**Risk**	
Earnings per Share Growth	20	Long-Term Debt/Total Capital	10
Share Price Growth	15	**Total QM&R (maximum 20)**	**15**
Total Growth (maximum 80)	**75**	**FINAL GRADE**	**90**

BACKGROUND

If you have already read about L'Oréal (see page 201), you know something about Synthelabo. This twenty-seven-year-old pharmaceutical company, 56% owned by L'Oréal, came into being when two older French companies, founded in 1834 and 1899 respectively, merged. It is the third largest drug company in France, a specialized player in an industry of global giants. Product development is focused on three key areas: the central nervous system, the cardiovascular system, and internal medicine (urology, gastroenterology, and allergy). And the company's marketing efforts are focused on seven key products, which represent 52% of its pharmaceutical sales. Among them are drugs for angina pectoris and hypertension, insomnia (including the world's leading hypnotic), schizophrenia, and "agitation and aggressiveness." Fifteen percent of sales, overall nearly $2 billion in 1996, are plowed back into Synthelabo's research efforts. Management has said it will bring out one new drug a year.

In 1995 Synthelabo also moved into the business of generic drugs when it bought Germany-based Lichtenstein Pharmazeutica and France-based Irex. While Germany is Europe's largest generic drug market, in France the generic drug market is only beginning and represents tremendous growth potential. Synthelabo has also begun expanding its over-the-counter drug business throughout Europe.

In terms of its international presence, Synthelabo has subsidiaries all over Europe and joint ventures in Japan and the United States. About 63% of its revenues are now generated outside France. And management is building on existing businesses in Africa, Asia, and Latin America.

COMPANY STATEMENT (from the 1996 annual report)

"In 1996, Synthelabo once again progressed much faster than the pharmaceutical market, while at the same time bringing its research technologies up to the highest levels and posting further profit growth.

"Growth was particularly strong outside France, notably the rest of Europe and the United States. As in previous years, it was based on our policy of specializing in therapeutic fields, the quality of our products, and the efficiency of our European subsidiaries and of the American joint venture Lorex Pharmaceuticals. We were also active on the acquisitions front, with the strengthening of our operations in Germany and Switzerland and the setting up of new joint ventures in Thailand and Taiwan. . . . The foundations of future growth have been laid, with the full effect of the acquisitions made in 1996 due to feed through in 1997. . . .

"The future of the Group will be built on its strong position in Europe, the success of its international expansion strategy, the growth potential of existing products and the introduction of innovative products. Organic growth will be complemented by acquisitions as well as licensing agreements for Europe in our specialist fields. We are therefore convinced that Synthelabo will continue to grow faster than the market."

PERFORMANCE

Synthelabo gets high marks for growth, losing only a few points for consistency of share price performance (even so, the share price increased at a compound annual rate of 24%). In every other growth category, Synthelabo got a perfect score. Revenues in dollars, EPS, and EBDIT all increased in nine of the last ten years. Revenues showed compound annual growth of 18%, and both EPS in dollars and operating income showed compound annual growth of about 23%. Synthelabo also raised its dividend every year over the last ten years, from $0.25 in 1986 to $1.04 in 1996. Finally, the long-term debt to total capital ratio was a very comfortable 8% in 1996 and averaged 12% for the decade. The company lost a few points in the ROE category, with an average ROE of 13%; however, in 1996 ROE was just under 18%.

If you had invested $10,000 in Synthelabo at the end of 1986, you would have bought around 150 shares at $13 each. There was a five-for-one stock split in July 1993. By the end of 1996, you would have had about 770 shares worth an estimated $84,600. You would also have received dividend payments worth around $4,800.

SYNTHELABO

Ticker Symbol and Exchange: SYTBF—OTC   **SEDOL Code: 4872896**

OPERATING AND PER SHARE DATA
(in millions of French francs and francs per share)

	1986	1987	1988	1989	1990	1991	1992	1993	1994	1995	1996	CAGR
Sales	2,594	2,621	2,984	2,919	3,331	3,455	6,323	7,205	8,120	9,318	10,425	14.9%
EBDIT	305	318	355	382	490	488	941	1,124	1,269	1,549	1,881	20.0%
Net Profit	66	94	70	100	130	184	456	561	680	794	951	30.6%
EPS	3.16	4.41	3.23	4.56	5.81	8.12	9.45	11.62	14.09	16.44	19.69	20.1%
DPS	1.60	1.80	1.90	2.10	2.34	2.60	2.80	3.24	3.74	4.34	5.32	12.8%

OPERATING AND PER SHARE DATA
(in millions of U.S. dollars and dollars per share)

	1986	1987	1988	1989	1990	1991	1992	1993	1994	1995	1996	CAGR
Sales	403	437	501	458	612	613	1,195	1,273	1,466	1,868	2,040	17.6%
EBDIT	47.4	52.9	59.5	60.0	90.1	86.5	178.0	198.6	229.1	310.6	368.1	22.8%
Net Profit	10.2	15.6	11.7	15.7	23.9	32.7	86.2	99.2	122.8	159.2	186.0	33.6%
EPS	0.49	0.74	0.54	0.72	1.07	1.44	1.79	2.05	2.54	3.30	3.85	22.9%
DPS	0.25	0.30	0.32	0.33	0.43	0.46	0.53	0.57	0.68	0.87	1.04	15.4%

KEY RATIOS

	1986	1987	1988	1989	1990	1991	1992	1993	1994	1995	1996	AVG
EBDIT Margin	11.8%	12.1%	11.9%	13.1%	14.7%	14.1%	14.9%	15.6%	15.6%	16.6%	18.0%	14.4%
ROE	7.6%	10.1%	7.1%	8.9%	10.8%	12.0%	14.7%	16.4%	17.6%	19.7%	17.5%	13.0%
LT Debt/Total Cap	24.0%	24.1%	18.7%	17.3%	14.5%	10.5%	5.7%	3.6%	2.5%	1.8%	8.1%	11.9%
P/E (Projected)	19.0	15.8	18.9	14.8	14.2	20.1	20.0	16.6	13.1	15.6	24.8	17.5

STOCK PRICE CHART
(fiscal year-end closing price, in U.S. dollars, adjusted for capital changes)

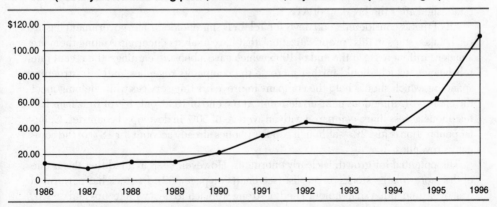

Note: Figures in U.S. dollars are translated from local currency using average exchange rates.

TELEBRAS (TBR—NYSE)

Address: SAS Quadra 6, Andar 6 / 70313 Brasilia-DF / Brazil
Tel.: (011) 55 61 415 2955   **Fax:** (011) 55 61 322 4153   **Web site:** http://www.telebras.com.br

BASIC INFORMATION

Country: Brazil
Industry: Telecommunications services
Investment thesis: Primary supplier of telecommunications services in Brazil

Market capitalization: $31.99 billion
Share status: ADRs trade on NYSE

COMPANY GRADING BOX

Growth Categories		Quality of Management	
Revenue Growth	20	Return on Equity	0
Operating Income Growth	20	**Risk**	
Earnings per Share Growth	15	Long-Term Debt/Total Capital	10
Share Price Growth	15	**Total QM&R (maximum 20)**	10
Total Growth (maximum 80)	70	**FINAL GRADE**	80

BACKGROUND

Telebras, the primary supplier of telecommunications service in Brazil, was the largest publicly traded company in Latin America as of the end of 1996, with a market capitalization of more than $23 billion. It is also a company in transition. During the summer of 1995, the Brazilian constitution was reformed to pave the way for the privatization and breakup of Telebras, actually a holding company for the country's regional operating systems. A few months later, the Brazilian government announced a massive reform program aimed at overhauling the company: upgrading the systems, bringing in greater foreign investment, moving toward privatization, and introducing a competitive bidding process in the granting of concessions. Since then, steps have been taken to open the country's cellular market to competition and to rebalance the tariff structure, allowing the cost of local service to rise and long-distance service to fall to a more reasonable level (high long-distance rates had been used to subsidize low local rates).

Assuming that Brazil's government continues along the path already established, within the next few years Telebras shareholders are likely to wind up holding shares in each of the regional companies, dubbed the "Baby Brases"—named after the Baby Bells established after the breakup of AT&T.

All of that is considered good news for Telebras shareholders. The government has already taken steps in this "preprivatization" that have analysts cheering. Among them are a major tariff increase at the end of 1995, which gave a boost to earnings; the recent rate rebalancing, which should further increase the company's revenues; and infrastructure spending, which should help the company improve existing services while helping meet the country's tremendous pent-up demand. At the end of 1996, only 9% of Brazilians had telephone access lines, compared with an average of 50% in developed countries. Cellular penetration is just 2%—although cellular phones already account for 18% of the company's revenues.

The potential for growth is clearly enormous. However, keep in mind that this is one of the more volatile stocks on our list (see charts on page 332). Its stock has performed well over time, but a shareholder needs a strong stomach to deal with its ups and downs.

COMPANY STATEMENT (from the 1995 annual report on Form 20-F)

"Telebras, through its 28 operating subsidiaries, is the primary supplier of public telecommunications services in Brazil. At December 31, 1995, Telebras owned approximately 94% of all public exchanges and approximately 91% of the nationwide network of local telephone lines. Through its subsidiary, Empresa Brasileira de Telecomunicaçãos S.A. Embratel, Telebras owns and operates all of the inter-state and international telephone transmission facilities in Brazil. Through the other 27 subsidiaries, Telebras is the primary provider of intra-state service. (Telebras and its 28 operating subsidiaries are referred to collectively herein as the "Telebras System"). The Telebras System also provides telephone-related services such as data transmission, cellular mobile telephone service, and sound, image videotext, telex and telegraph transmission. Telebras is the second largest company in Brazil. . . .

"At December 31, 1995, the Brazilian telephone system comprised 14.8 million installed access lines and 13.4 million access lines in service. Virtually all such installed lines were connected to automatic exchanges, including 46.7% connected to digital exchanges. At December 31, 1995, Brazil had approximately 9.3 access lines in service per 100 inhabitants."

PERFORMANCE

Telebras got high marks for share price performance (not consistency!), revenue growth, and a low long-term debt to total capital ratio, compiling a total score of 80 points in our grading system. Over the last five years, the share price saw compound annual growth of 40%. Revenues dipped a little in 1991 but have been rising dramatically ever since, with compound annual growth of almost 21%. EBDIT followed the same pattern, with compound annual growth of 24%. In terms of risk, the long-term debt to total capital ratio averaged a moderate 11% and was 7% in 1996. ROE averaged just 6% for the seven-year period but was a much improved 12% in 1996. EP/ADR and dividend growth were inconsistent but impressive, with compound annual growth of 22% and 43% respectively.

If you had invested $10,000 in Telebras at the end of 1989, you would have purchased around 1,350 ADRs at about $7.25 each (excluding commissions). During the following seven-year period, there was a 2.4-for-100 rights issue. By the end of 1996, you would have had around 1,400 shares worth an estimated $106,800. You would also have received dividend payments of around $7,600.

TELEBRAS

Ticker Symbol and Exchange: TBR—NYSE   **CUSIP No.: 879287100**

OPERATING AND PER SHARE DATA
(in millions of U.S. dollars and dollars per ADR)

	1986	1987	1988	1989	1990	1991	1992	1993	1994	1995	1996	CAGR
Net Revenues	N/A	N/A	N/A	N/A	3,920	3,442	4,696	5,131	7,743	8,884	12,020	20.5%
EBDIT	N/A	N/A	N/A	N/A	1,997	1,566	2,267	2,874	3,502	4,786	7,211	23.9%
Net Income	N/A	N/A	N/A	N/A	582	(155)	298	1,141	657	835	2,653	28.8%
EP/ADR	N/A	N/A	N/A	N/A	2.56	(0.63)	1.08	4.03	2.25	2.70	8.27	21.6%
DP/ADR	N/A	N/A	N/A	N/A	0.21	0.16	1.40	0.26	0.49	1.59	1.81	43.2%

KEY RATIOS

	1986	1987	1988	1989	1990	1991	1992	1993	1994	1995	1996	AVG
EBDIT Margin	N/A	N/A	N/A	N/A	50.9%	45.5%	48.3%	56.0%	45.2%	53.9%	60.0%	51.4%
ROE	N/A	N/A	N/A	N/A	11.2%	−1.6%	2.3%	9.2%	3.4%	3.6%	11.5%	5.7%
LT Debt/Total Cap	N/A	N/A	N/A	N/A	7.3%	17.0%	16.1%	10.8%	9.5%	7.2%	7.2%	10.7%
P/E (Projected)	N/A	N/A	N/A	2.8	(2.9)	18.4	4.2	15.1	16.6	5.7	7.5	9.2

STOCK PRICE CHART
(fiscal year-end closing price, in U.S. dollars, adjusted for capital changes)

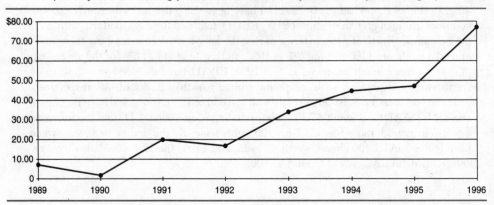

Note: Historically, hyperinflation in Brazil distorts local currency results; thus figures are quoted in U.S. dollars only.

TELECOM ITALIA (TLERF—OTC)

Address: 189 Via Flaminia / 00196 Rome / Italy
Tel.: (011) 39 6 3600 1273   **Fax:** (011) 39 6 3688 2263   **Web site:** http://www.telecomitalia.it

BASIC INFORMATION

Country: Italy
Industry: Telecommunications services
Investment thesis: Sixth largest telecommunications service provider in the world

Market capitalization: $20.86 billion
Share status: Foreign shares trade OTC

COMPANY GRADING BOX

Growth Categories		Quality of Management	
Revenue Growth	15	Return on Equity	0
Operating Income Growth	10	**Risk**	
Earnings per Share Growth	15	Long-Term Debt/Total Capital	0
Share Price Growth	10	**Total QM&R (maximum 20)**	0
Total Growth (maximum 80)	50	**FINAL GRADE**	50

BACKGROUND

In 1994 Telecom Italia—majority owned by Italy's STET Group—brought five Italian telecommunications companies under one name to form the sixth largest telecommunications company in the world. It covers every corner of Italy, has more than 86,000 employees, and serves 25 million customers. The emphasis has been on leading-edge technology, on customer service and on new product development that is responsive to consumers. The synergies between the five formerly independent companies has led to tremendous efficiencies of scale, as well as a profitable pooling of resources. Although Telecom Italia will face competition in the traditional voice-call business beginning in 1998, it has already dealt with competition in its other businesses. The challenge remains, but Telecom Italia has been bracing itself.

Like every successful telecommunications company, Telecom Italia pushes hard to stay ahead of the technological curve. At the end of 1996, more than 75% of Telecom Italia's networks were digitized, a far higher percentage than that achieved in many other countries. And all those lines have access to Telecom Italia's lucrative "value-added" services. Among the services currently available: national and international telephone credit cards, upgraded public telecommunications systems, video phones, centralized answering service, in-flight phones, and Telecom-On-Line for Internet access. Then there are the targeted business services, another important source of new business for Telecom Italia, including network management, virtual private network services, video communication services, and high speed dedicated networks.

Company management has said the ratio between telecommunications usage and gross domestic product in Italy lags far behind that for the rest of Europe, a fact that bodes well for the company's growth prospects. Internationally Telecom Italia has set up a subsidiary, Tele-Media International, with more than eighty offices outside Italy, to service multinational clients. In addition, Telecom Italia has an interest in Cuba's telecommunications operation, and won the competitive bidding for the privatization of Bolivian telecommunications. It also has operating responsibility for Telecom Argentina and Impsat, investments held by its parent company.

COMPANY STATEMENT (from the 1995 annual report)

"The Vision:

- To be a global operator of telecommunications services.
- To be a Company that is process-oriented, capable of achieving system-wide efficiency by constantly improving each individual corporate process with the goal of providing maximum satisfaction to internal and external end customers; integrated, capable of pursuing its objectives through synergy, teamwork, and simultaneous action; differentiated, able to provide specific responses for different market segments and individual customers; with a high level of capability, to ensure that the solution of each problem is based on outstanding knowledge, experience and skills.

"The Values:

- Competitiveness: We measure ourselves against the best and strive for excellence.
- Integration with our customers: We invest to gain in-depth understanding of the needs of our customers, whose satisfaction is the measure of our success.
- Skill: Our competitiveness stems from the effective and integrated management of our skills.
- Speed: The ability to respond promptly at all levels is essential.

"The Mission:

- To maintain and strengthen our leadership in the domestic market.
- To attain a significant position in the international market.
- To improve our ability to generate earnings and cash flow.

PERFORMANCE

Telecom Italia received an overall score of 50 in our grading system, with poor performance in the 1980s masking the company's excellent performance since 1993, in the wake of a restructuring. In dollars, revenues, EBDIT and EPS increased in each of the last three years, after stagnating for much of the previous period. Even so, for the ten-year period, revenues increased at a compound annual rate of 9%, EBDIT increased at a compound annual rate of 10%, and EPS increased at a compound annual rate of 19%. ROE also showed steady improvement, from a low of 4% in 1990 to a high of 9% in 1996. And the ratio of long-term debt to total capital steadily declined, from a high of 53% in 1992 to a low of 34% in 1996. Share price performance in dollars also started picking up in 1992, and averaged 18% for the ten-year period. One important feature of Telecom Italia, despite the slow growth years: the company maintained a very high dividend payout ratio of 56% for the decade, rewarding investors with a good source of income.

If you had invested $10,000 in Telecom Italia at the end of 1986, you would have purchased around 5,000 shares at about $19.25 each (excluding commissions). During the following ten-year period, there was a one-for-ten bonus issue in February 1990, a two-for-one stock split in February 1990, a four-for-25 rights issue in June 1991, a 13-for-100 rights issue in May 1995, and a spin-off in July 1995. By the end of 1996, you would have had approximately 20,800 shares worth an estimated $53,000. You would also have received dividend payments of around $10,000.

TELECOM ITALIA

Ticker Symbol and Exchange: TLERF—OTC

SEDOL Code: 4811565

OPERATING AND PER SHARE DATA
(in billions of Italian lira and lira per share)

	1986	1987	1988	1989	1990	1991	1992	1993	1994	1995	1996	CAGR
Sales	10,720	12,033	13,376	14,882	16,720	19,453	20,907	23,404	29,162	28,328	29,376	10.6%
EBDIT	5,142	6,018	6,624	7,031	7,750	9,249	9,702	11,294	14,165	14,556	15,415	11.6%
Net Profit	255	489	496	471	489	675	555	669	1,517	1,827	2,119	23.6%
EPS	38.25	67.31	68.23	64.83	53.79	64.79	53.23	58.29	101.35	222.64	258.28	21.0%
DPS	32.76	32.76	32.76	16.38	35.98	39.30	39.30	46.58	57.54	120.00	125.00	14.3%

OPERATING AND PER SHARE DATA
(in millions of U.S. dollars and dollars per share)

	1986	1987	1988	1989	1990	1991	1992	1993	1994	1995	1996	CAGR
Sales	8,006	10,373	10,258	11,746	14,875	16,930	14,203	13,647	18,091	17,839	19,162	9.1%
EBDIT	3,840	5,188	5,080	5,549	6,895	8,050	6,591	6,586	8,787	9,166	10,055	10.1%
Net Profit	190	422	380	372	435	587	377	390	941	1,150	1,382	21.9%
EPS	0.03	0.06	0.05	0.05	0.05	0.06	0.04	0.03	0.06	0.14	0.17	19.4%
DPS	0.02	0.03	0.03	0.01	0.03	0.03	0.03	0.03	0.04	0.08	0.08	12.8%

KEY RATIOS

	1986	1987	1988	1989	1990	1991	1992	1993	1994	1995	1996	AVG
EBDIT Margin	48.0%	50.0%	49.5%	47.2%	46.4%	47.5%	46.4%	48.3%	48.6%	51.4%	52.5%	48.7%
ROE	2.7%	5.0%	4.9%	4.5%	4.2%	5.1%	4.2%	4.6%	7.3%	8.0%	9.4%	5.4%
LT Debt/Total Cap	52.9%	52.6%	51.4%	52.3%	52.7%	48.3%	52.9%	50.9%	40.9%	40.3%	34.2%	48.1%
P/E (Projected)	9.6	6.4	10.4	14.6	9.4	13.4	13.3	19.4	10.4	9.5	13.9	11.8

STOCK PRICE CHART
(fiscal year-end closing price, in U.S. dollars, adjusted for capital changes)

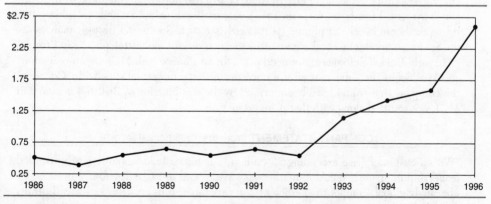

Note: Figures in U.S. dollars are translated from local currency using year-end exchange rates.

TELEFÓNICA DE ESPAÑA (TEF—NYSE)

Address: General Perón 38, Planta 1 / Edificio Master's 11 / 28020 Madrid / Spain
Tel.: (011) 34 1 556 8285 **Fax:** (011) 34 1 520 335 **Web site:** http://www.telephonica.es

BASIC INFORMATION

Country: Spain **Market capitalization:** $24.1 billion
Industry: Telecommunications services **Share status:** ADRs trade on NYSE
Investment thesis: Spain's dominant telecommunications company; extensive holdings in Latin America

COMPANY GRADING BOX

Growth Categories		Quality of Management	
Revenue Growth	20	Return on Equity	0
Operating Income Growth	20	**Risk**	
Earnings per Share Growth	15	Long-Term Debt/Total Capital	0
Share Price Growth	5	**Total QM&R (maximum 20)**	0
Total Growth (maximum 80)	60	**FINAL GRADE**	60

BACKGROUND

Telefónica de España is not just the largest telecommunications company in Spain (and, until recently, a monopoly), it is also the largest company in Spain, with a market capitalization of $24.1 billion and 1996 revenues of $15 billion. Of course, the era of deregulation has made business a bit tougher, but so far Telefónica de España's management has risen to the challenge. And when the Spanish government sold its remaining 21% stake in a public offering in February 1997, geared to the domestic market, it became the first widely held stock on the *bolsa*.

This is a company that reinvented itself with astonishing speed. Through 1992, it was considered a model of a telecommunications monopoly mired in bureaucracy. New management restructured and looked for growth prospects, including overseas expansion. Telefónica's growth prospects today? In the basic telephone business (now a duopoly, the market will be open at the end of 1999), there is tremendous potential for cost reductions and margin expansion. In its international business, Telefónica has put together stakes in companies in some of the fastest-growing telecommunications markets in the world, including Argentina, Chile, and Peru. In 1996, 17% of revenues were generated by the company's overseas businesses, up from 14% a year earlier. Finally, in mobile telephony, it is riding the boom in cellular phones (particularly strong in Southern Europe); analysts say the Spanish market is one of the most attractive markets for mobile telephones in Europe.

In early 1998, Telefónica announced plans for an alliance with MCI Communications and Worldcom Inc., one year after a once-promising strategic alliance with "Concert," the company that would have been formed by the combination of British Telecom and MCI, was scuttled along with that planned merger.

COMPANY STATEMENT (from the 1996 annual report)

"With a customer base exceeding 23 million, Telefónica holds a position of unrivalled leadership in Spanish-speaking markets. . . . We intend to make Telefónica become increasingly global, competitive, efficient and profitable, thus ensuring enhanced profits for shareholders.

"Our strategic objective, "Telefónica, a global operator," sets forth very positively our determination vis-à-vis a newly competitive telecommunications environment. As undisputed leader of Spanish-speaking markets, Telefónica is solidly positioned to face the challenge posed by the progressive liberalization of the telecommunications sector. We view the creation of regulatory authorities as a positive move to ensure a fair and equitable competitive environment which safeguards consumer interests. Our ability to compete has been put to the test and we are convinced of our ability to meet client needs in a broader marketplace.

"This new dynamism is fully compatible with our tradition of public service, a vocation which has strong roots in Telefónica's corporate culture. It takes the form of constant attention to client needs and demands, and our contribution to the economic development and technological advancement of our country."

PERFORMANCE

It is difficult to evaluate Telefónica over a ten-year period because the company has changed so much—with recent years being the key to its categorization as a growth company. Even so, Telefónica managed to garner 60 points with its ten-year history, enough to make it onto our list. In dollars, revenues and EBDIT increased in eight of the last ten years, with compound annual growth of 16% and 15%, respectively. EP/ADR increased in nine of the last ten years, with compound annual growth of 14%. Telefónica lost points for ROE, which averaged only 6%, and the long-term debt to capital ratio, which averaged 44%—although this is reasonable enough for a national telephone company. ADR price performance has been so-so compared with that of many of the other companies in this book, with the ADR price increasing at a compound annual rate of 13% over the last ten years; however, shareholders doubled their money in the last two years. They also received a nice dividend, as Telefónica maintained a payout ratio of 50 to 60% of earnings over the last five years.

If you had invested $10,000 in Telefónica de España at the end of 1986, you would have purchased around 450 ADRs (or ADR equivalents) at about $21.50 (excluding commissions). Over the next ten years, there were a number of minor changes to the capital structure. By the end of 1996, you would have had around 490 ADRs worth an estimated $33,900. You would also have received dividend payments of around $8,500.

TELEFÓNICA DE ESPAÑA

Ticker Symbol and Exchange: TEF—NYSE   **CUSIP No.: 879382208**

OPERATING AND PER SHARE DATA
(in billions of Spanish pesetas and pesetas per share)

	1986	1987	1988	1989	1990	1991	1992	1993	1994	1995	1996	CAGR
Sales	468	541	613	711	852	1,049	1,209	1,297	1,579	1,741	2,006	15.7%
EBDIT	271	305	349	398	475	607	690	744	887	1,011	1,102	15.1%
Net Profit	39	44	52	64	72	91	113	96	113	133	161	15.2%
EPS	45.16	51.24	56.07	69.19	77.45	98.49	121.79	102.55	119.79	141.70	171.04	14.2%
DPS	52.20	53.85	54.95	55.00	55.00	59.00	61.00	62.00	66.00	76.00	89.00	5.5%

OPERATING AND PER SHARE DATA
(in millions of U.S. dollars and dollars per ADR)

	1986	1987	1988	1989	1990	1991	1992	1993	1994	1995	1996	CAGR
Sales	3,567	5,033	5,410	6,496	8,921	10,837	10,499	9,070	11,994	14,317	15,301	15.7%
EBDIT	2,063	2,833	3,082	3,635	4,978	6,270	5,994	5,203	6,737	8,317	8,407	15.1%
Net Profit	299	405	456	585	752	943	980	674	855	1,095	1,226	15.2%
EP/ADR	1.03	1.43	1.48	1.90	2.43	3.05	3.17	2.15	2.73	3.50	3.91	14.3%
DP/ADR	1.19	1.50	1.45	1.51	1.73	1.83	1.59	1.30	1.50	1.88	2.04	5.5%

KEY RATIOS

	1986	1987	1988	1989	1990	1991	1992	1993	1994	1995	1996	AVG
EBDIT Margin	57.8%	56.3%	57.0%	56.0%	55.8%	57.9%	57.1%	57.4%	56.2%	58.1%	54.9%	56.8%
ROE	3.8%	3.8%	4.2%	5.1%	5.5%	6.9%	7.8%	6.6%	7.6%	8.9%	8.6%	6.3%
LT Debt/Total Cap	36.7%	35.9%	36.2%	39.5%	42.1%	50.1%	48.7%	48.4%	48.5%	46.5%	46.3%	43.5%
P/E (Projected)	17.4	18.4	12.8	11.5	8.5	10.1	11.1	15.6	11.0	9.8	14.7	12.4

STOCK PRICE CHART
(fiscal year-end closing price, in U.S. dollars, adjusted for capital changes)

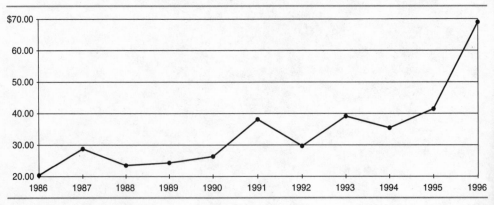

Notes: 1986 and 1987 year-end share prices are average of high and low. Figures in U.S. dollars are translated from local currency using year-end exchange rates.

TELECOM NEW ZEALAND (NZT—NYSE)

Address: 68 Jervois Quay / P.O. Box 570 / Wellington / New Zealand
Tel.: (011) 64 4 801 9000   **Fax:** (011) 64 4 473 6961   **Web site:** investor.infor@telecom.co.nz
or
Address: Investor Relations Department / Bank of New York/ 101 Barclay Street / New York, NY 10286
Tel.: (800) 524-4458

BASIC INFORMATION

Country: New Zealand
Industry: Telecommunications services
Investment thesis: Dominant telecommunications company in New Zealand

Market capitalization: $8.54 billion
Share status: ADRs trade on NYSE

COMPANY GRADING BOX

Growth Categories		Quality of Management	
Revenue Growth	10	Return on Equity	10
Operating Income Growth	10	**Risk**	
Earnings per Share Growth	20	Long-Term Debt/Total Capital	5
Share Price Growth	20	**Total QM&R (maximum 20)**	15
Total Growth (maximum 80)	60	**FINAL GRADE**	75

BACKGROUND

Telecom New Zealand, publicly traded since 1993, increased its operating revenues by 12.2% in 1996 and its net earnings by 15.6%, impressive growth for a telephone utility. But this company, with a market capitalization of $8.5 billion and 1996 revenues of around $2.2 billion, is hardly anyone's idea of a stodgy phone company. Not only is it New Zealand's primary basic phone service provider, it has involved itself in almost every part of the ongoing telecommunications revolution.

High on its priority list are the "value-added" phone services for private and corporate use—everything from voice mail and caller identification to international video conferencing and virtual private networks. New Zealand Telecom is also involved with mobile phones, the Internet, cable television, and telecommunications equipment. One subsidiary, Netway, provides outsourcing services to companies looking to contract out computer and telephone networks. Another is rolling out enhanced cable television services.

Telecom's two principal operating groups are Telecom Network, which operates and develops the company's fixed-line and mobile networks, and Telecom Services, which markets and sells those products and services. In 1996 about 34% of New Zealand Telecom's revenues were generated by its local services; 18% by national calls; 18% by international calls; and just over 29% by its various other activities. Telecom New Zealand's cellular network covers an area that includes about 96% of the population—though to date only about 11% of New Zealand's population has cellular phones; its DataLink service allows customers to send and receive faxes over the cellular network; its paging services are available to 95% of the population; and it has launched personal communications service (PCS), a new cellular technology growing around the world. PCS had its Southern Hemisphere debut in New Zealand.

In 1990 two U.S. Baby Bells, Ameritech and Bell Atlantic, bought Telecom New Zealand from New Zealand's government for $2.46 billion on condition they agreed to reduce their stake to under 49.9% by 1993. The following year, the two phone companies sold 31% of Telecom New Zealand to the public in an international public offering. They then sold another 19% in private deals. They remained major shareholders through 1997.

COMPANY STATEMENT (from the 1996 annual report)

"Telecom's goal is to be one of the best performing telecommunications companies in the world. The creation of value for shareholders is our ultimate measure of progress towards that goal. To add value for shareholders we must grow operating revenues and earnings while managing Telecom's assets with increased efficiency. For revenue and earnings growth we must provide Telecom services and products which are valuable to customers today and into the future. To ensure our business has a strong growth orientation we must be committed to innovation. In 1995–1996 Telecom developed innovative services for an everchanging marketplace while achieving growth in revenues, earnings and shareholder value.

"Ultimately, we recognize that success is determined by how well we perform in markets for Telecom services, now and into the future. Value-adding growth comes through meeting and exceeding the expectations of customers with services of real value to their working and personal lives. It comes also through market leadership with valuable, new services."

PERFORMANCE

Over the last nine years, New Zealand Telecom performed reasonably well in terms of revenues and operating income and excellently in terms of earnings and ADR price growth. Overall, the company received a total of 75 points in our grading system. Revenues grew by a steady 6% in dollar terms while consistent cost cutting and emphasis on value-added services helped EBDIT to grow at a compound rate of 7.5%. While other companies in our study had stronger growth in these two areas, consistently higher operating income growth led to a rising operating margin, which increased from 43% to 50% during this period, a signal that management was successful in improving profitability at the company. EP/ADR grew at a compound rate of nearly 17% per annum, rising from $0.83 in 1988 to $3.31 by 1997. ROE averaged 18.5%, a relatively high rate of return for a telephone company, while the long-term debt to total capital ratio remained moderate for the industry at 43% following announced restructuring and buyback programs.

Shareholders saw this strong operating performance rewarded by rising share prices. New Zealand Telecom's ADR price increased from a low of $21.75 in 1992 (when the company went public) to a high of $72.28 in 1997. Dividends increased from $1.14 to $4.30 during this period.

If you had invested $10,000 in New Zealand Telecom in March 1992, you would have purchased around 460 ADRs at about $21.75 each. During the following four years, the company made no significant changes to its capital structure. By March 1997, you would still have had 460 ADRs, but their value would have risen to an estimated $33,000. You would also have received about $6,700 in dividend payments.

TELECOM NEW ZEALAND

Ticker Symbol and Exchange: NZT—NYSE   **CUSIP No.: 879278208**

OPERATING AND PER SHARE DATA
(in millions of New Zealand dollars and dollars per share)

	Mar 87	Mar 88	Mar 89	Mar 90	Mar 91	Mar 92	Mar 93	Mar 94	Mar 95	Mar 96	Mar 97	CAGR
Sales	N/A	1,970	2,158	2,292	2,432	2,568	2,474	2,497	2,841	3,187	3,107	5.2%
EBDIT	N/A	850	925	946	1,074	1,209	797	1,358	1,526	1,683	1,537	6.8%
Net Profit	N/A	185	293	257	332	402	108	528	620	718	582	13.6%
EPS	N/A	0.08	0.12	0.11	0.14	0.17	0.05	0.23	0.33	0.38	0.30	15.8%
DPS	N/A	0.03	0.08	0.08	0.09	0.13	0.16	0.23	0.30	0.35	0.39	33.0%

OPERATING AND PER SHARE DATA
(in millions of U.S. dollars and dollars per ADR)

	Mar 87	Mar 88	Mar 89	Mar 90	Mar 91	Mar 92	Mar 93	Mar 94	Mar 95	Mar 96	Mar 97	CAGR
Sales	N/A	1,285	1,332	1,333	1,431	1,403	1,323	1,402	1,861	2,183	2,143	5.8%
EBDIT	N/A	554	571	550	632	661	426	763	999	1,153	1,060	7.5%
Net Profit	N/A	120	181	150	195	220	58	296	406	492	401	14.3%
EP/ADR	N/A	0.83	1.19	1.02	1.32	1.49	0.43	2.07	3.46	4.16	3.31	16.5%
DP/ADR	N/A	0.31	0.79	0.74	0.85	1.14	1.37	2.07	3.14	3.84	4.30	33.8%

KEY RATIOS

	Mar 87	Mar 88	Mar 89	Mar 90	Mar 91	Mar 92	Mar 93	Mar 94	Mar 95	Mar 96	Mar 97	AVG
EBDIT Margin	N/A	43.1%	42.8%	41.3%	44.2%	47.1%	32.2%	54.4%	53.7%	52.8%	49.5%	46.1%
ROE	N/A	7.8%	12.1%	10.4%	12.8%	14.9%	4.4%	23.6%	30.1%	33.5%	35.4%	18.5%
LT Debt/Total Cap	N/A	19.5%	23.2%	24.9%	29.2%	27.0%	24.6%	27.0%	23.5%	28.0%	42.7%	26.9%
P/E (Projected)	N/A	N/A	N/A	N/A	N/A	50.0	14.3	15.5	15.2	16.1	14.2	20.9

STOCK PRICE CHART
(fiscal year-end closing price, in U.S. dollars, adjusted for capital changes)

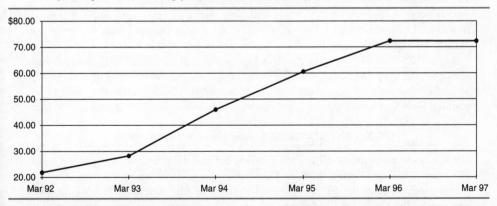

Notes: New Zealand Telecom shares began trading publicly in 1992. Figures in U.S. dollars are translated from local currency using year-end exchange rates.

TEVA (TEVIY—NASDAQ)

Address: 5 Basel Street / P.O. Box 3190 / Petach Tikva / Israel
Tel.: (011) 972 3 926 7267   **Fax:** (011) 972 3 923 4050

BASIC INFORMATION

Country: Israel
Industry: Health and personal care
Investment thesis: Manufacturer of multiple sclerosis drug Copaxone; a leading generic drug company

Market capitalization: $3.54 billion
Share status: ADRs trade on NASDAQ

COMPANY GRADING BOX

Growth Categories		Quality of Management	
Revenue Growth	20	Return on Equity	5
Operating Income Growth	20	**Risk**	
Earnings per Share Growth	20	Long-Term Debt/Total Capital	10
Share Price Growth	20	**Total QM&R (maximum 20)**	15
Total Growth (maximum 80)	80	**FINAL GRADE**	95

BACKGROUND

With a major blockbuster drug now being marketed in the United States, Israel-based Teva Pharmaceuticals has been in a lot of headlines recently. In December 1996 Teva received U.S. FDA approval to market the drug Copaxone, used for the treatment of multiple sclerosis. It has been under development since 1987, was launched in the United States in April 1997, and—according to analysts—could bring Teva as much as $300 million in additional revenues within three years.

Of course, there is a lot more to Teva than Copaxone. Teva is among the three largest manufacturers of generic drugs in the United States—with about 8% of the U.S. market—and is expected to be a prime beneficiary of efforts to bring down health care costs in this country. It also is the largest drug company in Israel (though the United States accounts for a larger share of Teva's revenues), selling drugs it manufactures under license from other companies, as well as drugs that are no longer covered by patents. Its networks serve Israel's drugstores, health care services, and hospitals. Teva Pharmaceuticals also has subsidiaries in Germany, Holland, Italy, the United Kingdom, and Hungary, as well as coordinating offices in France. And Teva has begun operating in the Far East, Russia, and Argentina. Altogether, brand-name and generic pharmaceuticals account for close to 80% of Teva's sales.

As for the rest of the company . . . Bulk Pharmaceutical Chemicals (BPC), which supplies chemicals to manufacturers of generic drugs, accounted for 13% of revenues in 1996; hospital supplies accounted for 9% of revenues; Israeli veterinary products accounted for 4% of revenues; and yeast products accounted for 2% of revenues.

COMPANY STATEMENT (from the 1996 annual report)

"1996 was a momentous year for Teva. Looking beyond the significantly improved financial results achieved during the year, the importance of 1996 lies in the marketing approval received from the FDA at the end of the year for Copaxone, Teva's innovative product for the treatment of Multiple Sclerosis. Teva is entering a new era as a one billion dollar company. In fact, annual sales in the second half of the year already exceeded this new order of magnitude. . . .

"Teva's highest-ever research expenses in 1996 ($90.4 million) were dedicated not only to Copaxone, but also to a number of other innovative projects, at least one of which is expected to develop into a commercial product by the end of the decade. Concurrently with Teva's efforts in innovative research, development and registration, the Company continued the pursuit of its goal of becoming a leading global generic company.

"Teva's overall business strategy has proven itself in the last decade both in sales and in income growth. We fully intend to maintain these growth rates in the coming years. We believe that a combination of innovative products such as Copaxone on the one hand, with a well planned merger and acquisition strategy in the US and in Europe on the other hand, can enable us to maintain this growth rate."

PERFORMANCE

Teva's overall grade of 95 in our grading system reflects the company's consistent impressive growth. Revenues and EBITDA in dollar terms increased in each of the last ten years, with compound annual growth of just over 20% and 22%, respectively. EP/ADR increased in nine of the last ten years, with compound annual growth of 15%. The long-term debt to total capital ratio averaged an acceptable 14%, although it hit 23% in 1996, following the acquisition of Biocraft. ROE averaged 16.6%—very good but not quite high enough for top marks (it reached 21% in 1993 and 1994).

If you had invested $10,000 in Teva in 1986, you would have purchased around 3,100 ADRs at about $3.25 each (fully adjusted for capital changes and excluding commissions). At the end of 1996, you would have had around 3,100 ADRs worth an estimated $157,000. You would also have received dividends of around $5,300.

TEVA

Ticker Symbol and Exchange: TEVIY—NASDAQ   **CUSIP No.: 881624209**

OPERATING AND PER SHARE DATA
(in millions of U.S. dollars and dollars per ADR)

	1987	1988	1989	1990	1991	1992	1993	1994	1995	1995	1996	CAGR
Sales	150	211	268	295	321	396	502	588	668	811	954	20.4%
EBITDA	20.8	31.4	40.6	47.4	49.0	72.8	107.6	130.2	135.8	132.4	153.2	22.1%
Net Income	16.2	12.0	16.1	18.7	23.3	31.7	57.5	71.7	83.8	74.3	88.3	18.5%
EP/ADR	0.35	0.28	0.37	0.39	0.46	0.61	1.07	1.32	1.33	1.22	1.44	15.2%
DP/ADR	0.07	0.07	0.08	0.09	0.09	0.11	0.21	0.26	0.26	0.26	0.28	14.9%

KEY RATIOS

	1987	1988	1989	1990	1991	1992	1993	1994	1995	1995	1996	AVG
EBITDA Margin	14%	15%	15%	16%	15%	18.4%	21.4%	22.2%	20.3%	16.3%	16.1%	19.1%
ROE	18.0%	12.1%	14.1%	15.3%	13.0%	14.6%	21.5%	21.0%	20.8%	15.4%	16.5%	16.6%
LT Debt/Total Cap	14.5%	17.0%	15.0%	12.1%	9.9%	5.6%	16.0%	19.1%	9.2%	16.2%	23.2%	14.3%
P/E (Projected)	11.6	9.2	15.0	12.5	15.4	21.0	22.8	18.2	38.0	32.2	19.3	19.6

STOCK PRICE CHART
(fiscal year-end closing price, in U.S. dollars, adjusted for capital changes)

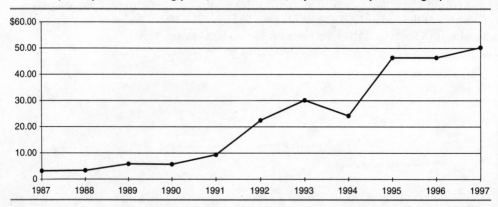

Notes: Teva acquired Biocraft in 1996 with stock. Historical data 1987 to 1995 show Teva's performance prior to the ac-quisition. We repeat 1995 showing results on a pro forma basis, including the effects of Biocraft. 1996 results are for the merged company. The 1995–96 results for the new company exclude merger expenses net of tax. The 1995 results for the old company exclude a $40 million write-off, net of tax.

TOMRA (TMRAY—OTC)

Address: P.O. Box 278 / 1371 Asker / Norway
Tel.: (011) 47 66 78 92 60   **Fax:** (011) 47 66 78 42 52

BASIC INFORMATION

Country: Norway
Industry: Industrial equipment
Investment thesis: Leading producer of machines for recycling cans and bottles

Market capitalization: $728 million
Share status: ADRs trade OTC

COMPANY GRADING BOX

Growth Categories		Quality of Management	
Revenue Growth	20	Return on Equity	10
Operating Income Growth	20	**Risk**	
Earnings per Share Growth	20	Long-Term Debt/Total Capital	5
Share Price Growth	20	**Total QM&R (maximum 20)**	15
Total Growth (maximum 80)	**80**	**FINAL GRADE**	**95**

BACKGROUND

A self-described "green" company, Norway's Tomra manufactures and distributes machines for recycling (or reusing) beverage containers. That means that when you put your old cans and bottles into a Tomra machine, it sorts, shreds, and compacts them (you may or may not get a deposit back, depending on where you are and what you put in). This company has an 80% share of the world market in a growing industry (55% of the market in the United States), with subsidiaries throughout Europe and North America. Among Tomra's major U.S. clients are A&P and Kroger supermarkets. Although it is one of the smallest companies on our list, with a market capitalization of $728 million, it has increased its earnings by 33.2% over the last ten years.

Worldwide key products include: the Tomra 200 Separator for glass and plastic bottles, which returns nonrefundable bottles to the customer; the Tomra 22 Plastic, which compacts or shreds and stores plastic bottles; the Tomra 42 Cans, which does the same for cans; the Tomra 62, which does the same for both cans and bottles . . . and the list goes on. Tomra tailors its machines to its markets and customers and monitors them with Tomra-developed software. The newest Tomra machines are linked by modem to a central computer to make them easier to program and monitor. A "just-in-time" production philosophy means a minimum of inventory sitting around. And direct deliveries to assembly lines means less intermediate storage and working capital.

Tomra was started in 1972 with the invention of the first reverse vending machine—"incorporating electro-optical recognition, a single reception point for all bottle types and a printed receipt for the deposit amount," according to an official company history. As recycling and bottle deposits started to catch on throughout Europe and the United States, Tomra was right there. It still is.

COMPANY STATEMENT (from the 1995 annual report)

"The ability and willingness to establish priorities and work towards long-term objectives is essential to create future growth. A long-term approach is perhaps the most important element in our planning up to the end of the century. In recent years Tomra has devoted considerable resources to:

- R&D, with the development of products for the future, new software solutions and reductions in the cost of existing products.
- Market development, where, for example, this year's breakthrough in Michigan (major new contract) is a result of three years' preparatory work in a new market.
- Organizational development, with quality as a target at all levels—Quality in recruitment processes, in customer relations and in the development of individual employees.
- Investment, the new premises and the acquisition of businesses in our core area are examples of investments to be viewed in a 20-year perspective.
- Further developments of our Corporate Identity. With our new corporate profile and logo, we believe we have created an even better impression of Tomra in relation to our customers and business environment.

"When making investments of a long term nature, it can often be difficult in the short term to evaluate results. Tomra, however, is enjoying a positive trend, with skilled and motivated employees both in Norway and abroad, capable through their professionalism of achieving the targets set. We believe this trend will continue and even be strengthened in the coming years."

PERFORMANCE

Tomra, small by comparison to many of the companies included in this book, received 95 points in our grading system, making it one of our top scorers. Its growth record is impressive, and its shareholders have been well rewarded: Tomra's share price in dollars increased at a compound rate of 40% per annum over the last nine years (of course, nine years ago this was a *very* small company). Revenues in dollars increased in each of the last nine years, recording compound growth of 26%. EBDIT and EP/ADR in dollars increased in eight of the last nine years, with compound annual growth of 33% and 26%, respectively. Tomra did not begin issuing a dividend until 1992, but since then the company has raised it every year. ROE averaged an impressive 24%. The long-term debt to total capital ratio averaged a moderate 27%—higher than some of our companies, but not excessive.

If you had invested $10,000 in Tomra at the end of 1987, you would have purchased around 9,000 ADRs (or ADR equivalents) at about $1.10 each (excluding commissions). During the following nine years, there were a one-for-ten bonus issue in April 1992 and a one-for-two rights issue in December 1993. By the end of 1996, you would have had approximately 13,300 ADRs worth an estimated $200,000. You would also have received dividend payments of around $1,900.

TOMRA

Ticker Symbol and Exchange: TMRAY—OTC   **CUSIP No.: 889905105**

OPERATING AND PER SHARE DATA
(in millions of Norwegian kroner and kroner per share)

	1986	1987	1988	1989	1990	1991	1992	1993	1994	1995	1996	CAGR
Sales	N/A	97	133	157	205	235	262	303	386	501	784	26.1%
EBDIT	N/A	15	25	26	34	35	23	36	64	116	206	33.5%
Net Profit	N/A	7	13	17	21	27	10	19	33	63	104	35.2%
EPS	N/A	0.34	0.66	0.86	1.24	1.45	0.31	0.65	1.00	1.85	2.72	26.0%
DPS	N/A	N/M	N/M	N/M	N/M	N/M	0.10	0.15	0.20	0.25	0.30	31.6%

OPERATING AND PER SHARE DATA
(in millions of U.S. dollars and dollars per ADR)

	1986	1987	1988	1989	1990	1991	1992	1993	1994	1995	1996	CAGR
Sales	N/A	15.6	20.3	23.8	34.9	39.4	37.7	40.2	57.1	79.0	121.4	25.6%
EBDIT	N/A	2.5	3.8	4.0	5.7	5.9	3.3	4.8	9.5	18.3	31.9	33.0%
Net Profit	N/A	1.1	2.0	2.5	3.6	4.5	1.4	2.6	4.9	9.9	16.2	34.7%
EP/ADR	N/A	0.05	0.10	0.13	0.21	0.24	0.04	0.09	0.15	0.29	0.42	25.5%
DP/ADR	N/A	N/M	N/M	N/M	N/M	N/M	0.01	0.02	0.03	0.04	0.05	34.0%

KEY RATIOS

	1986	1987	1988	1989	1990	1991	1992	1993	1994	1995	1996	AVG
EBDIT Margin	N/A	15.8%	18.6%	16.8%	16.3%	14.9%	8.8%	10.9%	16.6%	23.2%	26.3%	16.8%
ROE	N/A	35.2%	37.6%	32.0%	31.1%	26.2%	7.6%	13.6%	15.8%	15.9%	20.4%	23.5%
LT Debt/Total Cap	N/A	67.7%	49.8%	37.5%	24.7%	2.8%	13.3%	8.2%	23.3%	17.4%	20.3%	26.5%
P/E (Projected)	N/A	7.1	8.3	8.8	9.1	58.1	17.1	15.2	8.3	18.4	28.3	17.9

STOCK PRICE CHART
(fiscal year-end closing price, in U.S. dollars, adjusted for capital changes)

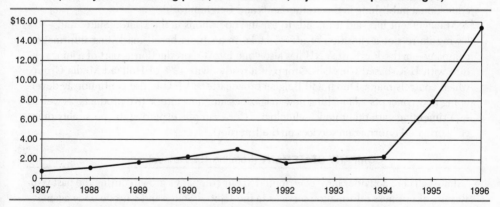

Note: Figures in U.S. dollars are translated from local currency using year-end exchange rates.

VNU (VNUNY—OTC)

Address: Ceylonpoort 5–25 / 2037 AA Haarlem / Netherlands
or
P.O. Box 4028 / 2003 EA Haarlem / Netherlands
Tel.: (011) 31 23 546 3681 **Fax:** (011) 31 23 546 3911

BASIC INFORMATION

Country: Netherlands
Industry: Printing and publishing
Investment thesis: Dutch publishing and information giant; extensive overseas operations

Market capitalization: $3.8 billion
Share status: ADRs trade OTC

COMPANY GRADING BOX

Growth Categories		Quality of Management	
Revenue Growth	10	Return on Equity	10
Operating Income Growth	15	**Risk**	
Earnings per Share Growth	10	Long-Term Debt/Total Capital	5
Share Price Growth	10	**Total QM&R (maximum 20)**	15
Total Growth (maximum 80)	45	**FINAL GRADE**	60

BACKGROUND

If you work in the movie, music, advertising, or restaurant business and subscribe to a trade magazine, chances are you are dipping into this company's stable of brand names. VNU is a Netherlands-based publishing and information company with more than 10,000 employees in eleven countries. Although its roots are in newspaper publishing, today the newspaper group accounts for just 20% of revenues.

The largest percentage of VNU's revenues in 1996, 35%, was generated by the magazine group, with operations in the Netherlands, Belgium, the United Kingdom, the Czech Republic and Hungary. Business Information USA, which operates in the United States and United Kingdom, accounted for 22% of revenues. In the United States, VNU is a leader in trade magazines (including titles such as *Billboard, Adweek, Hollywood Reporter, Restaurant Business,* and *Successful Meetings*), marketing and media information services, and trade shows (in 1996 VNU bought 15% of a California-based exhibition group—it lost out in a bid to buy a controlling interest). The rest of the company is made up of broadcasting and entertainment (7%), Business Information Europe (13%), and educational publishing in the Netherlands and Belgium (3%).

Management has said it intends to expand operations in the United States and—following its recent acquisition of a 26% stake in an India-based marketing information company—in the Far East. VNU has also gone into TV production as part of a joint venture with U.K.-based Chrysalis Group; it already owns 49% of Holland Media Group, which controls major Dutch and Belgian broadcasters. VNU is also continuously developing new concepts—launching new magazines and new interactive products, as well as experimenting with other new technologies (for example, exploring the possibility of locally oriented information services on the Internet).

COMPANY STATEMENT (from the 1996 annual report)

"Almost all core activities have contributed to our company's growth during the past year. Results of business information services in the United States and Europe once again increased substantially. Significant progress was realized by our consumer magazines in various countries and by our educational publishing companies. The progress at our newspapers was tempered by non-recurring costs due to the merger of our newspaper companies. We previously announced that results at our commercial broadcasting activities would continue to significantly decline as a result of intense competition in the markets in the Netherlands and Belgium. In 1996, a number of measures were taken which could result in a rebound in 1997. A further recovery could evolve if there is a consolidation in our commercial television markets.

"The quality of our portfolio of activities increased by successful product launches and acquisitions in various countries. All groups now participate in electronic media and multi-media services. Accordingly, the level of start-up costs increased. Well planned investments in new technologies are necessary for a strong future VNU. Almost half of VNU's United States revenues are derived from non-print related services. Our American experience and know-how will increasingly be used in the expansion of our European marketing information services companies.

"The main focus of VNU's present policy, which has proven to be successful, will remain unchanged. In order to realize our growth objectives and considering its size in The Netherlands, VNU will primarily expand internationally. Currently, 45% of our revenues are generated outside The Netherlands. Core areas for expansion are marketing information services, other clusters of business information in the United States and Europe, consumer magazines and audio-visual products for consumer markets. The allocation of our resources will take place in such a manner that our share in business information, which at present amounts to approximately 40% of net revenues, will further increase. These areas of development offer opportunities for continued growth for our company, additional improvement in margins and continuation of earnings per share growth."

PERFORMANCE

VNU received 60 points for its overall performance over the last ten years; though performance has generally been strong and consistent, a downturn in its performance in the early 1990s—before the company began its aggressive expansion—cost it points in most of the categories. Even so, revenues in dollars increased at a compound annual rate of 9.3%; EBDIT in dollars increased at a compound annual rate of 14%; and EP/ADR increased at a compound annual rate of 11%. The ratio of long-term debt to total capital also averaged 33%, higher than for many of our companies. ROE on the other hand, was excellent, averaging 28% over the ten-year period. The dividend payout ratio was also good, averaging 35%.

If you had invested $10,000 in VNU at the end of 1986, you would have purchased around 70 ADRs (or ADR equivalents) at about $144 each (excluding commissions). During the next ten years, there were a number of capital changes, including a ten-for-one stock split in February 1996. By the end of 1996, you would have had 2,778 ADRs worth $57,639. You would also have received dividend payments of around $6,000.

VNU

Ticker Symbol and Exchange: VNUNY—OTC   **CUSIP No.: 62945K202**

OPERATING AND PER SHARE DATA
(in millions of Dutch guilders and guilders per share)

	1986	1987	1988	1989	1990	1991	1992	1993	1994	1995	1996	CAGR
Sales	1,735	1,972	2,504	2,612	2,718	2,735	2,737	2,310	2,776	3,052	3,369	6.9%
EBDIT	187	215	296	331	327	325	379	382	478	507	550	11.4%
Net Profit	78	100	132	153	151	120	138	166	218	274	316	15.1%
EPS	0.72	0.85	1.00	1.08	1.06	0.85	0.93	1.08	1.21	1.44	1.66	8.7%
DPS	0.23	0.28	0.32	0.36	0.36	0.36	0.36	0.36	0.40	0.48	0.55	9.1%

OPERATING AND PER SHARE DATA
(in millions of U.S. dollars and dollars per ADR)

	1986	1987	1988	1989	1990	1991	1992	1993	1994	1995	1996	CAGR
Sales	796	1,114	1,254	1,368	1,618	1,599	1,504	1,185	1,605	1,896	1,936	9.3%
EBDIT	86	121	148	173	195	190	208	196	276	315	316	13.9%
Net Profit	36	57	66	80	90	70	76	85	126	170	182	17.7%
EP/ADR	0.33	0.48	0.50	0.57	0.63	0.50	0.51	0.55	0.70	0.89	0.95	11.2%
DP/ADR	0.11	0.16	0.16	0.19	0.21	0.21	0.20	0.18	0.23	0.30	0.32	11.6%

KEY RATIOS

	1986	1987	1988	1989	1990	1991	1992	1993	1994	1995	1996	AVG
EBDIT Margin	10.8%	10.9%	11.8%	12.7%	12.0%	11.9%	13.8%	16.5%	17.2%	16.6%	16.3%	13.7%
ROE	30.9%	33.6%	35.8%	23.5%	22.2%	16.2%	21.3%	27.2%	34.8%	30.4%	31.3%	27.9%
LT Debt/Total Cap	29.1%	27.4%	36.8%	27.4%	31.3%	35.6%	29.8%	36.0%	39.9%	35.3%	32.6%	32.8%
P/E (Projected)	9.2	7.2	6.8	9.6	9.6	7.4	8.1	14.3	12.5	13.3	18.5	10.6

STOCK PRICE CHART
(fiscal year-end closing price, in U.S. dollars, adjusted for capital changes)

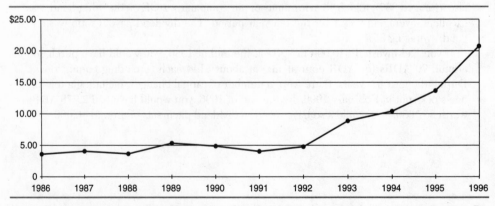

Notes: 1986–89 year-end share prices are the median of the high and low share prices for the corresponding years. Figures in U.S. dollars are translated from local currency using year-end exchange rates.

VODAFONE (VOD—NYSE)

Address: The Courtyard / 2–4 London Road / Newbury, Berkshire RG14 1JX / United Kingdom
Tel.: (011) 44 1635 33251   **Fax:** (011) 44 1635 45713   **Web site:** http://www.vodafone.co.uk

BASIC INFORMATION

Country: United Kingdom
Industry: Telecommunications services
Investment thesis: Largest U.K. provider of mobile telecommunications services; expanding abroad

Market capitalization: $13.97 billion
Share status: ADRs trade on NYSE

COMPANY GRADING BOX

Growth Categories		Quality of Management	
Revenue Growth	20	Return on Equity	10
Operating Income Growth	20	**Risk**	
Earnings per Share Growth	20	Long-Term Debt/Total Capital	10
Share Price Growth	10	**Total QM&R (maximum 20)**	20
Total Growth (maximum 80)	70	**FINAL GRADE**	90

BACKGROUND

Vodafone is one of our favorite plays in mobile telecommunications. With a thirteen-year operating history, it is the largest provider of mobile telecommunications in the United Kingdom with a reported 41% of the subscriber base (2.8 million people). It has been profitable since 1988 and has raised its dividends to shareholders every year since 1989. Today the company, which services more than 4 million subscribers overall, also has substantial overseas investments in twelve countries, the overseas businesses representing 20% of its total revenues and growing fast. By the year 2000 Vodafone expects that up to a third of its profits will be generated by its international activities.

With the continued expansion of the company's digital network, Vodafone is laying the groundwork for its future. Its Global Standard for Mobile Communications (GSM) systems provide its subscribers with "value-added services": voice messaging on mobile phones plus the ability to send and receive faxes, data, and short messages. GSM systems also provide automatic roaming between networks in different countries; roaming now represents 35% of airtime billed by Vodafone. New customers nearly all choose the digital network, and analog customers are gradually migrating to digital. The analog frequencies are all expected to be transferred to digital by the year 2003. Most recently, the British press has applauded Vodafone's pricing, considered both alluring for customers and profitable for the company.

Other divisions of Vodafone offer paging services and a radio-based public data network. Overseas, Vodafone has invested in mobile telecommunications in Australia, France, Germany, Greece, South Africa, the Netherlands, Hong Kong, Sweden, Malta, Fiji, and Uganda, as well as in Global Star in the United States.

COMPANY STATEMENT (from the 1996 annual report)

"Strong demand for mobile telecommunications services continues worldwide. The emergent new operators have made the UK cellular market more competitive. Vodafone operates the UK's largest digital network and, after repositioning its tariffs, is well placed to continue to be the market leader.

"In many of the overseas markets in which the Group operates, cellular penetration is low and this should enable the overseas businesses to grow and make a substantial contribution to Group profits.

"The Group's strategy is to concentrate on mobile telecommunications services, focusing on Western Europe and the Pacific Rim. The number of new overseas licenses being awarded is diminishing and the future expansion will be through increased shareholdings in existing network operators coupled with substantial organic growth.

"With the Group's prominence in the UK and expansion overseas, it is well positioned to deliver sustained growth and increased shareholder value."

PERFORMANCE

Vodafone received a total of 95 points in our grading system, receiving high marks for growth, ROE, and a low long-term debt to total capital ratio. EBDIT in dollars and EP/ADR increased in each of the last nine years, with compound annual growth of 28% and 31%, respectively. Dividends kept pace, increasing at a compound annual rate of 27%. The payout ratio averaged 30%. Revenues in dollars increased in seven of the last eight years, with compound annual growth of 30%. The ADR price lagged by comparison, increasing at a compound annual rate of 16% in the nine years since the company went public. ROE averaged an excellent 37%, and the ratio of long-term debt to total capital averaged about 9%.

If you had invested $10,000 in Vodafone in March 1988, you would have purchased around 290 shares at about $34.50 each (excluding commissions). During the next nine years, there was a two-for-one bonus issue in July 1994. By March 1997, you would have had 870 shares worth $37,000. You would also have received dividend payments of around $2,500.

VODAFONE

Ticker Symbol and Exchange: VOD—NYSE   **CUSIP No.: 92857T107**

OPERATING AND PER SHARE DATA
(in millions of British pounds and pounds per share)

	Mar 87	Mar 88	Mar 89	Mar 90	Mar 91	Mar 92	Mar 93	Mar 94	Mar 95	Mar 96	Mar 97	CAGR
Sales	N/A	138	240	405	537	585	664	851	1,153	1,402	1,749	32.6%
EBDIT	N/A	65	110	196	292	324	376	417	446	589	710	30.5%
Net Profit	N/A	26	62	119	169	184	222	231	233	310	364	34.2%
EPS	N/A	0.01	0.02	0.04	0.06	0.06	0.07	0.08	0.08	0.10	0.12	33.9%
DPS	N/A	N/M	N/M	0.01	0.02	0.04	0.02	0.03	0.03	0.04	0.05	28.8%

OPERATING AND PER SHARE DATA
(in millions of U.S. dollars and dollars per ADR)

	Mar 87	Mar 88	Mar 89	Mar 90	Mar 91	Mar 92	Mar 93	Mar 94	Mar 95	Mar 96	Mar 97	CAGR
Sales	N/A	260	404	666	938	1,016	1,005	1,262	1,870	2,139	2,669	29.5%
EBDIT	N/A	122	185	321	510	563	570	619	722	898	1,083	27.5%
Net Profit	N/A	49	105	195	294	320	336	343	378	473	555	31.1%
EP/ADR	N/A	0.16	0.35	0.65	0.98	1.06	1.11	1.13	1.24	1.55	1.81	30.8%
DP/ADR	N/A	N/M	N/M	0.13	0.31	0.63	0.35	0.41	0.54	0.61	0.73	27.4%

KEY RATIOS

	Mar 87	Mar 88	Mar 89	Mar 90	Mar 91	Mar 92	Mar 93	Mar 94	Mar 95	Mar 96	Mar 97	AVG
EBDIT Margin	N/A	46.8%	45.8%	48.3%	54.4%	55.5%	56.7%	49.0%	38.6%	42.0%	40.6%	47.8%
ROE	N/A	N/M	34.4%	44.0%	40.3%	40.8%	37.2%	33.1%	28.5%	30.3%	47.2%	37.3%
LT Debt/Total Cap	N/A	8.9%	0.9%	0.4%	0.4%	0.9%	5.6%	4.8%	15.1%	12.6%	40.6%	9.0%
P/E (Projected)	N/A	29.5	29.0	20.6	19.7	14.6	16.7	22.4	19.6	20.4	22.0	21.4

STOCK PRICE CHART
(fiscal year-end closing price, in U.S. dollars, adjusted for capital changes)

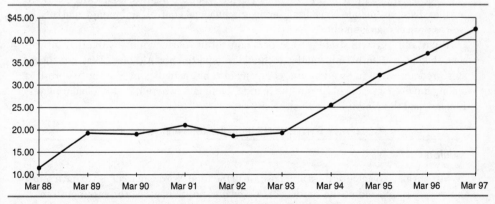

Note: Figures in U.S. dollars are translated from local currency using year-end exchange rates.

WM-DATA (WMDS.ST—STOCKHOLM)

Address: Sanhamnsgatan 65 / Box 27030 / 102 51 Stockholm / Sweden
Tel.: (011) 46 8 670 20 00   **Fax:** (011) 46 8 670 20 60   **Web site:** http://www.wmdata.com

BASIC INFORMATION

Country: Sweden   **Market capitalization:** $1.2 billion
Industry: Business services   **Share status:** Foreign shares trade on Stockholm Exchange
Investment thesis: Information technology outsourcing in Sweden, Denmark, Finland, the Netherlands, and Norway

COMPANY GRADING BOX

Growth Categories		Quality of Management	
Revenue Growth	20	Return on Equity	10
Operating Income Growth	20	**Risk**	
Earnings per Share Growth	20	Long-Term Debt/Total Capital	10
Share Price Growth	15	**Total QM&R (maximum 20)**	20
Total Growth (maximum 80)	75	**FINAL GRADE**	95

BACKGROUND

When WM-data was founded in Sweden in 1969, it was still the age of the mainframe computer, and WM-data got its start as a consultant to corporate mainframe users. It has come a long way—but its basic premise has not changed, just expanded. In 1980 the company added a Software Products division, and in 1989 it added a Computer Resource Services division, building out its niche with each foray. Years before anyone was using the term "outsourcing" to describe the contracting out of "noncore" functions, WM-data was offering its services to do just that. Now that outsourcing is all the rage, the folks at WM-data are the old hands. With workplace technology becoming ever more expensive, more complex, and more essential, WM-data's years of experience in the business give it a great competitive advantage. In 1996 WM-data's revenues topped $800 million, having increased at a compound annual rate of around 41% since 1986.

Today the company's various businesses include its original consulting group plus WM-data Dataservice, which operates computer systems and communications networks; various specialized consulting services; and an education group, which develops training materials and customer training programs. In 1995 WM-data added a leading distributor of personal computer products in Sweden to its mix when it bought NASDAQ-listed Owell. Smaller divisions include consulting services in financial control, and money markets, as well as project management.

As part of its growth strategy, WM-data now forms "partnerships" with other institutions, taking over entire information technology departments. Although WM-data operates predominantly in Sweden, the company also has activities in Norway, where it is among the five largest in players in the market; Denmark, where it is also a major player; Finland; and the Netherlands.

COMPANY STATEMENT (from the 1996 annual report)

"Vision:

"WM-data aims to achieve the same position in the total Nordic market as we have today in Sweden. By expanding the borders of our current position, we can offer our customers continued high quality, professionalism and service-mindedness.

"Goals:

- WM-data is a professional and service-minded computer services company and a natural choice when choosing a longterm and stable IT partner.
- Our customers can clearly see that co-operation with WM-data leads to the expected results and that the quality of our work is at least on a level with their expectations.
- The employees see WM-data as an attractive and reliable employer who can contribute to the employee's personal and professional development.
- WM-data's profit margin and financial stability are above average for the computer service companies in the Nordic region.
- WM-data plays an active role in the restructuring of the computer services sector."

PERFORMANCE

WM-data received top marks in almost every category, garnering a total of 95 points in our grading system. Share price performance in particular has been off the charts, increasing at a compound annual rate of 47%—though it is important to remember that back in 1987, when this company went public, it was much smaller and more difficult to invest in. Ironically, more recent investors have actually done better, although more inconsistently, in the stock (WM-data actually lost points for inconsistency of share price performance). Just in the last few years (1994–1996) investors made nearly six times their initial investment.

Altogether, WM-data has an enviable track record. In dollars, sales and EBIT increased in nine of the last ten years, recording impressive compound annual growth of 41% and 29%, respectively. EPS in dollars increased in seven of the last nine years, recording compound annual growth of 26%. ROE averaged a high 33%. And the long-term debt to total capital ratio was very comfortable, averaging 18%.

If you had invested $10,000 in WM-data at the end of 1987, you would have purchased around 630 shares at about $15.75 each (excluding commissions). In June 1994, there were a four-for-two bonus issue and a two-for-one stock split. By the end of 1996, you would have had approximately 3,780 shares worth an estimated $325,000. You would also have received dividend payments of around $11,000.

WM-DATA

Ticker Symbol and Exchange: WMDS.ST—Stockholm   **SEDOL Code: 4976903**

OPERATING AND PER SHARE DATA
(in millions of Swedish kronor and kronor per share)

	1986	1987	1988	1989	1990	1991	1992	1993	1994	1995	1996	CAGR
Sales	186	275	365	477	753	869	907	1,357	2,009	3,260	5,700	40.8%
EBIT	32	39	47	60	88	90	68	83	156	283	410	29.0%
Pretax Profit	41	48	58	71	99	103	86	105	172	316	434	26.6%
EPS	N/M	1.96	2.36	2.77	3.17	4.16	3.34	3.92	8.74	13.52	19.18	28.8%
DPS	N/M	0.33	0.40	0.47	0.79	0.84	0.84	1.00	2.50	4.25	5.25	36.0%

OPERATING AND PER SHARE DATA
(in millions of U.S. dollars and dollars per share)

	1986	1987	1988	1989	1990	1991	1992	1993	1994	1995	1996	CAGR
Sales	27.3	47.6	59.7	76.9	133.7	156.6	128.1	162.7	270.4	491.0	830.9	40.7%
EBIT	4.7	6.7	7.7	9.7	15.6	16.2	9.5	9.9	20.9	42.5	59.7	29.0%
Pretax Profit	6.0	8.4	9.5	11.5	17.5	18.6	12.2	12.5	23.2	47.6	63.2	26.5%
EPS	N/A	0.34	0.39	0.45	0.56	0.75	0.47	0.47	1.18	2.04	2.80	26.4%
DPS	N/A	0.06	0.07	0.08	0.14	0.15	0.12	0.12	0.34	0.64	0.77	33.4%

KEY RATIOS

	1986	1987	1988	1989	1990	1991	1992	1993	1994	1995	1996	AVG
EBIT Margin	17.2%	14.1%	13.0%	12.7%	11.7%	10.3%	7.5%	6.1%	7.7%	8.7%	7.2%	10.6%
ROE	38.8%	38.0%	38.8%	35.8%	38.6%	38.8%	25.1%	23.7%	28.1%	21.8%	36.4%	33.1%
LT Debt/Total Cap	0.8%	15.8%	28.4%	33.8%	25.7%	17.8%	19.6%	13.9%	14.4%	10.5%	17.2%	18.0%
P/E (Projected)	N/A	6.5	8.7	7.6	4.8	6.2	4.7	6.2	7.9	15.6	23.3	9.1

STOCK PRICE CHART
(fiscal year-end closing price, in U.S. dollars, adjusted for capital changes)

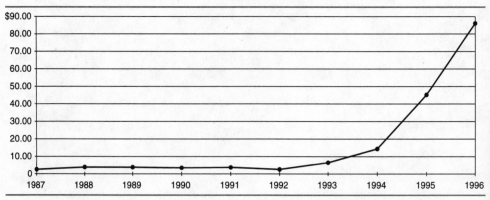

Note: Figures in U.S. dollars are translated from local currency using year-end exchange rates.

ZODIAC (ZODC.PA—PARIS)

Address: 48 Boulevard Gallieni / 92137 Issey-les-Moulineaux Cedex / France
Tel.: (011) 33 1 41 23 23 23   **Fax:** (011) 33 1 46 48 83 87
or
Address: Thompson Creek Road / P.O. Box 400 / Stevensville, MD 21666
Tel.: (410) 643-4141   **Fax:** (410) 643-4491

BASIC INFORMATION

Country: France   **Market capitalization:** $1.22 billion
Industry: Aerospace   **Share status:** Foreign shares trade on Paris Exchange
Investment thesis: Leading supplier of parts and products to the aerospace industry worldwide

COMPANY GRADING BOX

Growth Categories		Quality of Management	
Revenue Growth	20	Return on Equity	10
Operating Income Growth	20	**Risk**	
Earnings per Share Growth	20	Long-Term Debt/Total Capital	5
Share Price Growth	20	**Total QM&R (maximum 20)**	15
Total Growth (maximum 80)	80	**FINAL GRADE**	95

BACKGROUND

Zodiac fits in neatly with our theme of outsourcing, producing parts for the airplane manufacturing and aeronautical defense industries. Having recently celebrated its centenary, France-based Zodiac has a long and illustrious history in aerospace. In 1896 the company's founder began promoting balloons for recreational flying—and within a few years added "airships." By World War I, Zodiac was supplying airships, then airplanes, to the French military. Today the company is a supplier of civil and military aerospace equipment worldwide and is a major player in both the pool industry and the market for inflatable boats. It has a market capitalization of $1.2 billion, about 5,500 employees, and subsidiaries in eleven countries.

The company is divided into three primary divisions. First is aeronautical equipment, accounting for just under a third of Zodiac's revenue and providing design and production of emergency evacuation systems, braking systems and parachutes, de-icers, fuel tanks, air bags, and a few other miscellaneous industrial products. Second is the airline equipment sector, accounting for about a third of revenue and supplying the world's airlines with seats and cabin equipment—a business that is booming with the airlines' need to refurbish or replace their aging fleets. Finally, there is the "marine leisure" division, accounting for more than a third of revenues and manufacturing boats, inflatable rafts, pools, and pool-cleaning equipment. Zodiac's recent purchase of Baracuda, a world leader in automatic pool cleaners, consolidated its position in that rapidly growing industry.

COMPANY STATEMENT (from the 1995–96 annual report)

"1996/1997 Outlook

"Aeronautical Equipment Segment: We forecast a satisfactory growth in business linked to the civil aviation market, bearing in mind that the gains will depend on the capacity of airframers to accelerate their production rates. By contrast, we remain prudent in our forecast for the defense market, particularly in France. Overall, the Aeronautical Equipment segment should enjoy a positive but moderate growth. . . .

"Airline Equipment Segment: The passenger seat market is headed for sustained growth as the world civil aviation industry moves into a cyclical upswing. Zodiac's Airline Equipment segment, which commands a strong position here, should benefit from the trend. Most airlines are now back in profit and are placing orders for both new-aircraft fittings and retrofits on existing planes. . . .

"Marine Leisure Segment: For the third consecutive year, the marine division is expected to post a mild increase in sales and a steeper increase in profitability. We forecast an upturn in our business in the U.S., both in the leisure market (own-brand products and private labels) and in the professional/defense market—with some orders in the latter sector already booked. In Europe and the rest of the world, we believe the signs observed in 1996 herald a further improvement in 1997. The new product range has proved popular with retailers at the first boat shows of the season—a good omen for overall growth in the marine division.

"In the leisure division, we look forward to improved sales and profitability in 1997. A new Japanese distributor should help achieve that goal."

PERFORMANCE

Zodiac received an overall score of 95, getting top grades in all of our growth categories and for ROE. The only category in which it lost a few points was long-term debt to total capital ratio, which averaged 31% from 1986 to 1996. Revenues in dollars, EBDIT, and EPS in dollars all increased in eight of the last ten years, revenues had compound annual growth of 16%, operating income showed compound annual growth of 18%, and EPS had compound annual growth of 19%. Dividends rose in nine of the last ten years, at a compound annual rate of 17%. The share price increased at a compound annual rate of 22%. And ROE averaged 19%.

If you had invested $10,000 in Zodiac in August 1986, you would have purchased around 35 shares at about $275 each (excluding commissions). During the following ten years, there were a two-for-one stock split in May 1988 and a four-for-one stock split in March 1995. By August 1986, you would have had approximately 290 shares worth an estimated $75,000. You would also have received dividend payments of around $3,000.

ZODIAC

Ticker Symbol and Exchange: ZODC.PA—PARIS   **SEDOL Code: 4994693**

OPERATING AND PER SHARE DATA
(in millions of French francs and francs per share)

	Aug 86	Aug 87	Aug 88	Aug 89	Aug 90	Aug 91	Aug 92	Aug 93	Aug 94	Aug 95	Aug 96	CAGR
Sales	1,033	1,236	1,413	1,701	1,902	2,018	2,273	2,678	2,967	3,033	3,414	12.7%
EBDIT	123	166	192	227	289	300	342	342	395	415	486	14.7%
Net Profit	38	56	63	78	103	116	129	137	158	174	202	18.3%
EPS	9.95	14.77	16.75	20.56	26.76	29.55	31.86	30.70	34.78	37.57	43.22	15.8%
DPS	2.75	3.25	3.75	4.50	5.50	6.25	7.00	7.25	8.00	9.00	10.25	14.1%

OPERATING AND PER SHARE DATA
(in millions of U.S. dollars and dollars per share)

	Aug 86	Aug 87	Aug 88	Aug 89	Aug 90	Aug 91	Aug 92	Aug 93	Aug 94	Aug 95	Aug 96	CAGR
Sales	155	203	212	257	360	340	476	458	548	602	675	15.9%
EBDIT	18.5	27.3	28.8	34.2	54.7	50.6	71.6	58.4	73.1	82.3	95.9	17.9%
Net Profit	5.6	9.2	9.5	11.7	19.5	19.5	26.9	23.4	29.3	34.5	39.9	21.6%
EPS	1.49	2.43	2.51	3.10	5.07	4.98	6.67	5.25	6.43	7.45	8.54	19.1%
DPS	0.41	0.53	0.56	0.68	1.04	1.05	1.46	1.24	1.48	1.79	2.03	17.3%

KEY RATIOS

	Aug 86	Aug 87	Aug 88	Aug 89	Aug 90	Aug 91	Aug 92	Aug 93	Aug 94	Aug 95	Aug 96	AVG
EBDIT Margin	11.9%	13.4%	13.6%	13.3%	15.2%	14.9%	15.1%	12.8%	13.3%	13.7%	14.2%	13.8%
ROE	15.6%	20.8%	20.1%	20.6%	24.9%	21.3%	21.6%	15.4%	16.1%	16.1%	15.7%	18.9%
LT Debt/Total Cap	29.0%	37.3%	32.0%	29.5%	22.4%	26.4%	23.6%	39.8%	33.3%	32.6%	30.1%	30.6%
P/E (Projected)	15.6	16.4	8.4	11.5	9.2	8.8	9.2	13.4	15.3	15.3	26.6	13.6

STOCK PRICE CHART
(fiscal year-end closing price, in U.S. dollars, adjusted for capital changes)

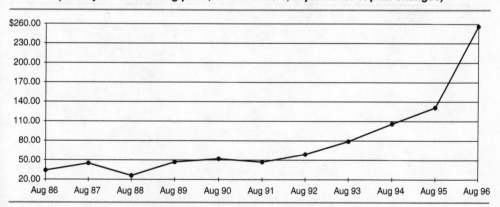

Note: Figures in U.S. dollars are translated from local currency using average exchange rates.

Appendix

A. BREAKDOWN OF COMPANIES
(by region, country, industry, sector, market capitalization and grade)

Number of Companies, Developed vs. Emerging Markets	
Developed Markets	81
Emerging Markets	19

Number of Companies by Market Capitalization	
Large Cap (over $5.0 bn)	46
Mid Cap ($2.0 bn to $5.0 bn)	29
Small Cap (under $2.0 bn)	25

Number of Companies by Grade	
One hundred	13
Ninety-five	21
Ninety	17
Eighty-five	14
Eighty	12
Seventy-five	5
Seventy	5
Sixty-five	1
Sixty	6
Fifty-five	4
Fifty	2

Number of Companies by Region and Country

Europe	62	Pacific Rim	18
Belgium	2	Australia	2
Denmark	2	Hong Kong	5
Finland	1	Japan	4
France	9	Malaysia	1
Germany	5	New Zealand	1
Ireland	3	Philippines	1
Italy	4	Singapore	3
Netherlands	9	Thailand	1
Norway	1		
Spain	3	**Americas**	**14**
Sweden	4	Argentina	1
Switzerland	4	Brazil	2
United Kingdom	15	Chile	3
		Canada	4
Other	**6**	Mexico	3
South Africa	3	Panama	1
Greece	1		
Israel	1		
Russia	1		

Number of Companies by Industry and Sector

Capital Equipment	17	Materials	4
Auto Equipment	1	Building Materials	1
Electrical and Electronic	8	Construction	1
Industrial Equipment	6	Mining	2
Telecom Equipment	2		
		Miscellaneous	**6**
Consumer Goods	**20**	Multi-industry	4
Brewing	2	Property	2
Food and Beverages	7		
Health and Personal Care	9	**Services**	**35**
Household Goods	2	Business and Public	6
		Industrial	4
Energy	**9**	Leisure and Tourism	2
Electric Utility	2	Office Equipment	1
Natural Gas	2	Printing and Publishing	3
Oil and Gas	4	Retailing	11
Oil Service	1	clothing	1
		food	5
Finance	**9**	specialty	5
Banking	5	Telecom Services	6
Financial Services	3	Temporary Employment	2
Insurance	1		

B. THE TOP TEN

(Shows the returns generated by a $10,000 investment in the ten largest companies, by market capitalization, over the last ten years)

Company	Mkt Cap U.S. $ (billions)	Country	Industry	Ticker Symbol	Start Shr Price	Shares Purchased	Initial Investment	End Shr Price	Ending Investment	Dividends
Novartis	$83.1	Switzerland	Pharma	NVTSY	$13.54	70	$947.83	$57.20	$4,004.10	$300.00
Roche	$70.0	Switzerland	Pharma	ROHHY	$6.55	145	$949.25	$77.72	$11,269.40	$420.00
HSBC	$61.0	Hong Kong	Banking	HSBHY	$31.00	30	$930.00	$214.00	$6,420.00	$1,130.00
Sony	$32.7	Japan	Electronics	SNE	$21.70	45	$976.50	$70.30	$3,163.50	$160.00
Telebras	$32.0	Brazil	Telecoms	TBR	$7.20	130	$936.00	$77.00	$10,010.00	$760.00
Ericsson	$31.0	Sweden	Equipment	ERICY	$1.50	635	$952.50	$30.76	$19,532.60	$1,250.00
Astra	$26.5	Sweden	Pharma	A	$3.67	260	$954.20	$47.96	$12,469.60	$590.00
L'Oréal	$25.8	France	Household	LORLY	$7.17	130	$932.10	$76.48	$9,942.40	$380.00
Telefonica	$24.1	Spain	Telecoms	TEF	$20.37	45	$916.65	$68.99	$3,104.55	$850.00
Carrefour	$23.7	France	Retailing	CRERF	$70.00	14	$980.00	$661.00	$9,254.00	$418.00
							$9,475.03		$89,170.15	$6,258.00

Purchases	$9,475.03
Commissions	$500.00
Cash	$24.97
Initial Invest	$10,000.00
Shr Value	$89,170.15
Cash	$ —
Dividends	$6,258.00
End Result	$95,428.15
CAGR	25.3%
Total Return	954%

Notes: Table assumes $50 minimum commission for each $1,000 investment.
Telebras investment is not made until end of 1989, when shares became available.
Returns are untaxed.
Sun Hung Kai Properties and Petrobras could have made it into the Top Ten,
but we excluded them to limit Hong Kong and Brazil to one company each.

INDEX

About the Authors

Peggy Edersheim Kalb and her husband, Scott E. Kalb, are uniquely positioned to write about international stocks. Each brings tremendous experience in the field to the project.

Peggy Edersheim Kalb is a Contributing Editor to *Smart Money,* the personal finance magazine of *The Wall Street Journal.* She has also freelanced for *The Wall Street Journal* and *New York Magazine.* Prior to this position, she worked for two years as a portfolio manager at Smith Barney International and previously as the producer of CNN's *Moneyline* with Lou Dobbs. After graduating from Yale University with a B.A. in history, Ms. Kalb began her career as a financial journalist as a staff reporter for *Manhattan Inc.*

Scott E. Kalb is currently Managing Director and senior portfolio manager with Salomon Smith Barney International Asset Management, which manages the $1.2 billion Salomon Smith Barney International Equities Fund, the $300 million globally invested Worldwide Funds, and about $700 million in institutional accounts. Before assuming his current position, Mr. Kalb was the Director of Smith Barney's International Equity Research department. Mr. Kalb began his career in finance as an economic consultant to the South Korean Ministry of Finance shortly after graduating from Harvard with a master's degree. He went on to work with James Capel and Drexel Burnham Lambert in Seoul, Tokyo, and London before joining Salomon Smith Barney in New York.